Philosophers
of
Consciousness

Polanyi
Lonergan
Voegelin
Ricoeur
Girard
Kierkegaard

Philosophers
of
Consciousness

Polanyi
Lonergan
Voegelin
Ricoeur
Girard
Kierkegaard

EUGENE WEBB

UNIVERSITY OF WASHINGTON PRESS
Seattle and London

Library of Congress Cataloging-in-Publication Data

Webb, Eugene, 1938–
    Philosophers of consciousness : Polanyi, Lonergan, Voegelin,
Ricoeur, Girard, Kierkegaard / Eugene Webb.
        p.   cm.
    Bibliography: p.
    Includes index.
    ISBN 0-295-96621-1
    1. Consciousness—History. 2. Philosophy, Modern—20th century
3. Philosophy, Modern—19th century.   I. Title.
B105.C477W43 1988
126'.09'04—dc19

The figure "The Fraser Spiral" is reproduced with the kind permission of its original publishers, John Wiley and Sons, Inc., from Ralph M. Evans, *An Introduction to Color* (New York and London, 1948), p. 153.

For my daughter Christina,

a book of her own

Contents

Preface   ix

Introduction   3

1. Michael Polanyi:
Consciousness as Focal and Subsidiary Awareness   26

2. Bernard Lonergan:
Consciousness as Experience and Operation   53

3. Eric Voegelin:
Consciousness as Experience and Symbolization   91

4. Paul Ricoeur:
Consciousness as a Hermeneutic Field   137

5. René Girard:
Consciousness and the Dynamics of Desire   183

6. Søren Kierkegaard:
Consciousness as Incarnate Subjectivity   226

7. The Differentiation and Integration of Consciousness
in the Individual and in History   284

Bibliography   319

Index   332

vii

Preface

THIS BOOK HAS grown largely out of the force of questions that arose during my earlier studies, *The Dark Dove: The Sacred and Secular in Modern Literature* and *Eric Voegelin: Philosopher of History,* but it has also grown out of conversations and correspondence with a number of friends and colleagues—especially John A. Campbell, Dale Cannon, Douglas Collins, Ray L. Hart, Howard V. Hong, Rodney W. Kilcup, Thomas J. McPartland, and William M. Thompson—who asked further questions, made suggestions, and pressed me for further clarification. If it now succeeds in communicating what I feel is the urgency of the questions it raises and in exploring and elucidating them to some extent, much of the credit is due to them. It also owes an enormous debt to my conversations with Eric Voegelin. Of course, my expressions of gratitude should not be interpreted as implying that all of those mentioned would endorse everything I have said in these pages. In some cases, the objections they raised forced me to clarify points that may in fact have sharpened rather than diminished our differences, but where that is the case I am grateful for their stimulus and for the friendship and patience they have extended. I wish also to express my most special thanks to my wife Marilyn, who for twenty-four blessed years has been my constant companion in all my explorations.

Seattle, January 1988

Philosophers
of
Consciousness

Polanyi
Lonergan
Voegelin
Ricoeur
Girard
Kierkegaard

Introduction

"Philosophers of Consciousness"—the reader may well ask what this title means. What might be meant here by "philosophy" and "consciousness"? And why the choice of these figures: Michael Polanyi, Bernard Lonergan, Eric Voegelin, Paul Ricoeur, René Girard, and Søren Kierkegaard—to be discussed under that heading? These are questions that could be discussed at length, and in fact the book as a whole will be an attempt at an extended answer to them, but I will try to respond to them briefly here at the beginning.

The term "philosophy," though somewhat slippery because of the variety of ways it has been used historically, is not inherently problematic. It has always referred to systematic, rational inquiry, with the particular type and scope of the inquiry varying according to the interests of those who engage in it. The pertinent question in the present context is what it means as a word for what the thinkers studied here are engaged in. What philosophy has been primarily for them is a reflective inquiry into what it means to function consciously as an inquirer and as a responsible agent. This means that they have focused not on questions regarding particular knowledge, such as that developed in the sciences, but on the development of a broad framework for the understanding of what knowing, valuing, deliberating, and deciding are as such and what it means to be the kind of being who engages in them.

Perhaps Lonergan can be taken to speak for the figures studied in this volume generally in his comments on the relation of philosophy as he conceived it to different schools of philosophy as well as to the various particular sciences:

3

Now the emergence of the autonomous sciences has repercussions on philosophy. Since the sciences between them undertake the explanation of all sensible data, one may conclude with the positivists that the function of philosophy is to announce that philosophy has nothing to say. Since philosophy has no theoretic function, one may conclude with the linguistic analysts that the function of philosophy is to work out a hermeneutics for the clarification of the local variety of everyday language. But there remains the possibility—and it is our option—that philosophy is neither a theory in the manner of science nor a somewhat technical form of common sense, nor even a reversal to Presocratic wisdom. Philosophy finds its proper data in intentional consciousness. Its primary function is to promote the self-appropriation that cuts to the root of philosophic differences and incomprehensions. It has further, secondary functions in distinguishing, relating, grounding the several realms of meaning [i.e., common sense, theory, and what Lonergan calls "interiority" or self-reflective consciousness] and, no less, in grounding the methods of the sciences and so promoting their unification.[1]

What this means is that—if Lonergan can indeed be taken to speak, to a certain degree and in his own special idiom, for this group of thinkers—the term "philosophy" as used in the present context refers to systematic reflection on consciousness as such, on the variety of ways it is possible to operate in a humanly conscious manner, and on the basic character of the various objective correlates of such operations.

This, of course, brings us to the more problematic question: what is consciousness? The term itself has had a long and complex history. I will try here simply to mention a few of the major emphases that have developed in the past and remain influential, and then I will indicate briefly how the present figures relate to some of these traditional meanings and what specifically I think the term tends to mean in their writings.

The earliest uses of the term "consciousness" cited in the *Oxford English Dictionary* are from the seventeenth century, where they pointed in two rather different directions: toward the sharing of knowledge in common and toward private, internal awareness. An example cited for the former is Thomas Hobbes, *Leviathan*, I, vii, 31 (1651):

1. *Method in Theology*, pp. 94–95.

"Where two, or more men, know of one and the same fact, they are said to be Conscious of it one to another." This is a use of the word that may now seem rather odd, since the latter emphasis has tended to eclipse it, but it is germane—as I hope will become clear in the latter part of this book—to the school of thought known in France as *la psychologie interdividuelle*, represented here by René Girard and Jean-Michel Oughourlian. Both hold that the human "self" or center of consciousness is not a strictly individual thing or attribute, but is continuously formed in and by relationships between different human beings (hence the term *interdividuel* or "interdividual," as will be explained in the chapter on Girard). They also see consciousness in this light not only as inherently social but as tending to be conflictual. This is an aspect of the problem of consciousness that has not been emphasized in philosophical discourse, but which I hope to show is much too important to neglect.

The predominant modern use of the term, however, derives from the latter of the two emphases mentioned above—that which refers to what are usually called the "inner perceptions" of what is conceived of as a more or less self-contained individual. John Locke, the other major philosophical figure among the *OED*'s early examples, offered the following definition in his *Essay Concerning Human Understanding*, II, i, 19 (1690): "Consciousness is the perception of what passes in a man's own mind." He went on to explain there (II, i, 20–24) that in his view this meant awareness first of sensations and then of the "operations" (as examples he lists "perception, remembering, consideration, reasoning, &c.") by which the data of sensory experience are processed in various ways.[2]

Roughly speaking, this is also the way most of the figures in the present study have tended to use the term—as when Voegelin speaks of what he calls the "noetic differentiation" of consciousness as "the rise of reason to articulate self-consciousness" or "the adequate articulation and symbolization of the questioning consciousness."[3] It was also this, of course, that Lonergan was referring to as the specific subject matter of philosophy in the passage quoted above; and he, too, frequently

2. Quoted from the Oxford University Press edition, ed. Alexander Campbell Fraser, reprinted in *Great Books of the Western World*, 35:127.
3. "Reason the Classic Experience," in Eric Voegelin, *Anamnesis*, trans. and ed. Gerhart Niemeyer, pp. 89, 93.

referred to the process involved as "differentiation of consciousness."

What principally distinguishes Voegelin's conception of consciousness, as well as those of Polanyi, Lonergan, Ricoeur, and Kierkegaard, from that of a Locke is the scope attributed to the experience reflected upon. In Locke's thought and that of other empiricists in his tradition, the notion of experience tended to be limited pretty much to sense data, while the operations by which the data were processed were treated almost like the workings of a mechanism. The persons studied in this book, on the other hand, have tended to place emphasis on the operations of consciousness and their experienced dynamism as themselves important data for philosophical reflection. Voegelin, for example, speaks of a fundamental "existential tension" that itself calls for interpretation as a structuring principle of human consciousness, while Polanyi, Lonergan, Ricoeur, and Kierkegaard all speak similarly of what they call "dynamism," "passion," or "concern." Lonergan in one place defined consciousness as "just experience," but the experience he was especially concerned with in that discussion was that of a "dynamic state," not a collection of sensations, and his purpose was to distinguish between consciousness as such and knowledge: "To say that this dynamic state is conscious is not to say that it is known. For consciousness is just experience, but knowledge is a compound of experience, understanding, and judging."[4] There is, in other words, experience that can be treated as constituting the objective pole of the intentional operations Lonergan lists, but there is also experience of the subjective pole of those same operations (i.e., the experience of performing them).

To speak of consciousness as structured in terms of objective and subjective poles is typical of this group of thinkers, and it constitutes another major difference from the pattern of thought exemplified in the passage from Locke, who still worked within a basically Cartesian framework that cast the issue in terms of "inner" and "outer" or "mind" and "matter." The shift from a discussion of such mutually exclusive realms to an analysis of "intentional consciousness" (a term made popular in our century by Edmund Husserl) as structured by a relation between subjective and objective poles has had, of course, a long history of its own, and much of that history has involved a continuing

4. *Method in Theology*, p. 106.

entanglement of these terms with Cartesian dualism and various versions of idealism.

It was to force a clear break with the idealist pattern of thought that William James presented his seemingly paradoxical argument against the existence of consciousness, in his famous essay, "Does 'Consciousness' Exist?"[5] James was arguing against what he believed to be a mistaken tendency, especially in German philosophy since Kant, to speak of consciousness as though it were a sort of substance in the metaphysical sense or the stuff of which a "transcendental ego" is constituted. He did not mean to deny, on the other hand, that we have experience and perform intentional operations. Rather he wanted to make a point very like Lonergan's when the latter said in the passage quoted above that consciousness is "just experience." As James put it in his own language:

> To deny plumply that "consciousness" exists seems so absurd on the face of it—for undeniably "thoughts" do exist—that I fear some readers will follow me no farther. Let me then immediately explain that I mean only to deny that the word stands for an entity, but to insist most emphatically that it does stand for a function. There is, I mean, no aboriginal stuff or quality of being, contrasted with that of which material objects are made, out of which our thoughts of them are made; but there is a function in experience which thoughts perform, and for the performance of which this quality of being is invoked. That function is *knowing*. (Pp. 3–4)

James went on to propose a corrective explanation of the phenomenon at issue that, despite its different terminology, resembles Lonergan's:

> My thesis is that if we start with the supposition that there is only one primal stuff or material in the world, a stuff of which everything is composed, and if we call that stuff "pure experience," then knowing can easily be explained as a particular sort of relation towards one another into which portions of pure experience may enter. The relation itself is a part of pure experience; one of its "terms" becomes the subject or bearer of knowledge, the knower, the other becomes the object known. (P. 4)

---

5. This was incorporated as the first chapter of his *Essays in Radical Empiricism* (1912). *Essays in Radical Empiricism and A Pluralistic Universe*, pp. 1–38.

James also went on to say that subject and object are not radically different, but can function interchangeably: as a quantity of paint may be merely "saleable matter" in a paintshop but in a picture "performs a spiritual function," "[j]ust so . . . does a given undivided portion of experience, taken in one context of associates, play the part of a knower, or a state of mind, of 'consciousness'; while in a different context the same undivided bit of experience plays the part of a thing known, of an objective 'content.' In a word, in one group it figures as a thought, in another group as a thing" (pp. 9–10).

Although Lonergan, who read extensively the major German thinkers from Kant through Husserl, shows little sign of the influence of James, he clearly shared a similar conception of consciousness as experience and operations or functional relations; and he, too, considered the subjective and objective poles of consciousness to be interchangeable, though with different implications than James would have argued for. The way Lonergan would have put that issue, if he had stated it in so many words, would have been to say that an object is whatever it is possible to ask questions about, so that to ask questions about a subject is to render the subject an object and even to make possible a conception of the subject as an entity.

The latter is a point, however, on which Lonergan and the other figures in the present study divide in a disagreement that will be seen to have important implications. For Lonergan, as will be explained in his chapter, one of the culminating points of philosophical reflection is what he calls the rational self-affirmation of the knower as a metaphysical entity, and he took strong exception to Voegelin for rejecting this move as well as the metaphysics of substances generally. As we will see Lonergan define the issue, this is a point that divides his own "critical realism," as he called it, from every form of "existentialism," which he himself rejected as the result of a failure to complete the movement from "naive" to critical realism.

It also divides him from James, whose *Radical Empiricism* was a major influence on Voegelin.[6] It was precisely the traditional metaphysics of entitative substances that James thought the idealists tended to carry

6. Cf. Voegelin's own account of this influence in his "Autobiographical Memoir," quoted in Ellis Sandoz, *The Voegelinian Revolution: A Biographical Introduction,* pp. 170–71. This memoir is a transcription of a series of taped interviews made by Sandoz in 1973 and quoted extensively throughout Sandoz's book.

forward with their notions of a "transcendental ego" or of a substantial "subject," and it was from this that Voegelin was trying to break free by interpreting the "subject" as a mythic concept that could be treated more adequately in the language of the philosophical myths of his own favored Greek tradition than in that of what he considered a reifying (or as he liked to call it, "hypostatizing") metaphysics. In the passage quoted above in which James spoke of "the subject or bearer of knowledge, the knower," James himself added a footnote in which he said, "In my *Psychology* I have tried to show that we need no knower other than the 'passing thought.'"[7] To put the matter another way that will bring it closer to Lonergan's language, if not exactly his conception, what we can actually experience, understand, and affirm is inquiring, thinking, and knowing—the operations themselves, that is, without the need to suppose a theoretical entity called a "subject" in addition to them.

Voegelin considered himself to be in line with James on this point, and indeed he said that it was his reading of James that stimulated him to consider the issue in this way even before he discovered a parallel line of thinking in Plato. As he recounted the development of his own reflections on this point in his "Autobiographical Memoir":

> At the center of consciousness I found the experience of participation, meaning thereby the reality of being in contact with reality outside myself.... Among the philosophers I found important confirmation from the radical empiricism of William James. James's study on the question—"Does 'Consciousness' Exist?" (1904)—struck me at the time, and still strikes me, as one of the most important philosophical documents of the twentieth century. In developing his concept of the pure experience, William James has put his finger on the reality of the consciousness of participation, inasmuch as what he calls pure experience is the something that can be put into the context *either* of the subject's stream of consciousness *or* of objects in the external world. This fundamental insight of William James identifies the something that lies between the subject and object of participation as the experience. Later I found that the same type of analysis had been conducted on a much vaster scale by Plato, resulting in his concept of the *metaxy*, the In-Between. The experi-

7. James *Essays*, p. 4. James was referring to his *Principles of Psychology*. The passage referred to may be found in *Great Books of the Western World*, 53:220.

ence is neither in the subject nor in the world of objects but In-Between, and that means In-Between the poles of man and the reality he experiences. . . . A good number of problems which plague the history of philosophy now become clear, as hypostases of the poles of a pure experience in the sense of William James, or of the *metaxy* experiences of Plato. By hypostases I mean the fallacious assumption that the poles of the participatory experience are self-contained entities that form a mysterious contact on occasion of an experience.[8]

It was on the basis of these considerations that Voegelin said he developed his own conception of how consciousness can best be interpreted:

> The term *consciousness,* therefore, could no longer mean to me a human consciousness which is conscious of a reality outside man's consciousness, but had to mean the In-Between reality of the participatory pure experience which then analytically can be characterized through such terms as the poles of the experiential tension and the reality of the experiential tension in the *metaxy.* (Ibid., p. 171)

The question whether a subject can be said to be an object must hinge, of course, on how one wishes to use such words, but there can be substantive issues implicit in the choice of language. Since this question will play a dramatic role in the clash between the intellectualist emphasis of Lonergan and the more existential emphasis of the other thinkers in the present study, it will be well to take a moment to clarify some of what it involves.

The fundamental issue in this case has to do not only with how a "subject" can be conceived but with what is meant by an "object." If, for the sake of simplicity, we limit our consideration for the moment to the objects of just three intentional operations—attention, understanding, and knowing—and speak of these in the simplest terms, we can identify the objects of these operations as experiential data, ideas or propositions, and verified propositions respectively. We "attend" to an experiential datum by focusing our awareness on it. We "understand" a pattern of such data or an idea or proposition by grasping the way its elements or parts relate to one another. We "know" the truth of a proposition when we have verified it in some way. In all of these cases,

8. Quoted in Sandoz, *Voegelinian Revolution,* p. 170.

there is a focusing of awareness on something in particular, whether it is an object of experience, understanding, or knowledge.

What Lonergan emphasizes is that it is possible to ask questions of some sort about absolutely anything: the objects of intentional operations, the operations themselves, and what might be called the inner or subjective source of the operations. And this is, of course, true. What the opposing, "existential" pattern of thought tends to emphasize, on the other hand—without denying that such questions can be asked—is that, to phrase it in the language we will shortly see Polanyi introducing, there is always an irreducibly "subsidiary" dimension to consciousness as compared with the "focal" awareness we are able to bring to bear on what becomes explicit as an object of intentional operations.

In attending to something, one might say, there is that which one attends to, and there is that which one attends through, and there is the attending itself. One can look through a lens, for example, at a landscape, and one can redirect one's attention from the landscape to the lens, thereby rendering the lens itself "focal," but one cannot actually attend to attending in the same sense as that in which one attends to a particular object, whether landscape or lens. Attending itself, that is, remains a subjective act, even if one can coin a word for it, imagine an example of it, or construct a definition of it. The idea of attention, no matter how it is conceived, always remains something distinct from the act itself of attending. To Polanyi and Voegelin quite explicitly, but also to Ricoeur, Girard, and Kierkegaard in their various ways as well, it makes a great deal of difference to keep clear about this distinction in experience and not to let a passion for understanding ideas lead one to lose sight of the ultimate irreducibility of the subjective dimension of consciousness. What this means in all of its implications will be a major topic running throughout the discussion of each of these thinkers.

My reason for choosing these six in particular to discuss is that considered together they raise a wide range of interrelated and searching questions on such matters as those just indicated and also that the very differences in perspective that divide them can be especially helpful in uncovering central issues that must be considered in exploring the phenomenon of human consciousness. They have enough in common to be placed together in dialogue, while at the same time they differ sufficiently within that common framework of discussion to uncover the actual or potential aporias of the traditions of thought that lie behind them. In doing so, they indicate where important problems for further exploration can be found.

This is not to say that there are not many other figures I might reasonably have chosen to substitute for one or more of these. It may be helpful, therefore, if I explain briefly how this particular selection developed. My initial intention was to write a study of the thought of Polanyi, Lonergan, Voegelin, and Ricoeur. The reason was that in my own reading, and especially in the writing of my earlier study of the thought of Eric Voegelin, I found these thinkers mutually illuminating with respect to questions regarding the structure and dynamics of human consciousness and the problems of how we can know it and how we can speak about it.[9] I made numerous references to Lonergan, Polanyi, and Ricoeur in that work because I thought them sufficiently complementary in their analyses to be helpful, through comparisons of their different formulations of an issue, for the clarification of some of the points Voegelin was concerned with. I also found from conversations with colleagues in a variety of fields (religious studies, philosophy, political science, literary theory) that anyone interested in one of these four tended to be interested also in two or three of the others. In fact Voegelin himself gave careful study to each of the other three, as had Lonergan as well—though neither Polanyi nor Ricoeur seem to have read the others. Since no study had been written to compare the four systematically with one another I thought such a work could be useful. I recognized, of course, that a thorough study of philosophical approaches to the theme of consciousness would have to include a great many other figures—such as Kant, Fichte, Hegel, Schelling, Martin Heidegger, Hans-Georg Gadamer, Henri Bergson, Jean-Paul Sartre, and Maurice Merleau-Ponty, just to name a few—but I also wanted to produce a book of manageable length (indeed I hoped for one much shorter than this). I did consider possibly including a chapter on Gadamer when I first began planning this project. As a former student of Heidegger's he would have brought into the work the Heideggerian perspective as well as his own special contributions to the hermeneutics of intellectual and cultural history to complement those of Voegelin, Lonergan, and Ricoeur. And he would also have fitted neatly into the historical time frame of the study as an approximate age mate of the other four.

9. Eugene Webb, *Eric Voegelin: Philosopher of History.*

On the other hand, I did not in the beginning think of including the other two of the present six. My reason for deciding that if a fifth were to be added it should be Kierkegaard was that as my study of Lonergan and Voegelin made me increasingly aware of the differences between them, I also realized that these differences paralleled those between Hegel and Kierkegaard in the nineteenth century. Since the issues that divided Lonergan from both Voegelin and Ricoeur in particular seemed so closely involved with the existential tradition as such and especially with the heritage of Kierkegaard, to whom both of the latter were linked through their common intellectual forebear, Karl Jaspers, I decided that it would be helpful to bring Kierkegaard explicitly into the discussion.

Of course it may seem odd at first glance that Kierkegaard's chapter comes after the discussion of all the others, but that is precisely because his work seems to me so seminal for all of the issues explored here. If I had intended a historical study of the philosophy of consciousness, Kierkegaard would have had to precede the others, and he would probably have had to be accompanied in that position by a number of other nineteenth-century figures. As it is, however, my plan has been to begin with the more recent group and draw the more significant figures from the background (such as Kant, Hegel, and Schelling) into the discussion as they become relevant to an understanding of these figures. In the case of Kierkegaard, I chose to bring him in after the others so that the issues that arise in their own "dialogue" could be brought into focus before turning to Kierkegaard to see what his contribution to it might be. In contrast to the other five of my figures, Kierkegaard seemed well enough known not to need a general exposition, and an attempt to provide that for so rich a figure would have required far too much space if it were to do him justice. His chapter is the longest of the book even so, although his thought is explored only with an eye to the ways in which his interests and interpretive strategies link up with and can serve to illuminate the explorations of the other five.

The other remaining figure among the six, Girard is another twentieth-century thinker. He is not an age mate of the other four, however, but a full generation younger, and is probably the least known in the English-speaking world, although his reputation has been growing rapidly in France, where his psychological and sociological theories have had considerable influence on thinkers in a wide variety of disciplines. His principal value for the present discussion lies in the new approach he offers to an understanding of human psychology.

In exploring the issues raised by the others, I found myself led to feel increasingly that a treatment of human consciousness that does not give serious consideration to possible distortions of consciousness through various forms of unconscious bias will inevitably be tempted toward distortions of its own. One of the major contributions of Paul Ricoeur has been his attempt to bring together the philosophical tradition of reflection on consciousness and the psychological critique of unconscious bias pioneered by Freud. As Ricoeur himself phrased it, a hermeneutic that works through openness and trust toward a tradition of thought in the hope or recovering its sound insights needs to be balanced by a "hermeneutic of suspicion" that will help it to resist what there may be of naiveté and bias in that tradition. In Girard's psychology of mimetic desire, I found what seems to me a much more searching hermeneutic of suspicion than either Ricoeur or Freud seems to have suspected possible. I therefore chose to draw Girard's thought into the present analysis along with Ricoeur's in order to provide what I believe is a necessary balance to the more traditionally philosophical emphasis of the other thinkers. In the final chapter, "The Differentiation and Integration of Consciousness in the Individual and in History," I will also discuss the thought of Girard's close collaborator, the psychiatrist Jean-Michel Oughourlian.

The actual order of the chapters and the sequence of the thinkers introduced in them is in accord with what came to seem to me the immanent logic of this particular inquiry. It begins with Polanyi, because as a scientist turned philosopher of science, Polanyi introduces in a fairly basic and straightforward manner some considerations regarding the way thought and systematic inquiry demand to be understood. Polanyi was stimulated to this by what he believed was the inadequacy of the positivist paradigm that was predominant during his lifetime in the philosophy of science. The succeeding chapter proceeds to Lonergan because, even though Lonergan was a religious thinker whose immediate stimulus lay in the questions of theology, his thought, like Polanyi's, took its theoretical starting point in a reflection on the practice of scientific inquiry. Also, Lonergan seems to me to have gone further into some of the questions Polanyi raised regarding cognitional theory, even in relation to the natural sciences, than did Polanyi himself.

The philosophy of science tends to concentrate on questions regarding methods of knowing objective reality. Polanyi's and Lonergan's analysis of such knowing, however, introduces the question of the subjective dimension of consciousness and its role in objective cognition. Lonergan was more insistent than Polanyi on developing "objective" knowledge of subjectivity, with the result that within the internal dialectic of Lonergan's thought there developed what, according to my reading of him, seems a persistent tension between the thrust of questioning toward the specifiability of the objective pole and what for Polanyi always remained the unspecifiability of the subjective pole, or, as he frequently called it, the "tacit dimension."

One way to state this issue would be to say that although Lonergan genuinely appreciated the unique qualities of subjectivity and never completely abandoned the idea that the subjective dimension of consciousness is not entirely reducible to an object of science, the logic of questioning as he conceived it suggested a movement in that direction. Lonergan's later works placed increasing emphasis on what he came to call the "existential subject," but he never developed an analysis of that topic parallel in depth and thoroughness to the analysis of objective cognition he offered in his *Insight*. Even the reference to the focus of that topic as a "subject," moreover, tends to connote for it, as was suggested above, an entitative status. This may be largely a matter of emphasis, but for the other thinkers studied here the notion of what Lonergan referred to as the "existential subject" suggests rather a mode of operation than an entitative operator. Even as a matter of emphasis, the ambiguity of the notion and its Lonerganian phrasing calls for some clarification, and much of the present book is devoted to the ways the other thinkers sketch out possibilities of clarifying it.

The exploration of human subjectivity in a way that would go beyond any entitative connotations was a central concern of Voegelin's thought. This is not to say that Voegelin, or any of the other thinkers discussed here, failed to appreciate the demands of cognitive objectivity. In fact all of these thinkers not only respected but genuinely understood the exigences of scientific thought, including Kierkegaard, who is often—wrongly, as I shall argue—thought of as an antiscientific irrationalist. All of them, however, have made a point of calling attention to, as Kierkegaard liked to put it, the difference between what one does know and what one does not know. Or to put it in the language of

Gabriel Marcel, who will be discussed as an important influence on both Ricoeur and Girard, they tended to emphasize the importance of recognizing the difference between a mystery and a problem. As the discussion of Voegelin, Ricoeur, and Kierkegaard will attempt to make clear, the latter distinction closely correlates with that between the subjective and objective dimensions of consciousness.

It was with this issue in mind that Voegelin placed such emphasis on the way in which human beings have always felt a need to explore the mystery of subjectivity and have done so through the analogical medium of the mythic imagination. Lonergan, as we shall see, sometimes spoke of myth as though it were simply a prescientific and inadequate substitute for science. Voegelin, on the other hand, valued science as highly as any other modern thinker, but he also considered myth or, to be more precise, metaphor to be an indispensable mode of thought in relation to the subjective dimension of consciousness, and his own thought took as its starting point the ways in which such metaphoric exploration of human and divine mystery developed and functioned historically from the time of our earliest records to the present. He imaged human existence as a drama in which all of us can discover ourselves to be actors called on to play our roles well, but without clear knowledge of what those roles are or could be. The variety of myths human beings have developed, Voegelin thought, have grown out of their effort to develop some notion of the script of the drama they find themselves caught up in. Because this drama is experienced as a task in which either success or failure is possible, moreover, and in which a possibly transcendent meaning of existence is at stake, the question of human evil comes to be experienced as having a more than theoretical urgency.

Ricoeur has shared Voegelin's interest in the mythic imagination and the problems of understanding the human calling as oriented both toward action in the world and toward some form of potential transcendence, and he has also shared his concern with understanding our ways of thinking about human evil. Ricoeur's own reflections, however, led him to place more emphasis than Voegelin on the possible dangers of the mythic imagination and the consequent importance, as was mentioned above, of the hermeneutics of suspicion as a counterbalance to the temptations of both myth and philosophy. Voegelin's strategy tended to be one of identifying, on the grounds of their historically originary, or, as he called it, "primary," symbolism those myths that can be considered existentially authentic and authoritative. Such myths express what Voegelin termed, following Bergson, "open" existence as distinct from those that expressed "closed" existence and constituted examples of philosophical and existential "derailment." Voegelin was not at all naive about the need to look suspiciously at the guiding myths of human communities, but Ricoeur would probably suspect that he may nevertheless have been somewhat naive in his belief that they can be so neatly separated into the categories of authentic and inauthentic. Ricoeur has a strong affinity for the Adamic myth of universal human fallenness. The hallmark of the hermeneutic of suspicion that he came to find of value in Freud, therefore, is that from such a point of view suspicion is directed first and foremost against oneself and one's own susceptibility to the temptation of self-serving and deceptive images. Myths, Ricoeur might say, may lead us astray as well as guide us toward existential truth, and each myth itself brings into our lives a chiaroscuro of mingled insight and temptation that calls for us to be always on our guard.

Girard's special contribution in this context lies in the way he has sought to discover the psychological mechanisms that govern our imaginations and drive us, as long as we leave them to control us unconsciously, toward the evils either of mutual destruction or of victimization. Both Voegelin and Ricoeur have tended to treat human evil as a mystery in Marcel's sense. Girard, on the other hand, treats it as a problem with a definite intelligible structure, even if its solution may involve a dimension of mystery. The reason human evil has always seemed to us a mystery, he suggests, is that the controlling mechanisms of human psychology have not only lain undetected but they have actually been systematically falsified by a variety of what he terms "romantic" evasions—of which Freud's emphasis on the objective force of sexual desire has been one example among a multitude. Girard and Oughourlian believe that all human beings are moved on the most fundamental level by a drive to unconscious imitation not only of the objective behavior but also of the subjective attitudes of others. This has led them to a thoroughgoing revision of the entire framework of Freudian psychopathology. In Girard's thought, especially, it has led to a radical critique of traditional religiousness and its mythologies. To explain how all this is worked out will have to wait for Girard's chapter and the final one, but a simple way to put its implications for the study of Voegelin and

Ricoeur is to say that whereas both tend to seek wisdom in mythic thought through a hermeneutic of recovery, even if it is balanced to some degree by a hermeneutic of suspicion, Girard makes the hermeneutic of suspicion central and directs it against all mythic thought as such. Whereas Voegelin and Ricoeur seek to discern in the universal drama of human life and its mythological expressions some outline of a true script that would offer clues to the inherent meaning of human existence, Girard believes he has discovered the essential outline of the mythic script, and he has found it thoroughly sinister: the endlessly duplicated, mindless, and compulsive killing of a sacrificial victim.

Girard speaks of this with a prophetic fervor because he also believes that compulsive as this scenario is, it is nevertheless not inevitable. The deciphering and demystifying of this sinister script and the unmasking of the mechanism that drives us repeatedly to enact it can serve, he believes, at least partially to disarm it. He is hardly an optimist about this possibility, however. In fact he believes the *mécanisme victimaire* or "victimizing mechanism" is so deeply rooted in human nature that the most we can hope for is through consciousness of its insistent workings to win some very small clearing in our lives for the exercise of genuine freedom. This demands constant vigilance—above all, a vigilance against ourselves. And even at its most lucid, this vigilance will never root out from our lives the power of the mechanism and the potential seductiveness of the mythic thinking it uses to entice us into its trammels.

I referred above to the fact that even if Girard conceives of human evil as a problem in Marcel's sense rather than a mystery, its solution for him retains a dimension of mystery. Despite his distrust of all traditions of mythic thinking and his strong criticisms of what he calls "historical Christianity," Girard draws on Christian theological language to speak of the possibility of transcendence. His works through *Violence and the Sacred* say nothing of this, but his subsequent writings, mostly as yet untranslated from the French, speak of Christ as the incarnation of the nonviolent God who is both intelligence and love and who stands always on the side of the victim. In Girard's developed religious thought, Christ becomes not only the symbol but the actual living presence of what some of the other thinkers in this study would speak of as fully developed existential subjectivity. At the same time, however,

Girard is as critical as anyone of the notion of an entitative subject, which he considers mythological not just in the pre-scientific sense, but much more importantly in what he thinks is the distinctly sinister sense that it is part and parcel of the sacrificial mentality born of the *mécanisme victimaire*. Girard considers "historical Christianity," with its idea of Jesus as an expiatory sacrifice, to be a reversion to this mentality and the betrayal of what he believes is the essential truth of the Christian faith.

The theological anthropology toward which Girard rather sketchily points involves a much more radical demythologizing than either Lonergan or Rudolf Bultmann ever considered. It also implies a theology and Christology that would emphasize both that the true God is to be found in Christ and that Christ is not to be understood as a sacralized entitative subject, but is to be looked for only in the transcendent life that is the potentially universal subjective presence of the incarnate God.

To speak in such a manner, of course, is to use the language of Kierkegaard and to begin to probe the themes of such works as the *Philosophical Fragments* and *Concluding Unscientific Postscript to the Philosophical Fragments* as well as such other central works in his canon as *Fear and Trembling, The Sickness Unto Death,* and *The Concept of Anxiety.* I think that by the time the reader has worked his way through the dialectic of the other five thinkers he will see a variety of reasons why this inquiry culminates appropriately in a reconsideration of the thought of Kierkegaard and its implications for Christian philosophy in our period.

One of the major points in common between the figures studied in the present volume is that all of them have been in some manner or another closely associated with the tradition of Christian thought and have tried to point directions for its future development, even if in some cases their relation to it has been somewhat problematic from the point of view of the orthodox.

There has been a good deal of controversy in Voegelin's case, for example, as to whether he was in any sense at all a Christian thinker despite his numerous positive references to Christ and the doctrine of the Incarnation. I explored this issue myself in an article in *The Thomist* in 1978 and in the "Philosophy of Religion" chapter of my book on

Voegelin.[10] There is no need for me to go into the details of that discussion here. It will suffice perhaps if I state again my basic conclusion that although Voegelin was not a churchgoer and clearly not an *orthodox* Christian, he still thought of himself as a Christian thinker and that it makes sense to speak of him as one. He was not the first important heterodox Christian thinker, and he will not be the last one—and it may eventually turn out to be very important for the health and future of Christianity that there continue to be dissenting figures who nevertheless take Christianity seriously and see it, despite what they consider its historical decay, as a bearer of spiritual truth.

One of the things I said about Voegelin's thought in the earlier discussion that may help to clarify his relevance for the question of a Christian philosophy in our own period and among the present set of thinkers was that "from Voegelin's point of view the Incarnation is not something that takes place exclusively in Jesus, but is the same mystery of divine-human participation in which all human beings are involved—to the extent that they actually rise to their potential humanity."[11] I also quoted Voegelin himself as saying, "Transfiguring incarnation . . . does not begin with Christ, as Paul assumed, but becomes conscious through Christ and Paul's vision as the eschatological *telos* of the transfiguring process that goes on in history before and after Christ and constitutes its meaning."[12]

This brief quotation should make clear where the orthodox would probably find the major difference between their own thought and Voegelin's. Read in the light of the discussion of Girard above, it should also make clear something of what he and Voegelin have in common. I hope that the chapter on Kierkegaard will also make clear what the thought of each has in common with the latter's reflections on the meaning of the Christian faith.

Polanyi did not speak as much about Christian thought in his writ-

---

10. "Eric Voegelin's Theory of Revelation," *The Thomist* 42 (1978): 95–122; *Eric Voegelin: Philosopher of History*, pp. 211–36. The article on Voegelin's theory of revelation has also been reprinted in *Eric Voegelin's Thought: A Critical Appraisal*, ed. Ellis Sandoz, pp. 157–78.

11. *Eric Voegelin*, p. 233.

12. *Order and History*, vol. 4: *The Ecumenic Age*, pp. 269–70, quoted ibid., pp. 233–34.

ings as Voegelin did, but he makes numerous references nevertheless to the gospels, and he always thought of himself as closely related to the Christian tradition, even if slightly to one side of it. He too was unchurched, but at various times in his life he seems to have made more effort than Voegelin did to try to align himself with a church tradition. His son, John Polanyi, has told me that his father liked to attend the Church of England on its major feast days and on occasion discussed with various priests the possibility of a formal affiliation. These discussions never actually bore fruit, but the fact that they took place indicates both a sense of affinity on Polanyi's part for the Christian tradition and a sense of awkwardness in relation to some aspects of its traditional expression. Ricoeur's protestant Christianity, on the other hand, has always been clear, but his explorations of the tradition have also been as original, searching, and even challenging in their way as were those of Voegelin and Polanyi.

Of course Lonergan was an eminently orthodox priest and theologian of the Roman Catholic church. He is less known to the general public than such figures as Karl Rahner, Hans Küng, or Edward Schillebeeckx, to name just a few other prominent modern Catholic thinkers, but as professor of systematic theology at the Gregorian University he trained a whole generation of theologians in the 1950s and 1960s, and he attempted—it seems with a good deal of success, to judge by his influence—to lay the methodological foundations for theological thinking well into the next century.

Lonergan may also, however, be the only one among these figures who did not include Kierkegaard among his formative influences or perhaps even among the figures he ever actually took up for study. As a traditionally educated Catholic theologian he was steeped in the thought of St. Thomas Aquinas, and he also speaks of Hegel, despite his criticisms of him, as marking a major point of return to the rediscovery of the world of interiority that Aquinas had explored before Scotus and Ockham had led subsequent thinking down another path. The particularly Protestant emphasis of Kierkegaard, on the other hand, does not seem to have evoked Lonergan's special interest.

I spoke earlier of how a comparison of Lonergan and Voegelin led me in the course of my own research for this volume to reflect that the difference between them involved an important parallel to that in the preceding century between Hegel and Kierkegaard. To a large extent Hegel and Kierkegaard may be said to have established the line of demarcation along which the possibilities of modern Christian philosophy necessarily divide, and the tensions, or even clashes, between Lonergan's thought and that of the other thinkers represented here reflect that fundamental division.

To state the issue in the simplest terms, Hegel considered the goal of human thought and spiritual development to lie in an ultimate transcendence of the difference between subject and object. This was to be attained in the contemplation of the Absolute Idea in which all of human and even cosmic history would find its culmination. The affinity of Lonergan's thought for the Hegelian thrust can be seen in those parts of his *Insight* in which he linked the question of the existence of God with that of "the idea of being," which he said "would be the content of an unrestricted act of understanding that primarily understood itself and consequently grasped every other intelligibility" (p. 657). The idea of the ultimate union of subject and object at the peak of the hierarchy of being is further emphasized by the way Lonergan refers to God as the "primary being" who is to be understood as "spiritual in the full sense of the identity of the intelligent and intelligible" (p. 658). The difference between Lonergan's thought and Hegel's lies in the fact that this notion of being is designated by Lonergan as supernatural and discontinuous with human intellectual development. Still, from the point of view of a Kierkegaard or of some of the other figures here discussed who emphasize the ultimate irreducibility of the subject-object distinction, this difference between Lonergan and Hegel may not be as important as the similarity it attempts to negate.

In one of the philosophical myths sketched in his *Phaedrus*, Plato has his Socrates picture the universe as marked by a line of division between the cosmos and what is beyond the cosmos. The gods are able, Socrates says, to mount to the peak of heaven and gaze with direct and clear vision on the realm of the Ideas that lies beyond. Human beings also may, by drawing on the power of a god, ascend to the heavens, but they are unable to catch more than fragmentary and confused glimpses of the Ideas. This myth was a favorite of Voegelin's, and he emphasized the importance of accepting the limitations of man's place in the cosmos as there delineated. What Voegelin called "gnostic" derailments from genuine philosophy consisted, according to his way of thinking, in the presumptuous claim to be able to transcend the human condition and look directly, in the manner of Plato's gods, on the contents of the Beyond. Voegelin's constant criticism of Hegel was that he thought such vision not only possible but the essence of the philosophical calling.

It may be, however, that Voegelin did not note sufficiently the inherent ambiguity of Plato's myth: it clearly places human beings below the gods in the hierarchy of knowledge, but it also depicts that hierarchy as culminating in a realm in which ideal knowledge and perfection of being are one and the same. Depending on which aspect one emphasizes, the myth can be taken to point either toward the imperfection of human knowledge of the Beyond or toward the idea that at least some glimpses of it are possible to man and that perfect knowledge of it is possible to knowers who transcend the human condition. Hegel was drawing as clearly in his own way as was Voegelin in his on the actually quite ambiguous implications of Plato's imagery.

Much of the Western tradition of philosophy since Plato has involved exactly the type of thinking and aspiration Hegel gives expression to. Arthur O. Lovejoy's classic study, *The Great Chain of Being,* is a tracing of the manifold ways in which ideas of ontological hierarchy were explored from the time of Plato through the German Idealists of the nineteenth century. What is significant for the present consideration is that in the picture Lovejoy unfolds, it is clear that the difference between an Aquinas and a Hegel in this tradition seems little more than one of emphasis or of shading, with the family resemblance far outweighing any differences. Both thinkers, along with the Lonergan of *Insight* as their intellectual descendant, could be said in this respect to stand within the general tradition that conceived of God and man as embraced within an overarching order of being that has the ultimate character of logical ideality and that culminates in the identity of thought and being.

There was also, within the European Christian tradition, an opposing school of thought, of which William of Ockham became a major spokesman in the century after Aquinas. This held that God must not be conceived of in a way that would reduce his absolute freedom and sovereignty by subordinating these to the necessity of an overarching ideal order.[13] For Ockham, to say that God willed the good by a necessity of his nature, as Aquinas had said, suggested that God was constrained by the immanent logic of his own being or essence. Ockham's own solution was to emphasize God's sovereign autonomy, even to the point of declaring that God could actually will evil and make evil good by the *fiat* of his command. Much of Christian thought in the past has been torn between these extremes of objectivistic essentialism and subjectivistic existentialism—between a God of logical structure on the one hand and a monstrous caricature of voluntaristic human egoism on the other.

Both of these earlier paths in Christian thought now seem to have largely exhausted themselves and lost their clientele, as may Christianity as a whole if it cannot develop into something different from the rationalization of a decaying mythology. A further value, therefore, at least for some readers, to the study of the six thinkers in the present volume is that, as explorers of new possibilities for religious philosophy, they have engaged in a serious effort to find a path beyond such earlier impasses by addressing the question of the relation between subjectivity and objectivity in consciousness. I will try in what follows to make clear how they have done so and how in the process, through the exploration of both intellectual and psychological considerations, they have brought new issues to the fore that will have to be taken into account by any Christian thought of the future that wishes to be taken seriously.

Not all readers of this book, however, will have a special interest in these thinkers as specifically religious philosophers—and for understandable reasons. Many modern inquirers feel generally wary of the highly connotative languages of religious traditions, and for some of these the language of psychology has come to function as an effective replacement for it. I think myself that an adequate philosophy of religion in our century, just as much as an adequate philosophy of consciousness, will need to take into account the insights developed by the various schools of pyschoanalysis, and in my last chapter I will examine in some detail the specifically psychological theories of Girard's collaborator, the psychiatrist Jean-Michel Oughourlian.

13. For a study, explicitly intended as a complement to Lovejoy's, on this topic, see Francis Oakley, *Omnipotence, Covenant, and Order: An Excursion in the History of Ideas from Abelard to Leibniz.*

Whatever the reader's specific interest and point of departure—philosophical, theological, or psychological—it is my hope that the study of the six thinkers who are the focus of the present volume can serve to open up for exploration the depths of problem and mystery at the heart of all human experience. The fundamental philosophical challenge that faces us all in the world of modern thought is that of finding a way to reconcile the demands of the differentiation of consciousness with our parallel need for an integration of consciousness. This is not an entirely new challenge, of course. Rather as Voegelin insisted, it is one that began for those of us in the European tradition with the first stirrings in ancient Greece of systematic reflection on the structure and dynamism of the questioning consciousness. It is a challenge, however, that has been continuously increasing in pressure to the point that there is no longer scarcely anyone among us who does not experience acutely the insistency of its claims and who does not also feel somewhat threatened as a result with a possible loss of psychic wholeness and sense of spiritual direction. Many of the disturbances of modern culture derive in fairly obvious ways from attempts on the part of individuals or groups to recover a sense of such wholeness and direction by setting aside this challenge in favor of some form of claim to immediate intuition of truth or being or the good. Whatever their differences, the six thinkers studied here all agree that this is not a genuine alternative and that the only path to a truly adequate integration of consciousness is the one that leads not around but directly through the experience of its differentiation. Our challenge, they suggest, is to follow that path faithfully to its end, where they also hope we will discover the fullness of life that we long for.

CHAPTER 1

Michael Polanyi

Consciousness
as Focal and Subsidiary Awareness

OF THE FOUR thinkers to be studied in this book, Michael Polanyi is the only one, with the possible exception of Eric Voegelin, to offer anything especially colorful in the way of biographical background. Even in Polanyi's case, it must be said, the color lies less in his own life than in that of his family: the Polanyis came out of Hungary in the early part of this century to dwell in diverse milieux and to play prominent, if very different, roles in each of them. Peter Drucker, who was a close friend of Polanyi's elder brother, Karl, wrote about the family recently in his memoir, *Adventures of a Bystander*. He says their father "was born between 1825 and 1830 in a small Jewish settlement in the Hungarian mountains" and that after participating in the Hungarian revolt against the Habsburgs in 1848 he "escaped to Switzerland where he studied engineering and became a stern Calvinist" (p. 127). There, says Drucker, he married an anarchist Russian countess who had also fled to Switzerland in the aftermath of a bomb plot (for which she had built the bomb in the chemistry laboratory of the Czar's School for Daughters of the Nobility). In the 1920s the eldest of the Polanyi brothers, Otto, became a major industrialist in Italy, where he changed his name to Otto Pol.[1]

---

1. I should note, however, that it is difficult to determine exactly how reliable Drucker's account of the family history is. He presumably received his information from Karl. I tried to confirm the account with Michael Polanyi's son, John, who followed his father into the field of physical chemistry and is now a professor at the University of Toronto. John had not heard some of the material Drucker recounts, and in some cases his impression of the family history was quite different. In this case, for example, John had never heard of his uncle Otto, and the account of his grandfather as a "stern Calvinist" and his grandmother as a Russian countess was also completely new to him. His own impression was that his

He also became a Marxist and a financial backer of the socialist newspaper *Avanti*, of which Mussolini was the editor. Later Otto became disillusioned with Marxism and converted to a nationalistic political ideology of class unity based on a corporate state. This was, of course, the ideology that later became known as fascism. Otto evidently played a major role in converting Mussolini to it also. Subsequently, however, he became disillusioned with both fascism and Mussolini and ended, says Drucker, "a broken, bitter old man" (p. 129). The next brother in age, Adolph, emigrated to Brazil, where he sought "an interracial society in which whites, blacks, and Indians would meld to create a new civilization, modern yet tribal, free yet not individualist" (p. 129).

After Otto and Adolph came their sister, Mousie, who around 1900 at the age of nineteen became a leader in the Hungarian folk movement.[2] This had an artistic side (Bartok and Dohnanyi) as well as a political and social vision: of a life centered in the communal village. Mousie Polanyi edited a magazine of this movement and through this organ helped to define and direct it. One of her followers was Josip Broz, later Marshal Tito, whose ideas about the self-governing village community and the self-governing factory community were not Marxist, says Drucker, but based on Mousie Polanyi's movement of "rural sociology" (pp. 130–31).

Karl Polanyi, who eventually became a professor of economic history at Bennington and Columbia, was between Mousie and Michael in age. When Drucker first met him in Vienna in the depressed period after World War I, he was editing the *Austrian Economist* and living in poverty while giving most of his income to the relief of Hungarian refugees. Karl is now best known for his study of the social and cultural effects of the rise of capitalistic market economies in *The Great Transformation*, which he wrote after emigrating to the United States shortly before World War II. Its central argument was that the significant factor in

Jewish ancestors had by the time of his grandfather's generation become liberal agnostics. It may be, however, that these aspects of the family history were simply not discussed in John's home after Michael had left that other world behind when he moved to England to escape Hitler's Germany. And of course Drucker, as a member of Karl's generation and a long-term friend of the family, would have had a firsthand acquaintance with events that would have been long past by the time John was growing up.

    2. John Polanyi says that his aunt's proper name was Laura, but that it is true everyone called her Mousie.

that development was the extension of the market system and its impersonal law of supply and demand from goods and capital, where it could function appropriately, to land and especially labor, with the effect that people came to be considered commodities with a purely economic value. To counteract this dehumanizing tendency, Karl advocated redistribution of wealth and reciprocity of commitments and obligations according to social and political rather than economic norms. He hoped to find some precedent in history for such a system, an illustration of a possible alternative and a proof of its viability, but although he spent the remainder of his life searching for it, he could never find an example that stood up to careful scrutiny. He believed nonetheless that the logical and inevitable end of capitalism would lie in fascist tyranny unless his alternative could be realized. The driving force of his life was his need to keep trying against all frustrations to oppose this impending tragic destiny. "If there was one article of faith," says Drucker, "to which all the Polanyis subscribed—from Karl's father on—it was that the 'laissez-faire' Liberals of the nineteenth-century Manchester School were wrong in their assertion that the market is the only alternative to serfdom. Indeed the market creed of the Manchester Liberals may be called the hereditary enemy of the House of Polanyi" (p. 138). "But the more Karl delved into prehistory, primitive economics, and classical antiquity," he goes on to say, "the more proof did he find for the hated and despised market creed of Ricardo and Bentham, and also of Karl's contemporary bogeymen, Ludwig von Mises and Frederick Hayek of the Austrian School" (p. 138).

Michael Polanyi, too, suggests Drucker, was looking for an alternative in the form of what he calls, rather strangely in the light of Polanyi's actual writings, "Michael's stoic desire-free individual" (p. 138). "At first," Drucker says, "like all the Polanyis, he was concerned with society and social processes. He looked to science to find the way out between a bourgeois capitalism that denied community and a Marxist socialism that denied freedom and the person. But very soon he gave up on society and became instead a humanist philosopher, opposed alike to the positivism and rationalism of the traditional 'Liberal' and to the anti-human collectivism of the Socialists and Marxists. Human existence for Michael Polanyi is existence as an isolated individual; and the individual is grounded in values and ethic, rather than in logic and reason" (pp. 131–32).

This last comment would probably have bewildered Polanyi, since his writings, besides having important political and social implications, were devoted primarily and with passionate intensity to an effort to understand and clarify the workings of genuine intelligence and thereby to open a clearer path for the life of reason. It was this above all else that he looked to for a solution to the problems that in his and his father's generations had become insistently conscious among the various Polanyis. Far, however, from giving up on society, he held that only in cooperation with others in the development of understanding and in responsible action can the full development of human personhood take place.[3] Nor is it clear what in Polanyi's writings Drucker could have taken as advocacy of the ideal of a completely "desire-free" individual, since he argues against the idea of the totally detached scientist and in favor of the necessary role of intellectual passion in inquiry (*Study of Man*, pp. 36–37).

It is worth mentioning this background of political and cultural concern, because it makes clear what might otherwise be easy to overlook as a result of the emphasis of the present study on theoretical issues having to do with consciousness and cognition. In fact, the practical, ethical, and political implications of such issues have been of central importance to each of the thinkers to be studied. Voegelin is of course well known as a political philosopher, and he was himself very closely involved during his Vienna years in the intellectual circles of Karl's two "bogeymen," Hayek and Mises. Despite his largely unwarranted reputation as a "conservative" thinker, moreover, Voegelin also differed from these political economists in the same way Drucker indicated that Michael did. Despite his distrust of coercion, even for commendable ends, on the part of a centralized state, Voegelin would have been as opposed as any Polanyi to an ideology of "laissez-faireism." The fundamental principle of such a creed in practical terms is the centering of all genuine value in the egoistic desires of economic agents, a principle Voegelin explicitly criticized in his study of Helvetius, where he pointed out the parallel of Helvetius's concept of "amour de soi" to what Augustine called the "amor sui" in opposition to what he considered the true center of the soul's life in the "amor Dei."[4]

---

3. See, for example, his *Study of Man*, p. 60.
4. *From Enlightenment to Revolution*, ed. John H. Hallowell, pp. 45–51.

Paul Ricoeur has also been interested in political issues as an author of political essays and a member of the editorial board of the left-Catholic periodical, *Esprit,* and was himself involved actively in the political events in France in the late 1960s as rector of the University of Paris at Nanterre.[5] René Girard, Ricoeur's younger compatriot, has not been especially involved in politics, perhaps in part because he has made his academic career outside France, but the political and social implications of some of his ideas have attracted a great deal of attention among contemporary French thinkers, including economists, political scientists, and sociologists.[6]

Bernard Lonergan, who spent his entire career as a Jesuit professor of theology, would seem the least likely of these figures to be directly concerned with political and economic issues, but as recent studies of his thought have shown, Lonergan's writings embody a highly developed philosophy of history, and his own major scholarly efforts of the last decade before his death in 1984 were directed toward completing a book on economic theory which he began in the 1930s.[7]

The apparent paradox that thinkers whose writings have emphasized what might seem rather abstract theory should also have been intensely concerned with culture, society, politics, and economics is easily resolvable. It is an expression of their common belief in Plato's principle that social and political order flows from and depends on right order within the individual: that intelligent and appropriate action in the world depends upon adequate understanding of both oneself and one's situation within the comprehensive framework of reality.

To return, however, to Michael Polanyi, his own career was that of a scientist who eventually turned to reflection on the cognitive process he had experienced in the practice of science. His scientific work was distinguished, and it has been said that he was at one time considered as a

5. For translations of some of Ricoeur's political writings, see his *Political and Social Essays,* ed. David Stewart and Joseph Bien.

6. See, for example, the essays of the Colloque de Cerisy of June 1983, *Violence et vérité: Autour de René Girard,* ed. Paul Dumouchel.

7. On Lonergan's philosophy of history, see the dissertation of Thomas J. McPartland, "Horizon Analysis and Historiography: The Contribution of Bernard Lonergan Toward a Critical Historiography" (University of Washington, 1976). On Lonergan's economic theory, see William Mathews, "Lonergan's Economics," *Method: Journal of Lonergan Studies,* 3, no. 1 (March, 1985): 9–30.

possible candidate for a Nobel Prize in either physics or chemistry.[8] His work extended into both disciplines. In 1923 he was elected to the Kaiser Wilhelm Institut für Physikalische Chemie and was made a life member in 1929, though he resigned that in 1933 when he left to take up permanent residence in England and become professor of physical chemistry at Victoria University in Manchester. In 1944 he was elected a fellow of the Royal Society.

From his own description of it, it seems that Polanyi's interest in philosophical reflection on science and cognition in general developed in large part out of his dissatisfaction with the currently prevalent account, which was that of positivism. This had been represented in the Vienna of his youth by Ernst Mach and later in England by the influence of figures from Moritz Schlick's "Vienna Circle." To make clear the issues involved it will be helpful to consider briefly what the positivism was with which Polanyi would have been most familiar.

Although the term "positivism" derives from Saint-Simon and Auguste Comte, the central European positivist tradition was more strongly influenced by the earlier British philosophers John Locke and David Hume. The history of this development is well told by David F. Lindenfeld in his *Transformation of Positivism: Alexius Meinong and European Thought, 1880–1920*. From the British empiricists, says Lindenfeld, came three central assumptions: (1) the atomistic model of both mental contents and corresponding reality, (2) the analytic approach to knowledge, and (3) the introspective criterion, the idea that all real knowledge comes from inner perception of mental contents. With reference to the atomistic model, he says that it was Locke who established the idea of the mind as consisting "primarily of a number of distinct, nugget-like experiences called 'ideas' or 'presentations'" (p. 17). Coupled with this in Locke's conception was a corpuscular theory of physical reality and a tendency to assume that the "ideas" and the corpuscular physical units were basically alike both in structure and in their constancy over time.

Closely related to the atomistic model was the analytic approach, the belief "that the best way to describe a complex topic, say the human mind or the properties of gross physical bodies, was to break it down

8. Drucker, *Adventures*, p. 131. His son, John Polanyi, did win the Nobel Prize for Chemistry in 1986.

into its simpler conceptual elements or 'parts' and describe these separately" (p. 22). The natural result of this approach was, of course, "a tendency to reductionism—that is, to derive all ideas from a single homogeneous type" (p. 19). A reality that could be truly known only in terms of atomistically conceived elements could never, without intellectual inconsistency, be conceived of as involving comprehensive systems with a unity, totality, and integrity of their own.

The special contribution of Ernst Mach, who succeeded to Franz Brentano's chair at the University of Vienna, was to revive and clarify these principles as derived from the British Empiricists. "Mach's role in the transformation of positivistic thinking," says Lindenfeld, "may be summarized as follows: he succeeded in bringing positivism back into line with the empiricist tradition by stressing the atomistic model and the analytical approach which Comte and Spencer had both spurned. Unlike John Stuart Mill and Brentano, Mach interpreted these notions reductionistically: the homogeneity of elements is one of the most striking features of his thought. Like Mill and unlike Brentano, however, Mach did not value the introspective criterion so highly" (p. 85).

The advantage the analytic approach to knowledge seemed to offer was precision, the reduction Descartes had advocated of all supposed knowledge to "clear and distinct ideas" known with immediate, intuitive certainty. The opposite of this would be the "holistic" approach represented in the earlier Germanic tradition by such figures as Goethe and Hegel, and by such later figures as Freud or Wolfgang Koehler—the idea that to try to understand a part without consideration of the whole is to distort it. Polanyi is himself clearly in the line of such holistic thinkers as against the atomistically analytic, and, as we shall see, he has been criticized by analytic thinkers for lack of precision as a result.

Polanyi had several objections against positivism as a philosophy of science. One was that in attending analytically to the elements of a system, positivism failed to appreciate the synthetic relations that united them on a higher, more comprehensive level. Another was that although positivism had some real value as a critique of false assumptions, it lacked fecundity of its own: it could clear some cobwebs, but could not itself lead to genuine knowledge. Applied consistently, he said, a positivistic theory of science would not only fail to guide a real process of discovery, but would actively inhibit it.

Polanyi began expressing these criticisms as early as 1946 in *Science*,

Faith, and Society. "The positivist movement was undoubtedly justified and successful," he wrote, "in pressing for the purification of science from tautologies and unwarranted implications, but the great discoveries resulting from this process cannot be credited to any purely analytical operation. What happened was that scientific intuition made use of the positivist critique for reshaping its creative assumptions concerning the nature of things" (p. 88). The true creativity and discovery in science, however, come not from positivist methodology but from the scientist's fundamental belief that reality was objectively knowable even if the process by which it was known could not be rendered fully explicit. The purgative value of positivism, Polanyi recognized, derives from its heritage of skepticism regarding what cannot be known explicitly. But his own reflections on the method of actual science convinced him that the working scientist does not in reality proceed on the basis of strictly positivist conceptions. Contrary to positivist claims and to popular belief influenced by them, a consistently positivistic attitude, once it had cleared away the bits of deadwood it is adequate to deal with, would undermine the work of an actual scientist: " ... it would destroy, in fact, belief in truth and in the love of truth itself which is the condition of all free thought" (p. 76).

That a positivistic philosophy of science, which Polanyi traces back to Bacon and Descartes, has been predominant for so long without effectively inhibiting actual science "only shows," Polanyi said, "that people can carry on a great tradition even while professing a philosophy which denies its premises. For the adherents of a great tradition are largely unaware of their own premises, which lie deeply embedded in the unconscious foundations of practice" (p. 76). Even where the scientist himself fails to notice or clearly understand them, the fruitful premises of science embodied tacitly in his practice continue to function: "Thus science has been carried on succesfully for the last 300 years by scientists who were assuming that they were practising the Baconian method, which in fact can yield no scientific results whatever. Far from realizing the internal contradiction in which they are involved, those practising a tradition in the light of a false theory feel convinced —as have been generations of empiricists descending from Locke—that their false theories are vindicated by the success of their right practice" (pp. 76–77).

Polanyi believed that he knew from his own work as a scientist what a scientist actually does when he is developing scientific knowledge. But he also saw the hold that the positivistic account had on the imagination, which, he believed, unconsciously falsified the history of scientific discovery to accord with positivist assumptions. His principal theoretical treatise, *Personal Knowledge,* begins with a discussion of this problem. Arguing on the basis of Einstein's actual process of discovery of the theory of relativity, Polanyi explains how the story of this discovery, far from confirming the positivist view as has been widely supposed, provides excellent evidence for its refutation.

According to the standard textbook accounts, he says, Einstein developed his theory in order to account for the negative results of the Michelson-Morley experiment in 1887, which had been undertaken in order to measure what was assumed would be the difference between the speed of light in the direction of the earth's motion and its speed away from it. Michelson and Morley found out to their surprise that the speed of light was constant, no matter what the state of motion of the observer. This took place well before Einstein published his theory; but, as Polanyi says he confirmed with Einstein himself, the theory of relativity was not based on news of that experiment but on entirely independent thought begun before it: "Its findings were, on the basis of pure speculation, rationally intuited by Einstein before he had ever heard about it" (p. 10). The positivistic account, says Polanyi, is therefore "an invention" and "the product of a philosophical prejudice": "When Einstein discovered rationality in nature, unaided by any observation that had not been available for at least fifty years before, our positivistic textbooks promptly covered up the scandal by an appropriately embellished account of his discovery" (p. 11).

The implications of this example for a critique of the positivist theory of science are far more significant, believed Polanyi, than the mere fact of the fictionalizing of scientific history would indicate. Einstein said that Ernst Mach's *Die Mechanik in ihrer Entwicklung* (1889) had a "profound influence" on his thought.[9] This influence was a positive force in the development of relativity theory, but the irony is that it was not the sort of influence Mach himself could have imagined having. It grew out of Mach's objection to Newton's idea of absolute space, on

9. *Albert Einstein: Philosopher-Scientist* (Evanston, 1949), p. 21, quoted in *Personal Knowledge,* p. 11.

the ground that since it could not be tested by experiment it was mean-ingless. Einstein, however, accepting the empiricist criterion that space is what can be measured, went on to show that Newton's conception of space could indeed be tested and proven not meaningless but false. As Polanyi describes it, the fecundity of Mach's criticism of Newton lay not in its positivism but in intimations pointing in a quite different direction:

> Mach's great merit lay in possessing an intimation of a mechanical uni-verse in which Newton's assumption of a single point at absolute rest was eliminated. His was a super-Copernican vision, totally at variance with our habitual experience. For every object we perceive is set off by us in-stinctively against a background which is taken to be at rest. To set aside this urge of our senses, which Newton had embodied in his axiom of an "absolute space" said to be "inscrutable and immovable," was a tremendous step towards a theory grounded in reason and transcending the senses. Its power lay precisely in that appeal to rationality which Mach wished to eliminate from the foundations of science.... Thus Mach prefigured the great theoretic vision of Einstein, sensing its in-herent rationality, even while trying to exorcise the very capacity of the human mind by which he gained this insight. (P. 12)

The shift from belief in absolute space and time to relativity has im-portant implications in the thought of each of the first three thinkers studied in this book. Lonergan offered his own reflections on this prob-lem from the point of view of cognitional theory in connection with his analysis of the distinction between empirical and rational conscious-ness.[10] Voegelin has discussed Newton's commitment to absolute space, as compared with Leibniz's rejection of it, in connection with his cri-tique of scientism.[11] For Polanyi its main interest is as an illustration of the way the process of scientific knowing actually takes place and in so doing transcends any artificial restrictions placed on it by a false theory of heuristics.

Whatever the scientist may have learned to think about what he is doing, claims Polanyi, his actual work begins from a question in search of implicit rational order and proceeds to a solution on the basis of a

10. *Insight: A Study of Human Understanding*, pp. 152–72.
11. "The Origins of Scientism," *Social Research* 15 (1948): 467–70, 477–82.

fundamental trust that reality is inherently intelligible and knowable. The process of scientific knowing begins from experience that suggests a possibility of understanding and culminates in the testing of understanding against experience, but it is the anticipation of the actually intelligible, says Polanyi, that is the driving force of the entire process. As he stated the issue in his essay "Knowing and Being" (1961), "To hit upon a problem is the first step to any discovery and indeed to any creative act. To see a problem is to see something hidden that may yet be accessible. The knowledge of a problem is, therefore, like the knowing of unspecifiables, a knowing of more than you can tell. But our awareness of unspecifiable things, whether of particulars or of the coherence of particulars, is intensified here to an exciting intimation of their hidden presence. It is an engrossing possession of incipient knowledge which passionately strives to validate itself."[12]

The process of inquiry that begins and moves in this way, as Polanyi indicated by his reference to knowing more than you can tell, contains an element of unspecifiability which constitutes what he calls the "tacit dimension" of knowing. His own major philosophical contribution consisted mainly of his analysis of the structure of cognitive consciousness in the light of this irreducibly implicit dimension within knowing. The positivists as well as the entire rationalist tradition of epistemology before them, from Descartes through Kant, had emphasized the principle that genuine knowledge must not only itself be fully explicit but also be attainable by steps that are equally explicit. Its generally acknowledged paradigmatic form among the rationalists was geometry, in which self-evident premises and deductive step-by-step reasoning led to results that were seen to be logically certain and necessary.

This amounts to a demand that not only knowledge but also the entire knowing process be rendered perfectly objective. Polanyi was not opposed to objectivity as such, but to what he considered an exaggerated objectivism based on naiveté about what actually takes place in knowing. He believed, that is, that the positivist demand that all subjectivity be finally eliminated from knowledge was impossible to fulfill. To insist on its elimination, moreover, would be potentially destructive of actual intelligence, which includes by its very nature an irreducibly

---

12. *Knowing and Being: Essays by Michael Polanyi*, ed. Marjorie Grene, pp. 131–32.

subjective element. This objectivistic demand is in effect founded on the assumption that there could be knowing without the active involvement of a knower.

Polanyi has offered a number of illustrations to make clear what is involved in this issue. To cite just one, in *The Study of Man* he refers to the way we use a map to help us find our way through unfamiliar terrain. Both men and animals, he says, are able to use tacit knowing in the form of direct, unarticulated observation to find their way. Human beings, however, are also able to make use of maps, which make at least part of our knowledge of the terrain no longer just tacit, but explicit and communicable from one person to another. This has distinct advantages, but also certain hazards: the map might be incorrect in some details and therefore needs to be checked critically against one's direct observation of the scene. "The peculiar risk that we take in relying on any explicitly formulated knowledge," he says, "is matched by a peculiar opportunity offered by explicit knowledge for reflecting on it critically" (p. 15).

A map is constructed according to strict rules on the basis of systematically collected observations. The function of critical thought is to reexamine both the data and the chain of logical steps in search of some weak link. When no weak link is found, we know that the map is reliable. It is understandable, therefore, that we should aspire to render all knowledge explicit and critical in this way. As Polanyi says, "it seems almost inevitable then . . . to accept as our ideal the establishment of a completely precise and strictly logical representation of knowledge, and to look upon any personal participation in our scientific account of the universe as a residual flaw which should be completely eliminated in due course" (p. 18).

To make such total explicitness our aim, however, says Polanyi, would involve us in self-contradiction. It would be to overlook that the inherently tacit process of knowing is not identical with the explicit knowledge it arrives at. For one thing: "Even if we admitted that an exact knowledge of the universe is our supreme mental possession it would still follow that man's most distinguished act of thought consists in *producing* such knowledge" by acts that rely on "the kind of plunging reorientation which we share with the animals": "Fundamental novelty can be discovered only by the same tacit powers which rats use in learning a maze" (p. 18). Even more important, because it is grounded in the structure of consciousness itself, is the fact that there can be no knowledge without knowing, no objective cognitive product without subjective cognitive process, and that in that process "everywhere—at all mental levels—it is not the functions of articulate logical operations, but the tacit powers of the mind that are decisive" (p. 19).

Essentially, what Polanyi meant is that knowing is subjective: it is a consciously enacted process. It is oriented toward an objective pole, but it can never so totally objectify itself that only an object remains. Or to put it differently, there is no way that the actual performance of the operations by which we inquire, understand, and know can be turned into nothing more than a formulation—for this is what the demand that knowing be rendered totally explicit and objective amounts to. As Polanyi himself stated it, "Though the intellectual superiority of man over the animal remains due to his use of symbols, this utilization itself —the accumulation, the pondering and reconsideration of various subject matters in terms of the symbols designating them—is . . . a tacit, a-critical process. It is a performance. . . . Our whole articulate equipment turns out to be merely a tool-box, a supremely effective instrument for deploying our inarticulate faculties" (p. 25).

The process of knowing, therefore, inevitably involves an implicit or tacit dimension as its subjective pole along with its explicit, articulated objective pole.[13] Even if everything in reality, including the steps and levels of the knowing process itself, could in principle be rendered an explicit object of human knowledge, these various facets of objective reality could not all be known simultaneously. The knower would have to attend first to some, then to others, because at least some of reality, according to Polanyi, would be embodied in his own performance of operations bearing on objects other than the performance itself.

It is from this fact that Polanyi derived the central principle of his cognitional theory: his distinction between focal and subsidiary awareness. Consciousness, he found, involves the objective pole upon which subjective operations may be said to focus, but it also necessarily involves a nonfocal substratum of immediate experience and performance. Only what is focal can be rendered explicit and thereby known

13. Cf. The Tacit Dimension, p. 87.

with full clarity and critical objectivity—and then only for the duration of the time that it remains focal. What is subsidiary remains tacit and inherently "a-critical," so that we are obliged, whether we wish to or not, to place our trust in it even if to do so carries with it the risk of potential error. As he put it in *Personal Knowledge,* "the tacit coefficient is an act of confidence, and all confidence can be conceivably misplaced" (p. 250).

This last point makes clear the radical difference between Polanyi's epistemology and that which at least until recently was predominant in modern Western thought. Descartes had demanded irrefutable certainty and made skepticism its foundation; only what could withstand every possible doubt could be trusted. And Kant, though he differed from Descartes in many ways, continued to think that genuine knowledge must be demonstrably universal and necessary. Polanyi, on the other hand, said that his principal purpose in writing *Personal Knowledge* was "to achieve a frame of mind in which I may hold firmly to what I believe to be true, even though I know that it might conceivably be false" (p. 214). This was not an expression of irrationalism on Polanyi's part. Rather it expressed his recognition that our knowledge of empirical, contingent reality is never certain, but is a matter of judgment. It also expressed his acknowledgment of the fact that our actual process of knowing is inextricably involved through its tacit dimension in the realm of contingent events we seek to know. Polanyi also recognized the necessity of basic trust in the possibility of performing adequately the tacit operations that go into knowing.

Without this willingness to trust one's powers of critical reflection and judgment, every inquirer would be crippled; no one could ever take a first step on the path of discovery. Nor could one yield oneself to the love of truth that invites pursuit of that path and quickens and guides the mind on the journey. Referring in *The Tacit Dimension* to Karl Popper's claim that the scientist must seek not to verify but to falsify, Polanyi said, "This is not only contrary to experience, but logically inconceivable. The surmises of a working scientist are *born of the imagination seeking discovery.* Such effort *risks* defeat but never *seeks* it; it is in fact his craving for success that makes the scientist take the risk of failure" (pp. 78–79). Objectivity is sought because the love of truth demands it, but a naive demand for pure objectivity would erode the basic trust upon which all actual knowing inevitably is founded.[14]

This makes clear the nature of Polanyi's departure from the Cartesian methodology of systematic doubt. He also spoke of what he considered the fundamental inadequacy of Kantian thought. This derived in part, he said, from Kant's acceptance of the Cartesian principle of indubitability as stated in the *Critique of Pure Reason:* "Reason must in all its undertakings subject itself to criticism; should it limit freedom of criticism by any prohibitions, it must harm itself, drawing upon itself a damaging suspicion."[15] That no prohibition of questions regarding possible error should be imposed on inquiry Polanyi would agree, but as Polanyi interpreted him Kant took this to mean that in the absence of perfect, critically explicit proof of every step, a reasonable person must abstain from any judgment of truth.[16] Polanyi pointed out what he considered the fundamental fallacy in this commitment in his essay of 1962, "The Unaccountable Element in Science."[17] The fallacy lay in this program's impossibility of execution, a fact that he says was recognized by Kant himself: " . . . even a writer like Kant, so powerfully bent on strictly determining the rules of pure reason, occasionally admitted that into all acts of judgment there enters, and must enter, a personal decision which cannot be accounted for by any rules. Kant says that no system of rules can prescribe the procedure by which the rules themselves are to be applied" (p. 105). What makes the actual decision in the applications of rules, according to Kant, is our ultimately inscrutable "mother-wit," "a skill so deeply hidden in the human soul that we shall hardly guess the secret trick that Nature here employs."[18] For Kant to admit this at all, however, was implicitly to undermine the entire critical enterprise as he conceived it. "One may wonder," says Polanyi, "how a

14. One might reasonably object, however, that in this case Polanyi seems to have failed fully to grasp Popper's point, which is that a serious seeker of truth will want to subject his hypotheses to the most careful testing rather than settle for a facile confirmation. No more than Popper did Polanyi wish to justify facile judgment.

15. B 766, quoted in *Personal Knowledge*, pp. 271–72.

16. *Personal Knowledge*, p. 273. Polanyi's reference here is to *Critique of Pure Reason*, B 851. For a more recent criticism of Kant's demand for absolute rigor in philosophy and also of his inconsistency in pursuit of it, see Walter Kaufmann, *Discovering the Mind*, vol. 1: *Goethe, Kant, and Hegel*, pp. 106–9, 189–90. The particulars of Kaufmann's critique of Kant will be discussed in the chapter on Kierkegaard.

17. *Knowing and Being*, pp. 105–20.

18. *Critique of Pure Reason*, A 133 and A 141, quoted in *Knowing and Being*, p. 105.

critique of pure reason could accept the operations of such a powerful mental agency, exempt from any analysis, and make no more than a few scattered references to it. And one may wonder too that generations of scholars have left such an ultimate submission of reason to unaccountable decisions unchallenged. Perhaps both Kant and his successors instinctively preferred to let such sleeping monsters lie, for fear that, once awakened, they might destroy their fundamental conception of knowledge. For, once you face up to the ubiquitous controlling position of unformalizable mental skills, you do meet difficulties for the justification of knowledge that cannot be disposed of within the framework of rationalism" (p. 106).

It may reasonably be questioned whether Polanyi himself succeeded fully in meeting those difficulties, but his thought has the strength that it begins not with a shunting aside of this basic problem but with its clear recognition. Polanyi recognized that knowing took place before there was philosophy to reflect on it and that it can be genuine even if one cannot perfectly explain it. His own effort aimed not so much at a full justification of knowing as at an adequate description of the process of knowing as we experience it. Fundamental to this descriptive effort was his recognition within that process of "unformalizable mental skills" that operate implicitly even when we do not notice them explicitly.

All of Polanyi's philosophical work consists of commentary on this fundamental fact of consciousness. His distinction between the tacit and explicit dimensions of knowing is simply a statement of this fact, and his parallel distinction between focal and subsidiary awareness is the core of his analysis of it. From this derives his distinction between "knowing that," which has to do with the truth of focal, explicit knowing, and "knowing how," which is a matter of skillful performance experienced in subsidiary awareness. Also from the subsidiary-focal distinction derives his notion of "indwelling" or bodily presence as fundamental to the act of knowing. In *Personal Knowledge* he illustrates these concepts with examples of our experience of using tools.

First he takes up the example of using a hammer: "When we use a hammer to drive in a nail, we attend to both nail and hammer, *but in a different way*. We *watch* the effect of our strokes on the nail and try to wield the hammer so as to hit the nail most effectively" (p. 55). We are aware of the feelings in our palm and fingers, but our attention centers on the impact of the hammerhead on the nail. "The difference," Polanyi says, "may be stated by saying that" the feelings in the hand "are not, like the nail, objects of our attention, but instruments of it. They are not watched in themselves; we watch something else while keeping intensely aware of them. I have a *subsidiary awareness* of the feeling in the palm of my hand which is merged into my *focal awareness* of my driving in the nail" (p. 55).

To appreciate Polanyi's meaning it is important to realize the *functional* character of subsidiary awareness and not to confuse Polanyi's distinction between subsidiary and focal awareness with other distinctions that might be made from the point of view of other interests. Polanyi is not, for example, talking about a difference between focal and what might be called peripheral awareness. As he insisted in his essay "The Structure of Consciousness" (1965), "It is a mistake to identify subsidiary awareness with subconscious or preconscious awareness, or with the fringe of consciousness described by William James."[19] Both focal and subsidiary awareness are fully conscious. The difference is that the subsidiary consists of the experience of actually performing the process of knowing, while focal awareness centers on the object on which the process bears. The subsidiary, that is, consists of immediate experience, while the focal consists of that on which awareness is brought to bear by means of (i.e., by the mediation of) operations and instruments, of which some may on occasion be themselves rendered focal.

After the example of the hammer in *Personal Knowledge* Polanyi shifts to that of using a probe, such as a scientist might use in examining something hidden in a cavity or a blind man might use to feel his way along a street. When a person uses such a device, his attention is no longer focused at his fingertips, but at the tip of the instrument. His corporeal organism and the instrument together form a single unit, an extended "body" indwelt by his subsidiary awareness:

> Our subsidiary awareness of tools and probes can be regarded now as the act of making them form a part of our own body. The way we use a hammer or a blind man uses his stick, shows in fact that in both cases we shift outwards the points at which we make contact with the things that we observe as objects outside ourselves. While we rely on a tool or a probe,

19. *Knowing and Being*, p. 212.

they are not handled as external objects. We may test the tool for its effectiveness or the probe for its suitability ...but the tool and the probe can never lie in the field of these operations; they remain necessarily on our side of it, forming part of ourselves, the operating persons. We pour ourselves into them and assimilate them as parts of our own existence. We accept them existentially by dwelling in them. (P. 59)

This carries with it the implication that, as a commentator of Polanyi's put it, "our experiential field is bifurcated into two regions": one lies on the side of subsidiary awareness and the operating subject, including both the organism and all of its instruments; the other lies on the side of the objects he focally attends to.[20] This, Polanyi suggests, is the experiential basis for our concrete understanding of the difference between self and other, within and without, consciousness and its objects. "Externality," he says, "is clearly defined only if we can examine an external object deliberately, localizing it clearly in space outside."[21] Or as he put the same issue in *The Tacit Dimension,* considering it in terms of the subjective rather than the objective pole of consciousness, "when we make a thing function as the proximal term of tacit knowing, we incorporate it in our body—or extend our body to include it—so that we come to dwell in it" (p. 16).

Obviously what Polanyi means by "body" here is not exactly what we mean by the term in commonsense usage. He is referring rather to the complex of instruments of subsidiary awareness and performance which serves as the starting point for all extraverted attention and inquiry. It is both a strength and perhaps a weakness in Polanyi's writings that he tends to use commonsense words even when he is trying to develop their meanings along more theoretical lines. It is a strength in that it is probably one of the principal reasons he has had a larger audience among the reading public as a whole than have the other contemporary figures discussed in this study; but it is also a weakness in that it makes for a certain ambiguity. Lonergan, as we shall see in the next chapter, has moved much further than Polanyi toward a fully explicit expression of the theoretical conceptions that are fundamental to the issues Polanyi addresses. For the moment, however, it will suffice to say that what

20. Robert Innis, "The Logic of Consciousness and the Mind-Body Problem in Polanyi," *International Philosophical Quarterly* 13 (1973): 83.
21. *Personal Knowledge,* p. 59.

Polanyi means is that the commonsense notions of "internal" and "external" or of "mind" and "body" are inadequate for a serious inquiry into the relation between subject and object as poles of consciousness.

Polanyi's own way of approaching this matter is akin to that of Aristotle: in the act of knowing, the knower and known are in some manner united, and they are distinguished not by being spatially inside a corporeal form or outside it, but rather by what might be called the subject-object polarity. On the side of the subjective pole there is subsidiary awareness and operation; on that of the objective there is focal awareness and that which is intended in the operation. Otherness, from this point of view, although it is commonly thought of as a matter of externality, is not a function of spatial location but of the relation between the subjective and objective poles of the acts that constitute consciousness.

This principle extends also to immaterial elements, such as beliefs and interpretive frameworks, for example, or language. These, too, function subsidiarily to extend the reach of our awareness. And this reach is reduced, at least temporarily, in the moment in which we direct our attention to them focally. "Subsidiary awareness and focal awareness," Polanyi points out, "are mutually exclusive. If a pianist shifts his attention from the piece he is playing to the observation of what he is doing with his fingers while playing it, he gets confused and may have to stop" (*Personal Knowledge*, p. 56). Similarly, the fluent use of language depends on its "transparency." One must attend focally to the meaning intended, not to the particulars of sound, typography, and so forth. "All particulars," he says, "become meaningless if we lose sight of the pattern which they jointly constitute" (p. 57).

This last point has a bearing on both the subjective and the objective aspects of the process of knowing, that is, on the structure of what is known as well as on the performance of the operations by which we know it. The "indwelling" of subsidiary awareness extends into the object as well, on the level of its particulars, so that just as one attends *from* one's sensations *to* the object at the tip of a probe, one also attends *from* the discernible elements within an object *to* the whole which is their meaning. Polanyi speaks of this in *The Tacit Dimension* as constituting a "structural kinship between subject and object" (p. 30). He gives as one example our understanding of a performance we witness: "Two kinds of indwelling meet here. The performer co-ordinates his moves by dwelling in them as parts of his body, while the watcher tries to correlate these moves by seeking to dwell in them from outside. He dwells in these moves by interiorizing them. By such exploratory indwelling the pupil gets the feel of a master's skill and may learn to rival him" (p. 30). Another example is a chess game, from the moves of which one may develop a sense of the mind that produced them. But the principle, says Polanyi, applies equally to any object, animate or inanimate: "For an inanimate solid object, too, is known by understanding its particulars, *from which* we attend *to it* as an object" (p. 31). From this it follows, Polanyi believed, that there is at the root of all knowing a "correspondence between the structure of comprehension and the structure of the comprehensive entity which is its object" (pp. 33–34).

This implies also the corollary that to attend to the parts focally may mean to miss the whole of which they are integral elements. Just as shifting focal attention to what had been subsidiary changes one's relation to it and may bring a performance to a halt, so to focus on seemingly discrete elements may prevent one from appreciating the unity they exhibit when considered from a viewpoint that integrates them. "Let loose an army of physicists and chemists to analyse and describe in utmost detail an object which you want to identify as a machine," Polanyi wrote in *The Study of Man*, "and you will find that their results can never tell you whether the object is a machine and if so, what purpose it serves and how" (pp. 47–48). An engineer could tell you, but a chemist qua chemist could not. Attention to the elements can tell you something about the conditions that make operation on a higher level of integration possible, but they cannot explain the operations themselves.

From such observations Polanyi concluded that reality as a whole, both subjective and objective, is a "universe filled with strata of realities, joined together meaningfully in pairs of higher and lower strata," which link together into "a series forming a hierarchy" (*The Tacit Dimension*, p. 35). As illustrations of such systems of levels he offers the roles of brickmaker, architect, and town planner in building and the roles of voice, words, sentences, style, and composition, in the giving of a speech. Many more could be given, including the functioning of the parts in a watch to tell time and the integration of mineral, vegetable, animal, and rational levels within a human being. Whatever the system or the sets of levels, Polanyi says, "each level is subject to dual control; first, by the laws that apply to its elements in themselves and, second, by the laws that control the comprehensive entity formed by them" (p. 36). You cannot derive a vocabulary from phonetics or the grammar of a language from its vocabulary, and you cannot explain life by the laws that govern inanimate matter or explain sentience by the principles of mechanics.

Rounding out his picture of the structural kinship between knowing and known and between levels of organization in reality is Polanyi's discussion of the tacit operation by which one moves from knowledge of one level to that of another. In "The Structure of Consciousness" he explains this with reference to the way in which we can view a three dimensional scene through stereoscopic photographs. In this case we attend through the two pictures, of which we are aware subsidiarily, in order to focus our attention on the three dimensional scene. We do not look at the two pictures as such, "but see them as clues to their joint appearance in the stereo-image" (*Knowing and Being*, p. 212). What is important is the *way* in which they serve as clues: "The relation of clues to that which they indicate is a *logical relation* similar to that which a premise has to the inferences drawn from it, but with the important difference that tacit inferences drawn from clues are not explicit. They are informal, tacit" (p. 212). Also, they must not be misinterpreted as clues from which one *deduces* a conclusion: "The fusion of the two stereoscopic pictures to a single spatial image is not the outcome of an argument; and if its result is illusory, as it can well be, it will not be shaken by argument. The fusion of the clues to the image on which they bear is *not a deduction* but an *integration*" (p. 212). The key concept here, with regard to both subjective and objective poles, is "integration": "Active consciousness achieves coherence by integrating clues to the things on which they bear or integrating parts to the wholes they form. This brings forth *the two levels of awareness:* the lower one for the clues, the parts or other subsidiary elements and the higher one for the focally apprehended comprehensive entity to which these elements point" (p. 214).

What is centrally at issue here, one might say, hinges on the difference between an inference or argument on the one hand, and on the other, a realization or act of insight. It is the difference, as one of Polanyi's recent commentators has put it, between a process and an act: "Now the crucial epistemological importance of this integrative character of our knowledge of mediated reality lies in noting the distinction between it and the process of inferential reasoning. . . . To begin with, the one is an *act* whereas the other is a *process*. This is not to say that an integrative act does not take place in time, but only that it is an 'all or nothing' phenomenon, what Gilbert Ryle calls a 'got it' verb. Inferring on the other hand is a step-by-step procedure about which it makes sense to say, for instance, that one was interrupted while engaged in it."[22] Another difference between the integrative act and an inferential process is that the former is not reversible. One can trace back through the steps of an argument, but except by forgetfulness one cannot undo an insight. Or, as in the case of the stereoscopic image, one can remove the joint photograph from the stereopticon to look at it directly and thereby replace, as Polanyi puts it, "a comprehensive entity" with "its relatively meaningless fragments" (*Knowing and Being*, p. 213).

Polanyi, however, was not fully consistent with regard to the distinction involved here, and seems to have failed to work out the issue with complete clarity. Sometimes he noted this distinction, but at others he talked of both tacit and explicit knowing as though they were forms of inference, as in his essay "The Logic of Tacit Inference" (1964).[23] The lapse is significant as an indication of the limits of Polanyi's analysis. The remainder of this chapter will trace some other limitations as well.

The problematic character of Polanyi's efforts to elucidate cognitive process and the question of what we come to know through it is further indicated by the type of criticism that philosophers of the analytic school are able to bring against him. A good recent example is the criticism offered by A. Olding of what he calls Polanyi's "illicit mixing together of ontological and what may be loosely called methodological claims."[24] Following the steps of Olding's attack will bring out the most important points of vulnerability in Polanyi's thought, and it will also

---

22. Jerry H. Gill, "Reasons of the Heart: A Polanyian Reflection," *Religious Studies* 14 (1978): 147. Gill has also discussed the possible relation of this difference between inference through steps and the instantaneous grasp of wholeness to recent research into the relation between the left and right hemispheres of the human brain. See p. 148, and also his "Of Split Brains and Tacit Knowing," *International Philosophical Quarterly* 20 (1980): 49–58.

23. *Knowing and Being*, pp. 138–58. Cf. Gill, "Reasons of the Heart," p. 148.

24. A. Olding, "Polanyi's Notion of Hierarchy," *Religious Studies* 16 (1980): 97.

serve as an occasion to discuss a further major concept of Polanyi's, that of what he calls "emergence."[25] This concept is not actually central to Polanyi's thought in the way that the notion of the tacit dimension is, but it is important nonetheless, and its importance as a theme will become clearer when we turn to the discussion of Lonergan, who makes better use of it than Polanyi succeeded in doing.

Olding begins his attack at a point at which Polanyi left himself particularly susceptible: his discussion of the parallel between the genetic code in the DNA molecule and the meaning of a printed text. Olding quotes Polanyi: "As the arrangement of a printed page is extraneous to the chemistry of the printed page, so is the base sequence in a DNA molecule extraneous to the chemical forces at work in the DNA molecule."[26] Polanyi's idea here is familiar from our preceding discussion: he is talking about his conception of the part-whole relation as connected with tacit knowing. It has to do with the difference in level in the object that is correlative to the difference in level between subsidiary particulars and the focal whole in which the particulars are integrated. One can understand why Polanyi would see a parallel. In both cases the structure of knowing is the same; and if there is, as he supposed, a structural kinship between knowing and known, the levels in these two different kinds of object should also be parallel.

Olding infers that Polanyi rejects the framework of mechanistic determinism: "The conclusion must be that the structure of particular DNA molecules is not due to the way its constituents as originally independent entities bumped up against, and reacted with, each other... " (p. 98). To speak of the order of bases in the molecule as functioning as a code, he goes on to say, is simply to confuse a literal idea of "information content" (as one speaks of it in connection with a text) with a metaphorical one in reference to the molecule, "as if acting as a code," in this case, "involved something over and above acting chemically." And then to speak of this code as being "read" by the developing organism is only to compound the error. "This blatant mystery-mongering," says Olding, "has its purpose. For Polanyi wishes to regard the

25. For Polanyi's discussion of emergence, see, for example, *Personal Knowledge*, pp. 382–404, and *The Tacit Dimension*, pp. 29–52.

26. Polanyi, "Life's Irreducible Structure," in Marjorie Grene and Everett Mendelsohn, eds., *Topics in the Philosophy of Biology* (D. Reidel Publishing Co., 1976), p. 132, quoted in Olding, "Polanyi's Notion," p. 98.

DNA molecule as a mixture of blueprint and engineer which somehow *constructs* the living organism" (p. 99). Similarly, when Polanyi speaks of a machine's parts as being "harnessed" by its design, this usage, says Olding, "is at most a misleading metaphor" (p. 99). In reality, "There is no question here of higher and lower 'principles,' and, therefore, no threat to the reductionist's position" (p. 99). The essence of the matter lies, he says, in Polanyi's "confusion of ontological with methodological questions in that bringing in the engineer brings in a consideration of *interests*" (p. 100).

Upon this sort of confusion, moreover, says Olding, depends all of what Polanyi has to say about "emergence," the evolution of significant forms from an initial matrix of randomness. Here Olding detects a kind of "vitalism," and he has a point. In *Personal Knowledge* Polanyi said, "Randomness alone can never produce a significant pattern, for it consists in the absence of any such pattern; and we must not treat the configuration of a random event as a significant pattern . . . " (p. 37). And yet out of randomness, though uncaused by randomness itself, emerge instances of order and "intensity of coherent existence" (p. 37). How can this happen? Discussing the emergence of life from inanimate origins, Polanyi says, "It is clear that for such an event to take place two things must be assured: (1) Living beings must be possible, i.e., there must exist rational principles, the operation of which can sustain their carriers indefinitely; and (2) favourable conditions must arise for initiating these operations and sustaining them. In this sense I shall acknowledge that the *ordering principle* which *originated* life is the potentiality of a stable open system; while the inanimate matter on which life feeds is merely a *condition* which *sustains* life, and the accidental configuration of matter from which life had started had merely *released* the operations of life. And evolution, like life itself, will then be said to have been *originated* by the *action* of an ordering principle, an action *released* by random fluctuations and *sustained* by fortunate *environmental conditions*" (pp. 383–84).

In itself this does not appear to involve any logical contradictions on Polanyi's part, and if this were all of the matter, Olding's objection to his idea of emergence would seem to express only a difference in fundamental assumptions. Clearly, of course, there is such a difference. When Olding concludes his essay with a dismissal of the idea of a higher level of "vital forces" in favor of their reduction to "bits of the universe interacting with other bits and, in particular, the complex chemical systems which are living organisms," he is saying in effect that he prefers mechanistic solutions to vitalistic ones.[27] Polanyi has a point when he says that in the case of conscious beings and of man in particular there seems to be something more involved than merely interacting particles. To recognize that, however, is not to explain it, and the stabs Polanyi makes toward explaining it might have offered Olding some additional material for criticism if he had cared to pursue the issue further.

The crux of the matter lies in the question of teleology, to which Olding alluded when he spoke of an illegitimate intrusion of the idea of "interests" into Polanyi's treatment of DNA. Polanyi addressed the question of teleology explicitly when he discussed "the rise of man" in the last chapter of *Personal Knowledge*. Here, with reference to human action, he could claim confidently that an adequate treatment must "fall into two parts, the first dealing with determinism *a fronte* by the universal target of a commitment, the other with determinism *a tergo* by the bodily mechanism of the person entering on a commitment" (p. 395). He is right, most would probably agree, that human actions cannot be explained entirely in mechanistic terms but must take into account the person's commitments to standards he tries to live up to. In the case of the development of actual human intelligence, he says, "all the time the creative mind is searching for something believed to be real; which, being real, will—when discovered—be entitled to claim universal validity. . . . Such are the acts by which man improves his own mind; such the steps by which our noosphere was brought into existence" (p. 396).

In the case of man, can it really seem an exaggeration to speak in this way? Only if a person were to maintain that his own processes of thinking never aim at careful understanding of objective reality or that it is of no significance that they do so. But Polanyi's conclusion of this line of thought and its extension to lower forms of life is more questionable:

> Descending therefore from the person of a great man down to the level of the newborn infant and beyond that to the lowest animals, we find a continuous series of centres whose a-critical decisions account ultimately for

27. Olding, "Polanyi's Notion," p. 102.

every action of sentient individuality. Thus the personal pole of commitment retains its autonomy everywhere, exercising its calling within a material milieu which conditions but never fully determines its actions. Unopposed, the circumstances of a commitment would overwhelm and wipe out the impulse of commitment; but a centre actively committing itself resists and limits these circumstances to the point of turning them into instruments of its own operations. (P. 397)

We are left, it seems, with a vision of amoebas not only "reading" their DNA codes in order to construct their bodies, but striving to write better ones. Perhaps Polanyi did not intend this, but a critic would not be merely carping to wonder if he might have and to point out that it seems implied in his approach.

Here in the case of the term "commitment" we find another instance of ambiguity like that which Olding pointed out when he compared the literal meaning of the term "code," as in the meaning of a text, with its metaphorical use in the case of the DNA molecule. In fact, Polanyi, despite his pregnant intuitive insights into the actuality of our processes of knowing, constantly had difficulty precisely formulating what it was he grasped in those insights. The result, as was mentioned earlier, was a considerable residue of ambiguity in his basic concepts.

An instance of such ambiguity can be seen in his concept of a person's "body" as that system in subsidiary awareness from which one's attention proceeds as it directs itself toward the objects of focal awareness. This means, as was explained above, that what we ordinarily think of as "external objects" (for example, a pencil or screwdriver) can become incorporated into one's "body" when it is used in such a way that it becomes an instrument of one's processes of consciousness—as, for example, when it is used as a probe. Now this way of speaking of the body does make sense in the context of Polanyi's theory of cognition, but it also stretches the meaning of the term "body" beyond its recognizable commonsense connotations—in particular, the connotation that what is referred to is an objective entity separate from the "mind." What was needed was a more extensive discussion than Polanyi supplied of the broader implications of the shift from the commonsense notion to the concept he was developing. In the later discussion, in the final chapter of this book, of the idea of what it is to be a "person" I will suggest that

Polanyi's approach to the idea of the "body" can make a valuable contribution to understanding the notion of incarnate subjectivity, but it remains an idea that he did not develop to full clarity.

Still another ambiguity can be seen in Polanyi's use of the term "knowing." Polanyi's emphasis on the importance of the tacit dimension in cognitive process is a valuable corrective to the unrealistic critical demand that all knowledge be accountable in terms of steps that could all be rendered fully explicit. But are we to take the inescapability of the tacit dimension to imply that we can have some objective knowledge that is susceptible to no critical examination or verification of any kind? If so, can the term "knowing" have the same meaning with regard both to that and to what *is* verifiable? And if, as Polanyi suggests, some or all of the content of the tacitly known may be unspecifiable, does this mean that we can know something without knowing what it is we claim to know?

This leads, finally, to the question why tacit knowing is really a form of knowing. What is it we do when we are doing it that makes it an instance of knowing? This question might be answered by way of an analysis of cognitive process into a field of experience and a set of normative operations that take place in relation to it, but that is left largely implicit in Polanyi's own discussion. Bernard Lonergan developed a conceptual framework that can serve to complete the analysis Polanyi only hinted at and to resolve his various ambiguities by means of more precise theoretical formulations, but this means that Polanyi's valid insights cannot be fully vindicated until we proceed to a consideration of Lonergan's thought. The effort to translate Polanyi's conceptions into Lonergan's language and to place them in Lonergan's analytic framework should help to clarify and draw out the implications of the ideas of each.

CHAPTER 2

Bernard Lonergan

Consciousness
as Experience and Operation

LONERGAN'S MAJOR philosophical work, *Insight,* contains a passage that sounds very like something that might have been said by Polanyi: "The simple fact is that a man cannot reconstruct his mind by the process of explicit analysis; for explicit analysis takes more time than the spontaneous procedures of the mind; it has taken each of us our lifetime to reach by spontaneous procedures the mentalities we now possess; and so if it were necessary for us to submit our mentalities to a total explicit analysis, it would also be necessary for us to have twofold lives, a life to live, and another longer life in which to analyse the life that is lived" (pp. 716–17). The similarity is clear, but the same passage also implies some significant differences between the two thinkers. Lonergan agrees with Polanyi in principle about our inability to render all of our knowing explicit at a given time. What he is referring to in the passage quoted, however, is, within its context, rather more specific: the fact that each of our thoughts is founded on layers of accumulated beliefs that it would be impracticable to review one by one. This is a fact that does not preclude the possibility that any particular item of implicit belief could be rendered explicit and checked for accuracy if the effort were made. Polanyi used his concept of the tacit dimension to encompass everything in consciousness that at any moment was implicit, some of which might be capable of explication and some of which could not. One characteristic difference between the two thinkers which is exemplified in this case lies in the greater specificity of Lonergan's thought — its reference to judgments of truth rather than to all the steps and elements of implicit thought process and its clarity regarding what in particular he thinks must remain implicit and why.

A more important place, however, to look for the similarity as well as the difference between Polanyi and Lonergan is in their ways of interpreting the phenomenon both take as the starting point of their reflection: the fact of inquiry. Both, for example, have discussed the problem presented in Plato's *Meno:* how can we seek knowledge of something unless in some way we already know it. What is hidden and yet questionable constitutes for Lonergan a "known unknown," something of which we cannot yet give an explicit account but about which we nevertheless know enough to ask questions.[1] Polanyi speaks similarly in *The Tacit Dimension* when he says, "The kind of tacit knowledge that solves the paradox of the *Meno* consists in the intimation of something hidden, which we may yet discover" (pp. 22–23). Explaining what he means, however, Polanyi suggests an approach that itself raises more questions than it answers. He says that "the *Meno* shows conclusively that if all knowledge is explicit, i.e., capable of being clearly stated, then we cannot know a problem or look for its solution" (p. 22). Quite apart from whether Plato could really be said to have proved Polanyi's theory of tacit knowing, one might reasonably wonder, as was suggested at the end of the last chapter, whether the word "know" can have the same meaning when referring to tacit inklings and to considered judgments of truth. Polanyi's analysis did not probe that question, but Lonergan's does.

Lonergan's answer is that it is necessary to differentiate two distinct conceptions of knowing: that which is simply an apprehension of experiential data and that which is the fruit of understanding and critical reflection. That which is prior to explicit understanding and reflective judgment Lonergan does not consider to constitute knowledge in the full and proper sense of the term. It is conscious, but within the field of consciousness Lonergan distinguishes between experience in the strict sense, which is simple awareness of experiential data, a mere starting point for inquiry, on the one hand, and knowledge in the proper sense on the other. Experience may or may not be understood. When it *is* understood, the correctness of the understanding may be questioned, and when correctness is determined, one has "knowledge" in the sense in

---

1. See, for example, *Insight*, p. 546.

which Lonergan uses the term. Knowledge in the proper sense, that is, is consciously correct understanding, and its object alone is what can properly be called reality. "The real," says Lonergan, "is the verified; it is what is to be known by the knowing constituted by experience and inquiry, insight and hypothesis, reflection and verification" (*Insight*, p. 252). He goes on to say, however, that "besides knowing in that rather complex sense, there is also 'knowing' in the elementary sense in which kittens know the 'reality' of milk. . . . Both types of knowing possess their validity. One cannot claim that one is concerned with mere appearance while the other is concerned with reality. For elementary knowing vindicates its validity by the survival, not to mention the evolution of the animal species. On the other hand, any attempt to dispute the validity of fully human knowing involves the use of that knowing. . . . " Experience may be noticed and attended to, but only when it is interpreted and the interpretation is verified does it constitute the substratum of knowledge in the proper or critical sense.

Polanyi and Lonergan do not disagree on this point, but Lonergan has gone further than Polanyi did in developing a precise technical terminology for it and working out in detail the implications of the break it represents with the empiricist conception of knowledge, according to which the most incontestably genuine knowledge of which we are capable is the sort we have of sense data and in which the only active role the knower has to play is that of an attentive observer.

One of the more dramatic and revealing statements Lonergan has made about the history of philosophy appears on page 372 of *Insight*, where he says: "Five hundred years separate Hegel from Scotus. . . . that notable interval of time was largely devoted to working out in a variety of manners the possibilities of the assumption that knowing consists in taking a look. The ultimate conclusion was that it did not and could not." This statement indicates Lonergan's own situation within this history as one whose philosophical roots lie in thinkers both earlier and later than that episode and who considers himself to be working out the implications of the realization that knowing is much more than a look, that it cannot be a primarily passive process in which an object impresses itself or its image on an observer.

When Lonergan said that the ultimate conclusion of the five hundred year test of the theory of passive cognition was that it did not hold up, he was not speaking for many thinkers, and even those who would accept the same conclusion have found it difficult to apply its implications consistently. He was, however, speaking for some, among whom the philosophers discussed in this study are prominent; and when he designated Hegel as the historically epochal figure in the modern movement away from passivist epistemology, he showed a sound appreciation of Hegel's role as well as of the main tenor of his thought.

Hegel has been widely misinterpreted. For example, Hegel's supposed dialectic of thesis and antithesis culminating virtually mechanically in a synthesis is simply a myth; as Walter Kaufmann has convincingly shown, it is not to be found in Hegel's writings.[2] What was genuinely central to Hegel's thought was the idea that all knowing involves a relation between subjective and objective poles in the cognitive act. This was, in effect, a return to something more like the Aristotelian conception, according to which knowing always involves some active involvement on the part of the subject and a formal union or isomorphism between subject and object.[3] Kaufmann cites a passage from the preface to Hegel's *Logic* that makes clear the classical roots of Hegel's thought and that also finds echoes subsequently in the work of Lonergan: " ... ancient metaphysics had ... a higher concept of thinking than has become prevalent in recent times. For it assumed that what in things is recognized by thinking is what alone in them is truly true; thus not they in their immediacy, but only they as lifted into the form of thinking, as thought. This metaphysics thus held that thinking and the determinations of thought were not alien to objects but rather their essence, or that *things* and the *thinking* of them ... agree in and for themselves."[4]

Implicit in this way of thinking are three principles that are also fundamental to Lonergan's thought: (1) knowing is an active process; (2) this process results in a commonness of structure between the subjective and objective poles of the process; and (3) this formal identity of structure unites the knower with the known.

These assumptions were shared by Polanyi as well, but Lonergan goes much further in drawing out their implications. To read Polanyi is for the most part to remain fairly comfortably situated within the world

2. *Hegel: A Reinterpretation.* See, for example, p. 161. The actual source of the tripartite schematism, says Kaufmann, was Fichte.

3. Cf. Aristotle, *On the Soul,* bk. 3, ch. 8: 431b, 20–28; cf. also Aquinas, *Summa Theologica,* I, q. 14, a. 2.

4. 1812 edition, p. v; 1841 edition, p. 27; quoted in Kaufmann, *Hegel,* p. 179.

of common sense, where it is still easy to imagine a clear division between subject and object in something like spatial terms. Polanyi, as we
saw, does correlate "inner" and "outer" with subsidiary and focal
modes of awareness rather than with spatial location, but to explain
those concepts he tends to use images of visual perception (of probing a
cavity, looking through a stereopticon, and so on) that reinforce us in
our habit of assimilating theoretical conceptions to the imaginatively familiar world of sensory perception—to that world, that is, in which the
real is what is supposedly "out there" and is to be known by "taking a
look."[5]

Lonergan, however, presses his discussion forward completely into
the realm of theory. This demands both a refinement of language to
technically precise meanings and a radical break with the imagination.
The imagination is rooted immediately in the data of experience and
constitutes an initial and rudimentary step toward form; the form it discovers, however, is only an experiential pattern, and no matter how
"real" or "meaningful" it might feel, it is neither critically grounded nor
fully intelligible. It is a great challenge to make the break with imagination that Lonergan believed is demanded if one is to take adequately
into account all the implications of developed theoretical thinking, a demand that is becoming increasingly insistent as theoretical inquiry proceeds in the various sciences.

The prevailing paradigm of knowledge until recently was perceptualist: it was assumed that all genuine knowing took place by clear and accurate observation. But for modern science this is no longer tenable.
Heinz Pagels, in his history of the development of quantum physics,
stated the issue in almost precisely these terms: "As Max Born put it,
'The generation to which Einstein, Bohr and I belong was taught that
there exists an objective physical world, which unfolds itself according
to immutable laws independent of us; we are watching this process as
the audience watches a play in a theater.' . . . But with the quantum
theory, human intention influences the structure of the physical
world."[6] Lonergan himself would probably state the last point slightly
differently, since the idea of "influence" still connotes the image of an

5. Cf. Lonergan on what he considered the fallacy of the "already, out, there, now,
real," *Insight*, pp. 251–52.
6. *The Cosmic Code: Quantum Physics as the Language of Nature*, p. 95.

already constituted external object that is altered by our observation of it. To say that would be to assume that reality in the proper sense is to be found on the level not of the interpreted and critically verified but of the datum. Lonergan's own way of putting the point would be to say that the object as datum is simply experiential and that only as an element of the known or potentially knowable can it meaningfully be said to be real. The major problem for human reflection, from this point of view, is to break out of the hold that uncritical images have on our attempts at understanding. As Lonergan put it in the introduction to *Insight*, "Even before Einstein and Heisenberg it was clear enough that the world described by scientists was strangely different from the world depicted by artists and inhabited by men of common sense. But it was left to twentieth-century physicists to envisage the possibility that the objects of their science were to be reached only by severing the umbilical cord that tied them to the maternal imagination of man" (p. xxi).

Polanyi would not disagree. On the contrary, he was as convinced as Lonergan that the real in the strict sense is what is known through an act of critical intelligence rather than through sensation or imagination. This was why, as was mentioned in the last chapter, he considered a strictly theoretical conception of space ("a super-Copernican vision, totally at variance with our habitual experience") to be such an important advance on the absolute space of Newton, as "a theory grounded in reason and transcending the senses" (*Personal Knowledge*, p. 12). Polanyi was as fully committed as Lonergan to a consistently theoretical conception of the real, although his way of expressing himself sounded less forbiddingly austere, which may be one reason for his comparatively wider readership.

The perceptualist paradigm of knowing was perhaps the most fundamental assumption of the philosophical epoch of which Hegel marked the close. Although this framework of thought was not born with the late Middle Ages, but had always been the attitude of extraverted common sense, it took on a more theoretical character among thinkers of that period. It eventually became a major presupposition linking such disparate figures as Scotus, Ockham, Descartes, Locke, and Kant.[7] Its

7. For a discussion of Kant in relation to Lonergan, see Giovanni Sala, "The *A Priori* in Human Knowledge: Kant's *Critique of Pure Reason* and Lonergan's *Insight*," *The Thomist* 40 (1976): 179–221.

characteristic tenet was that the object one knows is a thing "out there," entirely separate from the individual who knows it; the knower looks over at it across a gap that is both physical and ontological, and if he gives it a good look and nothing distorts his vision, he receives accurate impressions of it. The major problem from the point of view of such an epistemology is, of course, how to be certain the object is really there or that its impressions are accurately transmitted across the gap. The question of certainty became the characteristic preoccupation of the epistemological epoch referred to, and its force is still widely felt by those who continue to share its assumptions. What a thinker of the other pattern looks for is less certainty than rationally grounded confidence, or what John Henry Newman, who was himself a major influence on Lonergan, called "certitude."[8]

Of course a person convinced of a perceptionist epistemology would ask at this point how one can be certain regarding one's certitude, but from Newman's point of view and Lonergan's, the true ground of intellectual confidence is the knower's awareness of the basis of his judgment of truth and of the care with which he performs it. As Newman put the matter, "certitude is not a passive impression made upon the mind from without, by argumentative compulsion [or, Lonergan might add, by the perception of an empirical datum], but in all concrete questions . . . it is an active recognition of propositions as true such as it is the duty of each individual himself to exercise at the bidding of reason, and, when reason forbids, to withhold."[9] Everyone who wishes to arrive at genuine knowledge, that is, must perform for himself the operations that produce it.

Newman only began the analysis of cognitional process, and his approach was largely descriptive, but in his emphasis on the role of judgment he made a major contribution to the line of thought Lonergan has developed. Hegel gave this function comparatively little attention. As Lonergan stated, "Hegel's range of vision is enormous; indeed, it is unrestricted in extent. But it is always restricted in content, for it views

---

8. Regarding Newman, Lonergan has said, "My fundamental mentor and guide has been John Henry Newman's *Grammar of Assent*," "Reality, Myth, and Symbol," in Alan M. Olson, ed., *Myth, Symbol, and Reality*, p. 34. For a general account of the influence of Newman on Lonergan, see George S. Worgul, "The Ghost of Newman in the Lonergan Corpus," *Modern Schoolman* 54 (1977): 317–32.

9. John Henry Newman, *An Essay in Aid of A Grammar of Assent*, p. 262.

everything as it would be if there were no facts" (*Insight*, p. 373). What Lonergan drew from Hegel, or at least found congenial in him, was his concept of *Aufhebung* (usually translated as "sublation" or "sublimation") and his idea of development in consciousness: "As his *Aufhebung* both rejects and retains, so also in their own fashion do our higher viewpoints. As he repeatedly proceeds from *an sich,* through *für sich,* to *an und für sich,* so our whole argument is a movement from the objects of mathematical, scientific, and common-sense understanding, through the acts of understanding themselves, to an understanding of understanding" (p. 374 n.). Judgment, however, was not Hegel's focus, whereas for Newman it was as central as it subsequently became for Lonergan.

What Newman offered to Lonergan was a starting point for the systematic investigation of human cognitive operations. This inquiry, as Lonergan conceives it, is directed by three basic questions: (1) What are we doing when we are knowing?(2) Why is doing that knowing? (3) What do we know when we do it? The answer to the first, he calls cognitional theory. The answer to the second is epistemology. That to the third is metaphysics.

It is the first that he takes to be most fundamental; we begin with a cognitive process that is already going on and we proceed to an understanding of it by discovering what it is we are engaged in. By attending carefully to our cognitive operations, Lonergan says, we can discover that they fall into three basic categories: attention, understanding, and judgment.

These three operations, according to Lonergan's analysis, are the building blocks of every genuinely cognitive act, and they form an invariant sequence; that is, they build upon one another. The judgment of truth is founded upon an interpretation, and interpretation is founded upon some sort of experience. For Lonergan these terms refer not to objects but to acts: experiencing involves an active attending to data, either of sense or of consciousness; interpreting is a construing of the data in a formal pattern that can relate them to one another; judging is the culmination of a process of reflection regarding the adequacy of a construing to the data it attempts to take into account. What happens in practice is that an initial, relatively passive experience of some datum gives rise to a question, which becomes the moving force of a closer attending and of the further operations of questioning about meaning. As

Plato and Aristotle did before him, Lonergan also believed that the beginning of philosophy lies in the experience of wonder. It is the force of the wondering question that impels one to attempts at interpreting and to reflection upon the adequacy of the interpretation to the data it construes.

The cognitive process culminates, when it is fully accomplished, in a reflective judgment to the effect that the interpretation is sufficiently comprehensive and careful and is at least the best one can think of for the time being. Further questioning, of course, always remains a possibility: additional data may be noticed that will need to be accounted for or new possibilities of interpretation may turn up. This need not impede the definite "yes" or "no" of judgment, however, because even though a judgment may regard an interpretation that is only relatively adequate, the judgment itself may be fully adequate to the extent that it takes the relative into account. If, for example, one were to assess a probability at something above 50 percent, the judgment of truth would not be a declaration that the event in question was certainly going to happen; it would simply declare that as far as the evidence indicates, the event is more likely to happen than not and by some measurable margin. Or, to take another example, if one were to consider the question of the adequacy of Newtonian physics as compared with quantum physics, an eighteenth- or nineteenth-century thinker could have judged quite reasonably that Newton's physics explained with sufficient precision the phenomena one was at that time interested in explaining, and such a judgment would not in itself necessarily imply a belief that no better system of physics would ever be possible. The latter belief would have been unreasonable, but it would have been so not because it referred to what was only relatively adequate, but because it failed to recognize the relativity involved. Judgments are made, and when they are, they necessarily take the form of a Boolean expression: yes or no, true or false. A judgment is always definite, even when it regards the relative.

This is not, of course, to imply that judgments will always be sound. They depend for their own adequacy on the acts of attention and interpretation that underlie them as well as on the sensitivity of intellectual conscience of the inquirer, who may terminate his efforts of investigation too soon or let himself be distracted by other interests than a radical love of truth. Careful judgments can, however, take place, and when they do, says Lonergan, they constitute the only knowledge a human inquirer can ever have: that which is constituted by the set of interrelated, cumulative operations he describes.

Lonergan's account of knowing as constituted by the operations of attention, interpretation, and judgment could seem so obviously true as to be trivial, and there is a sense in which this is the case. Any attempt to establish that these three operations play no role in knowing or that any of them could be dispensed with would soon destroy itself by an unintended *reductio ad absurdum*. Lonergan has himself described the implications quite bluntly:

> Despite the doubts and denials of positivists and behaviorists, no one, unless some of his organs are deficient, is going to say that never in his life did he have the experience of seeing or of hearing, of touching or smelling or tasting, of imagining or perceiving, of feeling or moving; or that if he appeared to have such experience, still it was mere appearance, since all his life long he has gone about like a somnambulist without any awareness of his own activities. Again, how rare is the man that will preface his lectures by repeating his conviction that never did he have even a fleeting experience of intellectual curiosity, of inquiry, of striving and coming to understand, of expressing what he has grasped by understanding. Rare too is the man that begins his contributions to periodical literature by reminding his potential readers that never in his life did he experience anything that might be called critical reflection, that he never paused about the truth or falsity of any statement, that if ever he seemed to exercise his rationality by passing judgment strictly in accord with the available evidence, then that must be counted mere appearance for he is totally unaware of any such event or even any such tendency.[10]

Despite the inherent obviousness of the invariant structured pattern of cognitive operations, there are several reasons why pointing it out is not trivial at all. One is that so many epistemologies have been founded on other assumptions, especially those of perceptionism. Another is that however fundamental the operations may be, they can be easily overlooked in practice (probably the major reason for the popularity of rival epistemologies). Still another is that to apply consistently the principle that what can be known is what we know by performing these opera-

10. *Method in Theology*, pp. 16–17. This work will subsequently be referred to as *Method*.

tions leads to conclusions about our objects of knowledge that conflict with most of our habitual assumptions. The deficiency of perceptionist epistemologies has already been discussed. Let us consider the last two of these points in turn.

A helpful example with which to illustrate both the presence of the three basic operations and the difficulty in practice of noticing them might be a visual figure such as the Fraser Spiral (see Figure 1). This

Figure 1. Fraser Spiral

figure is used by Sir Ernst Gombrich in his *Art and Illusion* as an example of what he calls "the etc. principle."[1] By this term Gombrich refers to the fact that when there are several visual cues of a certain pattern in a picture, the tendency of the beholder is to assume that the pattern is repeated consistently. In this case, the cues suggest convergence

11. *Art and Illusion: A Study in the Psychology of Pictorial Representation*, 5th ed., p. 184.

of the various lines upon the center of the picture, and for this reason we tend to perceive what appears to us to be a striped spiral moving in from the periphery toward the center. In fact, however, although there are various hints at a spiraling pattern, there is no spiral in the picture. To determine this, one can try tracing the apparent spiral with a pencil; one discovers that the pencil always returns to its starting point and that the figure is actually a set of concentric circles. This usually comes as a surprise. If it does, that is because the observer feels convinced that the picture represents a spiral. That feeling of conviction grows out of an unnoticed process of interpretation and uncritical judgment. Gombrich's "etc. principle" refers to the interpretative phase of this process. The feeling of conviction arises from settling uncritically for the nearest interpretation at hand, the one that springs spontaneously to mind. None of this process, of course, is actually conscious, which is to say that it is not noticed or adverted to. The data of the figure—the black, gray, and white markings and their shapes—are noticed, but the interpretative process is not. The operations by which the data of sense in this case are processed and packaged take place within a conscious person, but the person is not conscious of those operations and in fact cannot be said as subject to be performing them; he is conscious only of the data and of the perceptual package that is the product of the process that takes place within his nervous system between the point of sensory stimulus and the finished package. The only operation he can be said to be performing consciously is his attending to the data and to the spiral he believes he sees; in other words, his only consciously intended operations are empirical, not intellectual or rational.

To put the matter in Polanyi's language, the marks on paper are configured in perception into a spiral, and this perceptual spiral is focal in the subject's awareness. Both the interpreted data and the interpreting are subsidiary. The process by which the data are packaged into an interpreted form is what Polanyi would have called "tacit knowing":

> This act of integration, which we can identify both in the visual perception of objects and in the discovery of scientific theories is the tacit power we have been looking for. I shall call it *tacit knowing*. It will facilitate my discussion of tacit knowing if I speak of the clues or parts that are subsidiarily known as the *proximal term* of tacit knowing and of that which is focally known as the *distal term* of tacit knowing. In the case of percep-

tion we are attending to an object separated from most of the clues which we integrate into its appearance; the proximal and the distal terms are then largely different objects, joined together by tacit knowing. This is not so when we know a whole by integrating its parts into their joint appearance, or when the discovery of a theory integrates observations into their theoretical appearance. In this case the proximal term consists of things seen in isolation, and the distal term consists of the same things seen as a coherent entity.[12]

In the case of the Fraser Spiral, the marks on paper are proximal and subsidiary in Polanyi's language, and the apparent spiral is focal. It is characteristic of the difference between the perspectives of Lonergan and Polanyi that Polanyi concentrates his attention on the distinction between focal and subsidiary, or distal and proximal, while Lonergan directs his attention toward discovering the operations by which one can move from the one to the other. It is also characteristic that Polanyi distinguishes between perception and scientific theorizing, but does not elaborate on the significance of the distinction. For Lonergan, on the other hand, the distinction is of crucial significance.

Lonergan has not been especially concerned with perception, but has concentrated on theoretical inquiry so as to distinguish it from what he calls "common sense" (of which the perceptual world would be a component). For this reason Lonergan's own discussion of cognitive operations refers to operations performed with conscious intention, but the example of the Fraser Spiral is useful nevertheless, because it shows how pervasive interpretative operations are and because it helps to make clear why rival epistemologies based on the assumption that knowing is a simple matter of taking a look could develop and maintain such a hold on the imagination. In most cases, the perceptions that grow out of unconscious processes of interpretation are sufficiently accurate for our purposes, and so we feel no need to probe more deeply how we know what we know. The classic pattern for the development of a skeptical attitude begins with an initial naive acceptance of the products of such automatic interpretation as though they were not interpretations but a direct vision of naked reality. Then when the budding skeptic notices that sense perception is not necessarily accurate

12. *Knowing and Being*, p. 140.

(as in the classic example of the stick that looks bent in the water), he is tempted to conclude that all supposed knowledge is illusory. The naive assumption is that if real knowledge were possible, it would come by way of a "look," and if "looks" are suspect, there can be no certitude. If one continues the inquiry further than such a collap. e into skepticism, Lonergan would say, one can begin to discover the role of understanding and judgment in cognition. At that point one is in a position to find out what went wrong in the case of a misperception, like that of the stick in water or of the Fraser Spiral.

Since Lonergan was concerned primarily with the conscious operations by which knowledge in the proper sense is achieved (he would not consider Polanyi's "tacit knowing" to be knowledge in the proper sense, since it is not critically verified), it would be appropriate to consider briefly his conceptions of consciousness and of the subject who is conscious. The topic of consciousness is central to each of the philosophers this book deals with, but Lonergan, characteristically, is the only one to offer a technical definition of it. Probably his most succinct definition of what he means by "consciousness" appears in a Latin textbook written for his course in Christology at the Gregorian University (in which he discussed the consciousness of Jesus in a way that subsequently gave rise to some controversy among Catholic theologians): "Consciousness is an internal experience of one's self and one's acts, where experience is taken in the strict sense."[13] "Experience," he says, "can be taken either in a broad sense or in a strict sense. Broadly speaking experience is practically the same as ordinary knowledge. Strictly speaking, it is a prior rudimentary knowledge which is presupposed and completed by intellectual inquiry." Experience in the strict sense, as Lonergan uses this term, is made up of mere data, which as taken up and subsumed by further inquiry may become the elements of an interpretation.

By "internal experience" Lonergan meant something very like what

13. *De Constitutione Christi Ontologica et Psychologica* (Rome: Gregorian University Press, 1956), part 5, section 1. I am quoting from the typescript of an English translation prepared by the Reverend Timothy P. Fallon, S. J., of the University of Santa Clara. For Lonergan's reply to a critic of his approach to the consciousness of Christ, see his "Christ as Subject: A Reply," in *Collection: Papers by Bernard Lonergan, S. J.*, ed. Frederick E. Crowe, S. J., pp. 164–97.

Polanyi did when he spoke of the "body" as that from which we attend in subsidiary awareness toward some focal object. For Lonergan, the distinction between "internal" and "external" and that between subject and object are essentially equivalent. As Lonergan explained it: "What we experience externally is apprehended as an object and by an act peculiarly its own. We see colors as objects, hear sounds as objects, taste flavors as objects. . . . But what we experience internally does not enter the field of knowledge in an act peculiarly its own nor is it apprehended as an object. In the very act of seeing color I find two elements entering the field of knowledge: color on the objective side, and both the one seeing and the act of seeing on the subjective side" (ibid.).

Polanyi would say that the experience of the act of seeing is subsidiary to what is seen (i.e., to what is focal); Lonergan would essentially agree, but he would also say that in this case the subsidiary is the experiential in the strict sense, and that this is precisely what consciousness is. One experiences on the subsidiary level one's operations, but one can also shift one's focus of inquiry toward the operating subject and come to "know" oneself as well as simply experience oneself operating: "Now this awareness of the one seeing and his act of seeing, of the one understanding and his act of understanding, of the one judging and his act of judging, is presupposed and fulfilled, first when one inquires what the one who sees, the one who understands, the one who judges is, and what seeing, understanding, and judging are, and second, when one judges about the ideas formed in answer to this inquiry. Therefore this awareness too is prior and rudimentary. It is, also, what we call experience in the strict sense" (ibid.).

To make fully clear what Lonergan means here, it is necessary to emphasize that when he is speaking of inquiry leading to knowledge of the subject, he is not speaking of a quasi perception or a special introspective mode of consciousness. On the contrary, he says that "consciousness is one thing and introspection quite another. . . . Consciousness is prior and rudimentary knowledge of oneself and one's acts; introspection is consequent intellectual inquiry in which you grasp the intelligibility, quiddity, truth, and being of what you grasped by consciousness as experienced" (ibid.).[14] The only introspection possible to a human

14. Cf. *Method*, pp. 8–9.

knower, in other words, is rational inquiry; the idea of being able to know oneself as subject by "taking a look" is just as much a will-o'-the-wisp as any other such perceptionist aspiration.

Consciousness, for Lonergan, is the experience of a subject, not the perception of an object; nor can consciousness be said to know anything at all as an object (*De Constitutione Christi,* 5, 3). Consciousness has no objects; it is the subject who by his operations intends objects. It is not consciousness, that is, but the conscious subject who through his attending, interpreting, and verifying comes not only to sense but also to understand and know the objects of experience, understanding, and knowledge. These operations are the conscious acts that constitute the subject, for as Lonergan puts it, "Subject or 'I,' as conscious, is this man existing and psychologically operating in his capacity as a subject experiencing his coming to know. . . . No-one is conscious unless he is operating psychologically" (ibid., 5, 2). As he stated it in his 1968 lecture "The Subject": "The study of the subject . . . is the study of oneself inasmuch as one is conscious. It prescinds from the soul, its essence, its potencies, its habits, for none of these is given in consciousness. It attends to operations and their centre and source which is the self. It discerns the different levels of consciousness, the consciousness of the dream, of the waking subject, of the intelligently inquiring subject, of the rationally reflecting subject, of the responsibly deliberating subject. It examines the operations on the several levels and their relations to one another."[15]

To be a subject, as Lonergan uses the term, is to be a performer of intentional operations, and one actually exists as subject to the exact degree that he consciously performs those operations. When he only experiences, he remains in simple immediacy and exists only as an experiencing or empirical subject, not an intellectual or rational subject. When, however, a person not only attends to immediate experience but also pursues meaning and through that pursuit arrives at insight into intelligible form, comprehending the empirical fragments as the elements of a coherent, structured whole, he exists as an understanding as well as experiencing subject. When he reflects critically on the adequacy of his understanding to the experiential data that it construes, he operates as a rational as well as an empirical and intellectual subject. If an individual

15. Lonergan, *Second Collection,* ed. William F. Ryan, S. J., and Bernard J. Tyrell, p. 73.

neglects to notice that it is precisely and only in his operations that he exists as an actual subject, then he may fail to perform those operations and miss the opportunity to exist as one. As Lonergan put it in "The Subject": "The neglected subject does not know himself. The truncated subject not only does not know himself but also is unaware of his ignorance and so, in one way or another, concludes that what he does not know does not exist" (p. 73). Contrasting with the neglected and truncated subject, on the other hand, there is the existential subject, the one who knows what it is to act and consciously does so: "Such doing, at first sight, affects, modifies, changes the world of objects. But even more it affects the subject himself. For human doing is free and responsible. Within it is contained the reality of morals, of building up or destroying character, of achieving personality or failing in that task. By his own acts the human subject makes himself what he is to be . . ." (p. 79).

The subject as conceived by Lonergan is, then, the conscious performer of intentional operations. This means that the subject must be considered under three aspects: as conscious, as operating, and as capable of operating.

Consciousness, as was said, Lonergan defines as simply experience. It is a central feature of the operating subject, but it is not itself a distinct operation; rather it is the immediate self-presence of the subject in operations. Consciousness, he says, "is not another operation over and above the operation that is experienced. It is that very operation which, besides being intrinsically intentional [i.e., oriented toward objects], also is intrinsically conscious" (*Method*, p. 8). Or as he put it in *Insight*, "by consciousness we shall mean that there is an awareness immanent in cognitional acts. . . . To affirm consciousness is to affirm that cognitional process is not merely a procession of contents but also a succession of acts" (p. 320).

The conscious operations of the subject are dynamic intentions. Specifically they intend the noticing of data of sense and consciousness, the understanding of what is potentially intelligible, the verifying of understanding as truth, and ultimately the deciding for the good, which is to say, the truly desirable. "The operations," says Lonergan, "then, stand within a process that is formally dynamic, that calls forth and assembles its own components, that does so intelligently, rationally, responsibly," and it is the unifying force of this dynamism that explains "the unity and relatedness of the several operations" (*Method*, p. 16).

The active capacity for such unified, conscious, dynamic intentions Lonergan called a "transcendental notion." Unfortunately Lonergan, who usually gave definitions for his key terms, not only did not define what exactly he meant by a "notion" but used the term in different ways in different connections. Frequently he used it in the ordinary way of common speech to refer to a rough idea of something (I will call this meaning "sense A"). Sometimes, however, he used it in a less common way (which I will call "sense B") with an emphasis on subjective activity, as when he refers in *Method* to transcendental notions as "the active potencies . . . revealed in questions for intelligence, questions for reflection, questions for deliberation" (p. 120). When he goes on immediately afterward (p. 121) to speak of this conception of subjective operation as displacing such outmoded ideas as "the notion of pure intellect or pure reason" and "the notion of will," on the other hand, he is using the term in sense A. Perhaps the best way to elucidate Lonergan's "notion" (in sense A) of a transcendental "notion" (sense B) would be to say that by the latter term he meant not an idea or concept, even in a rudimentary sense, but rather a dynamic anticipation of the goal of intention. Interpreted in this way, the transcendental notion of the intelligible, for example, is one's active anticipation of a possible understanding. One has some experience that is not yet understood but which seems to contain some latent possibility of meaningfulness; then one strives by efforts of construing to reach from that "buzzing, blooming, confusion," as William James called it, toward a pattern that will satisfactorily subsume and order the data. The notion is transcendental in the sense that it is an anticipation of the intelligible as such, rather than of any particular pattern, which would be, in Lonergan's terminology, "categorial" rather than "transcendental." (By "transcendental" Lonergan simply meant that which cuts across the boundaries of particular categories; he did not mean anything like "otherworldly" or "mystical.") What Lonergan seems to have meant is that what the transcendental notion of the intelligible intends is not so much the particular intelligible object, but the satisfying act of understanding that the subject will be capable of performing when the process of interpretation is completed.

There are several transcendental notions in Lonergan's schematism—one for each type of operation. The transcendental notion of truth is the dynamic anticipation of verified knowledge, that of the good is the anticipation of satisfaction as such. (Thus Lonergan can speak of truth as the good of intellect.) The transcendental notions, in other words, are the dynamic anticipations of the fulfillment of the human longing to experience, to understand, to know, and to take appropriate action within the context of reality. "The transcendental notions," says Lonergan, are the dynamism of conscious intentionality. They promote the subject from lower to higher levels of consciousness, from the experiential to the intellectual, from the intellectual to the rational, from the rational to the existential" (*Method*, pp. 34–5). And not only do they "promote the subject to full consciousness and direct him to his goals" in this way, says Lonergan, but "they also provide the criteria that reveal whether the goals are being reached. The drive to understand is satisfied when understanding is reached but it is dissatisfied with every incomplete attainment" and so impels one to further questions (p. 35). Similarly the drives to truth and value come to rest only when the conditions for a reasonable assent or wise choice are fulfilled. In this way the transcendental notions move the subject in a process that is his coming to be as an actual rather than merely potential subject on the successive levels of conscious operation.

The levels of consciousness, like the operations that constitute them, are interrelated and cumulative, and so are the dynamic notions that give rise to them. Understanding builds upon the experience it understands; critical reflection reflects upon the understanding it seeks to verify; and the question of what to do pursues appropriateness of action in the real situation that is experienced, understood, and known. It is in this dynamic integration of the operations on the several levels that Lonergan's parallel to Hegel's *Aufhebung* or "sublation" is to be found. In Lonergan's words, "we describe interiority in terms of intentional and conscious acts on the four levels of experiencing, understanding, judging, and deciding. The lower levels are presupposed and complemented by the higher. The higher sublate the lower" (*Method*, p. 120). Understanding sublates experience in that without experiential data there would be nothing to understand; and the experience does not disappear when it is understood, but becomes experience understood. So also understanding does not disappear when it is judged correct; rather there is a single consciousness made up of distinct but mutually involved acts intending an object that is experience understood and verified. To phrase the issue in Polanyi's language, the lower levels of operation and their objects become subsidiary for the higher levels as the objects of the higher levels become focal. Reality or truth is focal for judgment, but that is intended *by way of* the subsidiary particulars of experience and understanding.

As these levels of intentionality succesively sublate one another, the unity into which they are integrated is an achieved unity; it is the result of consciously performing the operations. When we considered the example of our perception of the Fraser Spiral, that was not an instance of such an achieved unity of operations, because the only conscious operations involved were those on the empirical level: the attending to marks on paper and to the spiral pattern that was the result of an unconscious process of packaging that took place in the central nervous system. The higher levels of operation can have unconscious analogues, but they are the operations of an actual subject for Lonergan only when they are consciously performed.

Besides the achieved unity of consciousness that is the fruit of successive, sublating operations, there can also be an apparent unity like that of the perceiver of the Fraser Spiral. In such a case there are several distinct operations, but not all of them are conscious, and therefore they are not all genuinely subjective operations, but only processes that impinge upon the subject insofar as the subject notices their results. The resulting consciousness, however, despite the subject's impressions, is neither intellectual nor rational, but only empirical. Or else, in a case where there is not only experience but some conscious interpreting that is nevertheless uncriticized, there may be intellectual as well as empirical consciousness, but not rational.

The development of the capacity to perform the different operations distinctly and purposefully Lonergan calls "differentiation of consciousness." Ordinarily an individual begins with a mentality that easily leaps to conclusions, blurring the operations or letting certain ones lapse altogether, noticing only what is obvious or apparently advantageous, mistaking fantasy or dream for reality, and so on. It is usually only difficulty and disappointment that lead to reflective self-awareness and the development of a capacity for distinguishing the various cognitive operations and performing each with care. Even a person capable of performing them distinctly when he wishes will frequently respond as though they were not distinct at all, but a single power through which the true or the good is immediately grasped. Polanyi's "tacit knowing" as described above was precisely this sort of undifferentiated response;

in it, to phrase the issue in Lonerganian terms, the operations are experienced but not distinctly; they are performed, but not adverted to.

In one of his works on the history of theology Lonergan gave a brief account of the differentiation of consciousness in the following terms: "Consciousness is undifferentiated where the whole person is involved, operating simultaneously and equally with all of his powers. Differentiated consciousness, on the other hand, is capable of operating exclusively, or at least principally, on a single level, while the other levels are either entirely subordinated to the attainment of the goal of that level, or at least are held in check, so that they do not hinder its attainment. . . . the scientist, or the speculative thinker, tends towards a goal that is not that of the whole man, but only of his intellect. The will is therefore restricted to willing the good of intellect, which is the truth; imagination throws up only those images that induce understanding or suggest a judgment; feelings and emotions, finally, are as if anaesthetised, so firmly are they kept in control."[16]

Corresponding to the distinction between undifferentiated and differentiated consciousness is a parallel distinction between realms of meaning. To undifferentiated consciousness corresponds what Lonergan calls the world of "common sense." This is made up of our ordinary experience and our comparatively unreflective, though not necessarily inadequate, interpretations and judgments. It tends to be a world of widely shared assumptions and intuitions which most individuals believe to be true because they feel natural and seem obvious to them—as if they knew them by "taking a look" at objective facts—and because so many other people believe them unquestioningly. To differentiated consciousness, on the other hand, correspond two distinct cognitive realms, depending on whether the focus is the objective or the subjective pole of consciousness: the realm of theory and that of what Lonergan calls "interiority."[17]

When one realizes that what one knows objectively is what one can know only to the extent that one has noticed experiential data, interpreted them, and critically verified the interpretation, then, if one

---

16. *The Way to Nicea: The Dialectical Development of Trinitarian Theology,* translated by Conn O'Donovan from the first part of *De Deo Trino,* pp. 2–3.

17. See *Method,* pp. 81–85. Lonergan also refers briefly in these pages to a fourth realm of meaning, that of "transcendence," which will be discussed further in the later part of this chapter.

wishes to communicate, one is eventually led to realize also that it is necessary to develop a precise language with which to describe the objects of such theoretical inquiry. The world of common sense we can describe in ordinary language, and everyone we speak to will know approximately what we are talking about, because the conceptions as well as the language are shared, even if imprecisely. The commonsense realm of discourse—in which all of us participate in our ordinary living and conversation—is not one in which precise meanings are in great demand. The shift to theory, on the other hand, brings with it a need for precision, since only what is precisely formulated can be critically tested, and theoretical inquiry cannot be satisfied with vague hypotheses or unverified assertions.

Historically the realm of theory opened up earlier than the realm of interiority, says Lonergan, because thinkers became aware of the need for precise description of the objective before they became aware of the ground of objectivity in subjective operations carefully performed. In other words, the transition from common sense to theory has taken place gradually, and there has been an interim period of transition—not yet completed for many thinkers—during which it has been widely assumed that theoretical objectivity is to be achieved by a passive receptivity in the subject (the epistemology of the naked look) rather than by an active, internally differentiated process of careful interpretation.

The opening of the realm of interiority, however, has also been a process in human history, and Lonergan insists that in the final analysis it is inexorable, because the epistemology of the look does not hold up in practice but leads, when it breaks down, to questions about the ground of knowledge. These impel the discovery of interiority, which, as Lonergan uses the term, refers to our cognitive operations considered in their aspect as consciously performed by a subject moved by the dynamism of the transcendental notions. The discovery of interiority is, in fact, precisely what was referred to above as the introspective objectification of consciousness through inquiry into its operations. As Lonergan put the matter in Method in Theology, "the transition from common sense and theory to interiority promotes us from consciousness of self to knowledge of self" (p. 259). In doing so it provides the critical ground for the realm of theory, since clarity regarding interiority makes clear what our habitual commonsense perspective can so easily obscure: that the only reality we can ever actually know is that which we are able to understand and verify.

In the language of common sense, "reality" is made up of "external objects" that we can perceive through our senses. In the world of theory, on the other hand, reality is not what is sensed but what is critically known, and what is known in that way is not directly the object of experience, but of understanding and reflective judgment. The world of theory, as Lonergan states it, is a world mediated by meaning, and its objects are of a quite different character from those intended in the world of common sense:

> There are, then, two quite disparate meanings of the term, object. There is the object in the world mediated by meaning: it is what is intended by the question, and it is what becomes understood, affirmed, decided by the answer. To this type of object we are related immediately by our questions and only mediately by the operations relevant to answers, for the answers refer to objects only because they are answers to questions.
>
> But there is another quite different meaning of the term, object. For besides the world mediated by meaning there also is a world of immediacy. It is a world quite apart from questions and answers, a world in which we lived before we spoke and while we were learning to speak, a world into which we try to withdraw when we would forget the world mediated by meaning, when we relax, play, rest. In that world the object is neither named nor described. But in the world mediated by meaning one can recollect and reconstitute the object of the world of immediacy. It is already, out, there, now, real. It is *already*: it is given prior to any questions about it. It is *out*: for it is the object of extroverted consciousness. It is *there*: as sense organs, so too sensed objects are spatial. It is *now*: for the time of sensing runs along with the time of what is sensed. It is *real*: for it is bound up with one's living and acting and so must be just as real as they are." (*Method in Theology*, pp. 262–63)

It was over the distinction between these two worlds—the world of theory with its critically affirmed conceptions and the world of common sense with its felt conviction regarding the "already, out, there, now, real" object—that we saw a representative of the analytic school of philosophy clash with Polanyi in the last chapter. In Lonergan's terms, the encounter between Olding and Polanyi could be described as one between a commonsense perspective on the one hand and an incompletely developed theoretical one on the other. Analytical philosophy tends, as its emphasis on "ordinary language" might suggest, to begin from commonsense assumptions about reality and then to ask theoretical questions about the implications of those assumptions. Its contributions to deflating the claims of inadequate theory have been considerable, but it has always had some difficulty itself with the transition from common sense to adequate theory. The problem Olding pointed out in Polanyi's discussion of the part-whole relation in composite things, however, is a real one and worth considering for the light it can throw on the difference between Polanyi and Lonergan as well as on the question of the nature of theoretical reality.

Polanyi's discussion of the "tacit dimension" and the relation between subsidiary and focal awareness was a probe into the field of what Lonergan calls interiority, but as his use of the term "tacit" indicates, Polanyi left much of that territory implicit. In particular, although he had a sound appreciation of the roles of the distinct cognitive operations Lonergan discusses, he did not emphasize their distinctness, and in his discussion of the tacit dimension he seemed to assume that it was not especially important to advert to them distinctly.[18] One result was that Polanyi did not develop the clear distinction Lonergan did between differentiated and undifferentiated consciousness.

Another result was that when Polanyi came to explain the correlation between the subjective and objective poles of knowing, the only way he had developed to understand this was in terms of the relation between focal and subsidiary awareness. So when Polanyi discussed the relation between part and whole in an objectively real entity, he spoke of the parts as subsidiary and the whole as focal, since in knowing the thing as a whole we can be said to notice its elements but focus on their synthesis within a unity. Lonergan would agree that in consciousness lower levels are sublated by higher and are in that respect subsidiary to them, but he

18. Even so, the entire schema of intentional operations that Lonergan emphasized was articulated also by Polanyi in closely similar terms. See, for example, pp. 28–39 of *The Study of Man* where he describes "the act of understanding" as "a process of *comprehending:* a grasping of disjointed parts into a comprehensive whole" (p. 28) then goes on to speak of an "intellectual passion which impels us towards making ever closer contact with reality" (p. 34) and thereby seeks "satisfaction" or "intellectual joy" (p. 37) in the judgment of "fact" and also grounds the "appreciation of values."

would not consider that, by itself, a sufficient account of the relation between elements and the wholes they constitute as objective realities. It is
possible, from Lonergan's point of view, to distinguish sensory data
from structured form, and therefore it can make sense to speak of them
as related in a manner parallel to that between subsidiary and focal
awareness when the form is actually understood and is consequently the
focus of intention. But it is also possible to discuss the discovery of
coherent form (the "whole") through efforts to render explicit the possibilities of pattern latent in a set of experiential data by construing
them as related in some manner. The first way of speaking is actually
metaphorical, since from the point of view of intentionality analysis,
understanding (the operation in which a grasp of structure takes place)
is distinct from attention considered in itself. When Polanyi spoke, as
we saw, of a machine's parts as being "harnessed" by its design, Olding
was justified in pointing out that this was at most a suggestive metaphor
and not a theoretical explanation. Similarly he was justified in pointing
out the uncritically vitalistic connotations this kind of language introduced into Polanyi's discussion of the emergence of forms out of the
randomness of particulars. With little more than the focal-subsidiary relation to work with, Polanyi did not have a very refined set of conceptual instruments for the analysis of such phenomena. The problem with
the language of focal and subsidiary awareness, Lonergan would probably say, is that it connotes an ocular analogy that implies that knowing
is a kind of "look"—which from Lonergan's point of view, of course,
would be a fundamental misconception in cognitional theory.

Lonergan's own discussion of these issues is more detailed, precise,
and rigorous. Let us consider the examples of his treatment of the concepts of the part-whole relation in a unified "thing" and of "emergence" (emergence, that is, of increasingly complex syntheses or patterns of interrelatedness), both of which were mentioned at the end of
the last chapter as having remained somewhat ambiguous in the
thought of Polanyi.

As we saw, there are, according to Lonergan, two distinct types of
knowing: the experientially immediate and that which involves mediating processes of inquiry, interpretation, critical reflection, and verification. The first type Lonergan terms "elementary"; the second he refers
to as "fully human knowing," since it calls into play the full range of
possible human cognitive operations whereas elementary knowing we

share with other animals. It is in this elementary sense, we saw him say, that "kittens know the 'reality' of milk" (*Insight,* p. 252). Both types of knowing have their validity, and their respective objects are genuine, though different.

Problems arise when the types of knowing are confused. As Lonergan put it: "The perennial source of nonsense is that, after the scientist has verified his hypothesis, he is likely to go a little further and tell the layman what, approximately, scientific reality looks like! Already, we have attacked the unverifiable image; but now we can see the origin of the strange urge to foist upon mankind unverifiable images. For both the scientist and the layman, besides being intelligent and reasonable, also are animals. To them as animals, a verified hypothesis is just a jumble of words or symbols. What they want is an elementary knowing of the 'really real,' if not through sense, at least by imagination" (p. 253). What all of us wish, in other words, at least at times, is to be able to know a world of "already, out, there, now, real" things not by critical judgment but by a look.

Confusing the types of knowing in this way results in confusing their objects. The objects of experientially immediate or elementary knowing are apprehended by sense and imagination as wholes, but their unity is not critically comprehended. To distinguish these from the objects of theoretical inquiry, Lonergan makes a distinction between "body" and "thing" (p. 253). By a "thing" in this technical sense he means "an intelligible concrete unity." Among "things" he further distinguishes the idea of "a thing for us, a thing as described," on the one hand, and "a thing itself, a thing as explained" on the other. Description pertains to the thing for us, the thing as it relates to our powers of observation; explanation pertains to the relations of the elements of the thing to one another. By a "body" Lonergan means "a focal point of extroverted biological anticipation and attention" (p. 254). The milk is a "body" in this sense to the kitten, but so also are most of the objects that fill our commonsense world, since in the context of that world what we know is mostly packaged into chunks of data that are taken to be "already, out, there, now, real."

In his discussion of metaphysics, Lonergan analyzes the thing itself, the real object in the world of theory, in terms of relations in the thing that correlate with relations in knowing. The simplest explanation why our knowing has its particular structure, he says, is that "proportionate being has a parallel structure" to our knowing (p. 499). By "proportionate being" he means reality insofar as it is suited to knowing by the means available to human inquiry. Proportionate being, he says, is intrinsically intelligible because it is precisely that which we are able to inquire into. Traditional Aristotelian metaphysics distinguished within the structure of "things" between potency, form, and act. Lonergan considered these terms still useful, but he also recognized that his analysis and Aristotle's have very different points of departure, in that Aristotle was oriented primarily toward descriptive knowledge and still had one foot in the world of sensory extroversion and common sense, while Lonergan aimed at explanatory knowledge and accepted fully the implications of the shift to theory (p. 433). Aristotle could speak of matter or potency, form, and act as though they were simply objective. Lonergan correlated them directly with the proportionate operations by which they are known. Correlative to Aristotle's potency or matter, from Lonergan's point of view, are the data of experience. Correlative to intelligible structure or form is insight. Correlative to act, the existence of the real thing, is the judgment by which it is known as actual. The correlations, moreover, are perfect, because from Lonergan's point of view there is no way one can ever know about a real thing in the world of theory except by experience, understanding, and judgment. What is not yet understood and judged actual is not known as a real thing at all; it is apprehended merely as a manifold of experiential data.

To state simply the issue Lonergan was concerned with, cognition necessarily involves two poles, the subjective and the objective, and these correlate with one another. There is no object that is not known or is not at least knowable through some subjective operations; nor is there a cognitive subject that does not intend some object through some operations.

Of course this must sound odd to common sense, but that, Lonergan would have said, is simply because common sense is not theory and knows nothing of theoretical objects. To a thinker who cannot or will not proceed past common sense to theory and its grounding in interiority, Lonergan would probably sound like an idealist because it would sound as if he were talking about the objects of the world of common sense and denying that they have external reality. In fact, however, Lonergan was not talking about the same sort of object at all, but about the objects of theoretical inquiry. The difference is really not one between two different ways of looking at a single object, but between differentiated and undifferentiated consciousness. The subject of differentiated consciousness can engage, with a clear awareness of its distinctive procedures, in theoretical inquiry, but he can also engage in "looking" (i.e., in perceiving). What is important is that differentiated consciousness knows the difference between them and does not confuse these two ways of "knowing" or their objects. Undifferentiated consciousness, on the other hand, is aware of only one procedure and one world, even if it sometimes finds itself drawn to ask questions that probe into the realm of theory. Undifferentiated consciousness, that is, always thinks it is "looking" at things "out there," even when it may actually be doing something quite different.

The distinctions between these different ways of knowing and their correlative objects make it possible to carry further the analysis that was suggested only briefly and incompletely in the last chapter with regard to the clash between Polanyi and his empiricist opponent regarding the emergence of wholes by way of the synthesis of their elements. Olding, as we saw there, espoused a mechanistic view of the combination of particulars in nature, and in this respect he was like philosophers of the analytic school generally, who tend to conceive of reality as made up of the external objects of common sense, "bits of the universe," as he phrased it, "interacting with other bits."[19] It is to be expected, Lonergan would say, that such a pattern of thought would clash with that which seeks to understand the emergence of higher forms from the synthesis of lower. "Mechanistic determinism," he says, "is bound to conceive all things as of a single kind. For mechanism posits things as instances of the 'already out there now real.' Determinism makes every event completely determined by laws of the classical type. And the combination of the two views leaves no room for a succession of ever higher systems; for mechanism would require the higher component to be a 'body,' and determinism would exclude the possibility of the higher component modifying lower activities" (*Insight*, p. 255).

The notion of the theoretical entity as that which is explained by the relations among elements in a system, on the other hand, points in the direction of a world of different kinds of things explainable in different ways through the different sorts of relations among their elements.

19. Olding, "Polanyi's Notion," p. 102.

From this point of view, one can explain the workings of a machine by the interaction of elements that by themselves could be construed as "bodies" in the commonsense meaning (hence the appeal of mechanistic conceptions to common sense), but one can also explain nonmechanical systems in terms of different types of elements and relations. Lonergan's account of theoretical knowing, as described above, would be an example of precisely this sort of explanation. The elements of theoretical knowing are experiential data, three types of cognitive operation and the transcendental notions that impel, guide, and measure them, and they are related as mutually dependent and cumulative. The source of these operations is the fundamental dynamism of consciousness itself, of which the transcendental notions and the particular operations they motivate are immediate expressions. When these operations are successfully carried out in relation to one another and the data they work with, they result in an integrated unity of consciousness that is attentive, intelligent, and reasonable, and this in turn can become the cognitive foundation for wise decisions about courses of action. When they are not successfully carried out—when attention is only partial, understanding is unclear, or judgment is insufficiently critical—then they result in fragmented consciousness and an incoherent life, the life of what Lonergan referred to as the "truncated subject" (*Second Collection,* p. 73).

By analyzing human consciousness in such terms, as a nonmechanistic system, one is able to explain success and failure in the project of human existence without reducing humanity to a form of mechanism and thereby eclipsing what calls for explanation. And one is able to explain the specifically human in this way without any implication that this should entail interpreting lower organisms or machines vitalistically, as though their operations were intentional (in the case of machines) or (in the case of lower organisms) involved higher levels of intentionality than they are capable of.

The difference between different types of explanation, as Lonergan interprets it, is the difference between lower and higher viewpoints. Lower viewpoints are adequate to the explanation of the patterns that emerge on a lower level of organization within a system. The laws of subatomic elements explain the patterns of organization among such entities. They cannot, however, explain the patterns found on the level of molecular chemistry, biology, or human culture. The same is true of mechanistic explanation; it can explain machines as mechanisms, but it cannot address the further questions that could arise regarding the possible purposes machines could serve, their influence on society and culture, and so on. In this respect, "the lower viewpoint," says Lonergan, "is insufficient for it has to regard as merely coincidental what in fact is regular" (*Insight*, p. 256).

Higher levels of organization require their own sciences to explain them, just as the lower levels require theirs, and to confuse them is simply to fail to consider carefully what is at issue. The introduction of the higher autonomous science does not, says Lonergan, "interfere with the autonomy of the lower; for the higher enters into the field of the lower only insofar as it makes systematic on the lower level what otherwise would be merely coincidental" (p. 256). The laws of psychic stimulus and response, for example, elucidate the systematic features of what otherwise, on the level of the nervous system alone, would be "merely coincidental aggregates of neural events" and by themselves would seem meaningless without reference to the psychic system they serve (p. 263).

The emergence of higher levels of organization in the object, from this point of view, correlates directly with the discovery of intelligible pattern and does so because what Lonergan calls proportionate being is by its very nature correlative to the operations by which it can be known. The reason we find hierarchy in reality is that the reality we can know is proportionate to our knowing. As understanding presupposes attention to experiential data, and verified knowledge presupposes some act of understanding that needs testing, so we also discover in reality itself structural patterns that constitute the objective pole of a variety of interrelated lines of inquiry. As Lonergan explains, "The prototype of emergence is the insight that arises with respect to an appropriate image; without the insight, the image is a coincidental manifold; by the insight the elements of the image become intelligibly united and related; moreover, accumulations of insights unify and relate ever greater and more diversified ranges of images, and what remains merely coincidental from a lower viewpoint becomes systematic from the accumulations of insights in a higher viewpoint" (p. 483).

It is in accordance with this principle that Lonergan is able to explain "a basic fact which a mechanistic viewpoint has tended to overlook and to obscure, namely, that immanent intelligibility or constitutive design increases in significance as one mounts from higher to still higher systems" (p. 264). Higher viewpoints are initiated by further questions. For example, the merely empirical is considered from a higher viewpoint when the question of relations between elemental data is raised; the merely intelligible is considered from a higher viewpoint when the question of adequacy to evidence is raised. Similarly, an organism or a machine is considered from a higher viewpoint when it is considered in the light of the questions raised by a biologist or engineer rather than those of, say, a chemist.

Polanyi understood this implicitly, but his failure to work out its foundation in cognitional theory left his position seemingly vulnerable to an attack from the standpoint of quasi-theoretical commonsense, and it is natural that from such a point of view Polanyi's leap across a gap of tacit knowing would seem a kind of fideistic obscurantism. Lonergan's more explicit discussion, on the other hand, makes clear that if anyone should claim that there is or could be a reality of any other kind than that which is proportionate to human insights and powers of verification, it is actually that person who demands of us an unreasoned assent to what is unintelligible and unverifiable in principle.

The clarity Lonergan is able by his method of analysis to bring to bear on the questions of what we know as reality and how we know it is impressive. Its value for any investigator will depend, of course, on his willingness to accept and live consistently within the constraints of Lonergan's distinction between the realms of common sense, theory, and interiority, and that will probably depend largely upon the need he feels for inquiry that reaches beyond common sense. The fact is that for most of us most of the time, the commonsense world is the only one that interests us, and we rarely feel a need to ask questions that reach beyond its limits. Almost any field of investigation, however, if inquired into deeply enough, eventually leads into the realm of theory with its more precise use of language and its more clearly delimited conception of what can and cannot be known in the strict sense of the word.

Even professional theorists sometimes find this disconcerting. Heinz Pagels writes that "Enrico Fermi, the Italian-American physicist, as he witnessed the proliferation of hadrons, commented that had he known this was to become the outcome of nuclear physics, he would have studied zoology."[20] Pagels also tells how after discovering relativity with equanimity, Einstein balked at the disturbing implications of quantum theory. Midway through his book, Pagels presents an imaginary philosophical dialogue between various contemporary schools of physicists over what the term "reality" can mean in a context in which what can be theoretically understood and experimentally verified runs so directly counter to all of our commonsense ideas about bodies in space. The dialogue concludes with some comments from Niels Bohr, who says that unlike most of the others in this imaginary "Reality Marketplace," he has come to terms with quantum reality: "There is no quantum world," he says, "like the ordinary world of familiar objects like tables and chairs, and we should stop looking for it. . . . Previous to the invention of the quantum theory, physicists could think of the world in terms of its objects independent of *how* they knew that world existed. Quantum reality also has things—the quanta-like electrons and photons—but given along with that world is a structure of information which is ultimately reflected in how we speak about quantum reality. Quantum measurement theory is an information theory. The quantum world has disappeared into what we can know about it, and what we can know about it must come from actual experimental arrangements—there is no other way" (p. 187). The quantum world, he says, is not visualizable, and to know and describe it adequately, one must refrain from projecting fantasies into it.

Pagels's imagined Bohr calls this "a minimalist approach to reality" (p. 188). It is in effect the same as Lonergan's, who could also be termed a "minimalist" of this sort; the real, in the only sense in which that term can be used with theoretical precision, is what we can know by critical reflection and judgment when the fulfilling conditions for judgment include experiential data—data of sense or data of consciousness.

Where, however, does that leave the inquirer himself? What he knows in this way can be termed real, but can he himself be spoken of as real in the same sense? For Lonergan he can, because, as was discussed earlier, he can consider himself as an object of inquiry, and in so doing can discover that "cognitional process is not merely a procession of contents but also a succession of acts" that are characterized by the immanent awareness called "consciousness" (*Insight*, pp. 320–21).

20. *The Cosmic Code*, p. 219.

Discovering these conscious acts within himself, the inquirer who knows what rational affirmation is can go on to his own rational self-affirmation as a knower—as one, that is, who consciously performs cognitive operations founded on the data of his experience.

Still, this may leave us feeling that Lonergan has framed the question in a way that overly restricts its scope and perhaps unconsciously presupposes an answer conforming to that favored by the scholastic metaphysics Lonergan was trained in. He has asked what, considered as a theoretical object, a person or subject could be judged to be; and he has answered that it is a certain type of entity, the type that we call a "subject." To say that we are such entities, however, ultimately suggests more questions, and perhaps thornier ones, than it answers. For one thing, it interprets the subject as a type of object, and it has seemed to many thinkers in traditions other than Lonergan's that an adequate understanding of subjectivity depends on a clear recognition of the absolute difference between subject and object. One can hardly help but feel, moreover, that the objective question of "what" a person is does not fully exhaust the potential significance of questions more oriented toward subjectivity. Such questions begin not with "what" but with "who" or "why" and explore what it means to exist subjectively—to exist, that is, as consciously and purposively operating, not as some type of theoretically defined, rationally affirmed metaphysical entity but as an indefinable, inherently perplexing, metaphysically questionable process. In the next chapter we will find Eric Voegelin drawing on the language of ancient myth and of classical philosophy to recover symbols for a much more subtly differentiated notion of the subjective dimension of human existence, and we will also find him objecting strongly to any tendency to reduce this to objectivity by reification, or what he called "hypostatizing."

When we discover ourselves in the midst of the drama of our lives, the "who" or "why" questions can seem to have both greater urgency and greater scope than does the more objective and comparatively abstract question of "what" we are. There may also be more than just a residue of commonsense habits of thought in our feeling that even if at our most lucid and fully actualized we may be described as attentive, intelligent, reasonable, and responsible subjects, there are some irreducibly "tacit," nonobjectifiable processes at work in us that we must take into account in seeking to understand our humanity.

Lonergan himself, in fact, shifted his focus during the course of his career from a relatively greater emphasis on the objective in *Insight* to an emphasis in his later works on what is sometimes called the "existential" dimension of human being—the dimension in which the task of the subject is not to ground critically his belief that he exists, but to discover in the depths of his existence, as immediately experienced and intended, the dynamism that moves him not simply to inquire about objective reality but to seek spiritual as well as cognitive self-transcendence. Lonergan's treatment of the subjective dimension and of what in his lecture "The Subject" he termed the "existential" level of consciousness, which expresses itself in the decision for subjective existence, remained, however, rather sketchy.[21] The denseness and painstaking explicitness of his analysis of the objectively oriented operations of insight and judgment in the first six hundred pages or so of *Insight* represent a truly remarkable theoretical contribution. His treatment of the "subject" in that context, however, was necessarily cast in objectifying terms because the argument of that work was structured as requiring culmination in the rational self-affirmation of the subject as a theoretical object.

Also possible, but not actually explored by Lonergan, might have been the move, favored by the existential tradition of philosophy, entirely beyond the perspective in which whatever exists must be conceived of as some type of object. It may be, in other words, that our preliminary theoretical notion of a "subject" cannot in the last analysis be adequately conceived as proportionate being, but must be radically revised if we are to discover the actuality it points toward. Considered in such a way, the concept of an objective "subject" would have to be interpreted as an analogical symbol standing for what is ultimately irreducible to an object of any sort. Analogy, however, is not a theme that Lonergan has treated with anything like the thoroughness of his discussions of strictly objective cognition.

It seems indicative of the sketchiness of Lonergan's treatment of existential subjectivity that in *Method in Theology*, after discussing at length the realms of meaning he distinguishes as "common sense," "theory," and "interiority," he mentions only briefly that there is also a realm of what he calls "transcendence," but scarcely defines it except to

21. *Second Collection*, pp. 79–86.

say that it is "the realm in which God is known and loved" (p. 84). Then when he returns to that topic in the chapter on religion, he defines "faith" not as a claim to objective "knowledge" in the sense in which he usually uses that term but as "the knowledge born of religious love" (p. 115). That this is not at all the sort of objective knowledge consisting of verified hypotheses that he usually refers to as knowledge "in the strict sense" is made clear by his statement that "besides the factual knowledge reached by experiencing, understanding, and verifying, there is another kind of knowledge reached through the discernment of value and the judgments of value of a person in love" (p. 115). This, however, is a fundamentally different kind of "knowing" from those Lonergan has elsewhere defined, and he never stops to explain how it happens that at this point he has to shift ground so radically and what the implications of that shift must be. It amounts, one might say, to a shift from what might be called "knowing from without" to "knowing from within," and it would seem to imply that there is something irreducibly subjective in the "object" Lonergan is trying to analyze.[22]

Lonergan's discussions of value, freedom, and decision, in which he believes the subjective dimension of human existence manifests itself most fully, are also comparatively brief. In *Insight* he approached these questions primarily in terms of the distinction between objects of desire on the one hand and "the good of order" on the other (pp. 596–98). This became the basis for a treatment of value that placed true value in the world mediated by meaning: whatever one desires is good at least in an elementary sense, but rational valuation takes account of the place of the object of immediate desire in the real situation as understood and known. Responsible decision, then, pertains to that which is known to be desirable within the context of an ordered system. This is a teleological approach to ethics and for that reason alone would probably seem suspect to most contemporary philosophers of the analytic persuasion. But there is nothing inherently illogical about teleology as such, and Lonergan's way of talking about it makes sense in relation to his general treatment of human operations and their objects. Still, it is hardly worked out with the care for detail Lonergan gave to the earlier levels of

22. For a discussion of the distinction between these two types of knowing in the context of a comparison between Lonergan and Voegelin, who places much greater emphasis on "knowing from within," see Webb, *Eric Voegelin*, chapter 3, "Philosophical Knowing as an Existential Process," pp. 89–128, especially pp. 92–95, 103–7.

operation, and in certain respects it leaves crucial concepts ambiguous.

This can be seen, for example, in a passage from *Method in Theology*: "The fourth level, which presupposes, complements, and sublates the other three, is the level of freedom and responsibility, of moral self-transcendence and in that sense of existence, of self-direction and self-control. Its failure to function properly is the uneasy or the bad conscience. Its success is marked by the satisfying feeling that one's duty has been done" (p. 121). There are in this passage several ambiguous or incompletely analyzed concepts that Lonergan does not address at any length either here or elsewhere in his works. "Duty," for example, is not a term he uses often or defines; in fact, it does not appear in the index of either *Insight* or *Method in Theology*. The term has been used in a variety of ways historically: as an obligation defined by a system of positive law or by divine decree, for example, or as one grounded in natural law, or, in a Kantian framework, as a transcendental imperative grounded in the a priori principles of rationality as such. Lonergan's use of "duty" in the passage quoted seems to be a commonsense use of the term, and would require a more theoretical development to integrate it into a systematic analysis of the sort he gave to the first three levels of intentional operation.

Similarly in need of further analysis are the concepts of "self-transcendence" and "existence." If the difference between the apparent good and true value is, as Lonergan's treatment in *Insight* implied, the difference between objects of unreflective desire and objects of well-informed desire, in what sense is the term "self" used in the phrase "self-transcendence"? If "self" is taken to mean "subject" in the sense of the metaphysical entity affirmed in *Insight*, could not what Lonergan here calls self-transcendence just as appropriately be termed self-discovery, since what is in question is the discovery of what one really desires—what one desires, that is, not in one's daydreams but in one's properly understood situation in reality? From this point of view, to discover one's true desires would be to transcend a misunderstood self in favor of one's true self. Or would Lonergan wish to define "self" in some other way that would make it quite distinct from his notion of a "subject"? To pursue such questions, however, would require an exploration of the range of possible meanings of the terms "self" and "subject" beyond any that Lonergan undertook.

Lonergan's use of the term "existence" in the cited passage is especially problematic. Here he associates "existence" with "moral self-transcendence," "self-direction," and "self-control." This is not in itself an unclear use—he means that one exists as an ethical agent only when one decides on action and carries it out. But the meaning of "existence" as used in this passage differs perhaps more radically than Lonergan noticed from its meaning in *Insight*, where it has to do with objectively verifiable rather than subjectively enacted existence. It has to do, that is, with existence as experienced and intended from within rather than hypothesized and verified from without.

Reading *Insight* it is difficult not to get the impression that for Lonergan existence is a property specifically of objects and of them only inasmuch as they can be clearly conceived and judged actual by a critical knower. If this were taken to be the normative meaning of the term, however, how could we explain the sense we have that we are already, even before the development of critical self-affirmation of the sort Lonergan described, inextricably involved in existing and are responsible for our success or failure in that project? The type of critical objectivity Lonergan analyzed so effectively in *Insight* is, after all, a late development in the history of mankind, and unless we want to make the claim that no one was properly human before us, it is necessary to find a way of exploring the nature of human consciousness and existence that can take adequate account of the broad range of ways of being human. Lonergan seems to have come to feel this himself as time went on—hence the shift in emphasis in his later works—but he never analyzed his notion of the "existential subject" in anything like the detail of his analyses of what we are doing when we are knowing and what, considered as correlative object, we know when we do it.

There seem to have remained throughout Lonergan's career two divergent tendencies in his thinking—one based on a scientific and objective model of knowing (what was referred to above as "knowing from without") and the other a fundamentally different model ("knowing from within"). It would seem to have been the appeal of the latter that made for Lonergan's continuing interest in, as well as his somewhat perplexed and ambiguous attitude toward, the thought of certain thinkers he liked to call "existential," probably the most important of whom for him was Eric Voegelin, whose writings both fascinated and perplexed him to the end. Voegelin and the other remaining thinkers to be studied in this book probed more singlemindedly and more deeply into the subjective or existential dimension of human being than Lonergan did. It remains to be seen, however, to what extent they have succeeded not only in discovering the dimension of depth in subjective existence but also in satisfactorily elucidating it while meeting, as far as it is possible to do so, the demands of critical intelligence that Lonergan so carefully and cogently analyzed.

CHAPTER 3

Eric Voegelin

Consciousness

as Experience and Symbolization

To turn to Voegelin's studies of the development of philosophical and religious thought is to plunge into a very different world from the realm of scientific inquiry explored by Polanyi and Lonergan. It is a world of myth, drama, and mythic images of the divine—all functioning as a language with which to give utterance to experiences that elude the grasp of objective science. Such symbolism, Voegelin believed, has been and remains a necessary language for human self-knowledge, because human existence in its subjective dimension is knowable only partially and indirectly by way of the mirror of such metaphorical symbols. In his earlier years Voegelin had intended to write a history of political thought in the traditional manner, emphasizing ideas and their logical connections and development. In the 1940s he wrote several volumes of typescript for this project, but eventually abandoned it after realizing that what really interested him and seemed to him the underlying force in human thought was the history of experiences and their symbolizations.[1]

This shift in focus and conception issued in his major work, *Order and History,* a five-volume study that begins with the early history of

---

1. Some of the material from the abandoned work has been published in an edition by John Hallowell as Voegelin's *From Enlightenment to Revolution.* There were plans in the later years of his life to arrange publication of some of the remaining material, but they were never carried out. These manuscripts are now housed in a special archive at the Hoover Institution for the Study of War, Peace, and Revolution at Stanford University. They are to be published in the *Collected Works* of Eric Voegelin in preparation by Louisiana State University Press.

human reflection in the ancient Near East in *Israel and Revelation*, then turns to ancient Greece with *The World of the Polis* and *Plato and Aristotle*, continues its historical survey with a consideration of the world of the Hellenistic and Roman empires and the Pauline beginnings of Christianity in *The Ecumenic Age*, and then concludes, in the fifth volume, *In Search of Order*, with theoretical reflections on the nature of experiences of transcendence and of the types of symbolism that have given expression to them historically.[2] Voegelin's best known work is probably *The New Science of Politics*, based on his Walgreen Lectures at the University of Chicago in 1951, but unfortunately this work is not altogether characteristic and does not give a fully accurate impression of Voegelin's thought and its radical originality. *The New Science* was something of a way station between the abandoned project and *Order and History*, and it is probably responsible for the widespread impression that Voegelin was a highly conservative thinker in both politics and religion and philosophically in sympathy with neo-Scholasticism. *The New Science* could give that impression, but Voegelin's later works present a highly original line of thinking that is radically critical of all versions of dogmatic orthodoxy, in politics, philosophy, or religion.

Perhaps the best way to get a sense of the special character of Voegelin's mature thought is to consider the picture of man he presents in the opening pages of the first volume of *Order and History*—a picture of man as emerging into consciousness in the midst of a drama he discovers himself already enacting before he knows himself or his role or even has a sense of the plot:

> God and man, world and society form a primordial community of being. The community with its quaternarian structure is, and is not, a datum of human experience. It is a datum of experience insofar as it is known to man by virtue of his participation in the mystery of its being. It is not a datum of experience insofar as it is not given in the manner of an object of the external world but is knowable only from the perspective of participation in it.
>
> The perspective of participation must be understood in the fullness of its disturbing quality. It does not mean that man, more or less comfortably located in the landscape of being, can look around and take

2. These volumes will subsequently be referred to by volume number as *OH*, 1, 2, 3, 4, or 5.

stock of what he sees as far as he can see it. Such a metaphor, or comparable variations on the theme of the limitations of human knowledge, would destroy the paradoxical character of the situation. It would suggest a self-contained spectator, in possession of and with knowledge of his faculties, at the center of a horizon of being, even though the horizon were restricted. But man is not a self-contained spectator. He is an actor, playing a part in the drama of being and, through the brute fact of his existence, committed to play it without knowing what it is.... Participation in being... is not a partial involvement of man; he is engaged with the whole of his existence, for participation is existence itself. There is no vantage point outside existence from which its meaning can be viewed and a course of action charted according to a plan, nor is there a blessed island to which man can withdraw in order to recapture his self. The role of existence must be played in uncertainty of its meaning, as an adventure of decision on the edge of freedom and necessity. (*OH,* 1:1)

The difference from Lonergan should be obvious. It was mentioned at the end of the preceding chapter that Lonergan's conception of being or existence emphasized the objective (as the object of judgment) and made no clear distinction between that and what might be called subjective existence. Voegelin's emphasis here—a year before the publication of Lonergan's *Insight*—was clearly on subjective existence and its ultimately unobjectifiable character. Lonergan characteristically conceived of man as at the center of a horizon of rational judgments that constitute objective knowledge, of himself, the universe, and God. Voegelin, on the other hand, considered such a perspective an oversimplification of the true complexity and range of human experience.

Even so, however, the two thinkers found much in each other's work with which they could sympathize. Although they grew up in very different worlds—Lonergan in a small town in the Canadian midwest, Voegelin in imperial Vienna—and met only in their later years, Lonergan and Voegelin probably knew each other better and took more interest in each other's work than did any of the other figures treated in this book. They were close to the same age and died within three months of each other—Lonergan in November 1984 just short of his eightieth birthday and Voegelin in January 1985 just past his own eighty-fourth. During the preceding two and a half decades they had taken considerable interest in each other's work and regarded each other with genuine, if somewhat cautious admiration. In their first initial mutual interest they were aware that they had much in common in their concern with the dynamic processes that constitute human consciousness. Over time, however, they also became increasingly aware that in some ways important to each they diverged.

One would expect differences and perhaps a certain distrust between a leading Catholic theologian, on the one hand, who when Voegelin first became aware of his writings was a professor of dogmatic theology at the Gregorian University in Rome, and a cultural historian and political philosopher, on the other hand, who, though he took a great interest in the Christian religion and its history, was himself unchurched and often outspoken in his opposition to dogmatism, either political or religious. The differences between them were more consequential than that, however, and had to do with the ultimate implications of the lines of thought that they developed from certain common central concerns.

It is in their points of convergence in such central concerns that the present study of approaches to the understanding of human consciousness finds much of its unity of theme. It is likewise where Lonergan and Voegelin significantly diverged that it also finds its central problem: the question of in what manner and how radically the understanding of human subjectivity differs from our understanding of that which is strictly objective. It is therefore at this point, as we turn from Lonergan to Voegelin, that the focus of the present inquiry shifts from a primary concentration on consciousness in its relation to the objective realm to the much more difficult question of the possibility of subjective self-understanding and its possible limits.

It seems to have been rather slowly that Lonergan and Voegelin began to grow wary of each other's relative emphases and their possible implications. In the 1960s Voegelin urged his students and friends to read Lonergan's *Insight,* and in his theoretical essay of 1966, "What Is Political Reality?" he adopted Lonergan's term "scotosis" to refer to the phenomenon of flight from reality and from clarity of consciousness, a topic that concerned them both.[3] By the late 1970s, however, Voegelin's enthusiasm for Lonergan's thought had diminished. He never wrote critically of Lonergan in anything he published, but privately he had reservations as to how far Lonergan's approach to the

3. Voegelin, *Anamnesis,* p. 201.

fundamental issues of philosophy and theology could be helpful to one for whom both enterprises were aspects of the active existential project that, following Plato, Voegelin called a *zetema*, a quest not for objective knowledge or information but for subjective "existence in truth."[4]

Lonergan, in turn, urged his own students and colleagues to read Voegelin's *Order and History,* and he referred to him frequently in his writings. His references to Voegelin were mostly favorable, although he would occasionally indicate reservations—as when he said in "Theology and Praxis," after speaking of the importance and even brilliance of Voegelin's distinction between "information" (i.e., knowledge of objective reality) and "revelation" (elucidation of the subjective dimension of human existence) and of his emphasis on "the self-transcending dynamism of human living," that he considered "Voegelin's criticism of doctrines and doctrinization to be exaggerated."[5]

There were occasions, however, when Lonergan directly impugned both Voegelin's thought and that of other "existential" thinkers like him. The most striking of these was in an interview in 1981, in which he said, "Behind the course I did on existentialism at Boston College in the summer of '57 was my reading of Jaspers' three books (about 1931) on philosophy. They are still useful, you know, if you want to understand Voegelin who gives you everything about the golden cord and the steel cord, but doesn't get any objective truth out of it; it is just he knowing himself."[6]

In this brief but densely packed reference Lonergan was pointing to what seemed to him the central difference between his thought and Voegelin's: the concentration in his own thought on knowledge of objective truth and the corresponding concentration in Voegelin's on the quest for existential or subjective truth. At the root of this difference lay divergent conceptions of philosophy itself. In Lonergan's conception,

4. For Voegelin's discussion of Plato's concept of *zetema,* see *OH,* 3:83–85.

5. *Proceedings of the Catholic Theological Society of America,* 1977–78, pp. 12–13. For Voegelin's distinction between information and revelation, see his "The Gospel and Culture" in D. G. Miller and D. Y. Hadidian, eds., *Jesus and Man's Hope,* 2:91. See also Eugene Webb, "Eric Voegelin's Theory of Revelation," *The Thomist* 42 (1978): 95–122 (reprinted in Ellis Sandoz, ed., *Eric Voegelin's Thought: A Critical Appraisal,* pp. 157–78).

6. *Caring About Meaning: Patterns in the Life of Bernard Lonergan,* in *Thomas More Institute Papers,* vol. 82, ed. Pierrot Lambert, Charlotte Tansey, and Cathleen Going, p. 117.

philosophy was reflection upon the procedures of objective knowing and had as its aim the perfecting of that knowledge. As he put it in *Method in Theology,* "Philosophy finds its proper data in intentional consciousness. Its primary function is to promote the self-appropriation that cuts to the root of philosophic differences and incomprehensions. It has further, secondary functions in distinguishing, relating, grounding the several realms of meaning and, no less, in grounding the methods of the sciences and so promoting their unification" (p. 95).

For Voegelin, on the other hand, philosophy was essentially an existential project. Developing as a direct expression of man's basic experience of what Voegelin called "existential tension," philosophy as he conceived it was a subjectively dynamic process that included the experience of seeking and being drawn toward and into adequacy of existence. What man longs for in the fundamental "tension" of his existence, Voegelin believed, is *to be,* and one's conscious engagement in the struggle to be constitutes philosophy. As he put it in the preface to *Israel and Revelation,* "Philosophy is the love of being through love of divine Being as the source of its order" (*OH,* 1:xiv).

Our relation to the divine source of being would be misconstrued, thought Voegelin, if one were to conceive of that as the focus of a speculative metaphysic aiming at objective knowledge of an entitative substance—what one might call a "God-thing." Rather, that which in the language of traditional myths is symbolized by the imagery of "the divine" manifests its presence in an irreducibly *subjective* way within our experienced subjectivity as the ordering force that Voegelin frequently referred to as "the tension toward the Beyond." The "Beyond," in this phrase, is not a thing beyond things, but a spiritual formative presence that energizes human existence from within and thereby constitutes it subjectively as a seeking for truth, both objective and subjective, immanent and transcendent, informational and existential.

The philosopher, for Voegelin, is one who heeds the pull of that experienced tension and yields to its formative influence. One of his favorite symbols for this process is the one Lonergan referred to in the passage quoted above: Plato's philosophical myth in the *Laws* (644d–645c) of man as a puppet moved by forces symbolized by cords of iron or gold, the golden cord representing the force of divine *nous,* to which we should harken and yield, and the iron cords representing the distracting power of the inferior passions and appetites, which we must resist if we are to remain sensitive and responsive to the gentler pull of the golden cord.[7]

In the 1981 interview Lonergan immediately followed his comment on Voegelin's use of this symbol with some remarks on Jaspers evidently intended to make clear how different his own way of thinking was from that of both Voegelin and Jaspers (whose lectures Voegelin had attended at Heidelberg in 1929 and who was an important influence on him): "Jaspers acknowledges *Existenzerhellung,* clarification of consciousness, and it is a sort of self-appropriation. But he says it isn't science. And it isn't—in the sense that science proceeds from sensible data. But it is science insofar as the data are data of consciousness; it uses intelligence just as natural science does, and it uses verification. It has better verification than you can ever obtain in natural science or in history or in interpretation, so it is more scientific than science." One of the interviewers then said, "Jaspers and Voegelin have no way of expressing the objectivity of the authentic subject," and Lonergan responded, "Yes."[8]

What Lonergan was asking from Voegelin was a metaphysical theory of man as an objective entity knowable through Lonergan's version of scientific method, whereas what Voegelin offered was only a myth that could be used to elucidate a philosophical experience in process.

How fundamentally different Voegelin's way of thinking was, and how explicitly opposed to such entitative metaphysics with respect to man, can be seen in the paragraph immediately following those quoted earlier in which human existence was likened to participation in a drama:

> Both the play and the role are unknown. But even worse, the actor does not know with certainty who he is himself. At this point the metaphor of the play may lead astray unless it is used with caution. To be sure, the metaphor is justified, and perhaps even necessary, for it conveys the insight that man's participation in being is not blind but is illuminated by consciousness. There is an experience of participation, a reflective tension in existence, radiating sense over the proposition: Man, in his existence, participates in being. This sense, however, will turn into nonsense if one forgets that subject and predicate in the proposition are terms

7. *Order and History,* vol. 3:231–32. See also "The Gospel and Culture," pp. 70–74.
8. *Caring About Meaning,* pp. 117–18.

which explicate a tension of existence, and are not concepts denoting objects. There is no such thing as a "man" who participates in "being" as if it were an enterprise that he could as well leave alone; there is, rather, a "something," a part of being, capable of experiencing itself as such, and furthermore capable of using language and calling this experiencing consciousness by the name of "man." The calling by a name certainly is a fundamental act of evocation, of calling forth, of constituting that part of being as a distinguishable partner in the community of being. Nevertheless, fundamental as the act of evocation is . . . it is not itself an act of cognition. The Socratic irony of ignorance has become the paradigmatic instance of awareness for this blind spot at the center of all human knowledge about man. At the center of his existence man is unknown to himself and must remain so, for the part of being that calls itself man could be known fully only if the community of being and its drama in time were known as a whole. (*OH*, 1:2)

It could be known, that is, only if man could stand outside the drama of being and contemplate it and himself within it as intentional objects. Lonergan thought it was possible to do exactly that through the science, "more scientific than [natural] science," that formulates and verifies a theory of man as an entity that performs intentional operations. Voegelin, on the other hand, considered such a formulation a mere abstraction, a verbal construction that can add nothing cognitively substantial to our experience of engagement in what he metaphorically imaged as a drama that includes all our acts and operations, but which remains itself inherently mysterious because of the "blind spot at the center," our inability to turn the subjective pole of our experienced "tension of existence" into an object of any kind at all.

This is essentially the same unavoidable blind spot we earlier saw Polanyi affirming in his discussion of the irreducibility of the tacit dimension of consciousness due to the fact that human consciousness is necessarily structured as a relation between the subsidiary and the focal. To construct and verify a metaphysical theory of man as an entity it would be necessary to be able, at least in principle, to render every element of the supposed entity focal so that explicit consciousness of it could enable it to serve as a datum for metaphysical theorizing. To do so would be, to recall Voegelin's image, to stand outside the immediacy of our existence and become our own spectators. The impossibility of doing so and thereby of bringing focal attention to bear upon the inevitably subsidiary subjective pole would make the kind of objective science of man that Lonergan demanded as impossible from Polanyi's point of view as it was from Voegelin's.

The "something" that he referred to as participating in being cannot, Voegelin believed, be adequately construed as a "thing" that performs operations; rather it is constituted by the very process of such operations and has no other "being" than the acts that make it up. To call it by a name and speak of it as though it had a specific entitative status is not to know it as an entity, but to give metaphorical expression to an aspiration; it is to aim toward and seek to "evoke" fidelity to the goal of the dynamic process. To live humanly is to live between potentiality and fulfillment, the Beginning and the Beyond. The transcendent goal of the process of human existence is not, in Voegelin's conception, that of becoming an objective entity, the sort of "thing" or metaphysical "substance" that could become the proportionate object of a metaphysical science. Nor did he believe that it was this sort of reality that the ancient mythographers and classical philosophers sought to evoke. Rather the ultimate goal of our striving is subjective, not objective; what we are called to is to act or operate well, to play well our roles in the drama of human and cosmic existence.

Wisdom for Voegelin, therefore, must consist of a harkening or patient attentiveness to the pull of transcendence in this sense, the pull of the golden cord toward the Beyond. What we need for our guidance is symbols that offer us practical clues as to how to give heed in this way to the tension that draws us upward and to resist the contrary pull of the iron cords toward distracting goals. Essential to such wisdom are both symbols of transcendence and clarity about the analogical character and the limitations of such symbols. In the paragraph following the passage just quoted, Voegelin goes on to speak of the way in which we must be heedful both of the type of knowledge available and of its limits:

> The ultimate essential ignorance is not complete ignorance. Man can achieve considerable knowledge about the order of being, and not the least part of that knowledge is the distinction between the knowable and the unknowable. Such achievement, however, comes late in the long-drawn-out process of experience and symbolization that forms the sub-

ject matter of the present study. The concern of man about the meaning of his existence in the field of being does not remain pent up in the tortures of anxiety, but can vent itself in the creation of symbols purporting to render intelligible the relations and tensions between the distinguishable terms of the field. (*OH*, 1:3)

Being, as man experiences it in the drama of existence, is a field of tensions, and man operating within that field has to draw as best he can on metaphorical maps to help him find his way in it. The sciences of nature have their place in this process, but they do not of themselves offer guidance in meeting our existential challenges. And to mistake our metaphors for science would be a serious blunder. What we need from the maps that myth and philosophy have to offer is essentially what Jaspers called the elucidation of *Existenz,* a term that he used to refer not to the objective existence that can be known in the objects of science but to the immediately experienced dynamic process of subjective existence.

This process, of course, is the *Existenzerhellung* Lonergan attacked in the 1981 interview. That reference echoes a closely parallel discussion of the same theme in *Method in Theology:*

An *a priori* rejection of the present approach [i.e., Lonergan's metaphysical anthropology] can stem from idealist tendencies no less than from linguistic analysis. Perhaps its clearest expression is to be found in the writings of Karl Jaspers who would contend that our self-appropriation is indeed an *Existenzerhellung,* a clarification of the subject's own reality, but it is not objective knowledge.

Now it is true, of course, that self-appropriation occurs through a heightening of consciousness and such a heightening reveals not the subject as object but the subject as subject. I should contend, however, that this heightening of consciousness proceeds to an objectification of the subject, to an intelligent and reasonable affirmation of the subject, and so to a transition from the subject as subject to the subject as object. Such a transition yields objective knowledge of the subject just as much as does any valid transition from the data of sense through inquiry and understanding, reflection and judgment. (P. 262)

Lonergan believed, both the interview and the passage from *Method* make clear, that the subjective pole of consciousness can indeed become its own object and know itself as an entity of the type called a "subject."

He discussed this point in other writings as well. *Insight* had been in large part an attempt to refound scholastic metaphysics on the basis of a cognitional theory compatible with modern scientific method and thereby make it possible for Catholic theologians to speak of such matters as the objective existence and reality of God and of the human soul with a degree of authority comparable to that enjoyed by natural scientists.[9] The "rational self-affirmation of the knower" that culminates the initial phase of the unfolding argument of *Insight* and issues into the discussion of metaphysics as a science is the assertion that the human "subject" is a theoretical "object" not fundamentally different in its metaphysical structure from any other object of theoretical science. This, therefore, would seem to be the "objective truth" that Lonergan meant Voegelin did not discover through his interpretation of such symbols as Plato's philosophical myth of the puppet and the golden and iron cords.

Voegelin, however, had a fundamentally different way of thinking, as the passages quoted above indicate. In some of his later writings he formulated the issue in terms of a distinction within consciousness of dimensions of "intentionality" and "luminosity."[10] By "intentionality" he meant essentially what Lonergan meant (i.e., the manner in which consciousness may be oriented toward objects through operations). By "luminosity," on the other hand, he meant the existential elucidation that was discussed above: the process of interpretation of human existence as experienced from within. To the limited extent that we can objectify this knowledge, Voegelin believed, it can only be in the mirroring medium of metaphorical symbols.

Voegelin had no quarrel with Lonergan's account of intentionality insofar as it applied to the sciences, and in fact he admired it; that is why he recommended *Insight* to others. His quarrel was with what he considered the mistake of failing to appreciate the fundamental difference

9. It has been suggested that Lonergan's analysis of the objective pole of consciousness in terms of categories drawn from Aristotelian metaphysics need not have been interpreted as essential to his theoretical enterprise, but is an accident reflecting the influence of his particular cultural milieu; see Charles Davis, "Lonergan and the Teaching Church," in Philip McShane, ed., *Foundations of Theology: Papers from the International Lonergan Congress 1970*, pp. 70–72.

10. See, for example, "Equivalences of Experience and Symbolization in History," pp. 221, 232.

between that and the dimension of "luminosity," with the irreducibly subjective element one must recognize at its core. A theory of man that failed to grasp this point, he believed, would falsify our experience in a way that would amount to something much more serious than a merely cognitive error—it would be a distortion not just of speculative knowledge but of the project of existence itself.

To Lonergan's complaint, therefore, that Voegelin "gives you everything about the golden cord and the steel cords, but doesn't get any objective truth out of it; it is just he knowing himself," Voegelin, would probably have answered, "Precisely," since although he had no wish to denigrate objectivity, the wisdom he sought was not objective knowledge but the practice of fidelity to the Greek maxim, "Know thyself."[11] And perhaps even more to the point, what Voegelin was interested in and tried through his writings to help clarify for others was the way in which the metaphorical symbols left to us by those who engaged in the drama of human existence before us might help us in our own efforts to respond to the invitation to participate consciously and faithfully in that divine-human enterprise. What Voegelin was looking for, to put it simply, was not metaphysical propositions offering answers to theoretical questions about theoretical objects. What he sought for himself and for others was to recover through an inward and experiential exegesis of the symbols of transcendence the kind of genuine, even if nonscientific, insight that could offer us practical help in the project of existing humanly, which is to say, with spiritual responsiveness to the mysterious subjective force symbolized by the gentle pull of the golden cord.

This divergence between Lonergan and Voegelin represents a fundamental difference not just between these two thinkers, of course, but also between Lonergan and a great many others, including Jaspers and his own intellectual and spiritual forebear, Søren Kierkegaard, and others who were influenced by both Kierkegaard and Jaspers, such as Paul Ricoeur, the subject of the next chapter, and Ricoeur's teacher, Gabriel Marcel. Jaspers wrote extensively about Kierkegaard in various works, such as *Reason and Existenz* where he credits Nietzsche and Kierkegaard together with paternity of the idea of *Existenz*, by which

11. It is perhaps worth mentioning that at a conference in 1984 at Santa Clara University in honor of Lonergan's eightieth birthday (which he would have celebrated later in the year if he had lived) I stated this very response on Voegelin's behalf at a plenary session with Voegelin seated next to me, and he nodded his agreement.

he meant basically what is meant in the present study by subjective exis-tence. It was Jaspers, whose lectures Voegelin attended at Heidelberg in 1929, who introduced Voegelin to the thought of Kierkegaard and stimulated him, as Voegelin told me in conversation, to read all of Kierkegaard's writings then available in German. Jaspers has also been a major influence on Ricoeur, who was introduced to his thought by Marcel, and who wrote his first two books on Jaspers.[12]

Could Lonergan's emphasis on the objectivity of the subject and that of existential thinkers such as these on the radical incommensurability of the subjective and objective poles of consciousness be considered complementary in some sense? Or must they, as Lonergan himself seems to suggest, be considered expressions of fundamentally opposing views? Even those in Lonergan's camp have diverged on this question. Although he finds what he considers an unconscious correlation be-tween Ricoeur's four myths of evil and Lonergan's four levels of inten-tional operation, Emil J. Piscitelli, as will be discussed in the next chap-ter, has interpreted Lonergan and Ricoeur in terms that emphasize their opposition.[13] David Rasmussen, on the other hand, in another compari-son between Lonergan and Ricoeur which bears closely on the issues that separate Lonergan from Voegelin as well, has expressed reserva-tions about Lonergan's idea that myth must finally give way to meta-physics, with its "unqualified assumption that the advance of one is the decline of the other."[14] "One can summarize the limitations of [Loner-gan's] approach," he says, "by understanding it as a hermeneutic of demystification based upon a uniform theory of cognition which has as its aim the reduction of mythic-symbolic manifestations to lower order significations in order to account for so-called higher significations. . . . The question is, can a hermeneutic of demystification engage a herme-neutic of recollection?" (p. 269). He suggests in conclusion that it might be more fruitful to consider "the symbolic products of cultures, myths artistic creations, literature, etc.," not as inadequate cognitive efforts that are left behind in the evolution of more differentiated conscious-

---

12. *Karl Jaspers et la philosophie de l'existence*, with Mikel Dufrenne; *Gabriel Marcel et Karl Jaspers: Philosophie du mystère et philosophie du paradoxe.*

13. "Paul Ricoeur's Philosophy of Religious Symbol: A Critique and Dialectical Transposition," *Ultimate Reality and Meaning* 3 (1980): 275–313.

14. "From Problematics to Hermeneutics: Lonergan and Ricoeur," in McShane, ed., *Language, Truth, and Meaning*, p. 267.

ness but as having an integrity of their own (p. 271). The implication is that Lonergan, despite the value of his cognitional theory as an explication of generalized scientific method, never produced an adequate theory of symbolism.

Probably the most extensive effort actually to broaden the Lonerganian framework along such lines has been that of Robert M. Doran in several essays and in his book, *Subject and Psyche: Ricoeur, Jung, and the Search for Foundations.*[15] Doran argues that Lonergan's analysis of man in terms of cognitional theory and his discussion of human development as involving differentiations of consciousness that manifest themselves in intellectual, moral, and religious conversion needs to be complemented by another mode of self-appropriation that Doran calls "pyschic conversion." Drawing on the work of both Ricoeur and Carl Jung, he suggests that there is a life within persons that cannot be appropriated entirely through theoretical objectification, but must be lived immediately in "the free and responsible decisions of the existential subject" and mediated for reflective consciousness through a dialectical interplay between that active living and its nontheoretical symbolic expressions (p. 301). "My insistence that intentionality analysis sublate psychic analysis," he says, "is parallel to Ricoeur's insistence that philosophical reflection must become in part a hermeneutic and dialectic of symbols. The basic level for both Ricoeur and myself is the level of transcendental reflection, of the 'movement of self-appropriation by self which constitutes reflective activity.' Ricoeur has correctly argued, I believe, that this movement is not exhausted by its cognitional moment, which for Ricoeur is represented by Kant, and for me by Lonergan. Symbols play an *a priori* role in this movement of self-appropriation because of the connection between reflection on the *Sum* of the *Cogito* and 'the signs scattered in the various cultures by that act of existing'"(pp. 151–52).[16]

If it does not include this process of existential and symbolic self-appropriation, suggests Doran, Lonergan's emphasis on theoretical

15. See also his "Psychic Conversion," *The Thomist,* 41 (April 1977), pp. 201–36; his "Subject, Psyche, and Theology's Foundations," *Journal of Religion* 57 (1977): 267–87; and his *Jungian Psychology and Lonergan's Foundations: A Methodological Proposal.*

16. Doran's quotations from Ricoeur in this passage are from *Freud and Philosophy,* p. 52. The "*Sum*" to which he refers, here, and to which Ricoeur also frequently refers is the "I am" of Descartes's "I think, therefore I am" (*Cogito ergo sum*).

cognition will render those who follow his path potential victims of an "intellectualist bias" (p. 302). "The radical crisis," he says, "is not cognitional but existential. It is the crisis of the self as objectified becoming approximate to the self as conscious. It is the exigence for a mediation of the transcendental infrastructure of the subject as subject that would issue in a second immediacy. This exigence is only initially met by the appropriation of *logos*. Psyche will never cease to have its say and to offer both its potential contribution and its potential threat to the unfolding of the transcendental dynamism toward self-transcendence" (pp. 302–3).

Lonergan himself responded favorably to Doran's suggestions about the importance of "psychic conversion" as a step in the psychological development of the subject.[17] So it is possible that if he had lived longer, he might eventually have worked out a resolution in his own mind of what evidently seemed to him at least at some times to be a fundamental difference between his thought and that of such thinkers as Ricoeur and Voegelin. It may be significant in this respect that he also responded favorably to my own book, *Eric Voegelin: Philosopher of History*, and that when asked once by a graduate student at Boston College which part he found most interesting, he answered that it was the chapter on "Philosophical Knowing as an Existential Process," which deals with the issues discussed here.[18] He read my book after the 1981 interview in which he spoke so negatively of Voegelin. As it is, however, he did not live to pursue the possibility of a different view of Voegelin, Jaspers, and other existential thinkers, and in his publications he has left us with the very strongly worded statements quoted earlier that emphasize his difference from them, such as that about Voegelin's failure to get any objective truth out of Plato's philosophical myth of the golden and iron cords.

Voegelin's likely response to that particular charge was discussed above. He would probably also have wanted to add, in response to Lonergan's further implicit charge of virtually narcissistic self-preoccupation ("... it is just he knowing himself"), that as one pursues symbolic self-knowledge in the life of the spirit, one may also discover in the

17. Lonergan, "Reality, Myth, and Symbol," in Olson, ed., *Myth, Symbol, and Reality,* pp. 36–37.
18. This was reported to me by the student, Mr. Paul Kidder.

depths of individual existence the presence of the universal—and one does so by continuously pressing forward in the process of development into authentic individual consciousness in its dimensions of both intentionality and luminosity. Or to put it another way, what Voegelin meant by the process of transcendence is the process of realizing concretely, on the basis of inward experience and its explication in the mirror of symbols, that the ultimate goal even of intentional operations is not intentional objects but adequately enacted subjectivity; and when this is discovered, it is found not as a theoretical object, but as a life.

Nor is this life the private possession of an individual ego or "thinking thing" who, speculating on his own essence and existence, affirms them as objectively real.[19] It is an expression, Voegelin believed, of a transcendent vital presence, the "divine Beyond," as he called it, that is discovered also as a "divine Within."[20]

Voegelin did not believe this presence was unique to himself or any individual, so that an attempt to develop sensitivity to it would constitute a narcissistic self-preoccupation. Nor did he believe it to be unique to the adherents of a particular creed or the members of a particular historical tradition of symbol and sacrament. He thought of it as the true constituent of universal humanity. Increasingly as his own thought developed, Voegelin expanded the horizon of his expectations regarding the divine presence in history and the possible plurality of forms in which it could manifest itself. The first three volumes of *Order and History* may have suggested that Voegelin thought of Western civilization as the central locus of the breakthroughs he referred to then as Reason and Revelation, but the fourth volume made it clear that he had come to believe that history cannot be understood as a single line of unfolding truth culminating in a privileged set of symbols possessed by a privileged group, but rather that history is "a disturbingly diversified field of spiritual centers," a "plurality of centers of meaning" or "spiritual outbursts" that can and do take place anywhere, among any people, at any time (*OH*, 4:3, 6). "I had to conclude," he said, commenting on the fourth volume's shift in emphasis on this point, that "[t]he process of

19. The echo of Descartes here is not out of place since Lonergan aligned his rational affirmation of the knower with Descartes's analysis of the subject as a *res cogitans*; his objection to Cartesianism was rather to the idea of the *res extensa*. See, for example, *Insight*, pp. 388–89.

20. *OH*, 4:324. See also *Anamnesis*, pp. 95–96.

history, and such order as can be discerned in it, is not a story to be told from the beginning to its happy, or unhappy, end; it is a mystery in process of revelation" (p. 6).

The term "mystery" here is important for the comparison between Lonergan and Voegelin, since it is a term both of them used; but they used it in significantly different ways, and these differences help to reveal how their thinking differed. Voegelin believed that one of the major impediments to a faithful response to the divine-human calling was "the general deformation of experiential symbols into doctrines" (*OH*, 4:48) that grows out of a "literalism" that "splits the symbol from the experience by hypostatizing the symbol as a proposition on objects" (p. 37). For Voegelin, being is not an objective property of cognitive entities but a mystery in which we are immersed as we finitely enact it. It is not something we can take hold of by an act of propositional assent but a life that we long for and give ourselves to in the tensional experience that Voegelin described as simultaneously a seeking and being drawn.

To a person interested in the question of how to be, it may not be helpful at all, and even a dangerous temptation, from Voegelin's point of view, to be told that, as Lonergan put it, "*esse* is reality affirmed in the world mediated by meaning" (*Method*, p. 264). To say this is to treat existence as the intentional object of a theoretical assertion, a vanishing point of cognitive content pointed to by a propositional affirmation or negation. For Voegelin, on the other hand, existence is an act we experience inwardly, in the doing of it, and the only knowledge we can have of it is the knowledge from within that is "luminosity," not the "intentionalist" knowledge on which Lonergan concentrated. Existence is a mystery for Voegelin precisely because it is not the proportionate object of operations of intellection and judgment.

It is significant that in his discussion of "mystery" in *Insight* Lonergan equated it with what he called the "known unknown," that area of experience about which we know enough to formulate questions but for which we do not *yet* have answers. I have emphasized the "yet" in this sentence, because this is what makes the difference between Lonergan's conception of mystery, as presented in *Insight,* and that not only of Voegelin but of other thinkers, such as Gabriel Marcel, who have used the term "mystery" to refer to that which cannot fit into a dialectic of question and answer at all, because it is something entirely different in character from any object of intellection, actual or potential. Marcel distinguished between a "problem" and a "mystery" on exactly this basis.[21] One might compare with Voegelin's image of human existence as a dramatic mystery a similar image Marcel used in 1968 in conversation with Paul Ricoeur: " . . . I have never been able to understand the question . . . 'How is it that something exists, that an entity is?' . . . this question today makes no sense at all because it implies a possibility which is not granted to us, the possibility of abstracting ourselves in some way from existence or of placing ourselves outside existence in order to behold it. But what we are able to behold are objects, things which share in objectivity. Existence, however, is nothing of the sort; existence is prior. . . . That is, existence is the very condition of any thinking whatsoever."[22] For Marcel, the inherently mysterious is discovered at the point at which, in one's quest for objective understanding, one comes up against the irreducibly subjective: when one discovers human existence not as an object but as constituted of one's acts.

For Lonergan, on the other hand, there was nothing that could not, in principle, be an object of intellection—if not for man, then at least for God. This is because for him it was a matter of basic principle that the real is completely intelligible. The real simply *is* that which can be intelligently understood and reasonably affirmed: "Being, then, is completely intelligible, for it is what is to be known by correct understanding; and it is completely intelligible, for being is known completely only when all intelligent questions are answered correctly. Moreover, the real is being. . . . Nor is the real merely some of the objects of both thought and affirmation but all of them" (*Insight*, p. 673).

It was on this principle, in fact, that Lonergan founded his own argument for the existence of God: that being is completely intelligible implies that there is an unrestricted act of understanding that understands everything about everything, and this act is God (pp. 673–74). Not many, even among Lonergan's admirers, seem to have found this argument altogether persuasive, but it is valuable for the present purpose as an indication of how fundamentally foreign to Lonergan was the idea of

21. See, for example, his *Mystery of Being*, 1:260–61.
22. "Conversations between Paul Ricoeur and Gabriel Marcel" in Marcel, *Tragic Wisdom and Beyond*, p. 221.

mystery as that which is radically incommensurate with any object of intellection.[23] But of course to say this is to say that for Lonergan there can be nothing that is absolutely or inherently mysterious in reality.

It might seem surprising to say this of Lonergan, since he wrote at some length about what he called the "notion of mystery" and even said, "Man by nature is orientated into mystery" (*Insight*, p. 546); but what he meant by mystery in this passage is only what he called, as was mentioned above, the "known unknown." Lonergan's realm of mystery, that is, at least as he conceived of it in *Insight*, was not inherently mysterious in Voegelin's or Marcel's sense but only a problem awaiting solution, a realm of potential objective knowledge. Hence he said in the same place that "the field of mystery is contracted by the advance of knowledge," and when he added that nevertheless "it cannot be eliminated from human living," the reason he gave was simply that "there is always the further question" (p. 546).

As such passages present it, then, mystery is only a relative matter; it can be converted piecemeal into verified propositions, even if the process of so converting it will be endless. The endlessness is simply a function of the unlimited reach of questioning. It would be a different matter if the process could not come to an end because even the most indefatigable formulator of questions and answers would eventually discover something about which no appropriate question could be asked because it was inherently different from any intentional object. For Marcel, mystery was inherently different in just this way, and in this respect he thought more like Voegelin or Jaspers than like Lonergan.

To render compatible a concept of inherent mystery with his claim that the real is completely intelligible, Lonergan might have been helped by a distinction between objective reality and the inherently subjective, such that the subjective would be the realm of mystery in the proper or absolute sense and objective reality the realm of mystery in the relative

---

23. Cf. the comment by Avery Dulles, S. J., in a review of *Method in Theology*, when it first came out: "L.'s treatment of transcendental method is, in my estimation, very lucid and helpful. I wish, however, that he had been able to give more emphasis to the notion of mystery and to bring out the positive value of symbols for clarifying and intensifying the experience of mystery. L. is perhaps too confident of man's power to conceptualize the transcendent, including revelation, in an objectifying way and thus to move beyond symbol—a term he regularly used in a pejorative sense as if to indicate a rather primitive form of knowledge." *Theological Studies* 33 (1972): 553–54.

sense of a field of potential answers or objects of intellection. Lonergan, however, did not make such a distinction, even if in some of his later writings, such as *Method*, it seemed to be called for.

In *Method*, for example, Lonergan *did* distinguish between "problem" and "mystery" along something like Marcel's lines (and perhaps on the basis of his formulation), but in doing so he was shifting to what was implicitly a quite different meaning of the term from that of *Insight*, and he was also making, without explanation, an exception to his fundamental principle that the real is completely intelligible. It is a mark, moreover, of the characteristically intellectualizing tenor of Lonergan's thought that in introducing this distinction he emphasized that his own central concern is with the problematic, not with mystery, because the theologian's task, as he saw it, is to facilitate right belief by solving problems: "Accordingly, while mystery is not to be confused with problem, the ongoing contexts within which mystery is adored and adoration is explained are anything but free from problems. Least of all at the present time is the existence of problems to be ignored. For now problems are so numerous that many do not know what to believe. They are not unwilling to believe. They know what church doctrines are. But they want to know what church doctrines could possibly mean. Their question is the question to be met by systematic theology" (*Method*, p. 345).

Lonergan uses the term "believe" here to refer to what we will see Kierkegaard calling "faith in the ordinary sense" as contrasted with the "eminent sense." Kierkegaard's "faith in the eminent sense" is the experience of absolute mystery in "inwardness" or subjectivity and is more akin to what Lonergan called "adoration." Both Marcel and Kierkegaard would probably say in response to Lonergan's conception of theology that the true task of theology is to make clear the difference between mystery and problem and disentangle them so as to help the believer, through a kind of Socratic midwifery, learn to approach absolute mystery, the proper concern of faith, not through right opinion but through prayer and adoration. It was something more like this that Jaspers intended in his conception of philosophy as *Existenzerhellung*, of which he said in *Reason and Existenz*, "It is only comparable to the prayer of religion ... " (p. 139).

With all of this in mind, it is possible to see that Lonergan's complaint about the *Existenzerhellung* of Jaspers and Voegelin may have grown out of not a superior understanding but perhaps a simple missing of the point. It looks as if Lonergan was so intent on the analysis of intentionality and its objects that it was difficult for him to develop a clear sense that there was any other aspect or dimension of consciousness that needed exploration—or that there was anything more to the notion of transcendence than an advance toward increasingly comprehensive solutions to cognitive problems. The heavy emphasis in Lonergan's thought on intentionalist objectivity ran basically counter to the emphases of Jaspers and Voegelin as well as to that of Ricoeur, as we shall see in the next chapter. This seems to have made it difficult for him to develop a clear sense of what they were interested in or even an accurate grasp of what they were saying.

In fact, if one looks at the relevant passages in Jaspers himself, one can see that if Lonergan did, as he said in the 1981 interview, read Jaspers's three-volume *Philosophy* at one time, he did not remember it clearly or else failed to understand it. To say of Jaspers's notion of *Existenz*, as he said in *Insight* (p. 669), that "such existence is the existence of man, not as intelligently grasped and reasonably affirmed, but as experiencing, inquiring, and reflecting, yet not obtaining any definitive answers to his questions about himself" is to cast Jaspers's *Existenz* in the form of a failed effort at metaphysics and thereby to miss its distinctive character. To make clear what this was, it will be helpful to consider what Jaspers actually said in those sections of his *Philosophy* to which Lonergan would seem to have been referring in the 1981 interview. Since Jaspers was a major influence not only on Voegelin but also on Ricoeur, to clarify this issue should be worth a brief detour.

In the first volume of his *Philosophy*, Jaspers made some crucial distinctions between "existence analysis," "elucidation of *Existenz*" (*Existenzerhellung*), and metaphysics. Metaphysics, as Jaspers conceived it, is "the systematic analysis of absolute objectivity"—that is, of all possible real contents of the objective pole of consciousness.[24] As such it is inherently general in character; it is the delineating of the main outlines of the structure of objective reality, but it does not penetrate to and elucidate the actual experience of existing on the part of a particu-

24. *Philosophy*, trans. E. B. Ashton, 1:72.

lar individual. The latter is the province of the two other types of inquiry: "existence analysis" (analysis of *Dasein*) and "elucidation of *Existenz*."

Existence analysis, in Jaspers's thought, is the analysis of consciousness and includes, though it was not confined to, what Lonergan called "intentionality analysis." "To analyze existence is to analyze consciousness" (p. 49), said Jaspers. In explaining what he meant by "consciousness," he went on to say: "To be conscious is not to be the way a thing is. It is a peculiar kind of being, the essence of which is to *be directed at objects we mean*. This basic phenomenon—as self-evident as it is marvelous—has been called intentionality" (p. 49). Existence analysis, as he conceived it, takes account of the "self-reflexive" character of consciousness and distinguishes between its subjective and objective aspects, between acts of meaning and the content of what is meant. It also includes consideration of the ways in which consciousness is able to know the objective world and of the ways in which it can be affected by "the psychological forces at work as libido, fear, worry, will to power, fear of death, death wish" and so on (p. 55).

The "objective truth" or "science" regarding the human subject of intentional operations that Lonergan presumed lacking in both Voegelin and Jaspers would seem, therefore, to be found in what Jaspers called "existence analysis"—so that Jaspers clearly was not lacking in it after all. He did not work out the details of intentionality analysis as extensively as Lonergan did, but he was not at all opposed to that kind of analysis—nor was Voegelin. It is just that his main focus was something different, and he considered it important to keep clear regarding the difference between the two. Far from minimizing the importance of such reflective analysis of intentional operation, Jaspers emphasized its fundamental importance even for that enterprise that goes beyond it: "The philosophical relevance of existence analysis lies not so much in itself as in its distinction from the elucidation of Existenz, which presupposes it: the clearer my analysis of existence [*Dasein*], the greater the lucidity I can achieve in Existenz" (p. 71). The reason is that carrying out the analysis of object-oriented subjectivity (i.e., intentionality) will bring out with increasing clarity the distinction between the subjective and objective poles of consciousness and thereby lead to appreciation of the inherently mysterious (in Marcel's sense) and therefore ultimately nonobjectifiable character of the subjective as such.

It was the latter that Jaspers referred to by the term *Existenz:* "Existenz is the never objectified source of my thoughts and actions. It is that whereof I speak in trains of thought that involve no cognition. It is what relates to itself, and thus to its transcendence" (p. 56). Jaspers's footnote to the passage just quoted explains further, "No definable concept —which would presuppose some kind of objective being—can express the being of Existenz. The very word is just one of the German synonyms for 'being.' The philosophical idea began obscurely, as a mere inkling of what Kierkegaard's use of the word has since made historically binding on us."

Jaspers's "existence [*Dasein*] analysis" expresses itself in general terms that can be readily grasped by anyone who reflects on such facts as the structured pattern of intentional operations that Lonergan analyzed so carefully and so well. *Existenzerhellung,* on the other hand, is a fundamentally different procedure, as should be clear from the following passage, despite its possibly confusing terminology, which I will try to link to Lonergan's concerns and terms as it unfolds:

Existence analysis and the elucidation of Existenz have heterogeneous meanings. Existence analysis is existentially noncommittal. It is performed in consciousness at large [i.e., it describes a pattern of operations that can be found wherever thinking takes place], which also comprehends itself in it [i.e., its objectification of its pattern of activity constitutes genuine knowledge or "science" in Lonergan's sense]. It shows the universal of existence [i.e., the general pattern of subjective operations]. In existence analysis everyone will recognize himself, not as this individual, but as an I at large [i.e., as the type of operating cognitive subject Lonergan believed could be intelligently understood and rationally affirmed]. It is unequivocally and directly communicable [i.e., it is objective, "scientific" knowledge]. Elucidation of Existenz, on the other hand, involves commitment. It speaks from the individual to the individual. Instead of general insights, it conveys possible lucidities, showing the potential of the individual in his unconditional roots and ends. Not everyone will recognize himself in it, but each one does so more or less, both in adoption and rejection, by translating it into his own reality as this very individual. Its communication has many meanings and may be misunderstood. Its appeal to the man to whom it appeals at all will be to involve his self. (P. 71)

It was this type of experiential insight that Voegelin referred to as the "pneumatic" (i.e., spiritual) differentiation of consciousness. He respected the importance of the "noetic" (i.e., intellectual) differentiation (hence his appreciation of Lonergan's *Insight* as a general account of it), but he had a special interest in the implications of the "pneumatic" differentiation, which he considered the major "leap in being" that took place in ancient Israel and the birth of Christianity and that could also take place anywhere in anyone who yields himself to the transcendent calling implicit in every human being's experience of the tension of existence. Both differentiations of consciousness were closely related, indeed mutually involved, for Voegelin, and both were important to him.[25] That Voegelin, like Jaspers, would not have called experiential insight into the fundamental difference between the objective pole of consciousness and the subjective a matter of "objective truth" does not mean that he did not appreciate objectivity; what it means is that he appreciated both objectivity and its limits. The issue, in this case, is not objective truth, Voegelin would have said, but subjective truth or what he himself called "the truth of existence," one's conscious and responsible engagement in the drama of being.[26] The centrality of Voegelin's concern with the "pneumatic" and the subjective "truth of existence" was a major reason for his emphasis on the necessary role of myth in philosophical exploration.

Lonergan was not himself uninterested in the spiritual dimension of human experience, but he seems to have found it more difficult to find a language for it than he did the strictly intellectual or rational dimension. He preferred the theoretical languages of science and technical philosophy to the language of mythic symbols, and in fact tended to consider the latter to have no special contribution of its own to make to our knowledge. This can be seen, for example, in his tendency in *Insight* to dismiss myth as a prescientific attempt at objective knowledge: " . . . mythic consciousness is the absence of self-knowledge, and myth is a consequence of mythic consciousness as metaphysics is a corollary of self-knowledge. Myth, then, and metaphysics are opposites. For

25. For further discussion of the relation between the "noetic" and "pneumatic" differentiations in Voegelin's thought, see Eugene Webb, *Eric Voegelin*, pp. 119–22.
26. See ibid., pp. 158–61.

myth recedes and metaphysics advances in the measure that the coun-ter-positions are rejected" (pp. 542–43).

For Voegelin, in contrast, myth could never be dispensed with in the exploration of human experience in its full dimensions, because beyond the philosopher's strictly objective reach, there would always lie the in-herently mysterious realm of the irreducibly subjective, for which myth offers the only symbolization adequate to guide and assist us in our *zetema,* the project of existential truth or spiritual fidelity that is the deep calling of our lives. As he expressed the issue in his *From En-lightenment to Revolution:* "The mythical language was, at the time of its original employment, the precise instrument for expressing the irrup-tion of transcendental reality, its incarnation and its operation in man.... It has become a 'myth' as a consequence of the penetration of our world by a rationalism which destroys the transcendental meaning of symbols taken from the world of the senses" (p. 21).

The "irruption of transcendental reality" as a subjective presence and energy in man referred to here is essentially identical with the "pneu-matic differentiation" mentioned above. This, as Voegelin conceived it, will amount to a major subjective reorientation, a transition from con-sciousness that conceives of itself as fully immersed in the cosmos (the world of particular entities) to consciousness that is aware of its exis-tence in tension between immanence in the cosmos and the pull of the transcendent pole beyond the cosmos. This constitutes, he believed, a qualitative change in one's mode of existence in that the realization of the ordering presence of the transcendent within the field of experience implies a radical restructuring not only of understanding but also of in-tention. As he put it in another passage from the introduction to the first volume of *Order and History:* "Existence is partnership in the community of being; and the discovery of imperfect participation, of a mismanagement of existence through lack of proper attunement to the order of being, of the danger of a fall from being, is a horror indeed, compelling a radical reorientation of existence" (*OH,* 1:10). When this takes place, said Voegelin, it is experienced as "a turning around, the Platonic *periagogé,* an inversion or conversion toward the true source of order. And this turning around, this conversion, results in more than an increase of knowledge concerning the order of being; it is a change in the order itself. For the participation in being changes its structure when it becomes emphatically a partnership with God, while the participation in mundane being recedes to second rank. The more perfect attunement to being through conversion is not an increase on the same scale but a qualitative leap" (p. 10).

This "conversion" is both the discovery of the pull of transcendence and a commitment to it. In this respect, then, it involves realization both of a passive state of being drawn and an active seeking, and according to Voegelin these two are to be understood as complementary aspects of what is experienced as a single existential event: the experienced tension of existence. This tension is experienced on the most fundamental level as simultaneously something we do and something that happens to us. "The terms seeking... and drawing... ," said Voegelin (commenting on the use of the terms in Plato), "do not denote different movements but symbolize the dynamics in the tension of existence between its human and divine poles. In the one movement there is experienced a seeking from the human, a being drawn from the divine pole."[27]

Our specifically human consciousness, according to Voegelin, is our experience of existing in this way—as a dynamic passion, a living and conscious response to an immediately experienced presence that quickens and engages us in that drama of existence of which we do not know the plot but within which the symbols of religious and philosophical myth can serve to some degree to orient us. What we can know through their elucidation of our existence is its character as a tension, a field of pull and counter-pull, structurally defined by the poles from which the drawing and the seeking are apprehended as proceeding.

This state of existence between immanent and transcendent, finite and infinite, Voegelin described most extensively through the use of Plato's symbol of the Metaxy (literally, "the between") from the *Symposium* and the *Philebus:*

> Man experiences himself as tending beyond his human imperfection toward the perfection of the divine ground that moves him. The spiritual man, the *daimonios aner,* as he is moved in his quest of the ground, moves somewhere between knowledge and ignorance.... "The whole realm of the spiritual (*daimonion*) is halfway indeed between (*metaxy*) god and man" (*Symp.* 202a). Thus, the in-between—the *metaxy*—is not

27. "The Gospel and Culture," in Donald G. Miller and Dikran Y. Hadidian, eds., *Jesus and Man's Hope,* 2:71.

an empty space between the poles of the tension but the "realm of the spiritual"; it is the reality of "man's converse with the gods" (202–3), the mutual participation... of human in divine, and divine in human, reality....

If man exists in the *metaxy,* in the tension "between god and man," any construction of man as a world-immanent entity will destroy the meaning of existence, because it deprives man of his specific humanity. The poles of the tension must not be hypostatized into objects independent of the tension in which they are experienced as its poles. (*Anamnesis,* pp. 103–4)

Here we are presented with a picture of human existence as existential tension structured as a relation between the poles that Plato called human and divine. To grasp properly what Voegelin means by his use of such an image it is important to take seriously his emphasis on the point that the Metaxy is not to be imagined in spatial terms and the poles of the tension are not to be conceived as things, but are to be construed strictly as poles, that is, as aspects of the experience of seeking and being drawn. The references to human and divine did not, in Voegelin's use, refer to entities called "human beings" or "the gods." Both terms are for Voegelin mythic symbols with which to express the structure of the existential tension considered as such. As Voegelin described it in "The Gospel and Culture": "When existence becomes noetically luminous as the field of pull and counter-pull, of the question of life and death, and of the tension between human and divine reality, it also becomes luminous for divine reality as the Beyond of the *metaxy* which reaches into the *metaxy* in the participatory event of the movement. There is no In-Between of existence as a self-contained object but only existence experienced as part of a reality which extends beyond the In-Between" (p. 76).

Despite the obvious differences, however, between Voegelin's language and Lonergan's, the conception Voegelin expresses of the ordering of the soul by the "tension toward the beyond" is very similar to Lonergan's about the role of the "transcendental notion" in consciousness as it was explained in the last chapter. Both begin, that is, from reflection on essentially the same experience: the dynamism of human consciousness in its orientation toward transcendence. For both philosophers, authentic human consciousness is structured as a questioning that strives toward clarity and adequacy of understanding and that finds its deepest satisfaction in the fulfillment of the desire to live consciously in reality; this is a task which, as both conceive it, involves not only knowledge of objective truth but also, on the side of the subject, a life of fidelity to the demands of the structure of questioning consciousness.

Voegelin's "the Question," one of his numerous terms for our experience of existential tension, clearly has a function in his analysis of mythic thought paralleling that which the "transcendental notion" has in Lonergan's analysis of what he called the realm of interiority. "The Question capitalized," says Voegelin, "is not a question concerning the nature of this or that object in the external world, but a structure inherent to the experience of reality. As a consequence, it does not appear in the same form at all times, but shares by its varying modes the advance of experience from compactness to differentiation. . . . In the setting of the primary [i.e., "undifferentiated"] experience, the Question appears as the motivating force in the act of symbolizing the origin of things through the myth, *i.e.*, by a story which relates one thing, or complex of things, to another intracosmic thing as the ground of its existence" (*OH*, 4:317). Even when it reaches out for understanding through mythic symbolism, according to Voegelin, "the Question" is nevertheless rational in that it involves an implicit process of critical reflection: "The function of the Question becomes apparent, furthermore, when the creators of the myth reflect on the adequacy of the myth as an expression of the questioning they are experiencing" (p. 317). The comments certain ancient Egyptian mythographers made about the reasons some myths were more adequate than others "leave no doubt," says Voegelin, "about a live critical consciousness in the mythopoetic act" (p. 317).

The image of "the Question" would be misleading, however, if it suggested that Voegelin thought man's existential tension is inherently oriented toward particular answers to particular questions or, as we saw Lonergan put it, toward "objective truth." Its goal, for Voegelin, is the subjective truth that is a mode of existence rather than an item of information. In this Voegelin was in accord with Jaspers and, as we will see, with Kierkegaard, but also, he believed, with the greatest master of philosophical myth, Plato. As he described the issue in his discussion of Plato:

Truth is not a body of propositions about a world-immanent object; it is the world-transcendent *summum bonum,* experienced as an orienting force in the soul, about which we can speak only in analogical symbols. Transcendental reality cannot be an object of cognition in the manner of a world-immanent datum because it does not share with man the finiteness and temporality of immanent existence. It is eternal, out-of-time; it is not co-temporal with the experiencing soul. When, through the experiences of the Socratic-Platonic type, eternity enters time, we may say that "Truth" becomes "historical." . . . By "historicity of Truth" we mean that transcendental reality, precisely because it is not an object of world-immanent knowledge, has a history of experience and symbolization. (*OH,* 3:363)

The central idea in this case could perhaps be made clearer by rephrasing it in terms of the distinction mentioned earlier between subjective and objective poles of consciousness. Stated in such terms, Voegelin's "transcendental reality" or "truth" considered as "world-transcendent *summum bonum*" is not a "world-immanent object" because it is not an idea or entity with what Lonergan would call categorial content. It is not, in other words, what in Lonergan's language would be called the proportionate object of an operation of understanding or judgment. What it is is subjective presence. Only analogically can it be called an object at all, and then only in the sense that it is what one is moved to reach toward in the experience of existential tension as it expresses itself both in spiritual aspirations and in intentional operations. It is both the source and goal, that is, of the fundamental tension of existence that becomes humanly self-luminous as it is simultaneously experienced in immediacy and symbolically objectified in the refracting medium of intentional consciousness.

It must be admitted, however, despite the importance of the point Voegelin insists on against Lonergan, that Voegelin's fondness for the language of philosophical myth and his reluctance to move from that to a more explicit and precise technical terminology can leave one wishing at times that he had been willing to try as hard as Lonergan to make clear exactly what he means. When Voegelin speaks, for example, of "existence experienced as part of a reality which extends beyond the In-Between," one cannot help but wonder what exactly "reality" must be if "existence" can be called a "part" of it. Also, the strongly spatialized imagery of such phrases makes it all the more of a challenge to Voege-lin's reader to heed his injunctions to avoid yielding to the reifying con-notations of his language.

Voegelin's "tension toward the beyond," considered simply as a lin-guistic symbol, draws from its Platonic origin a set of associations that not only are spatial and visual but that also, however Voegelin may himself have intended them, seem dualistic in implication. In Plato's parable of the cave (*Republic*, 7) one moves from the vision of shadows on the walls out into sunlight, where one discovers the true source of light in the sun above. Or in the *Phaedrus*, one imagines the soul as like a chariot guided by a charioteer (reason) and drawn by both noble and ignoble steeds (the passions) toward the vault of heaven, beyond which (and directly visible only to the gods) lies true being. Such imagery of movement toward a goal or of vision across a distance is pervasive in Voegelin's writings. He does not mean it to be taken literally—as his denial that "Truth" or "transcendental reality" can be a world-imma-nent object indicates—but he does not explain with Lonergan's sort of care exactly how he does intend it to be interpreted, and he does not clearly rule out all the connotations that the spatial and visual meta-phors carry with them into the description of the subject-object rela-tion.

Even without slipping into visualization or reification, one could still, taking his images at face value, interpret the relation between Voege-lin's poles of immanence and transcendence or "human and divine" as implying some form of dualism. Epistemological and ontological dual-ism of a sort that would isolate the spiritual and material, the eternal and the temporal, and so forth, from one another and devalue the latter member of such pairings has frequently been interpreted as a basic ten-dency of Platonistic thought, and Voegelin may not have worked as hard as he should at making clear the ways in which his own thought differed from this aspect of the tradition of imagery on which he drew so heavily.

Lonergan, on the other hand, explicitly criticized the dualistic, spa-tial, and ocular connotations of the Platonistic pattern of thought with its tendency to analogize knowing to "looking" at something across some sort of gap.[28] In this respect Lonergan's own conceptual frame-

28. See, for example, *Insight*, p. 412.

work, which derives more from the Aristotelian-Thomistic tradition than from that of Plato, has a certain advantage as a means to avoid slipping into dualism.

Lonergan's use of his term "transcendental," for example, derives not from the tradition of Plato or from myth but from that of medieval scholastic logic, in which the transcendental stands in contrast to the categorial as the universal to the particular. According to this pattern of thought, intelligibility is a quality shared by all understood particulars, and truth is simply adequacy of understanding and as such is what all critically reflective judgments seek to confirm. In Lonergan's usage there is no latent dualism; he makes it quite clear that the transcendental notion implies no inherent discontinuity between subject and object as though they were two entities separated by some sort of epistemological or ontological gap. Rather, as was explained in the last chapter, his transcendental notions seem best interpreted as anticipations of acts of understanding, judging, and deciding—acts which can be and are performed at the culmination of the processes the transcendental notions guide. Lonergan's explicitness in his use of technical language enabled him to make it clear that he was not describing things in the commonsense world of space and time. It also helped to make clear his belief that human consciousness involves a dynamic tendency toward the performance of the specific operations by which actual knowing and moral commitment take place.

Voegelin, especially in his polemics against what he calls "gnosticism," argued against the belief that one can have a direct vision of transcendent reality and thereby derive irreformable knowledge about the true and the good. In this, he was arguing in effect against the same epistemology of the look that Lonergan opposed, but because he did so without addressing cognitional theory directly, he often leaves the reader with the impression of a dualistic picture of man as drawn by an insatiable longing toward a goal of direct vision that he can never reach, so that wisdom and fidelity to "the truth of existence" must lie in accepting the inevitable frustration of this longing.

This may not have been exactly what Voegelin intended, but the connotations of his favored myths suggest something like that meaning, and since he did not spell out a different meaning with full explicitness, it is difficult in the end to determine exactly how his mythic language is to be taken. There are times when the tragic tone of his language and imagery seem actually to express a sense of inevitable frustration in man's situation in the universe. Certainly there are passages that give the opposite impression, as when he says, for example, "In the Platonic-Aristotelian experience, the questioning unrest carries the assuaging answer within itself inasmuch as man is moved to his search of the ground by the divine ground of which he is in search. The ground is not a spatially distant thing but a divine presence that becomes manifest in the experience of unrest and the desire to know. The wondering and questioning is sensed as the beginning of a theophanic event that can become fully luminous to itself if it finds the proper response in the psyche of concrete human beings—as it does in the classic philosophers" (*Anamnesis*, pp. 95–96). It is not clear, however, that Voegelin thought of this experience of theophany as offering the individual anything more than a temporary, ultimately evanescent satisfaction. Nor is it clear that the satisfaction it offers must not leave still frustrated what in many other passages Voegelin seems to conceive of as man's insatiable longing for the direct vision of ultimate being that the *Phaedrus* attributes to the gods alone. Voegelin's own affinity for what he referred to as "the tragic experience of history" is suggested by his frequent references to the "truth" expressed in the sole surviving fragment of Anaximander: "The origin (*arche*) of things is the Apeiron [i.e., the boundless, the void]. . . . It is necessary for things to perish into that from which they were born; for they pay one another penalty for their injustice (*adikia*) according to the ordinance of Time."[29]

Such elusiveness regarding the ultimate implications of Voegelin's thought would seem to be one of the less fortunate effects of his preference for the language of myth over more explicit, theoretical language. Another effect is what might seem at times circularity of reasoning in the way he evaluates some symbols as having greater authority or truth than others because they are supposed to be more authentic expressions of the formative experiences of historical mankind. The seeming circularity is that of interpreting certain symbols as authoritative and then using those as criteria for the evaluation of other symbols. Whether this is really circular or not must depend on whether the initial selection can

---

29. *OH*, 4:174; see also 4:215–16, 226, and especially 241 and 269–70, where the Anaximandrian vision of coming into being and perishing is contrasted favorably with Paul's less "balanced" hope for resurrection into a life that will be imperishing.

be justified on theoretical grounds. Since Voegelin did not always make those grounds as explicit as he might have, however, his argument remains controversial on this point.

The authoritativeness of certain symbols became for Voegelin a matter of methodological principle. He began his *Order and History* with the statement, "The order of history emerges from the history of order" (*OH*, 1:ix). By this he meant that the intelligibility to be found in history is the unfolding of the structured, bipolar tension of existence in a process of experience and symbolization. This historical process is one in which human agents either respond to the experienced pull of transcendence with fidelity to its directional tendency or else resist it. Depending on their fundamental stance in relation to the inherent order of existence, their openness to it or resistance, they will image its structure in their lives and thought, or else they will embody and give expression to symbols of deformation.[30] Out of this process will be born, less by human intention than by a sort of spontaneous generation, symbols of existential order or disorder. "As long as the movements of the unconscious are allowed to express themselves in myth in free recognition of their nature," Voegelin said, "the soul of man preserves its openness towards its cosmic ground" (*OH*, 3:187). The most direct approach to an understanding of human existence, therefore, is to study the symbols that have appeared during the course of history out of the experience of people who lived in such openness and were thereby, as Voegelin terms it, "attuned" to the order of being (*OH*, 1:4).

In addition to the distinction between symbols expressing well-ordered or disordered existence, Voegelin made a further distinction between what he called "primary" and "secondary" (or even "tertiary") symbols. Primary symbols were for him direct expressions in symbolic form of the structure of the existential tension that he believed is the deep bedrock of reality. Once it is given utterance, the language of the primary symbolism may subsequently be misinterpreted by thinkers who have not shared adequately or understood well the original experience, and this results in what Voegelin called "secondary symbols." It is easy to see why, on these assumptions, Voegelin preferred to use histori-

---

30. On Voegelin's conception of existential "openness" versus "closure," see, for example, *Anamnesis*, pp. 97–98, and "On Hegel: A Study in Sorcery," p. 354. See also Webb, *Eric Voegelin*, pp. 147–48.

cal sources and to take the original expression of an experience as normative. In the introduction to *The Ecumenic Age* he emphasized this as the central concern of his work:

> In our time, the inherited symbolisms of ecumenic humanity are disintegrating, because the deforming doctrinalization has become socially stronger than the experiential insights it was originally meant to protect. The return from symbols which have lost their meaning to the experiences which constitute meaning is so generally recognizable as the problem of the present that specific references are unnecessary. The great obstacle to this return is the massive block of accumulated symbols, secondary and tertiary, which eclipses the reality of man's existence in the Metaxy. To raise this obstacle and its structure into consciousness, and by its removal to help in the return to the truth of reality as it reveals itself in history, has become the purpose of *Order and History*. (*OH*, 4:58)

It is also easy to see why, as a consequence of such principles, Voegelin tended to interpret most of the language of technical philosophy as a secondary symbolism. This tendency increased over time as the implications of his principles became clearer to him. In the comparatively early *New Science of Politics* (1952) Voegelin spoke critically of the rejection of metaphysics by modern social scientists, but in "What Is Political Reality" (1966) he himself described metaphysics as "the perversion of noetic exegesis by hardening its terms into a propositional science of principles, universals, and substances."[31] In the second volume of *Order and History* (1957) he spoke of myth and metaphysics as complementary in that "the compact symbols of the myth comprehend shades of experience that escape the differentiated concepts of metaphysics, while the language of metaphysics lends precision to meanings which remain inarticulate in the myth" (p. 127). In the fourth volume, on the other hand, his references to "propositional metaphysics" are more strongly negative in tone, as when he speaks of that of the Stoics as a "new intellectual game with imaginary realities in an imaginary realm of thought" growing out of a literalizing of mythopoetic symbols (*OH*, 4:43).

The principle that symbols that have developed historically as the

---

31. *New Science of Politics*, pp. 12, 20, and *Anamnesis*, p. 193. In both places Voegelin was referring primarily to the sort of metaphysics associated with Aristotle and Aquinas.

direct expression of experience and insight can speak to us with greater authority than can those that derive from the labored abstractions of epigones seems a sound one. It is obvious, however, that in practice the classification of certain types of symbol as primary and authoritative and other types as either false or secondary and possibly misleading will be a controversial procedure. For one thing, it can give rise to the suspicion of circularity mentioned above. For another it may carry a dualistic implication of its own: it may tempt one to trust certain symbols absolutely and to dismiss others with equal absoluteness, thereby underestimating the ambiguity inherent in all symbolism.

This could lead to a simplistic hermeneutic in which one might fail to appreciate the variety within the universe of myths—a point on which we will see that Paul Ricoeur has something valuable to offer. Or it might lead one to overlook aspects of mythic symbolism that do not fit into one's picture of what the primary symbols are supposed to convey. René Girard, as we will see, offers some incisive observations about the meaning of traditional myths that make them seem considerably less trustworthy as sources of philosophical guidance than Voegelin was inclined to suppose. Both Ricoeur and Girard put a great deal of emphasis on the way in which myths can both reflect and throw light on human evil. Voegelin, from his own historical experience as a victim of Nazi persecution and a critic of other versions of totalitarianism, was acutely aware of the problem of human evil. His analysis of it in terms of what he called political "gnosticism" or of utopianism, however, even if it throws valuable light on certain aspects of the problem, leaves unexplored other aspects that the thinkers just mentioned would probably consider even more central to our lives.

Girard in particular would challenge the wisdom of putting too much trust in any myth. Voegelin's assumptions about the spontaneous origins of primary symbolism in "experiences of transcendence," on the other hand, make it difficult even to consider looking skeptically at the kinds of implication we will see Girard uncovering in some of the very symbols that Voegelin credited with a high degree of authority, such as the philosophical myths of Plato and Anaximander. That discussion, however, must wait for Girard's chapter.

To get a sense of how some of the problems just mentioned manifest themselves in Voegelin's own treatment of the issues in which he was interested, let us consider some aspects of the way in which he drew on mythic imagery in his discussion of the experience and symbolization of the tension of existence. "The classic manifestation of the tension," Voegelin said, "is Plato's creation of the philosopher's myth," described as "the story of the gods that can claim to be true if it fits the cognitive consciousness of order created in the soul of man by the erotic tension toward the divine Beyond" (*OH*, 4:11). The experience in question, as Voegelin analyzes it, combines the inherent dynamism of consciousness that stirs us to inquiry and action with what seems a latently dualistic conception, imaged by *eros* in the *Symposium* or the *Phaedrus*, of deficiency longing for a tension-free sufficiency. In the *Symposium*, Eros is said to be the child of Poverty and Plenty, hence his always falling short and his perpetual longing for fullness. In the *Phaedrus* the human soul is likened to a chariot drawn by two steeds, one of which has a tendency to descend, the other a tendency to seek the heavens. Reason is like the charioteer, who has the task of redirecting the energy of the one steed while giving headway to the other. The chariot can ascend to the high point of heaven by following in the wake of a god—that is, by letting itself be possessed and drawn upward by a divine enthusiasm. Only the gods themselves, however, can ascend above heaven to gaze directly upon the true being beyond.

As Voegelin interprets the experience of existential tension, drawing on his particular reading of Plato's images, sufficiency is to be identified only with the Beyond, and the Beyond with absence of tension (since the tension is imaged as the Between or Metaxy, and the Beyond is its opposite). It is on such identifications that Voegelin based his opposition to what he called "gnosticism," which, in his interpretation, includes the belief that it is possible for a human being to arrive at a tension-free existence. Wisdom and the "truth of existence" for Voegelin lie in accepting the inevitability of tension (and by the implication of his images, deficiency) in the human experience of existence.

How did Voegelin determine that the experience of the dynamism of consciousness is adequately symbolized as a tension between poles and that these poles are related as inevitable deficiency longing for an unattainable sufficiency? Voegelin's own answer was that this is the interpretation of human experience that emerges from the study of "primary symbols," such as those just mentioned, which is to say those symbols that Voegelin takes to be authoritative. The circularity of such reasoning here seems both real and obvious: the symbols identified as authoritative are those that support the interpretation, and the interpretation is correct because it is the one suggested by these symbols. To point this out is not to imply that there is not some real wisdom in Voegelin's interpretation of human experience and of the folly of seeking to escape from its necessary conditions. It is only to point out that the interpretation lacks sufficient explicit critical grounding to be persuasive to one who does not already believe, perhaps on other grounds, in its validity and that however sound the interpretation may be, its validity is rather taken for granted than proven. Nor does it take into account other possible interpretations that might have different connotations and possibly greater truth.

The uncritical character of the interpretation, however, is inevitable considering the underlying assumptions of Voegelin's framework of thought. If the latent meaning of experience unfolds to consciousness through spontaneously generated symbols, it is difficult to imagine a way that the tacit process of symbolization could be rendered explicit so that it could be critically reflected on.

Even if Voegelin was correct about the nature of a primary symbol, moreover, it is not necessarily the case that all historical "primary symbols" must carry exactly identical connotations in every respect. There is no necessary reason to suppose that two primary symbolisms could not diverge in some aspects. Such divergences could have important implications. Plato's symbol of *eros* in the dialogues mentioned above is an element in a total framework of interpretation that emphasizes the analogy between knowing and the sense of sight and between the poles of the tension and mythic constructs involving a contrast between men and gods. That framework, largely by way of the connotations of these analogies, fixes an unbridgeable gulf between real being and human powers of vision or apprehension.

There is no necessary reason, however, why the experience of bipolar tension must be explicated in exactly this way, even if one accepts the idea that one of the poles is characterized by a deficiency relative to the sufficiency of the other. Even a shift from Plato to a thinker as close to him as Aristotle—whom Voegelin did not at least entirely dismiss— takes one into a different framework in which the analogy to ocular vision is replaced by an emphasis on the transition from potentiality to actuality. Potentiality might be called a deficiency relative to actuality, and the experienced dynamism of the movement from potentiality toward actuality could in the case of consciousness be described as a yearning toward sufficiency. Cast in the form of a transition from potentiality to actuality, the image would not suggest that the deficiency was inevitable or the sufficiency inherently unattainable. On the contrary, in such a framework the assumption of the unattainability of actualization would be patently nonsensical, since a potential that necessarily could not be actualized would be a potential without potential. With regard to the Platonic myth about the ability of the gods alone to gaze upon real being, the dualism the imagery implies is hardly necessary, especially if one interprets "the real" as that which is knowable by carefully performed intentional operations.[32] Alternative conceptions are possible even without discarding such symbols as human and divine or natural and supernatural. In an Aristotelian framework—such as that later developed by Aquinas in his concept of sanctifying grace—the actualization of human nature could be interpreted as constituting a real communion between man and the divine considered as the ultimate source of his actuality.[33]

This, of course, runs counter to Voegelin's emphasis on the quasi-tragic gulf between the human pole and the pole of the beyond, and Voegelin has expressed mixed feelings about the type of thought both Aristotle and Aquinas represent (as was explained earlier in connection with the topic of metaphysics), but there may be other differences between his thought and theirs other than their tendency to reify abstractions as metaphysical entities. It is also possible that they may have given expression to an alternative and possibly more valid symbolization of the experience Plato was reflecting on.

To assess the relative validity of either their symbolization or Plato's would require that experience (as datum) and interpretation (as a further process) would have to be explicitly differentiated, and this is precisely what Voegelin's assumption of spontaneous symbolization rules

---

32. If "real being" were interpreted as a symbol referring to strictly subjective existence, on the other hand, the mythic image of it as proper to the gods could have a very different point, as should become clear below in the chapter on Kierkegaard. Here again, a distinction between "reality" as objective and "existence" as subjective would seem helpful in clarifying such an issue.

33. For a study of Aquinas's theory of sanctifying grace as both operative (on the part of God) and cooperative (on the part of man), see Lonergan, *Grace and Freedom: Operative Grace in the Thought of St. Thomas Aquinas.*

out. As it is, Voegelin tended simply to assert his judgments about the relative adequacy and authority of different symbolizations. He also tended to speak as if any way of thinking that might seek an alternative to the dualistic vision implicit in the imagery of his favored myths is likely to reflect a "gnostic" or utopian tendency. This may have been justified in some cases, such as that of the Nazis or Marxist revolutionaries who in his historical situation were the opponents he was particularly concerned with. Even his own premises, however, need not necessarily imply that all nondualistic visions must be "gnostic" in the sense he attributed to the term. One can experience a dynamism in consciousness, and one can even call it a tension between deficiency and sufficiency and believe that the longed for sufficiency is attainable without necessarily construing the transition in what Voegelin would call "gnostic" terms. It need not, that is, be interpreted as an expression of the desire to attain an entirely tension-free existence in the possession of perfect and irreformable knowledge of the "Beyond" as though it were an object in the world. It could also be interpreted, for example, in terms of one's wish to perform well the intentional operations that seem called for in one's situation in the world.

This, in fact, is where Lonergan's language might have an advantage over Voegelin's. Lonergan believed, like Aristotle and Aquinas, that an actual subject is one who actually performs intentional operations and that the dynamism of consciousness is a tendency to seek actualization as a subject on all of the possible levels of operation. To do so is to pass from an unsatisfied longing to the satisfaction that Aristotle called *eudaimonia*. But it is not necessarily to attain irreformable knowledge of reality or to claim to have done so. Lonergan himself would only claim that knowing is possible and that one arrives at it by carefully performing the operations that constitute it—which means that even in attainment knowing is an active process involving the critical reflection that continuously seeks to reform a reformable understanding of objective reality.

Voegelin would immediately object, and perhaps with good reason, that to speak of man as "a subject" at all is to hypostatize the subjective pole of consciousness and naively to identify it with a mythic figure, namely "man." Even if that is the case, however, the point Lonergan was aiming at is a sound one and need not be interpreted in a hypostatizing way. It could even be expressed in a way that would fit quite well into Voegelin's framework: that human consciousness is experienced as a dynamism of seeking and being drawn toward the operations that constitute actual human subjectivity as well as man's communion with the "divine presence" that, as Voegelin phrased it in "Reason: The Classic Experience," "becomes manifest in the experience of unrest and the desire to know" and "is sensed as the beginning of a theophanic event" (*Anamnesis*, pp. 95–96).

To reflect on the possibility of alternative symbolizations, however, would be made difficult in the context of Voegelin's thought, as was mentioned above, by his assumption that the symbols that express our experience of existential tension emerge authoritatively in consciousness by a sort of spontaneous generation. Those to which he attributes authority he seems to treat as unquestionable. Since he never presented an explicit account of his conception of the generation of mythic symbols, it is possible that this was something he adopted from sources in his background, particularly the background of German philosophy he was exposed to in his youth.

To point out that Voegelin spoke of an early interest in the thought of Arthur Schopenhauer might throw some light on this tendency in his thought, since Schopenhauer, too, thought in terms of a dynamism of consciousness, which he called "the Will," and he believed that the Will revealed itself to consciousness indirectly by way of symbolic representations.[34] Friedrich W. J. von Schelling, whom Voegelin spoke of as the source of his realization that the history of ideas must give way to the history of experiences and their symbolizations, was another, even more important influence. Schelling, as will be discussed below, put great emphasis on the revelatory function of myth as a source of philosophical insight.

Perhaps equally important in inclining Voegelin to assume that the production of interpretive symbols must be a spontaneous, virtually automatic process may be the influence of a thinker who lies behind both Schelling and Schopenhauer as also behind almost any other individual educated in the German-speaking world since the early nineteenth century: Immanuel Kant. The influence of Kant was pervasive in the Viennese philosophical milieu Voegelin grew up in, and it therefore

---

34. For a brief account of Voegelin's early reading, see Webb, *Eric Voegelin*, pp. 24–25; for a more extensive account, see Sandoz, *The Voegelinian Revolution*, chapter 2.

would be likely to have played a role in the formation of Voegelin's mind before he ever took up the study of Plato, and may well have affected the way he eventually came to read the latter. There are obvious parallels, for example, between the implications of Voegelin's Platonic symbols and such Kantian assumptions as (1) that beyond appearances there is a noumenal reality which is spoken of as though it were cognitive in principle, though not to human knowing (cf. Plato's vision of the Beyond as attainable by the gods, though not by men), (2) that all we are ever able to know directly are phenomenal forms packaged for us spontaneously according to *a priori* forms of the sensibility and understanding by innate mechanisms of the mind (cf. Voegelin's spontaneous symbolizations of experience), (3) that the dynamism of human consciousness manifesting itself either as Reason (*Vernunft*) or as Spirit (*Geist*) orients us beyond all that we can know or imagine toward transcendental Ideals of totality and perfection (cf. Voegelin's "tension of existence" and Plato's "Beyond" and his "Idea of the Good"), and (4) that it would be a fundamental mistake to "hypostatize" the transcendental Ideal of the *ens perfectissimum* as an *ens realissimum* (cf. Voegelin's strictures against "hypostatizing" the Beyond).

Both Kant and Schopenhauer could be sources also of the quasi-tragic vision Voegelin sometimes inclined to. Schopenhauer cast his thought in a more obviously tragic mode than Kant's, but it is easy to imagine a reader of Kant, especially one who had been strongly impressed by Schopenhauer, experiencing as an endless frustrated yearning the impossibility of direct intuition (*Anschauung*) of the things-in-themselves hidden behind phenomena.

A major problem of any framework of thought that assumes, like the Kantian, that mental operations are largely automatic and unconscious is that it must also conceive of man as, in Lonergan's terms, a truncated subject, leaving him with the necessity of deciding on action but with no secure foundation for wise decision other than the practical wisdom enshrined in maxims, as in the case of Kant's ethics, or else, as in Voegelin's case, in the practical wisdom enshrined in "common sense" philosophical and prephilosophical myths.[35]

---

35. On this aspect of Kantian ethics, cf. Alasdair MacIntyre, *After Virtue*, pp. 42–45. Regarding "common sense" as a theme in Voegelin's thought, see for example the last pages of "What Is Political Reality?" *Anamnesis*, pp. 211–13.

Voegelin and Schelling are linked by even more similarities. Like Schelling, Voegelin was critical of Hegel for what he considered a virtually hubristic attempt to build a bridge between logic and existence by interpreting the cosmos as the unfolding in objectivity of the logical structure of absolute mind. For Voegelin as for Schelling, nature or the cosmos was to be understood ultimately not as a system of ideas, but as activity. Also in contrast to Hegel, both believed that human reason will always remain ultimately unfathomable to itself in its subjective source, because it, like the cosmos as a whole, is rooted in energy rather than in the logical structure of an absolute Idea. One might even say that the difference between Voegelin and Lonergan on whether the subjective pole of consciousness can become its own object is an echo of this difference between Schelling and Hegel and perhaps a result of their influence—Schelling's on Voegelin and Hegel's on Lonergan.

It is in Voegelin's way of thinking about the mythic structure of history that the influence of Schelling is especially clear. In Schelling Voegelin found the idea, which he took as a matter of fundamental principle, that insofar as human existence can be discovered as having meaning, that meaning finds its expression in an endless movement toward a supreme goal that can never be realized within history: the presence of God or the Absolute (two names in Schelling for the same reality).

History, in an image Schelling took from Jacob Boehme, has the structure of our, and the world's, return to God after a falling away—a cosmic Fall that is grounded in an impersonal, irrational impulse in the depths of the divine being. Following Boehme, Schelling spoke of the impulse behind this Fall as "the egoism in God," which serves as the initial impetus of the dynamic act of self-creation by which God produces and incarnates himself in history.[36] "Ideas, spirits," said Schelling, "had to fall away from their center and introduce themselves into separateness in nature, the general sphere of the fall, in order that afterward, as separates, they might return into the Undifferentiated and, reconciled with it, remain in it without disturbing it."[37] This image of a cosmic Fall from and return into the Undifferentiated in Schelling may throw some

36. Schelling, *Werke*, 4:330, quoted in Frederick Copleston, *A History of Philosophy*, 7 (1):163.
37. *Werke*, 6:57, quoted in Meyer H. Abrams, *Natural Supernaturalism*, p. 224.

light on Voegelin's frequently expressed affinity for the fragment of Anaximander quoted earlier on the origin of things from the Boundless and their perishing return to it, which he described as "the key symbolism for what may be called the tragic experience of history" (OH, 4:174).

Another related image of Schelling's that also became fundamental to Voegelin's thought is that of the history described above as a story told by God: "History is an epic composed in the mind of God. Its two main parts are, first, that which represents the departure of humanity from its center out to its furthest alienation [Entfernung] from this center, and second, that which represents the return. The first part is, as it were, the Iliad, the second the Odyssey of history. In the first part the movement was centrifugal, in the second it becomes centripetal.... "[38] In Voegelin's adaptation of this image he spoke of the story as a tale told cooperatively both by God and by the man, who enacts his role in the cosmic drama in a spirit of responsiveness to the divine drawing. As Voegelin described this process in the terms he was using at the very end of his life, in the first chapter of the posthumously published In Search of Order, "The event of the quest [for existential truth] is part of a story told by the It, and yet a story to be told by the human questioner, if he wants to articulate the consciousness of his quest as an act of participation in the comprehending story" (OH, 5:24). "The 'story' thus emerges," he goes on to say, "as the symbolism that will express the awareness of the divine-human movement and counter-movement in the quest for truth." The various myths that have found expression in historical traditions could be described from this point of view as a variety of transcriptions of the cosmic story told first by God and then by his responsive human partners in that story.[39]

Schelling believed, as did Voegelin, that human communities form and societies take shape under the guidance of myths that function as the first stage of God's revelation in history and as the immediate source of religious and political consciousness. "The peoples did not first come into being and then create their myths," says Ernst Benz, paraphrasing from Schelling's Philosophy of Mythology, "but the other way round: it

---

38. Werke, 6:42, quoted in Abrams, pp. 223–24.
39. Voegelin cites as a modern expression of such a conception of the relation of myth and history as divine-human story Thomas Mann's tetralogy Joseph and His Brothers. OH, 5:24.

is the mythology of a people that determines its character and history. . . ."[40] "A people exists as such," said Schelling, "only after defining itself and making its decision in its mythology."[41]

This pattern of thought in Schelling seems a likely source for Voegelin's principle that the order of history emerges from the history of order (*OH*, 1:9). The history of order is a story that begins with the birth of order in mythic symbolism and its incarnation in the life of communities. This is a revelation of the order of history because the myths of a people express not only their own conceptions of order as grounded in their own limited experience of history, but also the order of being itself as grounded in the inner history of the life of God.

Their ways of thinking about that life as manifest in our experience of existential tension is a further point of linkage between Voegelin and Schelling. As Schelling phrased it in his *Ages of the World*, God manifests his presence in the depths of his creation as "a state of perpetual desire . . . , an incessant seeking, an eternal, never quieted passion to be"—or, in Voegelin's language, as the deep source of man's experience of tension, seeking, and drawing.[42]

Schelling's way of thinking about the origins of myth and culture may also be an additional source of Voegelin's assumption that true, or "primary," mythic symbols are not the artificial products of particular human minds, but emerge spontaneously in history and speak in it with virtually divine authority. In Schelling's words:

Mythology comes into being through a necessary process (necessary in respect to consciousness), the origin of which loses itself in a suprahistorical realm. Consciousness may resist the process in certain particulars, but cannot impede, much less reverse, it as a whole. . . . Mythological ideas are neither invented nor voluntarily accepted.—Products of a process independent of thought and will, they were unequivocally and undeniably real for the consciousness subjected to them. Peoples and individuals are only instruments of this process, which they do not perceive as a whole, which they serve without understanding it. It is not in their

40. "Theogony and the Transformation of Man in Friedrich Wilhelm Joseph Schelling," in Joseph Campbell, ed., *Man and Transformation: Papers from the Eranos Yearbooks*, 5:213.
41. *Samtliche Werke*, 11:109, quoted in Benz, "Theogony," p. 214.
42. Schelling, *Samtliche Werke*, 8:231–32, quoted in Benz, "Theogony," p. 216.

power to cast off these ideas, to accept them or not to accept them: for these ideas do not come from outside but are within the mind and men never know how they arise: for they come from the innermost conscious-ness, on which they imprint themselves with a necessity that permits no doubt as to their truth.[43]

These various affinities in Voegelin for the thought of Schelling and especially for Schelling's conception of myth clearly place him in the tradition of German romantic philosophy. "Romanticism" is in fact a better word for the tradition in question than the more common desig-nation, "Idealism," although the latter term would fit Hegel well, since Hegel advocated the theory that reality itself is structured as a system of ideas grounded in the absolute Idea of which the universe and history are the unfolding in time. Despite his use of the term "Idealism" in some of his early writings, belief in idealist principles was never central to Schelling's thought, and in his later writings he explicitly attacked Idealism as such. Rather he believed, as the quotations already given indicate, that neither man nor God nor the comprehensive dynamic process that embraces both can ever be fully reduced to objects of intel-lection. For both Voegelin and Schelling man, God, and history are inherently mysterious; all three are to be understood as facets of a mys-tery that reveals itself to us in the images of religious and philosophical myth. All of these are central tenets of the cultural movement that has come to be known as Romanticism.

Romanticism, however, has its own questionable aspects, just as Idealism and Rationalism do. In particular, one may ask of it how one is to discriminate between those myths or aspects of myth that can be counted trustworthy and those that cannot. Voegelin was not naive about the dangers in mythological thinking, and one of his points of at-tack on Nazi and Marxist ideology was to unmask their uncritically mythic roots (it was his books on "The Idea of Race" and "Political Re-ligions," for example, that put him on the list of those to be arrested when the Nazis took over Austria).[44] His way of dealing with the criti-

43. *Samtliche Werke*, 11:212, quoted in Benz, "Theogony," p. 217.
44. *Die Rassenidee in der Geistesgeschichte von Ray bis Carus* (1933); *Die politischen-Religionen* (1938). It is my understanding that translations of these works are in prepara-tion for Louisiana State University Press to be included in the new collected edition of Voegelin's works. A translation of the latter volume has also recently been completed by Barry Cooper.

cal problem, however, tended to take the form simply of discriminating between those myths and symbols he believed give voice to existential truth and those that express existential deformation or spiritual perversion.

One may ask whether this approach may not reflect at least traces of a Manichean tendency that is itself an example of naively romantic thinking, a tendency to divide the universe of symbols up into those that are revelatory and completely worthy of trust and those that are the opposite. It will be helpful, therefore, in pursuing this issue to go on to consider two thinkers who have made mythic symbolism a central focus of their own work. René Girard is an explicitly antiromantic thinker who is highly critical of mythic thought as such, though far from inclined to dismiss it in a rationalist manner as merely unscientific. Paul Ricoeur, on the other hand, as we shall see in the next chapter, shares with Voegelin an inclination to seek wisdom in mythic symbols and to place trust in their guidance, and he even shares Voegelin's taste to a large degree in the myths he tends to look to. He has also, however—and this will be at least a part of his interest for us—come to believe in the importance of balancing his fundamental inclination toward a "hermeneutic of trust" with a complementary "hermeneutic of suspicion."

CHAPTER 4

Paul Ricoeur

Consciousness

as a Hermeneutic Field

THE EXPLORATION of the human calling, especially when this is conceived of as involving a sense of either love or obligation toward its goal, has frequently cast itself in the form of a consideration of human failure, guilt, and repentance. Often it is in realizing that we have failed toward what we love that we discover both what it is we truly care about and the depth of concern we feel for it. In doing so we also discover something of what it means to be human in the full sense of the word.

What exactly we discover when we discover this, however, is not easy to specify. Historically there have been many efforts to express a sense of the matter, whether in stories, rituals, or theories, but these, too, stand in need of decipherment. Of the thinkers considered in this book, Ricoeur has probably taken the greatest interest in this theme and has made it the most central to his thought. Two of his books—*Fallible Man* and *The Symbolism of Evil*—have made this their central focus, and most of his other writings have dealt with it at some length as well. His study of Freud, for example, is an exploration of the psychoanalytic approach to the phenomenon of double-meaning—that is, the ways in which symbols can express both literal or obvious meanings and figurative or hidden ones—but it also has to do with the radical dishonesty or flight from consciousness that can lead human beings to hide truth not only from others but from themselves.[1]

1. *Freud and Philosophy: An Essay on Interpretation*, trans. Denis Savage. This volume will subsequently be referred to as *Freud*.

As was mentioned in the last chapter, this last tendency is the same human phenomenon that both Lonergan and Voegelin called "scotosis" (a darkening of awareness and understanding in an attempt to escape from the tensional character of human consciousness).[2] Ricoeur shares with all three of the other thinkers studied so far the belief that human existence is characterized by an experienced passion that both energizes us and sometimes can terrify us so that we flee from it.

Like Voegelin, Ricoeur has framed his discussion of this experience of existential tension in terms of Plato's symbol of the Metaxy, as well as other equivalent symbolisms he draws from such figures as Descartes and Pascal. What Voegelin called the experience of existential tension, Ricoeur calls the "pathétique of misery," and he describes it as a "precomprehension" of what philosophy unfolds as it seeks to explicate human existence in language. The fact that philosophy is rooted in such an experience means, he says, that "the beginning in philosophy . . .can only be a beginning in elucidation whereby philosophy recommences rather than commences" (*Fallible Man*, p. 9).

This in turn means, as Voegelin also emphasized, that before philosophy developed its own language, the meaning "precomprehended" in the experience was already expressed in the language of myth, so that philosophy is born out of the womb of mythic symbolism as an effort to understand more clearly what the myth speaks of. Plato stands at the beginning of philosophy for Ricoeur because, as he has put it, "the whole precomprehension of 'misery' is already to be found in the myths of the *Symposium*, the *Phaedrus* and the *Republic*" (p. 12). "The myth," he says, "is the misery of philosophy," in the sense that myth is in tension toward a more explicit comprehension of its meaning, and philosophy itself, "when it wishes to speak of man . . . is the philosophy of 'misery'" in that it is an explication of the human soul, the "intermediate being *par excellence*," as "tendency and tension" (pp. 12–13). As he put it in his *Freud*, " . . . every *mythos* involves a latent *logos* which demands to be exhibited" (p. 19).

For Ricoeur this pattern of mythic explication is paradigmatic for philosophy. First there must be the implicit tensional structure of human existence grasped in experience, then an initial expression of this in condensed and ambiguous symbols, then a quest for clarity that seeks

2. Lonergan, *Insight*, pp. 191–203. Voegelin, *Anamnesis*, p. 201.

simultaneously to explicate the symbols in theoretical language and to trace back through them to the experience of "tendency and tension" that gave rise both to the initial symbols and to the dissatisfaction with them that drives us onward into philosophy. He has been drawn, therefore, to philosophical figures who have expressed a similar sense of human existence. It is this, he says, that appeals to him in Descartes—not the deductivistic rationalism of Descartes's epistemology, but his image of man as "a something intermediate between God and nothingness, that is to say, placed between sovereign Being and not-being in such fashion that... I find myself subject to an infinity of imperfections...."[3] In adopting the perspective expressed in such images, Ricoeur dissociates himself "from the contemporary tendency to make finitude the global characteristic of human reality" (*Fallible Man*, p. 6). His "man" is not a definite thing among the things of the objective world, but a movement or *eros* in tension between and participating in Pascal's two infinities of God and nothing.

Ricoeur is also as insistent as Voegelin on the importance of being on guard against the pitfall of hypostatizing the poles of the tension as things, with the Metaxy interpreted as a kind of region between them. His favored metaphor of man as an intermediate being, though he considers it the absolutely fundamental myth from which any adequate philosophy of human consciousness must begin, can also, says Ricoeur, be misleading:

> For to say that man is situated *between* being and nothingness is already to treat human reality as a region, an ontological locality or a place lodged *between* other places. Now this schema of intercalation is extremely deceptive: it tempts us to treat man as an object whose place is fixed by its relation to other realities which are more or less complex, intelligent and independent than man. Man is not intermediate because he is between angel and animal; he is intermediate within himself, within his *selves*. (Pp. 5–6)

Nor are the "selves" mentioned here reifiable either. They are not entities, but potentialities and images that serve to define the tensional structure of human existence. In his earlier volume, *Freedom and Nature: The Voluntary and the Involuntary*, Ricoeur had used phenom-

---

3. Descartes, *Meditations*, IV, quoted in *Fallible Man*, p. 5.

enological analysis to explore the difference between consciously intentional and involuntary human acts. *Fallible Man* then considered human existence as a movement between these as poles of human possibility, neither of which is ever so fully actualized that one becomes either a mere automaton of habit and neurological response or a completely volitional agent. It is the aim toward the latter that constitutes the ideal of being a "person," but this is a point of aim, never in our experience a full actuality: "Thus the Self, the Self as a person, is given first in an intention. . . . the person is primarily the ideal of the person . . ." (*Fallible Man*, p. 110). Man exists in tension between this ideal of a higher possibility and his experience of the involuntariness that impinges upon his consciousness from within himself, but which is likewise never his full actuality. "Character," as Ricoeur puts it, "is the narrowness of the 'whole soul' whose humanity is openness. My character and my humanity together make of my freedom an unlimited possibility and a constituted partiality" (p. 94). The Metaxy, for Ricoeur, is man's experience of tension between the poles of the voluntary and the involuntary, the personal and the impersonal, possibility and factitiousness, infinitude and finitude—all of which represent possibilities toward which he strives or from which he struggles.

Another Platonic theme that Ricoeur shares with Voegelin is "recollection," or as Voegelin, in an explicitly Platonic allusion, termed it in one of his titles, *anamnesis*. For Voegelin, the recollection or *anamnesis* in question was the elucidation through the interplay between symbol and experience of the fundamental existential tension that is the life of the *psyche*. For Ricoeur it is essentially the same; the theme of recollection in his thought flows logically from the idea that philosophy is the explication of what is "precomprehended" in man's experience of "tendency and tension." Ricoeur, however, has given more attention than Voegelin to the hermeneutic problem as such, and the reason is that he is somewhat less confident than Voegelin was that the symbols that articulate the structure of the experience of existential tension are entirely trustworthy.

As was mentioned in the last chapter, Voegelin tended to think of what he called "primary symbols" as spontaneous expressions of an individual's experience. The problematic character of symbolism as he conceived it arises when a person in flight from the fundamental experience of existential tension cannot adequately connect such symbols to the experience of existential tension that originally engendered them. The problem is one of "open" versus "closed" existence, as Voegelin phrased it. His supposition was that at least some individuals have existed in the open mode and have expressed their experience of open existence in symbols that adequately represent it. When individuals in flight from the tensional structure of the human experience of existence, on the other hand, try to interpret symbols of open existence, they cannot help assimilating them to what they are capable of comprehending, distorting them into expressions of their own experience of anxious flight from reality.

Ricoeur's thought on this issue differs in small but significant ways. An example can be seen in the differences between their attitudes toward Freud. Voegelin dismissed Freud—too readily and absolutely, I believe—as an example of existential closure and therefore of failure to grasp the meaning of the primary symbols of classical myth and philosophy.[4] Ricoeur, on the other hand, has attempted to take Freud's thesis with full seriousness while not giving up the important truth he believes is to be found in the idea of "recollection." As he put the issue near the end of his *Freud:* "'Symbols give rise to thought,' but they are also the birth of idols. That is why the critique of idols remains the condition of the conquest of symbols" (p. 543).

From this fact, Ricoeur believes, follows the need for two opposing theories of interpretation. One is a hermeneutic of "faith" or radical trust, "interpretation conceived as the recollection or restoration of meaning" (p. 9) that takes place through hearkening to the meanings implicit in the symbols of the sacred or of dreams or of the poetic imagination. This "is a rational faith," he says, "for it interprets; but it is a faith because it seeks, through interpretation, a second naïveté" (p. 28). The other theory is the hermeneutic of suspicion advocated by Freud, "interpretation conceived as the unmasking, demystification, or reduction of illusions" (p. 9).

Ricoeur's personal inclination is toward faith rather than suspicion, but he knows that trust can lead one into gullibility, and so his own approach attempts to balance this with critical reflection: "The contrary

4. See for example, *Anamnesis,* pp. 3, 102, 108, and "Eclipse of Reality," p. 190.

of suspicion, I will say bluntly, is faith. What faith? No longer to be sure, the first faith of the simple soul, but rather the second faith of one who has engaged in hermeneutics, faith that has undergone criticism, postcritical faith" (p. 28). At the same time, however, he insists that suspicion, while guarding against error, must not be allowed to undermine trust, lest one fail to benefit from its leading. Even the phenomenological "epoche" or "bracketing" of belief must have its limits if one is serious about discovering existential truth:

> But while the scientist as such can and must practice this method of bracketing, the philosopher as such cannot and must not avoid the question of the absolute validity of his object. For would I be interested in the object, could I stress concern for the object . . . if I did not expect, from within understanding, this something to "address" itself to me? Is not the expectation of being spoken to what motivates the concern for the object? Implied in this expectation is a confidence in language: the belief that language, which bears symbols, is not so much spoken by men as spoken to men, that men are born into language, into the light of the logos 'who enlightens every man who comes into the world.' It is this expectation, this confidence, this belief, that confers on the study of symbols its particular seriousness. (Pp. 29–30)

The difference between Ricoeur and Voegelin on this point is essentially between the confident belief on Voegelin's part that certain authoritative symbols speak to us in a manner that fully justifies our trust and a somewhat more cautious stance on the part of Ricoeur, who is willing to accept the idea that the hermeneutic of suspicion, even if it cannot have the last word, must nevertheless have a place in all hermeneutic process. The reason for this divergence between the two thinkers is directly connected with the centrality of the question of subjective evil for Ricoeur. Voegelin was not naive about the presence of evil in human life, and as a political philosopher he considered a willingness to take human evil seriously to be one of the criteria of philosophical maturity for individuals and for societies, but his tendency was to see it as a threat to what remains a genuinely possible human life of reason and open existence, not as the pervasive condition underlying and to some degree undermining every movement of the human soul. In this respect Voegelin is, as some of his Christian critics have suggested, a proponent more of "Greek" than of orthodox Christian thought.[5] Ricoeur, on the other hand, is an explicitly Christian thinker, and on this particular issue he stands in the tradition of Christian thought that emphasizes the radically problematic character of human existence. This is the idea that has been expressed in Western Christianity as the doctrine of Original Sin. Ricoeur has himself criticized that doctrine for its speculative clumsiness, but the underlying idea of radical fault that it tries to formulate is basic to his thought.[6]

It has been observed before that there may be a fundamental affinity, at least on one level of the symbolism, between the metaphor of Metaxy existence and the tragic vision of life in that both represent man as doomed to inevitable frustration of his deepest longings, and this was discussed in the preceding chapter in connection with Voegelin.[7] But while Voegelin tended to interpret this frustration as a result of man's longing to escape from existential tension into an imagined sufficiency, Ricoeur conceives the issue primarily in moral terms: the deficiency from which man inescapably suffers is not just lack of satisfaction but a failure to love sufficiently. The tragic vision in its classical form, Ricoeur points out, does not distinguish between fault and finitude, but this distinction has been a major theme for Ricoeur.[8] As he said in the autobiographical essay appended to the English translation of *La Métaphore vive*, this was the specific problem that occupied his mind in *Fallible Man* and *The Symbolism of Evil*, and it was for this reason that he gave the two volumes the general title of *Finitude and Guilt*. "I had the impression," he says, "... that these two terms tended to be identified

---

5. See, for example, Bruce Douglass, "A Diminished Gospel: A Critique of Voegelin's Interpretation of Christianity," in Stephen A. McKnight, ed., *Eric Voegelin's Search for Order in History*, pp. 139–54; John A. Gueguen, "Voegelin's *From Enlightenment to Revolution:* A Review Article," *The Thomist* 42 (1978): 123–34; John Hallowell, "Existence in Tension: Man in Search of His Humanity," *Political Science Reviewer* 2 (1972): 181–84 (reprinted in the McKnight volume, pp. 101–126); Gerhart Niemeyer, "Eric Voegelin's Philosophy and the Drama of Mankind," *Modern Age* 20 (1976): 28–39; and Frederick D. Wilhelmsen, "The New Voegelin," *Triumph* January 1975, pp. 32–35.

6. See his "Original Sin: A Study in Meaning," in Ricoeur, *The Conflict of Interpretations*, pp. 269–86.

7. Cf. Emil J. Piscitelli, "Paul Ricoeur's Philosophy of Religious Symbol: A Critique and Dialectical Transposition," *Ultimate Reality and Meaning* 3 (1980): 294.

8. Ibid., p. 295.

in classical existentialism at the cost of both experiences, guilt becoming a particular case of finitude and for that reason beyond cure and forgiveness, and finitude, on the other hand, being affected by a kind of diffused sense of sadness and despair through guilt."[9]

In Ricoeur's formulation, the Metaxy metaphor expresses inevitable imperfection—and this is in keeping with his affinity for the notion of Original Sin—but this imperfection is not identical with finitude. Rather finitude itself is only one of the poles man finds himself between: "Man's specific weakness and his essential fallibility," he said in the preface to *Fallible Man,* "are ultimately sought within this structure of mediation between the pole of his finitude and the pole of his infinitude" (p. xx).

The Symbolism of Evil, for which *Fallible Man* set the stage, was devoted to the problem of how actual subjective evil can be cognitively grasped. This was a matter, as Ricoeur put it in the opening sentence of that volume, of making "the transition from the possibility of evil in man to its reality, from fallibility to fault" (p. 3). This cannot be done by philosophical reflection as in *Fallible Man,* since that can grasp only abstract possibility. Rather it requires a meditation on the language of avowal of fault, "'re-enacting' in ourselves the confession that the religious consciousness makes of it" (p. 3). The doctrine of Original Sin, he says, is an abstract speculative theory explicating a myth of fallenness that itself is built upon the experience of the confession of sins, which in turn gives expression to deeper layers of experience and interpretation:

> "Guilt," in the precise sense of a feeling of unworthiness at the core of one's personal being, is only the advanced point of a radically individualized and interiorized experience. This feeling of guilt points to a more fundamental experience, the experience of "sin," which includes *all* men and indicates the *real* situation of man before God, whether man knows it or not. It is this sin of which the myth of the fall recounts the entry into the world and which speculation on original sin attempts to erect into a doctrine. But sin, in its turn, is a correction and even a revolution with respect to a more archaic conception of fault—the notion of "defilement" conceived in the guise of a strain [stain?] or blemish that infects from without. (Pp. 7–8)

9. *The Rule of Metaphor: Multidisciplinary Studies of the Creation of Meaning in Language,* trans. Robert Czerny with Kathleen McLaughlin and John Costello, p. 315.

At the root of all these symbols, believes Ricoeur, is an experience that cannot be articulated in any form of thought or captured adequately in any language; it can be referred to only in the language of paradox as a captive freedom or servile will, "the experience of being oneself but alienated from oneself" (p. 8). The entire process of self-discovery is a hermeneutic one, he says, in that at every step one finds symbols in need of decipherment, and it is never possible for human consciousness to go behind symbols to discover the self they point toward. For Ricoeur this is a matter of the greatest consequence: "There is something quite astonishing in this: the consciousness of self seems to constitute itself at its lowest level by means of symbolism and to work out an abstract language only subsequently, by means of a spontaneous hermeneutics of its primary symbols" (p. 9).

The underlying issue is whether actual self-knowledge is ever possible as anything more than a sense of the meaningfulness of metaphors — and not a substantial grasp of their meaning, moreover, but only a sense of a promise of meaning that may never be fulfilled.

In *The Symbolism of Evil* Ricoeur traced the variety of symbols in Western culture dealing with fault to their deepest roots in the confession of sin, and in the process he ranked the major ones according to the extent that they take into account the possibility of subjective evil and disclose it, as far as they can, in their symbolism. There he sketched a schema of four principal myths of the origin and end of evil. These can be listed in order of the seriousness with which they treat evil as grounded in something more than merely objective circumstance: (1) the myth of the drama of creation, (2) the myth of the exiled soul, (3) the tragic myth, and (4) the "Adamic" myth.

In the first of these, says Ricoeur, "the origin of evil is coextensive with the origin of things; it is the 'chaos' with which the creative act of the god struggles" (p. 172). Creation, however, is not evil in itself, and salvation for this myth lies in the completion of the process of creation by which chaos is brought under rule.

The myth of the exiled soul, on the other hand, which depicts man as a spiritual being who has strayed into or become imprisoned in an essentially alien body, tends to identify the created world as such with evil and therefore to treat evil as entirely objective. This myth, says Ricoeur, is the most heterogeneous in the group of four; the others all have an affinity for one another's vision of life, but the myth of radical dualism stands opposed to all the others in its fundamental denial of the possibility of goodness in creation. Salvation in this myth is deliverance from life in the world. Human evil tends to be associated with the flesh that situates man in a world, while man himself is identified with the soul, which in its essence remains untouched by evil.

In the tragic myth, man is fully incarnate and his true life is life in this world, but the world thwarts him in his quest for happiness. Here fault is attributed to the hero, but his fault is inevitable, not chosen, and is "indistinguishable from the very existence of the tragic hero; he does not commit the fault, he is guilty" (p. 173). Salvation in this vision of things does not lie in release from guilt, since fault is inevitable, but in understanding of tragic necessity, which leads to "pity with respect to oneself" (p. 173).

In the tragic myth, human freedom begins to emerge as a theme. In the case of the drama of creation, freedom belongs not to man but to the gods. In that of the exiled soul, the problem lies in captivity, not in the misuse of freedom. The tragic hero does not fall into fault through free choice either; rather he becomes free only when he acquires his freedom in the understanding of his situation. "Salvation of this sort," says Ricoeur, "makes freedom coincide with understood necessity" (p. 173).

In the "Adamic" myth, evil originates not in objective reality or circumstance but in the misused freedom of man. Even this myth, however, finds it almost impossible to bring into focus an idea of radically subjective evil. Rather it introduces symbols connoting suggestions of an external origin: " . . . the Adamic myth does not succeed in concentrating and absorbing the origin of evil in the figure of a primordial man alone; it speaks also of the adversary, the Serpent, who will become the devil, and of another personage, Eve, who represents the vis-à-vis of that Other, Serpent or Devil. Thus the Adamic myth raises up one or more counterpoles to the central figure of the primordial Man, and from those counterpoles it gets an enigmatic depth by which it communicates subterraneously with the other myths of evil . . ." (p. 234).

The vision that underlies the Adamic myth, on the other hand, believes Ricoeur, is unequivocally an ethical one, and the story of Adam was a partly successful effort of ancient mythographers to give it expression: "Hence, it is false that the 'Adamic' myth is the keystone of the Judeo-Christian edifice; it is only a flying buttress, articulated upon the ogival crossing of the Jewish penitential spirit" (p. 239). The function of the myth is to make clear, as it does despite the presence of peripheral figures, such as the serpent, who diminish to a certain degree the subjectivity of Adam's fault, that God is not in any way to blame for the emergence of evil in the world. "The myth of the fall is thus," says Ricoeur, "the myth of the first appearance of evil in a creation already completed and good. By thus dividing the Origin into an origin of the goodness of the created and an origin of the wickedness in history, the myth tends to satisfy the twofold confession of the Jewish believer, who acknowledges, on the one hand, the absolute perfection of God and, on the other hand, the radical wickedness of man. This twofold confession is the very essence of his repentance" (p. 243).

What is central, that is, is the experience that is expressed more directly and adequately in the avowal of sin than in the myth of sin's emergence in history. This, for Ricoeur, is the lived experience of freedom that is at the heart of human existence. The symbolic languages of myth and confession serve as a mirror in which one can approach as nearly as is humanly possible to self-knowledge. Even the ambiguity of the myth plays a valid part in this mirroring, since the experience itself is fraught with ambiguity. The serpent, for example, is not just a distraction from Adam's personal responsibility for his fault; it also expresses features of the actual experience of wrong choice:

> ... in the figure of the serpent, the Yahwist may have been dramatizing an important aspect of the experience of temptation—the experience of quasi-externality.... The serpent, then, would be a part of ourselves which we do not recognize; he would be the seduction of ourselves by ourselves, projected into the seductive object.... The serpent, then, represents this passive aspect of temptation, hovering on the border between the outer and the inner.... (P. 256)

Ricoeur cites St. Paul and St. James on this experience of the quasi-externality of evil, and like them he sides with the idea that despite appearances it does not negate subjective fault; rather the attempt to exonerate oneself through the excuse that the temptation came from without is a form of "bad faith" that avoids the realization that what has been projected outward is in reality one's own desire.

Although Ricoeur considers the experience of fault and repentance to be laden with an ambiguity that is appropriately reflected in its symbolic expressions, ultimately he looks toward a solution which, if it could actually be uncovered, would be unambiguous in itself: that man in his essence is a radically free subject who is genuinely responsible for the movements of his own evil will. Ricoeur does not deny that circumstances can play a role in the origin of evil, and for this reason he thinks the other three myths will always serve as necessary complements to the Adamic, since man in the Metaxy moves between the poles of the voluntary and the involuntary. But the Adamic myth has preeminence for him among the others because it alone gives central place to the voluntariness which every human being shares to a degree and which is the essential constituent of human personhood, to the extent that this becomes an actuality. The various myths of the origin of evil approximate to varying degrees the mystery of man as an "intermediate being," hovering between the impersonal and the personal, the involuntary and the voluntary, potential and actual, nothingness and being.

This leaves the reader of *The Symbolism of Evil*, however, facing an enigma, and Ricoeur acknowledges as much at the end of the volume. The image of the Metaxy sketches abstractly the potential for human fallibility, while the symbols that express the avowal of subjective evil image the concrete experience of its actuality. But this is an actuality that in the last analysis cannot adequately be figured in any image, nor can it be understood or known, but only, as Ricoeur puts it in his conclusion, "wagered" upon. The final image disclosed by the symbols of confession is that of a volition lost to itself, an enslaved will, a captive freedom—an image of what must always remain a contradiction for thought, an ultimate, irresolvable incoherence. Ricoeur had said in the preface to *Fallible Man*, "The riddle of the slave-will, that is, of a *free will which is bound and always finds itself already bound*, is the ultimate theme that the symbol gives to thought. Just how far such a speculative cipher of bad will is still capable of being '*thought*' is ultimately, from the methodological point of view, the most difficult question of this work" (p. xxiii). At the end of *The Symbolism of Evil*, he was no nearer a solution of the theoretical problem this poses; this volume only explicates more extensively the symbols that pose the problem.

Ricoeur's "wager" is a solution not to the problem of theoretical incoherence, but to the practical problem of the form his existence will take. As he expressed the dominant practical issue at the end of *The Symbolism of Evil*, "Beyond the desert of criticism, we wish to be called again" (p. 349), and the call he hears is "an appeal by which each man is invited to situate himself better in being" (p. 356). The symbolism of evil serves in this appeal or invitation not as a cognitive map, but as "an index of the situation of man at the heart of the being in which he moves, exists, and wills" (p. 356).

And yet even here, Ricoeur holds onto the hope that a synthesis of the theoretical and the practical may somehow prove possible. His wager, therefore, is an expression of hope and trust that the symbols of his myths, and especially of the Adamic myth, will point into the heart of human existence and open it up to rational as well as moral consciousness:

> I wager that I shall have a better understanding of man and of the bond between the being of man and the being of all beings if I follow the *indication* of symbolic thought. That wager then becomes the task of *verifying* my wager and saturating it, so to speak, with intelligibility. In return, the task transforms my wager: in betting *on* the significance of the symbolic world, I bet at the same time *that* my wager will be restored to me in power of reflection, in the element of coherent discourse. (P. 355)

Ricoeur's hope, as he indicates, is not only that through attending to the implicit meaning of the symbols he can become immediately aware of the experience they point to, but also that the wager will deliver him eventually from the incoherence of what in the symbols must remain a paradox. At the end of *The Symbolism of Evil*, nevertheless, this is only a hope, and the philosophical framework he alludes to there as one within which this hope could be fulfilled hardly seems to promise deliverance from paradox. It is the same Kantian framework, here made explicit, that we found implicit in Voegelin's picture of man in the Metaxy as doomed perpetually to fall short of knowledge of real being. Ricoeur hopes, however, for a knowledge sufficient to the human task:

> ... there opens before me the field of philosophical hermeneutics properly so called: no longer an allegorizing interpretation that pretends to find a disguised philosophy under the imaginative garments of the myth, but a philosophy that starts from the symbols and endeavors to promote the meaning, to form it, by a creative interpretation. I shall venture to call that endeavor, at least provisionally, a "transcendental deduction" of symbols. Transcendental deduction, in the Kantian sense, consists in jus-

tifying a concept by showing that it makes possible the construction of a domain of objectivity. Now, if I use the symbols of deviation, wandering, and captivity as a detector of reality, if I decipher man on the basis of the mythical symbols of chaos, mixture, and fall, in short, if I elaborate an empirics of the servile will under the guidance of a mythology of evil existence, then I can say that in return I have "deduced"—in the transcendental meaning of the word—the symbolism of human evil. In fact, the symbol, used as a means of detecting and deciphering human reality, will have been verified by its power to raise up, to illuminate, to give order to that region of human experience. . . . (P. 355)

Ricoeur's encounter with psychoanalytic thought in his next book, *Freud and Philosophy,* complicated this hope somewhat, but did not shift it from its basically Kantian orientation. It complicated the idea of trust in symbols in that it made Ricoeur more acutely aware that when symbols are trusted naively they can become idols—that the symbols that emerge from the human unconscious are not just ambiguous but also distorted and conceal human reality as much as they reveal it. "It is one and the same enterprise," he said there, "to understand Freudianism as a discourse about the subject and to discover that the subject is never the subject one thinks it is" (p. 420). It reaffirmed him in the conviction that the Kantian framework of thought was the only one that could deal adequately with the problem of the human subject, despite the appeal of both Freudian and Hegelian conceptions.

In the last part of that volume Ricoeur juxtaposed Freud and Hegel dialectically as examples of two tendencies in the quest for self-knowledge—Freud as one who emphasized the "archaeology" of consciousness and Hegel as one who emphasized its teleology. Freud, that is, attempted to understand the human subject as originating in impersonal drives—the Id—while Hegel treated the human subject as engaged in a process of personal becoming, an active striving toward a "self-consciousness" that unites immediacy of self-awareness with mediated self-knowledge (pp. 462–63). Ricoeur judged the dialectic between the "opposed poles" of archaeology and teleology—which he also found reflected *within* each of the two thinkers and not just between them—to be essential to the hermeneutic endeavor (pp. 494–95). And yet he returned at the end of the book, in commenting on the problem of subjective evil, to an affirmation of the preeminence of the

Kantian approach as the clearest explanation of why thought must arrive at a limit, beyond which the human subject remains unattainable to knowledge:

These symbols resist any reduction to a rational knowledge; the failure of all theodicies, of all systems concerning evil, witnesses to the failure of absolute knowledge in the Hegelian sense. All symbols give rise to thought, but the symbols of evil show in an exemplary way that there is always more in myths and symbols than in all of our philosophy, and that a philosophical interpretation of symbols will never become absolute knowledge. In short, the problem of evil forces us to return from Hegel to Kant—that is to say, from a dissolution of the problem of evil in dialectic to the recognition of the emergence of evil as something inscrutable, and hence as something that cannot be captured in a total and absolute knowledge. Thus the symbols of evil attest to the unsurpassable character of all symbolism; while telling us of the failure of our existence and of our power of existing, they also declare the failure of systems of thought that would swallow up symbols in an absolute knowledge. (P. 527)

To say this, however, is to return to the position in which Ricoeur left the problem at the end of *The Symbolism of Evil,* with the consequence that the human subject Ricoeur was in search of remains an enigma characterized in his innermost reality by a flawed will that can be known only as a contradictory combination of captivity and freedom. From this point of view, therefore, it would seem that Ricoeur's wager has not paid off in the "element of coherent discourse" he was hoping for.

A Lonerganian might add that this can hardly be surprising in view of Ricoeur's Kantian framework, since Kantianism is of its very nature not a solution to the problem of how one can arrive at knowledge of essential reality, but rather an explanation of why one cannot do so. Ricoeur has been criticized as a Kantian on just such grounds by one Lonerganian. Emil J. Piscitelli has said that "Ricoeur's project of a search for an adequate and critical philosophical method stands or falls on this ability to revise and expand the Kantian notion of limits."[10] For Kant, what is truly knowable is the realm of phenomena, of appearances, whereas es-

10. "Paul Ricoeur's Philosophy of Religious Symbol: A Critique and Dialectical Transposition," p. 276.

sential reality is hidden beyond appearances in the realm of the "thing-in-itself." "For Kant," says Piscitelli, "and we must conclude for Ricoeur, the human mind's grasp of the real remains bound to the level of sense impressions, it remains an immediate *Anschauung* [objective intuition] however much it is informed by the *a priori* concepts of the understanding or synthesized with these concepts in the act of judgment" (p. 277). Regarding the problem of self-knowledge for Ricoeur, Piscitelli goes on to say, "The grounding method for Ricoeur's ontology remains Kantian. As he puts it in his Kantian language: It is only within the movement of interpretation that we 'apperceive' the being we interpret. Apperception remains a 'perception,' the human subject remains in a stance of confronting himself and hence in principle divided against himself. . . . For Ricoeur's revised Kantian position as for Heidegger's end run around Kantianism the hermeneutic circle takes on the appearance of a kind of 'trap' in which human beings inevitably find themselves, because we can have no real self-knowledge on Kantian presuppositions . . ." (p. 281).

Since this criticism grows directly out of Lonergan's framework of thought and expresses a way of thinking that Lonergan himself considered to go to the heart of the difference between his own position and that of what he called "existential" thinkers, among whom he would probably have included Ricoeur just as he did Voegelin, it will be worthwhile to consider in some depth the issues involved in the Lonerganian critique of Kantianism and to assess the question of its relevance to an understanding of the issues that actually concern Ricoeur.

First let us consider Kantianism as such. Kant's position regarding knowledge of objects in the world might be described in Lonerganian terms as analogous to a sort of perceptionism, in that it treats knowing as the result of automatic, unconscious packaging of experiential data in categorial forms, rather the way a cognitive psychologist might say that our conditioning leads us to "perceive" the world in a way that accords with cultural conceptions. Knowing, that is, is not conceived as a process of conscious operations—attention to data, construing of the data as elements of some possible form, critical reflection on the fit between data and form, and so on—as it is for Lonergan. Rather the fact that some synthesizing operations have taken place can only be inferred, said Kant, from the fact that we find ourselves confronting their results. As Lonergan concisely put it in his essay "Metaphysics as Horizon": "a Kantian context is a context of contents that does not envisage performances."[11] According to Lonergan's description in *Insight* of the difference between his thought and that of Kant, Kant conceived of consciousness merely as empirical awareness; the operations of interpretation and judgment he conceived of as proceeding from a mechanism of which we never have immediate experience:

> Kant acknowledged an inner sense that corresponds roughly to what we have named empirical consciousness, namely, the awareness that is immanent in acts of sensing, perceiving, imagining, desiring, fearing, and the like. Besides this acknowledgment of inner sense, Kant deduced or postulated an original synthetic unity of apperception as the *a priori* condition of the "*I think*" accompanying all cognitional acts. On the other hand, Kantian theory has no room for a consciousness of the generative principles of the categories; the categories may be inferred from the judgments in which they occur; but it is impossible to reach behind the categories to their source. It is precisely this aspect of Kantian thought that gives the categories their inflexibility and their irreducible mysteriousness. It is this same aspect that provided Fichte and Hegel with their opportunity to march into the unoccupied territory of intelligent and raional consciousness. (*Insight*, p. 341)

The important difference between Kant and Hegel for Lonergan is that Hegel was not satisfied to treat the operations of understanding and knowing as unconscious automatisms, but sought to develop a theory of the human subject as actively intelligent and rational. This is why Lonergan said, as was mentioned in his chapter, that the long detour of Western philosophy into the theory that knowing is a kind of "taking a look" ran from the time of Scotus to a new beginning in the time of Hegel (ibid., p. 372). Hegel, that is, began the exploration of the alternative hypothesis that knowledge is not the product of an external thing's action upon a passive subject but the result of the subject's cognitive activity.

The place of Hegel in relation to Kantian epistemology is particularly important in the present context, because Ricoeur has never described his own position as a simple Kantianism but rather as an effort to develop a new approach based in part also on Hegel's conception of the

---

11. *Collection*, p. 207.

subject as consciously dynamic. As Ricoeur put it in his essay "Freedom in the Light of Hope": ". . . the Kantianism that I wish to develop now is, paradoxically, more to be constructed than repeated; it would be something like a post-Hegelian Kantianism. . . . chronologically, Hegel comes after Kant, but we later readers go from one to the other. In us something of Hegel has vanquished something of Kant; but something of Kant has vanquished something of Hegel, because we are as radically post-Hegelian as we are post-Kantian. In my opinion, it is this exchange and this permutation which still structure philosophical discourse today."[12] This suggests at least the possibility that Ricoeur's Kantianism may not have exactly the significance it might seem to have from the Lonerganian point of view.

Before addressing that issue, however, it will be helpful to explore a bit further the Lonerganian criticism of Kantian epistemology. In the

12. Ricoeur, *Essays on Biblical Interpretation,* ed. Lewis S. Mudge, p. 166. For a full discussion of the way in which Ricoeur considers his own thought "post-Hegelian," see the chapter "Renoncer à Hegel," in his *Temps et récit,* vol. 3: *Le temps raconté,* pp. 280–99. (This is the as yet untranslated third volume of Ricoeur's *Time and Narrative,* which will be discussed at greater length below.) There he speaks of Hegel's hope for the total objectification of Spirit as a temptation to be renounced, but he also indicates that it is a temptation he has himself felt keenly. Explaining how "we no longer think according to (*selon*) Hegel, but after (*après*) Hegel," he says, ". . . what reader, once he has been seduced like us by his power of thought, would not feel the abandonment of Hegel as a wound, and one which, precisely in contrast to the wounds of the absolute Spirit, does not heal? To such a reader, if he is not to yield to the weaknesses of nostalgia, one must wish the courage for a labor of grief" (pp. 298–99, my translation). That Ricoeur identifies himself as having been such a reader would seem to throw an additional light on his affinity for the tragic vision: we long to grasp the whole of existence and reality in a perfect objectification, but we must despair of it and always mourn its impossibility.

Could something of the same sort be said about Voegelin? Voegelin was strongly—indeed fiercely—critical of Hegelianism, but Thomas J. J. Altizer, in his review article on *The Ecumenic Age,* "A New History and a New But Ancient God?" suggested that Voegelin was actually "a clear descendant of Hegel" and that "Voegelin's hatred of Hegel is an attempted Oedipal murder of his father." *Journal of the American Academy of Religion* 43 (1975): 763. That may be putting it a bit strongly, but at the very least it would be surprising if any thinker whose mind was formed, as were both Voegelin's and Ricoeur's, in Europe in the first half of this century was not influenced to some degree by the framework of thought that includes both Kant and Hegel and that tends in its various forms to feel, if not to think or imagine, that ultimate reality is a sort of supreme objective of thought that we are doomed always to reach for, whether or not it can ever be attained. May it be that Voegelin's denunciation of Hegel and the "gnosticism" of the hope of attaining Absolute Knowledge was in part an attempt to exorcise a Hegelian longing that he had himself been instilled with by his culture and always continued to feel the pain of?

Kantian perspective there are two directions in which one might look in the search for knowledge: the objective and the subjective. The subjective, however, is precluded for the reasons just mentioned: it is approachable indirectly through a "transcendental deduction," but it can never actually be known. The objective direction remains open, but it too is limited by the structure of human knowledge in the Kantian framework. What can be known directly are phenomena—appearances made up of experiential data packaged into forms by the mysterious mechanisms of subjectivity. The noumenon or thing-in-itself, whether an object or a subject, is a reality that must remain always hidden from our direct gaze.

Lonergan objects that this conception of objective knowledge is fundamentally incoherent, since, according to his own analysis, what we can *know* in the proper sense is the verifiable, and verification must involve critical reflection on the full range of cognitive operations that begins with experience but proceeds through conscious steps of construing and verifying before culminating in the judgment that attains the real. It is precisely here that one finds the crucial difference between Lonergan and Kant: Lonergan believed that judgment actually does attain reality, since reality is what is knowable through a cumulative sequence of operations of experiencing, understanding, and judgment. The incoherence of Kantianism, for Lonergan, is that it insists on postulating a supposed reality that cannot be experienced, understood, or known but denies reality to what *can* be known. For Lonergan the question of correspondence between the known object and reality is nonsensical, because the knowable simply is the real and vice versa.

Regarding the question of objective knowledge, however, Ricoeur, despite his avowed affinity for Kant, does not necessarily think very differently from Lonergan. The reason I say "not necessarily" is that Ricoeur has not taken up our knowledge of objects as an explicit theme of discussion, and he has consequently not stated a clear position on that issue. But statements he has made in passing suggest that he would not necessarily wish to argue for an unknowable thing-in-itself corresponding to what we can know through objective inquiry. It is true that in the book on Freud he did speak as though Kant's treatment of physical reality were fully satisfactory even if something different might be needed with regard to human being: "In the area of physics, Kant has taught us to combine an empirical realism with a transcendental idealism. . . . Kant achieved this combination for the sciences of nature; our task is to accomplish it for psychoanalysis . . ." (pp. 432–33). But if one considers Ricoeur's discussion of the "finite perspective" of human knowledge in *Fallible Man,* what he says seems as close to Lonergan as to Kant, since he differentiates clearly, if in slightly different language, between the same three levels of cognitive operation that Lonergan does.

At the foundation of human knowing, he says, is a basic receptivity that is a function of the fact that "our primary relation to the world . . . is to 'receive' objects and not to create them" (*Fallible Man,* p. 37). Despite the fact that this way of speaking could be construed as implying that we "receive" real objects as such through perception (an interpretation that could be supported by Ricoeur's own use of the words "perception" and "perceptual" in the same passage), what Ricoeur actually seems to be speaking of here is what Lonergan would refer to as the fact that cognitive process begins with an apprehension of experiential data which as such are "given," rather than made up or imagined by the inquirer. The Latin word *data* could as suitably be translated "the received" as "the given."

The reason this idea of a starting point in the reception of data followed by a process of interpretive activity seems to be Ricoeur's actual meaning is that he goes on to speak of a necessary dialectic of "signifying and perceiving," which seems his equivalent of what Lonergan called interpreting and experiencing (p. 42). Here, too, of course, Ricoeur might be said to lean toward Kantianism in that he speaks of this dialectic as "absolutely primal" in the sense that "the project of a phenomenology of perception, wherein the moment of saying is postponed and the reciprocity of saying and seeing is destroyed, is ultimately untenable" (p. 42). But Lonergan's analysis of cognitive process does not rule out the idea of unconscious perceptual mechanism; it only denies that perception as such amounts to knowledge in the proper sense.

That Ricoeur does not mean to deny the distinction Lonergan would insist upon is made clear when he takes up the idea of the crucial role of judgment in knowledge. In fact Ricoeur introduces this idea by referring to Aristotle's epistemology, implicitly recapitulating Lonergan's own tracing of his critical realist position from the tradition of Aristotle and Aquinas, to whom Ricoeur also refers (p. 54). "Up to now," says Ricoeur, referring to the fact that in the previous discussion he had spoken in terms of what could be interpreted as a simple perceptionism, "we have pretended to ignore that the authentic 'significant speech,' as Aristotle calls it in the treatise *On Interpretation,* is the composite discourse which he calls *logos* . . . , the phrasing of the world or judgment" (p. 49).

The possibility of judgment, says Ricoeur, is founded on the "profound significance" of "the distinction between noun and verb." "Indeed," he says, "our whole meditation on the transcendence of speech over perspective [in Lonerganian terms, of the sublation of experiential data by the act of understanding] leads to a reflection on the verb" (p. 49). "Why put such stock in the significance of the verb?" he asks. One reason is that it expresses the judgment of actual existence: " . . . to say that 'Socrates is walking' is to posit the present existence of the walking" (p. 49). It expresses, that is, the judgment that culminates the transition from formal possibility to reality and serves as a sort of linguistic pivot between the two. It looks back, one might say, to the idea on the second level of operation and forward to the reality known on level three. In Ricoeur's words, "'Socrates is walking' means that the walk 'exists now' and that the walk is *'said of'* Socrates. In the verb's twofold intention the human sentence finds at once its unity of signification and its capacity for truth and error. . . . By asserting being, it introduces the human sentence into the ambiguous realm of the true and the false" (p. 50).

Ricoeur recognizes, therefore, just as clearly as Lonergan, that objective reality is known through operations of attention, interpretation, and judgment. The issue of a difference, within the realm of the objective, between the phenomenal and the noumenal is not, despite all his references to Kant, a theme of Ricoeur's thought. Rather, his emphasis, which has continued to increase in his later writings, on the linguisticality of the objectively knowable world, expresses the same conception Lonergan emphasized when he insisted that objective reality is made up not of "already out there now real things" in absolute space, but of the objective contents of verified hypotheses. Ricoeur's idea of the linguisticality of the world was virtually echoed by Lonergan when he said in a taped interview, "Data, questions, the different levels of questions, the answers you give, eh? It is all construction. Saying that it is all construction enlarges the notion that human knowledge is discourse" (*Caring*

About Meaning, p. 108). Similarly, Lonergan's rejection of faculty psychology in favor of intentionality analysis is echoed by Ricoeur when he says, " . . . it is better to abandon this faculty psychology altogether and substitute for it a theory of signification which (1) takes into account the radical distinction of nouns and verbs, and (2) links the volitional moment of affirmation to the proper signification of the verb" (*Fallible Man*, p. 56).

If Lonergan and Ricoeur are actually as close as this in their theories of cognition and reality, where do they diverge? The major divergence can be found in their treatment of the idea of a "subject" and the possibility of knowing such an entity objectively. Unlike Voegelin, who as we saw in the last chapter insisted explicitly that the subjective pole of consciousness must not be hypostatized as an entity, both Lonergan and Ricoeur speak as if there really is such a thing as "a subject." They differ, however, in how they intend this manner of speaking.

Lonergan intended it literally. As was discussed in the preceding chapter, he believed that the subject can be known as an objectively real entity in the same manner as any other—through experience, understanding, and judgment—although with the exception that the fulfilling conditions for the judgment in such a case are not data of sense but what he called "data of consciousness" (*Caring About Meaning*, p. 117). One can experience oneself attending to experiential data, interpreting the data, and verifying the interpretation. One can also interpret oneself as an experiencer, interpreter, and verifier, and one can verify this interpretation by reference to one's actual experience of the operations in question. This culminates in the "self-affirmation of the knower" (the title of chapter 11 of *Insight*). And the "subject" one knows in this way is as definitely an object as is any other. "Again, one may define a subject," said Lonergan, "as any object, say A, where it is true that A affirms himself as a knower in the sense explained in the chapter on Self-affirmation" (*Insight*, p. 375).

Ricoeur thinks quite differently. He believes, as was just explained, that the objects of the world are known in the way Lonergan described, but he also believes that human existence is not fully objectifiable; rather it is sketched analogously in mythic symbols that must always leave a residue of mystery. In fact, it would probably be better in Ricoeur's case to use his own term, "metaphor," rather than "analogy" for what he has in mind, since Lonergan himself used the term "analogy" to refer to a mode of cognition involving objective resemblances and correspondingly parallel subjective operations. "Metaphor" implies a definite break in continuity between the terms of a comparison, and it is such a break in continuity that Ricoeur wishes to suggest regarding the idea of the "subject."

Analogy, for Lonergan, is a straightforward affair: " . . . what is at work is the law, immanent and operative in cognitional process, that similars are similarly understood. Unless there is a significant difference in the data, there cannot be a difference in understanding the data" (*Insight*, p. 288). There is no fundamental discontinuity according to Lonergan between analogical thinking and fully developed conceptual thought; it is simply a matter of moving from the implicit to the explicit.

For Ricoeur, on the other hand, as he described the issue in his study of "Metaphor and Philosophical Discourse" at the end of *The Rule of Metaphor*, there is a basic discontinuity between what he refers to as metaphoric and speculative discourse. The latter attempts to explicate the former, but, in Ricoeur's words, "[b]etween the implicit and the explicit there is all the difference that separates two modes of discourse, and that cannot be eliminated when the first is taken up into the second" (p. 296). The two are related dialectically, says Ricoeur: "It can be shown that, on the one hand, speculative discourse has its condition of *possibility* in the semantic dynamism of metaphorical utterance, and that, on the other hand, speculative discourse has its *necessity* in itself, in putting the resources of conceptual articulation to work. These are resources that doubtless belong to the mind itself, that are the mind itself reflecting upon itself. In other words, the speculative fulfills the semantic exigencies put to it by the metaphorical only when it establishes a break marking the irreducible difference between the two modes of discourse" (p. 375).

This is, of course, just another way of stating Ricoeur's principle that the symbol gives rise to thought and does so by its hints of a surplus of meaning, of something that cannot be adequately objectified. The felt tension that the symbol thereby arouses stimulates a desire for explicitness, which demands first a systematic framework of possible meaning, then the formation of concepts themselves:

> . . . speculative discourse is the discourse that establishes the primary notions, the principles, that articulate primordially the space of the concept.

Concepts in scientific language as well as in ordinary language can never actually be derived from perception or from images, because the discontinuity of the levels of discourse is founded, at least virtually, by the very structure of the conceptual space in which meanings are inscribed when they draw away from the metaphorical process, which can be said to generate all semantic fields. It is in this sense that the speculative is the condition of the possibility of the conceptual. It expresses the systematic character of the conceptual in a second-order discourse. (P. 300)

In doing so, it establishes a framework in which the tension of inquiry can be resolved in the definiteness of objective knowledge: "Because it forms a system, the conceptual order is able to free itself from the play of double meaning and hence from the semantic dynamism characteristic of the metaphorical order" (p. 302). But does this mean that the inquirer is able to pass over completely from his state of tension to the contemplation of a static objective realm? Ricoeur thinks not: "My inclination is to see the universe of discourse as a universe kept in motion by an interplay of attractions and repulsions that ceaselessly promote the interaction and intersection of domains whose organizing nuclei are off-centered in relation to one another; and still this interplay never comes to rest in an absolute knowledge that would subsume the tensions" (p. 302).

The reason, he goes on to make clear, is that the ultimate goal of inquiry is not the stasis of verified ideas; what we seek is a way of knowing the dynamic as dynamic. Referring to a remark in Aristotle's *Rhetoric,* Ricoeur asks, "What does it mean for living metaphor 'to set (something) before the eyes'?" (p. 307). He goes on to answer: "Setting before the eyes, *Rhetoric* 3 replies, is to 'represent things as in a state of activity' (1411b24–25). And the philosopher specifies: when the poet infuses life into inanimate things, his verse 'represents everything as moving and living; and activity is movement' (1412a8)." The goal of inquiry, that is, is that of "signifying things in act," but what this means is itself difficult to state except in metaphors such as "seeing things as *actions*" or "seeing them as naturally blossoming" (p. 308). At this point, suggests Ricoeur, poetry and metaphysics touch one another as the poet becomes one "who reaches this 'source of the movement of natural objects, being present in them somehow, either potentially or in complete reality' (*Metaphysics* Delta 4, 1015a18–19), which the Greeks called *phusis*" (p. 308).

All of this amounts to a variety of ways of stating the central issue separating Ricoeur as well as Voegelin and other existential thinkers from Lonergan: the question of the radical incommensurability of the subjective and objective poles of consciousness. The subjective pole is the dynamic act of intending, in all the modes of intending that are possible. The objective pole is what is intended. In cognition the latter can be specified as determinate, and the adequacy of the construct so specified to the experience it construes can be tested—both Lonergan and Ricoeur would agree on this. But when what is intended is subjectivity itself—the very dynamism of intending—Ricoeur holds that this process of objectification must fall short. The subjective act can never be turned into the idea of itself; it will always remain irreducibly different from all of the objectifications that we use to represent it. There may be a sense for Ricoeur, as was mentioned above, in which the objective world is characterized by linguisticality, but the world is not existence, and existence is not language. A comment Ricoeur offered on the thought of Gabriel Marcel says a great deal about this aspect of his own thinking as well: "You," he said to Marcel, "have taken the body, rather than language, as the primary focus of your reflection on existence. Perhaps we should not forget this today when French philosophy is suffering from a kind of fascination with the problems of language. In joining a criticism of sensation as message to your criticism of the body as instrument, you opened the way to a philosophy of the body-subject, and gave philosophy the means for thinking embodiment."[13]

Objectifying formulations have their function in human consciousness, Ricoeur would say, but their true function is protected, not negated, by a recognition of their limitations. It is this recognition that makes the difference between live and dead metaphor.[14] "*Lively* expression," as Ricoeur put it, " . . . expresses existence as *alive*" (*Rule of Metaphor*, p. 308). Speculative discourse can do this only as long as it is

13. "Conversations between Paul Ricoeur and Gabriel Marcel," in Marcel, *Tragic Wisdom and Beyond*, p. 222.

14. *La Métaphore vive*, literally "Live Metaphor," was the title of the French original (Paris: Éditions du Seuil, 1975) of *The Rule of Metaphor*.

held in tension with poetic. If it tries to sever its roots in metaphor, it lapses into a system of static abstractions.

It is the maintenance of this epistemological tension with regard to "existence as alive" (existence in the subjective sense) that is the real function of the Kantian strain in Ricoeur's thought. As was discussed above, there is nothing especially Kantian about Ricoeur's conception of our knowledge of objects. Nothing that he says suggests that the idea of an unattainable noumenal reality in the objective realm plays a role in his thinking about the world. He does not, with regard to the things and facts of the objective world, maintain that there is an epistemological gulf between the objects we can know and the realities behind them. He only insists that existential actuality itself, in the subjective sense, even if it can be linguistically affirmed, cannot be turned into a static linguistic formula as though it were its own definition.

As far as objective knowledge is concerned, therefore, Ricoeur seems to be in accord with Lonergan's cognitional theory as a formulation of generalized scientific method. Where they differ is in the way they think about the subjective dimension of consciousness and the possibility of our being able to know a metaphysical "subject" by such inquiry. For Lonergan a subject is a type of object; for Ricoeur it is not. And one way to say that it is not is to say that it is beyond the direct grasp of cognitive operations—or, in Kantian terms, that it is noumenal. The quasi-Kantian noumenon in Ricoeur's thought, therefore, could probably best be described as a metaphor signifying, by the idea of its unattainability to objective knowledge, that the subjective pole of consciousness cannot legitimately be construed as an objective entity.

From this point of view, Piscitelli's objections to Ricoeur's Kantianism as an inadequate cognitional theory seem simply beside the point. The real issue is not our knowledge of objects proportionate to the operations of generalized scientific method but the problem of our relation to the mysterious subjective existence in which we are immersed and which we can only "know" in a metaphorical sense, or from within. It is true that in some of his writings, such as *The Symbolism of Evil*, Ricoeur speaks *as if* he were in quest of a metaphysical "self" or "subject" of the sort to which Lonergan attributed objective status. In this way Ricoeur's concretely failing individual—the individual who wants to love but fails in loving well—seems to lure metaphoric discourse like a thing-in-itself that must always escape our efforts to pin it down. But the point is that this image is precisely that: a lure eliciting metaphoric expressions for the tensional character of experienced existence. Ricoeur, therefore, shares with Voegelin an emphasis on the idea that the objectification of the subjective pole of consciousness does not capture it in its existential actuality, but only images it metaphorically.

Especially in his most recent writings, Ricoeur has also shared with Voegelin a tendency to prefer, in place of such potentially reifying images as that of a "self," the image of human existence as involvement in a drama or, in his own language, a narrative.

Ricoeur says in the preface to *Time and Narrative* that he conceived that work and *The Rule of Metaphor* as a pair, since in his conception metaphor and narrative both function to help us apprehend the possibilities of subjective existence. They do not describe an objective reality, he believes, but image the tensional structure of the subjective dimension of consciousness itself. Doing so, they seek to evoke the possible dynamic reality that would be a well-ordered human existence. Narrative in particular both images metaphorically the structure of subjective existence and sketches for us possibilities of action in the world. Or at least it does so, according to Ricoeur, when the narrative is true.

The idea that metaphor and narrative can be true, or possibly false, is an important point for Ricoeur that he sees differentiating him from much recent thinking, especially in France, regarding both history and literature. Structuralists and deconstructionists—the schools of thought deriving from Fernand de Saussure and Claude Lévi-Strauss, on the one hand, and Jacques Derrida, on the other—have both tended to treat the "text" as an autonomous network of internal semantic linkages without a referential function in relation to reality. As Ricoeur phrases the issue, such thought "rejects any taking into account of reference, something it regards as extra-linguistic, in the name of the strict immanence of literary language in relation to itself."[15] Describing his own thought, on the other hand, Ricoeur says:

> The study of living metaphor led me to pose, beyond the problem of structure or sense, that of reference or of its truth claim. In *The Rule of Metaphor* I defended the thesis that the poetic function of language is not limited to the celebration of language for its own sake, at the expense of

---

15. *Time and Narrative*, 1:79. This title will subsequently be abbreviated as *Time*.

the referential function, which is predominant in descriptive language. I maintained that the suspension of this direct, descriptive referential function is only the reverse side, or the negative condition, of a more covered over referential function of discourse, which is, so to speak, liberated by the suspending of the descriptive value of statements. . . . I even suggested that 'seeing as,' which sums up the power of metaphor, could be the revealer of a 'being-as' on the deepest ontological level. (*Time and Narrative*, pp. x–xi)

Time and Narrative develops this idea by way of a conception of the mimetic function of narrative, a theme Ricoeur traces to Aristotle's poetics, where plot was described as the mimesis of an action. For his own purposes Ricoeur distinguishes between three modes of mimesis, which he refers to as mimesis$_1$, mimesis$_2$, and mimesis$_3$, which are, respectively, "a reference back to the familiar preunderstanding we have of the order of action; an entry into the realm of poetic composition; and finally a new configuration by means of this poetic refiguring of the preunderstood order of action" (p. xi). This broad conception of mimesis gives what Ricoeur calls "emplotment" an existential significance. "I see in the plots we invent," he says, "the privileged means by which we re-configure our confused, unformed, and at the limit mute temporal existence" (p. xi).

Ricoeur's conception of how this reconfiguring takes place involves an aesthetic aspect and a teleological aspect. His reference to plot as a movement toward form suggests the first; his idea that it also points toward action suggests the second.

Here, perhaps, one does find a significant, formative influence of Kant's thought on Ricoeur's. It is the Kant of the *Critique of Judgment* that is relevant. Kant's concern in that work was not with speculative knowledge but with freedom. He distinguished there between aesthetic judgments and teleological ones. The former have to do not with the objective character of the world but with our possibilities of apprehending it as pleasing to taste. Teleological judgments have to do with the apprehension of the world as ordered toward ends. The two modes of judgment work together, according to Kant, to enable us to apprehend the world as a realm of values and a field of possible action. Neither is constitutive of the world in the manner of the categories of pure reason as analyzed in the first *Critique,* but they may be said to evoke a world by representing nature as a theater for the exercise of human freedom. In *Time and Narrative* Ricoeur says something similar: "For some years now I have maintained that what is interpreted in a text is the proposing of a world that I might inhabit and into which I might project my ownmost powers. In the *Rule of Metaphor*, I held that poetry through its muthos, redescribes the world. In the same way, in this work I will say that making a narrative [*le faire narratif*] resignifies the world in its temporal dimension, to the extent that narrating, telling, reciting is to remake action following the poem's invitation" (p. 81).

Ricoeur's stated thesis for that work has recognizably Kantian overtones: ". . . time becomes human time to the extent that it is organized after the manner of a narrative; narrative, in turn, is meaningful to the extent that it portrays the features of temporal experience" (p. 3). So also does his statement of how this organization takes place: in both metaphor and narrative, he says, "the semantic innovation can be carried back to the productive imagination and, more precisely, to the schematism that is its signifying matrix" (p. ix). This suggests that, as in Kant's theory of perception, the manifold of experience becomes apprehensible and intelligible to us only by way of the organizing forms under which it is apprehended, in this case the form of narrative. This first formulation of Ricoeur's thesis has an aesthetic emphasis; it is the ordering form and our innate receptivity to it that are central. His later reformulation of the thesis places the emphasis on teleology and possibilities of action: ". . . time becomes human to the extent that it is articulated through a narrative mode, and narrative attains its full meaning when it becomes a condition of temporal existence" (p. 52).

The alternation of emphases between the aesthetic and the teleological suggests a certain ambiguity in Ricoeur's thought regarding the role of metaphor and narrative as ordering principles in human existence. According to Ricoeur, human beings have a felt need for form and derive satisfaction from it when they can discover it. Does this mean that the value of possible human action is to be found in the satisfaction it can bring to taste, or is there some other criterion of appropriateness in regard to action, one that may have little or nothing to do with aesthetics? In Kant's case the answer is clear: his criterion was the categorical imperative. Ricoeur, on the other hand, does not discuss the ethical as such at any length; when he does, it is not in an especially Kantian manner.

Kant's principles, however, especially in his aesthetics, did leave open the possibility of another way of thinking about human action that could easily be taken to imply that it is the form of our story as such that we are mainly concerned with. If one were to follow out that line of interpretation, the criterion of right action could be an aesthetic one— one that evaluated action in terms of the way in which it can contribute to a dramatic effect valued for its own sake. Kant would have been repelled by such a notion, and Ricoeur probably would also if it were stated so bluntly, but here and there in Ricoeur's writings, and even in his discussion of his mimesis$_3$, one can discover a distinct note of aestheticism.

To say this, of course, is not necessarily to indicate a fault. An aesthetic approach to ethical value may have advantages over one that tries to derive judgments of value from the logic of abstract reasoning as Kant does. Kant's categorical imperative has a highly formalistic character that to many has made it seem more compulsive than compelling. An aesthetic approach may have the advantage that it can take into account that ethical values, too, must have some basis for concrete appeal. At the same time, it could bring dangers with it if it is not balanced with sufficient critical reflectiveness. To put the issue in the terms we will see René Girard using in the next chapter, there is the danger that our thinking can yield to romanticism and merely "reflect" rather than "reveal" an underlying dynamic that stands in need of criticism. But that discussion will have to wait until the next chapter. For the moment it is sufficient to point out that these are questions that must eventually be asked.

An example of Ricoeur's attraction to an aestheticizing mode of thought may be seen in his treatment of Aristotle's conception of tragic form. For Ricoeur what matters in this discussion is the central role of "plot." He sets aside as irrelevant to his own purposes Aristotle's distinctions between tragedy and other genres: " . . . I am not characterizing narrative by its 'mode' . . . but by its 'object,' since I am calling narrative exactly what Aristotle calls muthos, the organization of the events" (p. 36). Aristotle's tragedy (and narrative generally), according to Ricoeur, is a dynamic, productive mimesis of action.

This does not mean, he says, that it is a mimesis in Plato's sense, a representation of an ideal objective form. That would amount to an objectivistic aestheticism in which man would remain the passive spectator of forms that affect him. Rather it is constructive, with the emphasis on the subjective activity of poetic construction, emplotment (our active construing of a series of events as constituting a linked sequence moving toward an end). "Platonic mimesis . . . ," he says, "distances the work of art by twice over from the ideal model which is its ultimate basis. Aristotle's mimesis has just a single space wherein it is unfolded—human making [*faire*], the arts of composition" (p. 34). It is not an objectivistic aestheticism that appeals to Ricoeur, but one that places its emphasis on the subjective dynamism of emplotment in our "making"—both poetic and practical—of our lives.

Nevertheless, even with regard to the emplotment of our action, Ricoeur's emphasis retains a predominantly aesthetic character. In his further discussion of Aristotle he contrasts the *Poetics* with the *Ethics*. The *Ethics* subordinates action to character; the *Poetics*, on the other hand, does the opposite: "In poetics, the composition of the action by the poet governs the ethical quality of the characters" (p. 37). What is distinctive about such composition, moreover, is the fact that plot integrates "discordance" into its structure in such a way as to make even suffering a source of satisfaction: "The pitiable and the fearful are qualities closely tied to the most unexpected changes of fortune oriented toward unhappiness. It is these discordant incidents the plot tends to make necessary and probable. And in so doing, it purifies them, or, better, purges them. . . . By including the discordant in the concordant, the plot includes the affecting within the intelligible" (p. 44).

The pitiable and fearful, says Ricoeur, "constitute the major threat to the plot's coherence" (p. 43). The plot's construing of them, therefore, is a victory over incoherence, and Ricoeur's emphasis makes incoherence seem the major obstacle we need to overcome. The goal of human striving, that is, seems here to be a satisfying vision of formal coherence, and the value of tragedy, or narrative form generally, seems to be its ability to offer this.

This ability of tragedy to elicit pleasure from pity and fear becomes the core of Ricoeur's interpretation of Aristotle's theory of catharsis as "the integrating part of the metaphorical process that conjoins cognition, imagination and feeling" (p. 50). Ricoeur speaks of this "transformation of the pain inherent in these emotions into pleasure" as the result of a "subjective alchemy" taking place in the spectator's imagination by which the pitiable and fearful incidents are "brought to representation" (p. 50). Since this is explicitly presented as a discussion of mimesis₃, it calls into question what in other places seems a more ethical emphasis in the interpretation of the culminating activity of Ricoeur's "mimetic arc."

It may be that to highlight Ricoeur's aesthetic emphasis in this way could give a misleading impression of his ultimate intention. The point, however, is that to fail to note this strain in his thought would be to overlook an aspect of it that needs to be accounted for. It would have been possible, for example, for Ricoeur to develop his reflections on tragedy with a rather different emphasis. In the next chapter we will see a radically different theory of tragedy and catharsis in the thought of Girard. For the moment, however, it will be helpful to consider Voegelin's discussion of tragedy for the purpose of comparison, since he has a great deal in common with Ricoeur and demonstrates that beginning from the point of view of Ricoeur's own concerns a less aesthetic and more clearly ethical or existential emphasis might have been developed. In fact, as we shall see, a comparison of Voegelin and Ricoeur on a variety of points can be a great help in rendering explicit the underlying tenor of much of Ricoeur's thought.

In *The World of the Polis* Voegelin presents a conception of what, in the title of chapter ten, he calls "the truth of tragedy" that would harmonize well with the other side of Ricoeur's mind, that which emphasizes teleology and ethical concern. He begins his discussion with a characteristically historical and social focus, locating the origins of Athenian tragedy in the aftermath of the democratizing reform of Solon and the Athenian victory in the Persian War. In his great funeral oration, the Thucydidean Pericles praised Athens as the "school [*paideusis*] of Hellas," says Voegelin (*OH,* 2:243), and the Greek idea of "culture" or *paideia* took shape correspondingly as that of a process of education. In keeping with this orientation, Aeschylean tragedy was intended as having an educative function: "What the tragedy meant in the life of the Athenian democracy can be gathered . . . from the confrontation of Aeschylus and Euripides in the *Frogs* of Aristophanes. The poets appear as the educators of the people, holding up to them a model humanity; the quality of the people will depend on the type of humanity that is presented in the great performances at the Dionysian festivals. Aeschylus appears as the educator, the moulder of the generation of the Persian Wars; Euripides as the corrupter . . ." (p. 244). Voegelin considers

Aristophanes's play itself, with its partisan spirit and overt didacticism, to be a symptom of cultural decline from the great period of tragedy, and he says, "The disintegration of tragedy is complete when we reach the standard treatise on the subject, the *Poetics* of Aristotle," because here "[t]ragedy has become a literary genus, to be dissected with regard to its formal characteristics, its 'parts,'" and valued for its emotional effect: "We take Aristotle by his word, as we did Aristophanes; and we assume that he described to the best of his knowledge what an audience of the fourth century experienced when attending the performance of a tragedy. In its effect on the spectators, tragedy has become something like a psychological therapy. The events on the stage arouse pity and fear, and other emotions, in the spectators and thereby give relief to pent-up quantities of passion" (p. 246). Voegelin likens this conception of tragedy to that of modern theories of sports as offering spectators "virtual satisfaction of their aggressiveness." (This last phrase suggests a conception of tragedy explored, as we shall see in the next chapter, by René Girard.)

Voegelin goes on to say, however, that Aristotle still retained some sense of the earlier, educative function of tragedy and that this came out in his discussion of it as more "philosophical" than history. "The 'much-knowing' of the historian," says Voegelin, "is opposed to the 'deep-knowing' of the philosopher. The poet creates an action which conveys a 'general' insight; he participates in the great search for truth from Hesiod to the mystic-philosophers" (pp. 246–47).

Unlike Aristotle (as well as Ricoeur, implicitly), Voegelin takes as his classic example of a tragedy not *Oedipus the King* but Aeschylus's *Suppliants*, a considerably earlier play. It depicts a challenge to decision in a situation that suggests no clear solution to the question of right action. The fifty daughters of Danaus have been betrothed, in their homeland, Egypt, to their cousins, the fifty sons of Aegyptus. They have fled from the impending marriage and have come to seek refuge in Argos, the home of their ancestor, Io. This places the king, Pelasgus, and the Argive people as a whole, in a dilemma: Zeus is a protector of suppliants, but the gods are also committed to the rule of law, and in this case the Danaides are lawfully betrothed to the Aegyptians. Even for Zeus himself to take their side would expose him to a charge of injustice, but at the same time, to refuse the entreaty of the maidens may incur his wrath. An additional consideration is that the Aegyptians are on their way with a powerful force, so that to defend the maidens would bring grave danger to the city. Pelasgus explains that he cannot commit his citizens without their free assent, since this is the Greek way. "There is need of deep and saving counsel, like a diver's," Voegelin quotes him, "descending to the depth, with keen eye and not too much perturbed" (p. 249). The decision, says the chorus, must be in accord with *dike* (justice), but it must also be free. Pelasgus goes to consult the citizens and together they reach their decision: to defend the maidens, even at the peril of their city (which in the lost sequel, in fact, is supposed to have subsequently been defeated by the Aegyptians). "The descent into the depth was taken in common," says Voegelin, "and what the people found was the Dike of Zeus" (p. 250).

It is this type of search for right action that was the paradigm of Aeschylean tragedy, according to Voegelin: "We can speak of tragedy only when man is forced into the recourse to Dike. Only in that case is he faced with the dilemma expressed by the line 'to act or not to act.' Apparently Aeschylus considered as action only the decision in favor of Dike. A negative decision, an evasion through utilitarian calculus, or a mere insensitiveness toward the issue, would not be considered action" (p. 251). It is such action that in Voegelin's thought constitutes the existential "truth" tragedy aims at.

It was on the basis of such reflections, then, that Voegelin coined his own definition of tragedy: "The truth of the tragedy is action itself, that is, action on the new, differentiated level of a movement in the soul that culminates in the decision . . . of a mature, responsible man. The newly discovered humanity of the soul expands into the realm of action. Tragedy as a form is the study of the human soul in the process of making decisions, while the single tragedies construct conditions and experimental situations, in which a fully developed, self-conscious soul is forced into action" (p. 247).

Here the emphasis is more decisively on action and ethical decision than in Ricoeur's discussion of tragedy, but as was suggested earlier, Ricoeur's thought tends to be ambiguous on this theme. His thought may have an aestheticizing tendency, but he is not simply an aestheticist, and a comparison with Voegelin's treatment of tragedy helps bring into focus another current in Ricoeur's discussion of Aristotle. Ricoeur, too, speaks of a truth of tragic action in connection with his theme of mimesis. He says, for example: "The universals a plot engenders are not

Platonic ideas. They are universals related to practical wisdom, hence to ethics and politics" (*Time*, 1:41). He goes on to say that considerations regarding the audience's pleasure in the discerning of such universality point toward "a prospective theory of truth, according to which to invent is to rediscover," although he immediately adds that this "presupposes a more developed theory of mimesis than the one that simply equates mimesis with muthos" (p. 42).

What Ricoeur has in mind is made clearer both by his discussion of the "preunderstanding" that constitutes his mimesis₁ and by his discussion of Augustine's meditation on time in the *Confessions*. In both connections a comparison with Voegelin may again prove illuminating.

To turn first to the topic of the preunderstanding to which narrative form gives articulate expression, this is the same in essence as the experiential "precomprehension" Ricoeur spoke of in *Fallible Man* as the starting point of all philosophy. In *Time and Narrative* Ricoeur says: "Whatever the innovative force of poetic composition . . . may be, the composition of the plot is grounded in a preunderstanding of the world of action, its meaningful structures, its symbolic resources, and its temporal character" (p. 54). Actions, he says, unlike mere "movements," imply goals and motives, and they are understood by reference to agents. In the conceptual framework that makes it possible for us to think about action, "the infinite regression opened by the question 'Why?' is not incompatible with the finite regression opened by the question 'Who?' To identify an agent and to recognize this agent's motives are complementary operations" (p. 55).

To say this is to open up a field of questioning about human subjectivity that much of the remaining chapters of the present work will be devoted to exploring. This is the "who" question that was contrasted with the "what" type of question at the end of the chapter on Lonergan. For the moment, it will be appropriate to approach the issues involved in comparatively simple terms. What Ricoeur suggests here is that in order for us to think about action, we have to employ a conceptual framework in which actions are interpreted as having both subjects and goals. He also suggests that the hermeneutic of our representations of action must attempt to reach into the depths that underlie that conceptual framework and uncover the fundamental structure in our experience that makes it possible for us to conceive of action as such and thereby to discover the ground of right orientation. As Ricoeur puts it, "It is the task of hermeneutics . . . to reconstruct the set of operations by which a work lifts itself above the opaque depths of living, acting, and suffering, to be given by an author to readers who receive it and thereby change their acting" (p. 53).

To put this in Voegelin's language, it is the experienced tension of existence that energizes all human striving and makes orientation or what we might call "tensional polarity" possible. The resulting orientation is, as in Voegelin, from a pole of experienced deficiency to one of anticipated sufficiency conceived of as beyond our condition. This experienced tension is a preunderstanding that gives rise to symbols of transcendence reflecting the structure of the tension and enabling us to become reflectively conscious of its dynamism and its directional orientation. As will be explained in a moment, the ideas involved here could also be put in the language of Polanyi's discussion of "passionate thinking."

Ricoeur himself refers to Heidegger and Augustine for comparison. He likens his concept of the dynamic, tensional character of consciousness to Heidegger's concept of Care (Sorge) as the basic constituent of Dasein, Heidegger's term for our concrete experience of existence. This feature of Heidegger's thought, says Ricoeur, enables his philosophical anthropology "to overthrow the primacy of knowledge of objects and to uncover the structure of being-in-the-world that is more fundamental than any relation of a subject to an object" (p. 61). Ricoeur finds "the same powerful breakthrough" in Heidegger's discussion of our experience of time "as that 'within which' we ordinarily act" (p. 61). "This structure of within-time-ness (Innerzeitigkeit)," he says, "seems the best characterization of the temporality of action for my present analysis. It is also the one that accords best with a phenomenology of the voluntary and the involuntary and with a semantics of action."

In a manner that recalls Polanyi's discussion of the focal and subsidiary dimensions of consciousness, Ricoeur describes this concernful experience of time as the necessary preunderstanding that links time and narrative, mimesis$_1$ and mimesis$_2$. The experienced tensional structure of time, he suggests, is that which we must attend through in order to think in the narrative manner. In Polanyi's terms, it is the necessary subsidiary component that makes it possible for us to attend to the narrative symbol as focal. And again as in Polanyi, this subsidiary-focal relation within consciousness is what gives "embodiment" to consciousness; we "indwell" the stories by which we live and thereby enter a process of becoming what they image us as. Such embodiment or incarnation seems to be what Ricoeur has in mind by his mimesis$_3$.

This embodiment of consciousness is both paradoxical and problematic for Ricoeur. It is a paradox in that human consciousness seems to share simultaneously in the characteristics of time and eternity. By the concern that draws it into concrete relations it becomes involved in the world and time. And yet we find ourselves able to step back, as it were, from this involvement and reflect upon it, and we experience this capacity as an involvement with eternity and transcendence. Our problem is that the concern that founds in us both orientations also calls upon us to decide how to relate them to one another. We are threatened with two reciprocal dangers: to lose the world and to lose ourselves *in* the world. This is more complicated than a simple Manichean either-or. The two dangers are not exclusive but reciprocal in that for Ricoeur the one loss tends to bring with it the other. Referring again to Heidegger, Ricoeur says that in its actual character as human existence, "within-time-ness or being-'within'-time deploys features irreducible to the representation of linear time," which reduces the concretely human "now" to an abstract instant (p. 62). And yet our concern with objects and affairs in the world tends constantly to draw us into such objectivistic abstraction. "The existential now," he says, "is determined by the present of preoccupation, which is a 'making-present,' inseparable from 'awaiting' and 'retaining'. . . . It is only because, in preoccupation, Care tends to get contracted into this making-present and its difference with respect to awaiting and retaining is obliterated, that the 'now' so isolated can become prey to the representation of 'now' as an abstract moment" (p. 63).

Although more explicitly articulated, so that it is freed from any latent dualism in the images, the issue is essentially the same as that for which Voegelin found a symbol in Plato's myth of man as a puppet drawn by golden and iron cords. We are drawn by the powerful pull of preoccupation (the iron cords) toward objects in time and the world. In order for us to discover our inward orientation toward transcendence we have to resist those pulls so as to become sensitive to the gentle pull of the golden cord of divine Nous and yield ourselves to its drawing. What keeps Ricoeur's picture of the situation clearly free from any Manichean tendency is that in his thought our highest possibility of subjective existence is that of responsible engagement with the objective dimension, the world of space and time, as a milieu of action. Voegelin's way of interpreting Plato's images also gave them the same ultimate thrust, however, as he made clear in "Reason: The Classic Experience," for example, when he said of man, "The *apeiron* and the *nous* reach into his *psyche* and he participates in them, but he is not identical with, or in control of, either the one or the other. This area of metaleptic reality is the proper domain of human thought—its inquiries, learning, and teaching. . . . To move within the *metaxy*, exploring it in all directions and orienting himself in the perspective granted to man by his position in reality, is the proper task of the philosopher" (*Anamnesis*, p. 107). For both thinkers the proper field of human existence is the Between, in which each person acts continuously in relation to both time and eternity, the objective dimension and the subjective.

Ricoeur's way of speaking of this in *Time and Narrative* is to say that human existence must be understood as involving "a hierarchization of levels of temporality or rather of temporalization," an analysis he says Heidegger developed on the basis of his ontology of Care (*Time*, 1:84). This is a rather abstract formulation, but in Augustine's discussion of time as *distentio animi* (the outward reaching of consciousness toward objects) and *intentio animi* (the inwardness of consciousness) Ricoeur found an image for its meaning comparable to that which Voegelin found in the myth of the cords. "Indeed," he says, "by describing human time as raised beyond its inside by the attraction of its polar opposite, eternity, Augustine gave credit in advance [i.e., of Heidegger] to the idea of a plurality of temporal levels" (ibid.).

"The notion of *distentio animi,* coupled with that of *intentio*," says Ricoeur, "is only slowly and painfully sifted out from the major aporia with which Augustine is struggling, that of the measurement of time. This aporia itself, however, is inscribed within the circle of one that is even more fundamental, that of the being or the nonbeing of time" (p. 7). Before discussing Ricoeur's interpretation of Augustine's philosophical anthropology, therefore, it will be helpful to consider this question, which Ricoeur himself considers fundamental. It was this very question with which he opened his 1984 Aquinas Lecture at Marquette University: "What does the term 'real' signify when it is applied to the historical past? What do we mean when we say that something really happened?"[16] In *Time and Narrative* Ricoeur quotes Augustine as asking, "What, then, is time?" and continuing, "I know well enough what it is, provided that nobody asks me; but if I am asked what it is and try to explain, I am baffled."[17] The reason for the bafflement, in Ricoeur's summary, is itself a series of perplexities: "How can time exist if the past is no longer, if the future is not yet, and if the present is not always?"

These are questions intentionality analysis of the type developed by Lonergan can be helpful in answering, since they have to do with what it means to say that time is objectively knowable. Regarding the reality of the historical past, the solution is fairly easy if we accept Lonergan's principle that objective reality is what we are able to know by operations of attention to data, interpretation, and critical judgment. In this case, the data are memories and various other forms of historical evidence such as documents, archeological remains, and so on. The interpretations are our attempts to construe such data as, in Ricoeur's phrase, a narrative. The historical past can be said to be "real" insofar as it can be interpreted this way and the interpretation judged adequate to the evidence it interprets.

Regarding the objective reality of the future one might say something similar: the evidence consists of observed tendencies and the interpretation consists of statistical probabilities extrapolated from these on the basis of reasonable anticipation. To the extent that one can arrive at a critical judgment that present indicators have been carefully taken into account and adequately interpreted, one can attribute to the future an objectivity comparable to that which the historian finds in the historical past, even if the probabilities involved in our knowledge of it are more tenuous.

On the other hand, is it necessary or does it even make sense to say that either the past or the future "exists"? Here again we come upon a point that was touched on earlier when I suggested that Lonergan might have been helped by a distinction between reality and existence. Such a distinction might also have enabled him to avoid his unfortunate attack on Voegelin and Jaspers—an attack that extended through them implicitly to any other thinkers in the existential tradition, including

---

16. *The Reality of the Historical Past*, p. 1.
17. *Confessions*, 11, 14:17, quoted in *Time*, 1:7.

Ricoeur. If we distinguish between the "real" as what we can know by the performance of Lonergan's interrelated set of intentional operations and "existing" as what we *do* in performing those or any other operations, then all the perplexities Augustine discovered in his meditation on time and eternity seem easily resolvable. The past and future are objectively real in that we can know them with probability. The present—or perhaps a better word would be "presence"—is our existence itself, our active intending in the human "now." It is here that time and the eternal come together, because it is always from here (in the *intentio animi*) that we reach out (in *distentio*) toward the objective world of space and time.

Such concrete experiential presence is subjective, not objective. It contrasts with what we above saw Ricoeur call the abstract "now" of linear time. The latter could, in terms of this analysis, be called the "objective present," but it would be utterly lacking in content, since anything that could be known of it on the basis of evidence would be no longer present but past—a continuously vanishing series of traces in memory, even if the memory is of a split-second ago. The present in this objective sense, the present that is an infinitesimal point on the line of time, would be precisely the present that "is not always," because in fact it never "is" in the subjective sense at all. Considered with regard to the question of its reality, it is simply nothing, since it has no knowable content. Subjective presence, on the other hand, always has the concrete content that is our experience of intentional operation.

Augustine, in fact, finds a resolution for his paradox of time in what seems exactly this way: " ... the more the mind makes itself *intentio*, the more it suffers *distentio*. ...that the soul 'distends' itself as it 'engages' itself—this is the supreme enigma" (p. 21). Ricoeur calls it "the most impenetrable enigma" of Augustine's thought. It is precisely as an enigma, however, that he finds it valuable: "Augustine's inestimable discovery is, by reducing the extension of time to the distention of the soul, to have tied this distention to the slippage that never ceases to find its way into the heart of the threefold present—between the present of the future, the present of the past, and the present of the present. In this way he sees discordance emerge again and again out of the very concordance of the intentions of expectation, attention, and memory" (p. 21).

It is a characteristic pattern in Ricoeur's thought to seek to bring aporias and enigmas to light and to elucidate them precisely as aporetic or enigmatic. It was noted above that at the end of *The Symbolism of Evil* he was no nearer to solving the problem of how to pin down a radically subjective source of evil than he was at the beginning of that inquiry. Rather the book functioned to explore the limits of thought in relation to that problem. The same pattern is to be found in *Time and Narrative*. Ricoeur begins in the first volume of that work with a set of aporias regarding time that has to do with the difficulty of understanding it as both knowable and mysterious, objectifiable and nonobjectifiable, and he ends the third volume with a parallel set of aporias and emphasis on "the inscrutability of time and the limits of narrative."[18]

All such aporias would seem to derive from the problem of trying to find a means to bring together the objective and subjective in a way that would unite them or indeed merge them into one. The Hegelian goal that both Ricoeur and Voegelin believe human beings are constrained to renounce was that of such a perfect union of subjectivity and objectivity, and the aporias Ricoeur keeps turning up are precisely those that make clear that this goal is unattainable.[19] If one were to accept, on the other hand, as a basic principle the idea that the subjective and objective poles of consciousness are fundamentally different and can never be merged into one another, the aporias referred to would cease to be problems. This does not mean, of course, that they would cease to be problems because they had been solved, but rather that they would not be defined as problems at all. The aporia referred to a moment ago with regard to our inability to combine in thought the subjective "now" of the experienced present and the infinitesimal "now" of objective, linear time is an example. To distinguish between existence as subjective and reality as objective so that they are considered as pertaining to two different dimensions of consciousness would, as I just suggested, do away with the problem by simply eliminating it. What one can discover in either dimension would, in this light, be a function of the different types of operation pertinent to them. On the other hand, as long as we continue seeking to put the objective and subjective poles of consciousness together in such a way that they will be no longer two but one, they will

18. *Temps et récit*, 3:374.
19. It is also the goal symbolized by, and represented as eternally realized by, the God of Lonergan's *Insight*, who knows everything about everything, including himself in his infinity.

go on repelling each other in a way that will lead us to talk of aporias. To draw out the implications of accepting the radical difference between subjective and objective as a function of the structure of consciousness itself, however, will require further explorations that will have to include other thinkers—especially Kierkegaard, who built his entire thought on this ground.

To return for now to Ricoeur, the enigmatic experience of simultaneous concordance and discordance that we just saw Ricoeur referring to as the "supreme enigma" is what functions, he says, as the dynamism of emplotment; and it is this, therefore, that relates Augustine and Aristotle for him: "But Aristotle's *Poetics* does not resolve the enigma on the speculative level. . . . It puts it to work—poetically—by producing an inverted figure of discordance and concordance" (1:22). The focus of Aristotle's concept of tragedy on "the play of discordance internal to concordance," he says, is what "makes the tragic muthos the inverted figure of the Augustinian paradox" (p. 38).

Perhaps the reason Ricoeur finds Augustine's formulation of human experience as simultaneously *intentio* and *distentio* so enigmatic is that it is incomplete without consideration of another related problem: the relation of subjective presence to eternity. Considered simply as an answer to the hypothetical skeptic's arguments against time, he says, Augustine's resolution seems satisfactory: "In this respect, the thesis that time is 'in' the soul and finds 'in' the soul the principle of measurement of time, is sufficient in itself inasmuch as it replies to the aporias found within the notion of time. In order to be understood, the notion of *distentio animi* requires no more than to be contrasted with the *intentio* immanent in the 'action' of the mind" (p. 22). Considered in the light of the meditation on eternity that surrounds it in the *Confessions,* however, Augustine's discussion of *distentio animi* points into an aporia that seems less problem than mystery. Ricoeur says he discerns "three major ways in which the meditation on eternity affects the speculation on time:" "Its first function is to place all speculation about time within the horizon of a limiting idea that forces us to think at once about time and about what is other than time. Its second function is to intensify the experience of *distentio* on the existential level. Its third function is to call upon this experience to surpass itself by moving in the direction of eternity, and hence to display an internal hierarchy in opposition to our fascination with the representation of linear time" (p. 22).

It is this last point that is crucial for Ricoeur and brings out the full significance of his central theme in *Time and Narrative*. "At the very heart of temporal experience," he says, this dialectic of time and eternity "produces a hierarchy of levels of temporalization, according to how close or how far a given experience approaches or moves away from the pole of eternity" (1:28). Similarly, in Augustine's attendant treatment of the relation between the Word of God and the word of man Ricoeur finds a formulation of the concept of existential truth he is himself developing. Augustine's "Word" is "that inner master, sought and heard 'within' (*intus*)" (p. 29). It functions, that is, as the "preunderstanding" that gives rise to the narrative structures which, as it were, echo it in their mimesis. But Augustine's way of formulating this notion says something more that is equally important to Ricoeur: it speaks of the relation of our preunderstanding to its transcendent source. This relation is what makes it meaningful to speak of existential preunderstanding as a form of mimesis (Ricoeur's "mimesis$_1$") and not just a model for the other levels of mimesis. "In this way," says Ricoeur, "our first relation to language is not just the fact that we talk but that we listen and that, beyond the external *verba,* we hear the inner *Verbum*" (p. 29). It is also why what we hear, when we listen to symbols expressing existential truth, is a call to transcendence: "The teaching, we could say, bridges the abyss that opens between the eternal *Verbum* and the temporal *vox*. It elevates time, moving it in the direction of eternity" (p.29).

All of this could serve quite well as an explication of Voegelin's conception of the meaning of the symbolism of the golden cord. Voegelin in turn could offer a commentary on Ricoeur's Augustinian imagery. Just as Ricoeur found in Augustine's meditation on time and eternity the foundation for a philosophical theory of narrative form as a metaphor for human existence, so Voegelin found in Augustine's image of exodus, itself a narrative symbol, an implicit philosophy of history. Both history and philosophy, for Voegelin, were processes that take place in a field of tension between existential truth and untruth. To express this idea he drew on Augustine's familiar image of the two cities—the *civitas Dei* or city of God and the *civitas terrena,* the worldly city or "Babylon"—as an image of the tension of transcendence and the pull into possible forgetfulness of transcendence. He saw these symbols combining with that of spiritual exodus in a passage from Augustine's *Sermons on the*

Psalms: "Incipit exire qui incipit amare. Exeunt autem multi latenter, et exeuntium pedes sunt cordis affectus: exeunt autem de Babylonia" ("He begins to depart who begins to love. Many there are who leave without realizing it. For their walk of departure is a movement of the heart. And yet they are departing from Babylon."[20] In his explication of this image Voegelin says, "Augustine places the conflicts between the Chosen People and the empires under the symbol of the exodus and understands the historical processes of exodus, exile, and return as figurations of the tension of being between time and eternity. Whichever figure the exodus may adopt—that of a real emigration or that of a collision, within the society, between the representatives of higher- and lower-ranking orders—the dynamism and direction of the process stem from the love of eternal being. The exodus in the sense of *incipit exire qui incipit amare* is the classical formulation of the material principle of a philosophy of history" (*Anamnesis*, p. 140).

Both Ricoeur and Voegelin share, therefore, a common conception of human existence as a dynamic process oriented by its tensional structure toward a paradoxical transcendence that is simultaneously a movement beyond time and a movement into history as the incarnation of the eternal in time. They also share a conception of the way in which the existential truth of this process becomes conscious in human life through its expression in symbols. Regarding such symbols, both believe in their indispensability for consciousness and in their irreducibility. In this they share what might be called a revelatory conception of existential symbols, the belief that such symbols come to us already formed from a deep source that is both within us and beyond us. Ricoeur, in the Kantian language he tends to use, refers to the process deeper than consciousness by which we receive them as the "productive imagination." Voegelin's similar affinity for the Kantian pattern of thinking in this regard was mentioned at the end of the last chapter. In both thinkers one finds a conception of revelatory symbols as emerging in consciousness out of an unconscious process of what might be called "packaging." Also in both cases there is an affinity for the language of

20. *Ennarrationes in Psalmos* 64. 2. 42–44. See Voegelin, "Eternal Being in Time," *Anamnesis*, p. 140, and "Configurations of History," in Paul G. Kuntz, ed., *The Concept of Order*, p. 33.

the divine and the sacred as an expression for the transcendence of which the symbols make us aware.

This conception of the relation between philosophy and the sacred seems to have come to Ricoeur at least in part from the influence of his teacher, Marcel. In his early book on Marcel and Jaspers, Ricoeur spoke of how for Marcel "concrete philosophy grows in a soil prepared by revelation."[21] In his comments there on the historical situation of Marcel's philosophy of religion, he said that it was a type of thought that arose at a time when the sense of mystery had become diminished or lost and when traditional rational apologetics had ceased to have any effective appeal. Such apologetics, said Ricoeur, were more dependent than their authors had realized on a preexisting sense of the sacred and of transcendence and on attitudes of faith and reverence. "The historical meaning of Marcel's thought," he said, "seems to be to restore these foundations for a possible theology, natural and supernatural, deeper than argument, at the level of sentiments and attitudes that root thought at once in existence and in being, in the flesh and in the Spirit—to restore 'a certain living order [i.e., hope] in its integrity,' at the heart of which a revealed Word may be heard in simplicity" (p. 276).

Ricoeur wrote these words in 1947, but they are echoed in the more recent statement quoted earlier from *Time and Narrative* about how "our first relation to language is not just the fact that we talk but that we listen and that, beyond the external *verba*, we hear the inner *Verbum*" (p. 29). Both early and late in the course of his philosophical career, Ricoeur has been oriented in the most fundamental way toward faith in this sense—in the sense of fidelity and of heedful sensitivity to the drawing of transcendence. He has at times spoken of the importance of balancing trustfulness and hope with critical reflection, as when we earlier saw him speaking in *Freud and Philosophy* of the need for a hermeneutic of suspicion as well as a hermeneutic of faith. His own inclination, however, has led him to give most of his attention to the hermeneutic of faith, just as did Voegelin. His suspicion, as we saw in the cases of *Fallible Man* and *The Symbolism of Evil*, was directed less

---

21. *Gabriel Marcel et Karl Jaspers: Philosophie du mystère et philosophie du paradoxe*, p. 272.

toward symbols and the productive imagination that gives them to us than toward an elusive center of radically subjective evil in human intentionality. Even if, as was mentioned earlier, he said in *Freud and Philosophy* that symbols can be the birth of idols and that the critique of idols is the condition of the conquest of symbols, Ricoeur's critique of symbols is never radical. As in the case of Augustine with his conception of Original Sin, Ricoeur's suspicion has been directed more toward man than toward the sacred.

Still, if it is important to listen in order to hear the Word beyond words, it must also be important for us to do everything we can to ensure that we distinguish carefully between that Word and any sources of interfering noise. The sacred may be precious and life-giving, but it can also be a temptation, and any philosophy that wishes to draw on its resources must be prepared also to resist its possible enchantments and the lure of the power it represents. It is worth remembering, for example, that Augustine, besides leaving us symbols of transcendence and meditations on time and eternity, also, in connection with the forcible suppression of the Donatists, wrote the first theoretical justification in Christian history of the persecution of heretics.[22]

It is rare for a modern thinker both to take the sacred seriously and at the same time to approach it with the greatest caution.[23] It is more common either to seek out and trust its manifestations or simply to condemn them as a temptation to gullibility and superstition. Before proceeding to the emphatically religious thought of Søren Kierkegaard, in which so much in Voegelin and Ricoeur is rooted, it will be helpful to prepare for that and for further exploration of the "who" question by considering the highly original approach to man and the sacred made by a recent thinker who represents a nearly unique combination of religious seriousness and critical penetration: René Girard.

22. Peter Brown, *Augustine of Hippo: A Biography*, p. 235.
23. Among the better known modern Christian thinkers, the poet W. H. Auden was remarkable for the balance he tried to maintain between respect for the experience of the sacred on the one hand and a radical critique of enchantment on the other. For a discussion of Auden's poetry and criticism in this light, see the chapter "W. H. Auden: The Ambiguity of the Sacred" in Eugene Webb, *The Dark Dove: The Sacred and Secular in Modern Literature*, pp. 237–63. The topic of the ambiguity of the sacred as well as Auden's relation to it will be discussed further in the concluding chapter of the present study.

CHAPTER 5

René Girard

Consciousness
and the Dynamics of Desire

IN THE THOUGHT of René Girard consciousness is something that must be struggled for and won from the unconscious. The thinkers we have studied so far have tended to move directly to the discussion of consciousness and its tensional structure. All of them have been aware to a certain degree—as who has not since Freud?—of our human tendency to flee from consciousness or to let our desires and fears govern our thinking, but none of them has been led by this consideration to an attitude of radical suspicion. Girard, therefore, has a special contribution to make to this study in exposing elements of naiveté that could vitiate an insufficiently critical philosophy of consciousness.

Girard began his career as a literary critic, in such works as *Deceit, Desire, and the Novel* and the essays collected in *Critiques dans un souterrain* ("Critical Essays from the Underground," an allusion to Fyodor Dostoyevsky's *Notes from the Underground*).[1] These works dealt with such figures as Dostoyevsky, Camus, Hugo, Valery, Cervantes, Stendhal, Flaubert, and Proust, among others. Girard's focus in these studies was a psychological process he called "mimetic" or "triangular desire." This interest in the dynamics of imitative desire and the behavior driven by it led him to the study of the anthropology and psychology of religion in his subsequent works: *Violence and the Sacred*

---

1. The original French title of the former was *Mensonge romantique et Vérité romanesque* ("Romantic Lying and Novelistic Truth." Paris: Grasset, 1961). The English translation appeared in 1965. Subsequent dates given will refer to the original dates of publication, not the dates of translations. *Critiques dans un souterrain* has not been translated; it includes essays dating from 1963 to 1972.

(1972), *Des choses cachées depuis la fondation du monde* ("Things Hidden Since the Foundation of the World," 1978), *The Scapegoat* (1982), and *La Route antique des hommes pervers* ("The Ancient Road of Wicked Men," 1985).[2] In the process of dealing with this material, Girard has explored a number of themes that carry forward from the thinkers studied in previous chapters. These include religion and the sacred, the nature of philosophy and its roots in religion, the problem of objectivistic metaphysics, the themes of mimesis, myth, and tragedy, and the problems of the "subject" and the nature of subjectivity. Before discussing these, however, it will be appropriate to begin with a brief exposition of the basic framework of Girard's thought as it unfolds from the study of mimetic desire to the founding of culture in the dynamics of the sacred.

All the elements of Girard's framework of analysis (in France it is sometimes called *le système Girard*) were already present in *Deceit, Desire, and the Novel.* That work not only sketched in some detail what Girard has subsequently come to call *la psychologie interdividuelle*, the system of psychology he considers a complement and corrective to Freud's, but it also discusses the roots of sacralization in "metaphysical desire" and the manner in which, as one of the chapter titles phrases it, "Men Become Gods in the Eyes of Each Other." He begins with what he calls "mediation" and the role in our psychology of models we seek out for imitation.

At the base of Girard's system is a distinction between "appetites and needs" on the one hand and "desire" on the other.[3] Appetites and needs are grounded in the biological life of human beings: when we need food or water, we feel hunger or thirst, and so on. Genuine appetites or needs can be genuinely satisfied. Desire, on the other hand, is always reaching past its ostensible objects and finds little or no real satisfaction in them. It is rooted in the proclivity we have to dramatize our lives in our imag-

---

2. *Des Choses cachées* and *La Route antique* were not yet translated at the time the present study was written. Translations from as yet untranslated works by Girard will be my own. (After this book had gone to press, translations of both these works were pub lished by Stanford University Press as *Things Hidden Since the Foundation of the World* and *Job: The Victim of His People*.)

3. See *Des Choses cachées*, p. 401. References to this work will be to the Livre de poche edition.

inations and to fall into fascinations with figures or objects that symbolize for us a perfection or fullness of being that we feel ourselves lacking.

Because we begin from a feeling of deficiency in ourselves, we tend to seek other, seemingly more substantial and imposing figures to imitate. These become our "mediators" or models. They are mediators in the sense that it is *through* and *by means of* them that we seek to gain access to true "being"—which is to say, power—and thereby to become "really real." We also become fascinated by the objects we feel that these powerful figures desire. Wanting to be like them, we imitate them in their desiring. In fact, of ourselves we are incapable of the kind of imaginative desire that goes beyond mere appetite or need (which is by nature fairly limited in scope). "The human subject," says Girard, "is incapable either of focusing his desire or sustaining its force"; rather "the rival has sole authority in matters of desire: he alone can confer on an object, by desiring it himself, the seal of infinite desirability" (*Des choses*, p. 478). Such an object becomes fascinating to us because we tend to feel that if our admired models desire it, it must be something they can discern as having power to confer on them a heightening of the superior reality and self-sufficiency we feel they must enjoy.

The ultimate goal of desire, therefore, is always something beyond the objects that symbolize its presence. In Girard's words, "The object is only a means of reaching the mediator. The desire is aimed at the mediator's *being*"; it is a "desire to absorb the being of the mediator" (*Deceit*, p. 53). This is why he sometimes uses the term "metaphysical" (or "ontological") desire; every desire is ultimately "metaphysical" in this way. "If the model, who is apparently already endowed with superior being, desires some object, that object," Girard says we feel, "must surely be capable of conferring an even greater plenitude of being" (*Violence*, p. 146).

At this point any reader with an interest in comparative religion will recognize the connection with the phenomenology of the sacred as studied by such scholars as Mircea Eliade, Rudolf Otto, or Gerardus van der Leeuw and will see that the logic of Girard's thought would have to lead into the psychology of religion. One might compare, for example, the following passage from Eliade's *The Sacred and the Profane*, which offers both a close parallel to Girard's theme of metaphysical desire and a significant contrast:

The man of the archaic societies tends to live as much as possible *in* the sacred or in close proximity to consecrated objects. The tendency is perfectly understandable, because, for primitives as for the man of all premodern societies, the *sacred* is equivalent to a *power,* and, in the last analysis, to *reality.* The sacred is saturated with *being.* Sacred power means reality and at the same time enduringness and efficacity. The polarity sacred-profane is often expressed as an opposition between *real* and *unreal* or pseudoreal. . . . Thus it is easy to understand that religious man deeply desires *to be,* to participate in *reality,* to be saturated with power." (Pp. 12–13)

The parallel is obvious, the contrast perhaps less so. The latter is equally important, however. Eliade is fairly typical of modern thinkers interested in religion in that he tends to focus his attention on the appealingness of the sacred. He is aware, as his accompanying exposition of Otto's analysis of the sacred as *mysterium tremendum et fascinans* (a mystery not only fascinating but also frightening) indicates, that the appealingness of the sacred is not its only feature. But in Eliade's perception it tends to become predominant. This is readily evident not only in his many volumes on the history of religions but also in his novels, which typically depict a scholar of Indian thought who feels attracted to the sacred but has difficulty making contact with it, and is both fascinated by and in some awe of those who can. This attitude leads Eliade to concentrate on the way his *homo religiosus* ("religious man," considered as an ideal type) seeks out manifestations of the sacred and tries to dwell as much as possible in its presence.[4] From Girard's point of view, this would constitute a "romantic" view of religion—"romantic" in the sense that he gave the term in *Deceit, Desire, and the Novel,* where he said that the "romantic" novel "reflects" mimetic desire, but unlike the "romanesque" ("novelistic") does not "reveal" it—that is, does not make us explicitly aware of it as a controlling mechanism in human psychology (pp. 16–17).

Girard's own view, in contrast, is a distinctly sober one in which the sacred is considered an imaginative divinization of essentially human violence. He may well have had Eliade in mind when he said in *Violence and the Sacred,* "Modern thinkers view the sacred solely as a mediating

4. Eliade's thought and its relation to the theme of the ambiguity of the sacred will be discussed further, at somewhat greater length, in the concluding chapter of this study.

force, because they try to interpret primitive reality in terms of a religion that has been purged of its maleficent qualities" (p. 267). Real
primitives, he says, are acutely aware of the latter and are consequently
more concerned with using their rites to keep the sacred safely at a distance than with trying to get close to it.

Since this way of thinking may seem surprising in a world that usually finds the loss of the sacred more of a problem than its presence, it
will be helpful to consider Girard's conception of religion in more
detail. It is founded in his theory of mimesis and triangular desire. In
fact it is its direct logical consequence. If each human being is caught up
from his or her earliest childhood in a mimetic process by which he
seeks to acquire the "being" and power of the models who impress him
—parents, teachers, peers, and so on—and if for this very purpose he is
drawn above all else to imitate his mediator's desires as explained
above, then it is virtually inevitable that at some point he will come into
conflict with his mediator as they become rivals for the same object. In a
world of limited resources this is simply a natural consequence of the
fact that the desire is mediated or, as Girard calls it, "triangular."

If all desires were for objects that were in infinite supply, or if desire
were spontaneous and unmediated so that convergence of two lines of
desire on a single object would be an accident rather than an inevitability, it might be possible for human beings to avoid conflict. This
only happens, however, when the individuals in question are prevented
by their situations or by cultural prohibitions from entering into conflict. In *Deceit, Desire, and the Novel* Girard cites the example of the
way Cervantes's Don Quixote models himself on Amadis of Gaul, a
hero of chivalric romance. The Don seeks a glory like that of Amadis,
but there is no question of his having to defeat Amadis in order to win
it; rather the greater the glory Amadis can represent both to him and to
an admiring world, the greater the glory he himself can aspire to. In this
case the fact that one is a real person and the other fictitious is what separates their fields of action and hence their possible fields of conflict.
Girard terms such a pattern of mediation "external." "Internal mediation," on the other hand, takes place when both agents operate within
the same field of action, as might, for example, two rivals for business
success or for the love of the same woman. External mediation can also
take place between individuals in the real world when cultural forms insulate them from mutual competition. In a feudal society, for example,

a nobleman and a commoner might have different culturally defined fields of action even if they live and act in close physical proximity. (The noncompetitive relationship between Don Quixote and Sancho Panza would be an example.) Much of the literature discussed in *Deceit* depicts the mimetic rivalries that became pandemic in nineteenth-century Europe as the democratization of society brought more and more people into relations in which collisions of desire were possible.

It may help to clarify this point, and also bring out its pertinence to a conception of religion and the sacred, if we consider briefly Girard's critique of Freud's theory of the Oedipus complex. Freud's Oedipal triangle, in Girard's view, would be an example of internal mediation, the father and son competing for the mother. From Girard's point of view, such rivalry would be an abnormal condition. Under normal cultural circumstances, he says, the family is a zone of protection from conflicts of desire, so that the father can function as an external mediator and, as he put it in *Des choses cachées*, "a model for apprenticeship" rather than a model of sexual desire (p. 490). Far from being the universal drama of mankind, as Freud believed, sexual rivalry between father and son, suggests Girard, is the peculiar product of the same cultural situation that made for the spread of envy as a social force in nineteenth-century Western Europe generally, namely the breakdown of the traditional patterns of social differentiation that had previously guarded against the dangers of internal mediation. As Girard describes the Oedipal situation in *Violence and the Sacred*, "the father can only become an obstacle when the diminution of his paternal authority has brought him into direct confrontation with his son, obliging him to occupy the same sphere. The Oedipus complex appears most plausible in a society in which the father's authority has been greatly weakened but not completely destroyed; that is, in Western society during the course of recent centuries" (p. 188).

Regarding the pertinence of Freud's theory to an understanding of religion and the sacred, Freud himself, in such works as *The Future of an Illusion, Totem and Taboo,* and *Moses and Monotheism,* argued that religion was a product of the Oedipus complex and of the conflict with the father that grew out of it. His argument was essentially that the libido of a male child spontaneously reaches out toward the female with whom he is most closely associated, usually his mother, and thereby brings him into rivalry with his father, whom he would like to kill and replace. These feelings, however, lead to an inner conflict in the child, since he also fears his father's power. In his naiveté the child even fears that the father can discern his murderous thoughts before they are expressed, so that as soon as he conceives them he begins to feel a need to propitiate the father. The terror all of this excites is so painful that the child represses consciousness of both thoughts and feelings, but unless he can raise them into consciousness again through psychoanalysis they will continue to influence his behavior all his life. Among people incapable of psychoanalytic self-awareness, religion has developed as the spontaneous product of their unconscious feelings of a need to propitiate an angry father. Their image of God is the illusion projected by their fears of the father's wrath, and their sacrifices and confessions of sin are attempts to appease him.

Freud also hypothesized, in the last two of the books mentioned above, that religion as a historical phenomenon developed out of a primordial father-murder for which human beings have been trying to expiate the repressed guilt ever since. This hypothesis has not won much support from scholars of religion, both because of the impossibility of finding historical evidence for a prehistorical murder and because of the tenuousness of the theory of genetic transmission of memory that the idea of inheritance of repressed guilt must depend on. Although Girard differs fundamentally from Freud in his psychological theory, he is perhaps the only serious inquirer into the origins of religion to take Freud's questions, at least, seriously and to try both to correct and to build upon his hypothesis.

The major difference between the two thinkers has to do, as one would expect, with their theories of desire. Fundamental to Freud's framework of thought was an assumption exactly antithetical to Girard's, namely that desire is the spontaneous product of the influence of a desirable object on a subject. Girard's theory is that desire is subjectively generated through mimesis (through imitation of what one feels is a supposedly spontaneous desire on the part of a model).

To say that desire arises through one's imitation of another person taken as a model is not, for Girard, to say that this is something one does consciously—that is, with awareness of what one is doing and with an intention to do it. On the contrary, this is precisely where, in contrast to Freud, Girard believes what could be called "the unconscious" is to be found. He is quite critical of Freud's theory of the unconscious as a supposed repository of experiences that were once conscious and then repressed. This seems to him both a clumsy hypothesis and another example of Freud's object-centeredness, in that the unconscious content is interpreted as a repressed objective "representation" of a past experience. He speaks of Freud as a sort of Platonist in his tendency to focus on what might be called "objective mimesis" of remote or hidden realities. Freud is so preoccupied with mental representations of objective contents that he overlooks subjective mimesis and thereby misses what is really essential in our unconscious lives, namely what we are *doing* without realizing it. "What is lacking to Freud," he says in the chapter "Mimesis and Representation" in *Des choses cachées*, "is the same thing Plato lacks: an understanding of the mimetic as desire itself and of this fact as the true 'unconscious'—assuming one is interested in continuing to use this perhaps overly equivocal term. Such nonrepresentational mimesis is fully and solely capable of bringing about all triangular rivalries..." (p. 499).[5] What is imitated, he goes on to say, is not objective content at all; rather "it is a desire which the imitator not only need not but even cannot form a representation of for himself."

Freud's consistent tendency was to give precedence to the objective in every area and thereby to reduce human subjectivity to almost complete passiveness before the power of objects either to repel (as in the case of repressed traumatic memories) or to attract. "In Freud," Girard says, "the desire for the material object is intrinsic; this is fundamental, and it is inconceivable that it might itself need to be founded, especially on another desire. It is this intrinsic nature of desire for the mother, along with the element of narcissism, which is likewise interpreted as intrinsic," that constitutes for Freud what is specifically human about human desire (*Des choses*, p. 489). He then quotes Freud as saying that "man has two original sexual objects: himself and the woman who nurses him (*das pflegende Weib*)."[6] And both of these are completely spontaneous. "Mimetic desire," he says, "never shows up anywhere in Freud; he never mentions it in connection with the Oedipus complex, and one can easily see that the two notions are mutually exclusive" (pp. 489–90). In his chapter on "Freud and the Oedipus Complex" in *Vio-*

5. Cf. p. 501 on Freudian heresies (C. G. Jung and Melanie Klein) as neo-Platonisms. Jung, Girard says, expelled all traces of the theme of rivalry from psychoanalysis and ended, like Plotinus, in a sort of mystical contemplation of archetypes.

6. Girard cites the *Gesammelte Werke*, 10:154.

lence and the Sacred, Girard does say there are "traces" of the notion of mimetic desire in Freud's work, but he thinks Freud "saw the path of mimetic desire stretching out before him and deliberately turned aside" (p. 171). He says that in his earliest formulation of his theory, Freud came very close to a conception of desire as mimetic when he spoke of "identification" with the father as developing independently of sexual cathexis (fixation of desire) toward the mother and subsequently coming together with it to reinforce it, since as Freud himself put it, the child "would like to grow like and be like" his father "and take his place everywhere."[7] But in his later formulation, in *The Ego and the Id,* Freud turned away from this initial, half-formed intuition to commit himself to the theory of the primacy of object-desire, with the effect that he left his concept of identification vague and ambiguous and without any clear function in his framework.

Freud could not deny the phenomenon of identification with the father altogether, but his commitment to the libido theory and object-desire made it necessary for him to find a way of accounting for it in their terms. This drove him into what, from Girard's point of view, seems a bit of theoretical patchwork as clumsy and unconvincing as the epicycles of Ptolemaic astronomy: Freud's theory of latent bisexuality as a foundation for homosexual attraction to the father. What struck Freud, he says, and needed to be accounted for was the fact that over time the child experiences an increasing fascination for his rival, beyond the interest he has in his mother. Bound as he was to the idea of libidinous object-desire as man's fundamental motive, Freud was forced to interpret this as a homosexual fascination: " . . . a passive homosexual desire with regard to the father, a desire to be desired by the father as a homosexual object!" (*Des choses,* p. 503).

Girard, on the other hand, claims that the entire network of relations Freud tried to explain by way of his Oedipal theory, including the child's tendency to increasing fascination with the father even as the father thwarts him, is explainable very neatly and simply in terms of his own mimetic theory. Let us consider Girard's alternative account of these phenomena in *Violence and the Sacred.* Here he suggests that one

7. *Violence,* p. 170, quoting from Freud's *Group Psychology and the Analysis of the Ego* in *The Standard Edition of the Complete Psychological Works of Sigmund Freud,* ed. and trans. James Strachey, 18:105.

begin by trying to trace out the path that Freud might have taken if he had not turned aside from his early intimations of the role of mimesis in the child's identification with the father. From this point of view it would be the child's desire to "be like" his father and "take his place everywhere" that would lead him to desire the mother. He would learn that desire from his model by imitation. He would also learn from the model to interpret it as clashing with the model's, since the child, who does not come into the world with an innate idea of exclusive rights of possession, could not be expected himself to see any problem in sharing his mother with the father he admires. "Only an adult," says Girard, "could interpret the child's actions in terms of usurpation. Such an interpretation comes from the depths of a cultural system to which the child does not yet belong, one that is based on cultural concepts of which the child has not the remotest notion" (p. 174).

Since the child is encouraged by the father and the surrounding culture to model himself on the father, the prohibition of the mother in this case must put him in what Gregory Bateson, whom Girard cites frequently, called a "double-bind"; he is commanded, "Imitate me. Don't imitate me." The double bind turns what had been a simple model into something more problematic: a model-obstacle. To the child who in all innocence only wanted to please his model and discover through his tutelage how to live up to his example and share his values, the countermanding command is both confusing and painful. If the father reacts with anger or violence to what he sees as a rivalrous threat from the child, this is all the more traumatic to him, since in his emotional dependence on his father and in his own inability to defend himself he is doubly vulnerable.

It is at this point that the remarkable originality of Girard's analysis and its fruitfulness for an understanding of the dynamics of the sacred becomes evident. He says:

> Faced with the model's anger, the disciple feels compelled to make some sort of choice between himself and the model; and it is perfectly clear that he will choose in favor of the model. The idol's wrath must be justified, and it can only be justified by some failure on the part of the disciple, some hidden weakness that obliges the god to forbid access to the holy of holies, to slam shut the gates of paradise. Far from reducing the divinity's prestige, this new attitude of vengeful spite serves to increase it. The disci-

ple feels guilty—though of what, he cannot be sure—and unworthy of the object of his desire, which now appears more alluring than ever. Desire has now been redirected toward those particular objects protected by the *other's* violence. The link between desire and violence has been forged, and in all likelihood it will never be broken. (P. 175)

This is, of course, an account of the type of interfamilial rivalry that Freud believed he had discovered as a phenomenon in the world of his patients. Its implications are not dependent on strictly Oedipal, father-son conflict, however. The basic pattern would be the same wherever rivalry could develop between a model and a disciple, and it would have the same implications: the model's violence in defense of his own claims would increase the disciple's fascination both with the model himself and with his objects. The reason is that what we are drawn to above all else, as was explained earlier, is power, interpreted as "plenitude of being." "Desire," says Girard, " . . . is attracted to violence triumphant and strives desperately to incarnate this 'irresistible' force. Desire clings to violence and stalks it like a shadow because violence is the signifier of the cherished being, the signifier of divinity" (p. 151).

As a result of this process, which in *Des choses cachées* Girard calls "the sacralization of the model-obstacle" (p. 536), the model himself becomes the object and source of fascination, the hidden center within one's subjectivity from which radiates the power of all other fascinations. This is the direct result of the sacralization that establishes what feels to the disciple like a vast gulf between himself and his mediator: what creates fascination, says Girard, "is the appearance of absolute incompatibility between the desiring subject and the desired object, which in reality is not at all an object, properly understood—it is hardly necessary to underline this—but the model-obstacle himself" (p. 536).

This still does not bring us to the origins of religion, of course, even if it says a great deal about how our ideas of "divine" power can originate and take on a "sacral" fascination for us. Girard believes, however, that there is a sequence of natural connections between the various moments of the psychological processes he outlines that makes socially inevitable the development of religion and, with it, of properly human consciousness (according to his theory of hominization). The links are as follows:

Mimesis of desire will lead at some point to convergence on a common object and thereby to rivalry and conflict, which will in turn lead, in the manner described, to an intensification of desire into fascination. Influenced by each other's patterns of desire, that is, several and eventually many individuals will come to desire the same object. This process of mimetic rivalry, if allowed to continue unchecked, will lead to ever-increasing conflict and further exacerbation of desire in a kind of vicious spiral culminating in pandemic mutual hostility. The reason is that the object itself is not the controlling factor either in eliciting or allaying desire. The various antagonists, without realizing it, pursue their objects primarily as symbols of the sufficiency of being (i.e., power) they hope to acquire through them. They will therefore seek out the objects most keenly desired and fiercely guarded by the most powerful rivals, since only those will seem worth aiming at: "Violent opposition, then, is the signifier of ultimate desire, of divine self-sufficiency, of that 'beautiful totality' whose beauty depends on its being inaccessible and impenetrable" (*Violence*, p. 148).

This quest for the unattainable produces the ironic, but understandable and readily observable, effect that whenever one wins out over an antagonist in mimetic conflict, both his prestige and that of his objects tend to evaporate. Whoever can be vanquished and whatever can be possessed will by that very fact come to seem merely ordinary, leaving the conqueror either having to face the emptiness his victory reveals or else having to seek out a new, more powerful rival who can reawaken his confidence in objective desirability. Girard thinks few will have the courage to choose the first alternative. As he put it in *Des choses cachées*, "Rivalry is difficult to endure, but the absence of rivalry is even more intolerable, since it places the subject before nothingness..." (p. 501). This leaves the victor with only the latter alternative: "He must then turn to an even greater violence and seek out an obstacle that promises to be truly insurmountable" (*Violence*, p. 148).

This, of course, implies constantly escalating levels of conflict among the members of any group. In the absence of some mechanism to defuse such conflict, human life on this planet could never have survived as long as it has. In *Des choses cachées* Girard speaks at length, under the heading "Philosophical Anthropology," about the evolution of man and the origins of society. It is both in the ability of human beings to pursue imaginative goals and in the development of a solution to the problems arising from that pursuit that Girard sees the significant differences between the human species and lower animals. Girard thinks one of the great advantages of his theory of mimetic behavior is that it serves to explain both the continuity between men and animals and their discontinuity without the need to minimize either or to invoke the supernatural as an explanatory principle.[8] Primate societies, he points out, are governed like ours by mimetic mechanisms, but in the case of animals there are instinctive responses that stop the resulting conflicts short of death while allowing them to serve to organize the group around the strongest animal as leader. Human beings lack such instincts, and in their absence they have come to depend unconsciously on another mechanism for the termination of conflict.

This is what Girard calls le mécanisme victimaire, or "the victimizing mechanism." It is continuous with the mimetic mechanism and grows out of it naturally. To understand its dynamics Girard suggests we imagine a group of primitive human beings who have become caught up in an escalating spiral of violence and desire of the sort sketched above but who have not yet developed a cultural solution to its dangers. This would be a situation in which each human being is caught up in a maelstrom of constantly rotating rivalries as he turns again and again from defeated rivals to new and supposedly more powerful ones. Under such circumstances, says Girard, all the members of the group tend to become "monstrous doubles" of one another, each alike in snarling antagonism. Unchecked, this state of reciprocal violence would lead to mutual destruction. But at a certain moment the mimetic mechanism itself will bring a form of deliverance.

The way this can be expected to happen is as follows. At some point, in the midst of this mutual fear and hostility, some individual, perhaps because of a distinctive characteristic that draws attention to him or a perceptible weakness that makes him seem an easy mark, will be attacked by two or more others. If this happens, the very mimetic mechanism that drew all into mutual antagonism will also draw them to imitate the attackers in their choice of that particular victim. As this happens, the combination of fear, fascination, and hatred that bound them in opposition will cease to float freely from one antagonist to another throughout the group, but rather will become fixed on one in "the polarization of violence onto a single victim who substitutes for all the others" (Violence, p. 161). This figure Girard terms the "surrogate vic-

8. See Des choses cachées, bk. 1, ch. 3, "Le Processus d'hominisation," pp. 118–45.

tim." (Of course this "single victim" need not be an individual, but could be a subgroup within the larger. One can think of the killing of twins in some tribes, for example, or more spectacularly, the Holocaust of European Jewry during World War II or the incarceration of Americans of Japanese descent during the same period.)

This polarization of violence will have far-reaching effects. Above all, it will transform what had been merely a collection of mutual antagonists into a community united in mutual hatred of a single victim. In their imitations of each other's hatred of the victim they will join in interpreting him as the source of all the previous trouble among them. In addition, the new peace and harmony they experience in this cooperative opposition to a single enemy will make it seem to them as if the expulsion or death of the victim must be its source. This will give him the duality characteristic of the sacred as *mysterium tremendum et fascinosum;* he will seem to them both the source of the ultimate evil, reciprocal violence, and the source of its antidote, mutual love.

This establishes, says Girard, the fundamental difference on which all culture is founded, the difference between the sacred victim and the ordinary humanity of the rest of the group. On this is erected the fundamental cultural institution: sacrifice—of which all other patterns of social differentiation, he believes, are varying figurations.

It also precipitates, according to Girard, the process of hominization, the birth of human society and of consciousness in the properly human sense. In *Des choses cachées* Girard says that as mimesis expands and intensifies among animals "beyond a certain threshold of mimetic power, animal societies become impossible. This threshold corresponds, therefore, to that at which the mechanism of victimization appears; this is the threshold of hominization" (p. 133). He also speculates that when this mechanism takes hold, it gives birth not only to the original form of human signification in the designation of the victim but also to a new quality of attention that constitutes the difference between animal and human consciousness: "Before even arriving at the sign, one must see, I think, in the mechanism of victimization in its most elementary form a prodigious machine for the awakening of a new order of attention, the first attention that is noninstinctive" (p. 139). In the stillness and peace following the murderous frenzy, the members of the horde discover a new object beyond the dominant animal or the objects of sexual or alimentary appetite: the cadaver of the collective victim. It is this cadaver, he says, that "constitutes the first object of this new type of attention" (p. 139).[9]

One may reasonably wonder at this point in Girard's argument whether he is speculating too broadly in trying to trace hominization and human consciousness itself to primordial events that, like those Freud speculated on in *Moses and Monotheism* and *Totem and Taboo*, must lie forever beyond the reach of verification.

Other hypotheses, moreover, are possible that might equally claim to account for the sacrificial violence that has marked so much of human history. The American sociologist, Eli Sagan, for example, has developed in his book, *At the Dawn of Tyranny: The Origins of Individualism, Political Oppression, and the State* (1985), a theory of the evolution of what he calls "complex societies" that also builds on the idea that such societies have always been intimately involved with and dependent on sacrificial violence (originally human sacrifice) administered by kings and priests. Sagan, however, maintains that it is only when one passes beyond the level of primitive (and yet genuinely human) society that social violence becomes central to culture. Sagan studies the comparatively recent preliterate complex societies of Buganda in Africa and of Hawaii, Tonga, and Tahiti in Polynesia, regarding them as examples that can give us an idea of the types of complex society that must have preceded the archaic literate societies of early history, such as those of ancient Mesopotamia and Egypt.

If Sagan is correct, there must have been a long period of human life in primitive, comparatively less violent societies before the emergence of the type of society in which sacrificial violence began to play an essential role. Sagan's own theory is that such violence probably developed in connection with the shift from a kinship-centered society to one in which a more complex and impersonal social system came to demand a shift of loyalty to remote authorities and the rule of codified law. Such systems originated as tyrannies, in Sagan's view, and tyranny required

---

9. This theory of hominization has subsequently been echoed by Girard's collaborator in *Des chose cachées*, Jean-Michel Oughourlian, in Oughourlian's book, *Un Mime nommé désir: Hystérie, transe, possession, adorcisme* (1982), p. 58: "Consciousness therefore originates in the attention fixed on the other and on that exceptional Other that is the scapegoat-victim, the source of all signifiers and itself the transcendental signified." (A translation of *Un Mime nommé désir* is in preparation by the present author for the University of Washington Press.)

cruelty both as an essential instrument of power in such a society (as a means of coercing obedience) and as a means of managing the anxiety generated by the breakdown of the kinship system and the sense of security it had given. Sagan and Girard agree in finding legitimated violence central to society as we now know it, but in Sagan's view there is no need to suppose that the sacrificial rites we now have records of must derive directly from attenuated versions of primordial acts of murder.

On the other hand, one must also acknowledge in Girard's favor that the anxiety of social change alone need not be taken as a solely sufficient explanation for the development of sacrifices. There is no reason to deny that envy and rivalry may also contribute in a powerful way to whatever sense of satisfaction human beings might derive from the killing of their victims, whether in ancient or in modern times.

Where Girard's speculation seems weakest is not in its conception of the affective dynamics of sacrifice but in its conception of the dependence of hominization on a prior mimetic crisis that culminates in a paroxysm of collective violence directed against a single victim. Here Girard's speculation rests on the assumption that the immediate ancestors of man in the animal kingdom must have drifted at some point into a runaway mimetic frenzy that could only end in the collective murder he hypothesizes. A weakness in this line of thinking would seem to be that it offers no explanation for the failure of the violence-defusing instincts he also attributes to prehuman animals. A possible explanation might be that the loss of instinctive defenses against runaway violence could itself be caused by hominization as a result of the mental complexity that process generates. But that same mental complexity could also bring with it other possibilities for the avoidance of runaway violence, such as reflective consideration of the possible consequences of violent rivalry and the development of social codes to avert or inhibit it. It may also be that only the mental complexity that comes with hominization could make possible the development of mimetic desire itself, since the phenomenon of desire requires a certain degree of ability to play mentally with imaginative possibilities.

The problem, in other words, is a "chicken or egg" one: did hominization make mimetic desire and murderous rivalry possible, or was the causal relation the other way around? In the absence of a method to test either theory, the point must remain moot as a historical hypothesis.

The presence of mimetic desire and rivalry as a fact of our social existence, on the other hand, is easily attested in our everyday lives, as are also the crises of collective violence and victimization that have marked the recent as well as the early history of our species. Girard's point need not ultimately depend upon the historical claim that a *meurtre fondatrice,* a "founding murder," has actually taken place at the origin of a given society or the origin of *Homo sapiens* as we know him. Even if mimetic rivalry among early hominids may not have proceeded unchecked so that it had to culminate in a collective murder followed by peace and social harmony, the *tendency* to rivalry based on mimesis of desire is an undeniable feature of human life, and it can be a powerful force in society *even if it does not proceed unchecked.* For this force to be effective, that is, it need not be involved with a memory of a historical founding murder; it is sufficient that the implicit trajectory of rivalrous desire be sensed as an intimation. An *anticipated* crisis of violence and collective murder can be as important a founding factor in social cooperation as one that has actually taken place, since the anticipation of such an event happening at all, whether for the second time or the first, is what could be expected to lead people to reflect on the danger that at some point the victim might be oneself.

Girard, therefore, has a point when he says that conflicts of desire can lead to dangerous levels of rivalry and that such rivalry always points *in the direction,* at least, of collective violence and the murder of some victim. Sacrificial rites, as Girard interprets them, have developed out of such fundamental human tendencies. In any society that practices these rites, they are an attempt to purge out of the community the purported source of violence (the scapegoat figure) and also to perpetuate the beneficent effects of the process of his expulsion. The original act of collective violence, as hypothesized by Girard, was spontaneous and fortuitous; the rites of sacrifice develop as an attempt to bring its power under control and to make it both safe and dependably available, so that it may be continuously life-giving for the community. This means that the selection and killing of the victim must be repeatedly reenacted, but in a way that prevents the violence involved from getting out of hand and reinfecting the group as a whole. Some standard strategies that have developed historically for ensuring this, according to Girard's hypothesis, are the establishment of strict ritual procedures, the setting aside of certain figures as priests to perform the rites, and the selecting of victims in a way that cannot give rise to acts of revenge.

The last makes for a pattern Girard calls "double substitution": "The first, which passes unperceived, is the substitution of one member of the community for all, brought about through the operation of the surrogate victim. The second, the only truly 'ritualistic' substitution, is superimposed on the first. It is the substitution of a victim belonging to a predetermined sacrificial category for the original victim. The surrogate victim comes from inside the community, and the ritual victim must come from outside; otherwise the community might find it difficult to unite against it" (*Violence and the Sacred*, p. 102). (It would probably be more precise to say that the original victim comes from inside the "group" rather than the "community," since before the victimizing mechanism comes into play, the group has not yet become a community or society in the proper sense; there is nothing positive they share, only fear and hatred of one another.)

Sacrificial rites serve to channel rather than to abolish violence, but they are perceived by the members of society as its opposite. "A trace of very real violence persists in the rite," says Girard, "and there is no doubt that the rite succeeds at least partially because of its grim associations, its lingering fascination; but its essential orientation is peaceful. . . . the rite aims at the most profound state of peace known to any community: the peace that follows the sacrificial crisis and results from the unanimous accord generated by the surrogate victim" (p. 103).

It was mentioned above that the surrogate victim has the duality characteristic of the sacred: he is perceived as the source both of the greatest evil that can afflict the group (reciprocal violence) and the greatest good (mutual peace and love). Both, for Girard, are faces presented by one and the same reality: violence itself. This dual significance of violence, he believes, is what underlies all religious ideas; the mythic symbolism of divinity is simply a language for this deeper, truly original level of meaning. In fact, the associations of the sacred alone could serve as the origin of religion and thereby of culture and society, quite apart from the symbolism of divinity: "Sacrifice . . .," says Girard, "can be defined solely in terms of the sacred, without reference to any particular divinity; that is, it can be defined in terms of maleficent violence polarized by the victim and metamorphosed by his death (or expulsion from the community, which amounts to the same thing) into beneficent violence" (p. 258). When the imagery of gods and demons or of the wrath and mercy of a single all-powerful God develops, it simply serves as a way of expressing this sense of the dual power of the victim to curse or bless.

The inflation of the surrogate victim into a figure incarnating transhuman violence is therefore the origin of all theology as well as of the mythology on which it is based. In fact, it is precisely the polarization characteristic of the victimizing mechanism that Girard thinks of as the fundamental mark of mythological thinking. Unlike Rudolph Bultmann, for example, Girard does not consider the essence of mythological thinking to lie in its contrast with science as a system of causal explanation. Rather it lies in its character as expressing a polarized view of violence. "Myths," he says, "are the retrospective transfiguration of sacrificial crises, the reinterpretation of these crises in the light of the cultural order that has arisen from them" (p. 64). "Sacrificial crisis" is his term for the chaos preceding the engagement of the victimizing mechanism that delivers the group from its runaway violence. Mythology expresses the polarized vision in which the victim comes to seem imbued with superhuman power for good or evil. From the victim's two aspects spring the imagery of beneficent or destructive superhuman forces, and the myth takes shape as a story about the manner in which the community is founded by their power or delivered by it from possible destruction. Mythic protagonists, whether divine or human, tend to take on a clearly positive role in stories of conflict, and their antagonists a clearly negative one. Myths typically depict a struggle between forces of order and chaos, with the outcome normally the triumph of the former. In this way they function to image and celebrate the memory of the collective murder of the surrogate victim.

Tragedy, for Girard, is myth's opposite, in the sense that the tragic vision restores at least a glimpse of the original chaos. Tragic antagonists tend to be neither clearly good nor evil, and their conflict takes on the character of the sacrificial crisis rather than its mythic resolution. "Tragedy," he says, "envelops all human relationships in a single tragic antagonism. It does not differentiate between the fraternal conflict of Eteocles and Polyneices, the father-son conflict of *Alcestis* or *Oedipus the King*, the conflict between men who share no ancestral ties, such as

Oedipus and Tiresias. The rivalry of the two prophets is indistinguishable from the rivalry between brothers" (p. 65).

Tragedy typically proceeds by beginning with a myth, then demystifying its polarized vision so as to restore our awareness of the possibility of sacrificial crisis, and then closing with a reconsolidation of the mythic vision and a corresponding recoalescence of the group. Like Aristotle and Ricoeur, Girard takes *Oedipus the King* as his classic example, but the ultimate thrust of his analysis is toward a conception of the function of tragedy rather more like Voegelin's. The story of Oedipus, as he describes it, grows out of an earlier myth in which Oedipus played straightforwardly the role of a violator of social norms and a source of ritual pollution for the city of Thebes. Sophocles's play begins with that situation, but it depicts Oedipus as basically well intentioned though unfortunate.

Aristotle, in a reversion to the mythic pattern of thinking, developed the theory of a tragic flaw—in the case of Oedipus, his irascibility—as the special fault of the tragic hero and an explanation for his downfall. Girard points out, however, that Oedipus's "flaw" is hardly peculiar to him: "... we cannot help asking ourselves whether these tantrums really serve to distinguish Oedipus from the other characters. ... If we look closely at the myth we notice that 'anger' crops up everywhere. It was a kind of suppressed anger that incited Oedipus's companion at Corinth to cast doubt on the hero's parentage. At the fateful crossroads it was anger that goaded Laius initially to raise a hand against his son. It was an earlier act of anger, preceding any actions by Oedipus, that prompted the father's decision to do away with his infant son. It is clear that Oedipus has no monopoly on anger in the play. Whatever the author's intentions, there would be no tragic debate if the other protagonists did not become angry in turn" (pp. 68–69). Far from his having a special fault that explains, and justifies, his role as victim, Oedipus is no more severely flawed in the play than are his opponents.

Apart from a shared susceptibility to envy and anger, the major source of the antagonisms in Sophocles's play—between Oedipus and Creon and Oedipus and Tiresias—is the naiveté of each in underestimating his own involvement in violence: "At first, each of the protagonists believes that he can quell the violence; at the end each succumbs to it. All are drawn unwittingly into the structure of violent reciprocity—which they always think they are outside of, because all initially come from the outside and mistake this positional and temporary advantage for a permanent and fundamental superiority" (p. 69). All believe themselves to be above the battle, but each is naive. Sophocles unmasks this naiveté and shows us how easily reciprocal violence can break out and draw all into it unless the mechanism of polarization can break the cycle. He also shows how that resolution can take place. It requires unanimity against one, and in this case it is brought about by the joining even of that one himself in the process of polarization: Oedipus at the end plucks out his own eyes and calls for his own expulsion from the community he had polluted with his presence.[10]

Girard differs from Ricoeur, therefore, in placing his emphasis not on the power of tragedy to make pain pleasurable by uniting discord with concord, but on its power to do just the opposite: to make us uncomfortably aware of the sources of discord within ourselves. From Girard's point of view, Ricoeur's conception of tragedy would really be closer to the mythic vision, since it is there that we find pleasure in perceiving the victim's destruction as the culmination of a dramatic conflict. In fact, Ricoeur's whole notion of narrative form would look suspiciously mythic from Girard's angle—more "romantic" and reflective of the power of the mimetic mechanism than revelatory of it.

Even if Ricoeur may not have been thinking about collective violence and sacrifice when he said that human beings have a need to conceive of their lives as moving from a beginning through a middle toward an end, the fact remains, according to Girard's way of thinking, that the dramatic culmination that grips our imaginations and draws us, even unconsciously, is the polarized collective violence we imagine to be the defeat of evil. Each of us would like to think of himself as free from this pattern of feeling and imagination, but in Girard's conception, every human life experiences the threat of violence and it feels the allure of the mechanism of polarization. None of us, anymore than Sophocles's antagonists, stands above the battle. Both Ricoeur and Voegelin symbolized human life as a story or drama in which each person is caught up without knowing the script. Girard believes that following the lead of the Greek tragedians, the prophets of Israel, the earliest Christians, and

10. On the importance of unanimity and the need of a community only barely removed from a condition of sacrificial crisis to draw the victim himself into his collective condemnation, see chapter 16, "Un procès totalitaire," in *La Route antique*, pp. 165–74.

a few others who have left tracings of the essential insight, he has uncovered the script—and it is not one to take pleasure in but to criticize
and win freedom from.

It is in this way that Girard arrives at a conception of Greek tragedy
more like Voegelin's than Ricoeur's, one that emphasizes tragedy's educative and cultural function. In *Time and Narrative* Ricoeur, as we saw,
took tragedy as paradigmatic of narrative generally and emphasized the
aesthetic satisfaction narrative form offers to human beings, who by the
basic constitution of their minds are organized to apprehend their lives
under the aspect of such form, just as Kant supposed we must apprehend all experience under the aspects of his fundamental categories.
From Girard's point of view one can speak of such a necessity in the
case of myth, but it is not rooted in a Kantian manner in the constitution of the individual mind. Rather its roots are in psycho-social process. It is an outgrowth of the fundamental dynamics of mimetic rivalry,
collective violence, and group formation as described above—a process
every one of us is involved in whether we are conscious of it or not.

Tragedy, in Girard's view, may serve to raise this process at least partially into consciousness and thereby to loosen, to some degree, the hold
with which the mythic vision grips us. "Tragedy has a particular affinity
for myth," he says, "but that does not mean it takes the same course.
The term *desymbolism* is more appropriate to tragedy than is *symbolism*" (*Violence and the Sacred*, p. 65). Tragedy partly uncovers the
meaning myth serves to mask. It arises, Girard believes, in a special social situation, one in which myth and sacrifice have already done their
work of bringing order, but also one in which there is a perceived
danger of return to reciprocal violence: "If the tragic poet touches upon
the violent reciprocity underlying all myths, it is because he perceives
these myths in a context of weakening distinctions and growing violence" (p. 65). Girard goes on to say that "tragic and prophetic inspiration" in "the true tragic spirit" arise from "a direct intuitive grasp of the
role played by violence in the cultural order and in disorder as well, in
mythology and in the sacrificial crisis" (p. 66). The writing of tragedies,
from this point of view, would be an attempt on the part of the tragedian to share this insight with his audience and thereby to elicit in them
a more reflective consciousness.

Such glimpses of social and human truth, however, are highly
precarious. They develop in moments when the danger is just enough to

elicit insight, but not quite enough to trigger the mechanism of victimization and flight to the mythic vision. Tragedy flirts, one might say,
with human self-knowledge, but stops short of a thorough dismantling
of myth. Voegelin thought of tragedy as aiming at a free decision for
justice on the part of a responsible, self-aware human being. Girard
would probably agree that tragedy arises out of an intimation of such a
possibility, but he would also be quick to point out that when people
begin to talk about justice, they frequently use that as a springboard for
a plunge back into a mythic vision of a world of clearcut good and evil,
with the legitimation this offers for further victimizing. Voegelin could
answer that certain tragedies, such as Aeschylus's *Suppliants* or *Per-
sians,* break out of that simple duality, but Girard might nevertheless
suspect that Voegelin shares, at least to some degree, Ricoeur's tendency to overlook the sinister side of the mythopoeic imagination and
the power it has to sneak up on us and undermine the supposed freedom and responsibility we like to flatter ourselves upon.

As it is, the tragedies Girard selects for analysis support his theory
that tragedians typically stop short of a radical critique of mythic thinking. "From the very fact that it belies the overt mythological messages,"
says Girard, "tragic drama opens a vast abyss before the poet; but he always draws back at the last moment" (p. 135). What makes him draw
back from too radical an exposure of the mythic vision and its underlying mechanism is the threat that such a critique might undermine the
power of polarized violence to deliver the community from the very
dangers tragedy depicts. Clarity of consciousness may have its attractions, but a community threatened with the outbreak of a sacrificial
crisis is likely to feel that the old remedy, sacrificial religion, is more
reliable—and "religion protects man as long as its ultimate foundations
are not revealed" (p. 135). Tragedy typically closes with a return to the
mythic vision because the tragedian at least dimly realizes that "[h]e is
exposed to a form of hubris more dangerous than any contracted by his
characters; it has to do with a truth that is felt to be infinitely destructive, even if it is not fully understood . . ." (p. 135).

To the modern reader that might seem a blameworthy failure of
nerve, but despite his own strong commitment to rational consciousness, Girard does not want to share what he thinks is a similarly mythic
and naive modern tendency to condemn sacrificial religion out of hand
and make victims of our own those who once relied on its protection.

"Because modern man clings to the belief that knowledge is in itself a 'good thing,'" he says, "he grants little or no importance to a procedure . . . that only serves to conceal the existence of man's violent impulses" (p. 82). Such optimistic naiveté "could well be the worst sort of ignorance," because it would deny the value of a form of protection that played a needed role in its time: "Men cannot confront the naked truth of their own violence without the risk of abandoning themselves to it entirely. They have never had a very clear idea of this violence, and it is possible that the survival of all human societies of the past was dependent on this fundamental lack of understanding" (p. 82). Before we can safely try to win freedom from the myths, rites, and taboos that constitute the religious foundation of culture, therefore, we will have to learn to take seriously the danger they have served historically to protect us against.

In *Violence and the Sacred* Girard insisted so forcefully that "we must acknowledge mankind's thorough dependence on religion" (p. 218) that he was frequently misinterpreted as a religious apologist by readers of that book. That this represents a misunderstanding his subsequent works have made clear—as if his own relentless exposure of the victimizing mechanism as the root of religion had not made it clear enough already. Girard has made his actual position quite explicit in *Des choses cachées,* where he tells us that in our own time we have no choice but to demystify and transcend the religious remedies that once served to protect us, since they are no longer able to do so effectively. "The surpassing achievement of present-day critical thought, the final and complete deconstruction of all religious and cultural mystification," he says, "corresponds to an increasingly radical deprivation of sacrificial resources" (p. 207). The old mechanisms of mimetic rivalry, reciprocal violence, and victimization are still with us, but the victimizing mechanism is less and less effective as a remedy. We have already become too conscious of what we are doing for the mechanism to work as it once did, though not yet conscious enough to gain release from its hold on us. Unable to get the same satisfaction out of the expulsion or killing of our victims, we make our sacrifices increasingly violent in an effort to make them effective once again "by constantly increasing the doses, immolating more and more victims in holocausts which always seek to be sacrificial but actually are so less and less" (p. 195). The enormous increase at present in our capacity for violence, coupled with our inability to return to a spontaneously mythic and sacrificial religion as a means of reducing its destructive potential, puts us in the position of having no choice but to press forward into full consciousness and in doing so to renounce radically the mechanisms we once relied on: "The whole of humanity now finds itself confronted with an ineluctable dilemma: men must reconcile once and for all without benefit of sacrificial intermediaries or they must resign themselves to the imminent extinction of mankind" (p. 208).

This calls for a radical demythologizing of all our thought, in every area where the mythic and sacrificial vision has been able to put down roots. The discussion of this vision so far has concentrated on Girard's critique of the sacrificial element in religious thought, but he also sees the sacrificial mentality as an important component of our philosophical tradition as well. Philosophy itself, he says, has its roots in religion, and "it is the religious one must understand in order to understand philosophy" (p. 26). No one has yet tried to read Plato in the light of ethnology, he says (p. 26), but that is what will be necessary in order to deconstruct the metaphysics that has grown out of Plato's focus on objective rather than subjective mimesis. Plato concentrated on the problem of objective representation and thereby amputated, according to Girard, an essential dimension of the problematic of imitation: appropriative behavior, "the acquisitive dimension, which is also the conflictual dimension" (p. 16).

Read in the light of our awareness of the way human society takes rise from the mechanism of victimization and reproduces its sacrificial pattern everywhere, Plato's dialogue form takes on a new significance in Girard's eyes as a dramatic medium for philosophy:

> Philosophy, like tragedy, can at certain levels serve as an attempt at expulsion.... This point, I think, has been brilliantly demonstrated by Jacques Derrida in his essay "La Pharmacie de Platon." He sets out to analyze Plato's use of the term *pharmakon*. The Platonic *pharmakon* functions like the human pharmakos and leads to similar results. The word is a pivot point between sophistic deception and sound philosophy, even though its role is no more justified or justifiable than the violence inflicted on the human scapegoat.... When Plato applies *pharmakon* to the Sophists, he generally uses it in its maleficent sense of "poison." When it is applied to Socrates or any Socratic activity, however, it means

"remedy." . . . between Socrates and the Sophists, the structure of the opposition belies not the difference that Plato would like to establish but
rather the reciprocity that is suggested by the recourse to one and the
same word. . . .

Plato's *pharmakon* is like Aristotle's *katharsis*. And whatever their
philosophic intentions may have been, it was their literary intuition that
led these two men to select terms that seem suggestive but the full
pertinence of which may have escaped them. . . . Behind the various
metaphors a scapegoat effect can always be discerned. (*Violence*, pp.
296–97)

The implication is that Plato and Aristotle both, like the other philosophers Girard occasionally discusses, such as Nietzsche and Heidegger,
express their thought in an idiom that is thick with the atmosphere of
sacred violence, with the result that they reflect more than reveal the
roots of mimetic antagonism.

Unfortunately for our purposes, Girard's critique of the tradition of
philosophy is only sketchy. He never gives it the attention he does religion and psychology. Still it is possible to see the implications of his
point of view for some of the issues that have come up among the various figures in the present study. An obvious one in the light of what was
discussed above is the role of philosophical myth as a means of knowledge. Clearly Girard would agree that myth plays a major role in philosophy and that reflection on that role is important. He would also warn
us, however, in opposition to the romantic tendencies of Voegelin's and
Ricoeur's approaches, that philosophical myth can be a lure leading us
into a polarized vision of man and the cosmos and one that overlooks
the extent to which this polarization originates in man. In this connection he would probably want to draw a parallel between the expulsion-
ary character of Plato's dialogues that was just referred to and the
dualistic tendency mentioned earlier, in the chapter on Voegelin, latent
in both Plato's and Voegelin's favored images. The entire set of ideas associated with "the Beyond" and with the image of existential tension,
for example, might well seem from Girard's point of view to amount to
a mythic masking and sacralizing of the process of mediation, although
he might also consider it to have some value as a strategy for deflecting
its power toward external rather than internal mediation.

Another point at which Girard might wish to take issue with Voegelin is the interpretation of the fragment from Anaximander that was quoted in that same chapter. This is a passage both Voegelin and Girard discuss. Voegelin considered Anaximander's image of the things of the cosmos arising from the Boundless and perishing back into it in expiation of their injustice to express a profound truth about existence. For Voegelin this was both the tragic truth that reality is "a cosmic process in which things emerge from, and disappear into, the nonexistence of the Apeiron" and also the philosophical truth that "to exist means to participate in two modes of reality: (1) In the Apeiron as the timeless *arche* of things and (2) in the ordered succession of things as the manifestation of the Apeiron in time" (*OH*, 4:174). From Girard's point of view, too, the Anaximander fragment expresses a profound, even if not fully conscious, truth, but this has to do with reciprocal violence and its destructive effects, "for the vengeance Anaximander alludes to is wholly human, not divine" (*Violence*, p. 308). Voegelin, he might suspect, unconsciously succumbed to a temptation to cosmize sacrificial violence. One should note in fairness to Voegelin, of course, that far from denying violence, Voegelin interpreted the symbol as meaning that human existence is inherently violent and that our perishing is both a proper punishment for our violence and a deliverance from the power it has within us. Girard, on the other hand, would consider the very idea of a cosmic power inflicting punishment, proper or not, to be a mythifying reflection of our own violence.

Girard would probably be especially critical of the romantic theory of symbolization Voegelin seems to have taken from Schelling regarding the spontaneous and transhuman generation of "primary" symbols. Voegelin and Schelling, as we saw, believed these symbols come to us from the heart of being itself and therefore speak with authority. To Girard this would probably seem just another cosmizing of the mechanisms that govern us; the symbols that we feel to be charged with sacred authority are simply those that image the drama we unconsciously and compulsively enact: the drama of mediation, rivalry, monstrous doubles, and victimization.

He would probably take a similar approach to Ricoeur's theory of "productive imagination": just as Voegelin learned from Schelling to project the symbolizing function onto the level of the cosmos, so Ricoeur learned from Kant to project it onto the level of an equally mythic noumenal self. Both strategies serve to sacralize the human imagination and its products and thereby to obscure their real source in mimetic desire and insulate this from serious criticism.

The tenacity of Ricoeur's basic orientation toward a hermeneutic of faith, Girard might say, prevented him from developing a really penetrating hermeneutic of suspicion. From Girard's point of view the hermeneutic of faith would itself seem largely an expression of the mechanism of mediation: Ricoeur's remedy for the dangers of internal mediation is the development of a highly sophisticated strategy for the support of a process of external mediation—one in which the traditional mythic image of a transcendent God is replaced by the Kantian notion of transcendental mechanisms that function somehow as the equivalent of the old God. Girard would agree, of course, that external mediation has distinct advantages over internal, but he would probably disagree that this can still be an effective option in our world or that its advantages outweigh its disadvantages. As sophisticated as Ricoeur's Kantian framework is, this way of imaging our controlling mechanism remains just one more strategy for masking and sacralizing it, and Girard believes this is a luxury we can no longer afford.

Comparing Girard with Lonergan, one finds considerable convergence in their discussions of objective knowledge. Even considering the issue strictly from the point of view of epistemology, Girard is just as critical as Lonergan of what the latter called "naive realism" and what Girard, following Derrida, refers to as a "metaphysics of presence." In contrast to any hope that the real is what can be known by perception, Girard advocates a science that would recognize the need to move through hypothesis and verification beyond data, which do not of themselves constitute reality: "The hypothesis has the character of science because it is not directly accessible to empirical or phenomenological intuition. For the philosophical mentality that still tends to dominate the sciences of the human, the very notion of hypothesis is inconceivable. All remains subject to an ideal of immediate mastery, of direct contact with givens that constitutes perhaps an aspect of what in our period is called 'metaphysics of presence'" (*Des choses,* pp. 597–98). We would like, that is, to believe that we are objective entities and that we know ourselves by an immediate intuition or perception of our own reality, and we found our supposedly scientific approaches to the study of the human on this naive assumption. In actuality, he goes on to say, "[a] discipline only becomes truly scientific when it renounces that ideal of direct mastery" and reaches beyond the givens toward a principle of systematic intelligibility "inaccessible to direct intuition": "Scientific thinking, in sum, is a sort of canny humility that accepts the separation from givens and seeks further out what it could not discover close up. . . . This separation that renounces a certitude which in reality is only deceptive assures instead the only possibility of verification that interests science" (p. 598).

Despite this area of agreement with Lonergan, however, Girard would be no more inclined than Voegelin or Ricoeur to follow him to the conclusion that what one can know about man, even by hypothesis, is that he is a type of ontological entity, a thinking thing. The hypothetical knowledge Girard believes we can have of man is the knowledge of a process rather than of a thing.

Clearly, therefore, despite the criticism he would offer of Voegelin's and Ricoeur's romantic attitude toward myth, Girard would stand on their side in the controversy over the relative merits of *Existenzerhellung* as compared with metaphysics. Girard's own way of reflecting on man could well be described as a sort of demythologized *Existenzerhellung*. His focus, like that of Jaspers, Marcel, Voegelin, Ricoeur, and, as we shall see, Kierkegaard, is not on the metaphysical objectivity of hypothetical entities but on subjectivity. His own way of elucidating human existence is by bringing to light what we are doing without realizing it in our acts of subjective mimesis and violence.

As was mentioned earlier, Girard calls for a radical deconstruction of metaphysics, which he considers the product of a mistaken concentration on objective, representational mimesis. To carry somewhat further the line of analysis implied by Girard's framework, the emphasis metaphysical thinking places on the objective status of entities would seem a direct outgrowth of the dynamics of mimetic desire itself. If what one seeks above all else in the subject one imitates and the objects he desires is "being," then the mimetic process by its very nature implies what might be called a metaphysical myth, a story of the quest for such "being," and any insufficiently critical metaphysical system would be merely a translation of that myth into technical language. The concern of traditional metaphysics with objective being would seem, therefore, to reflect the philosopher's fascination with the power and mythic self-sufficiency felt to belong to a figure of mediation. Mimetic desire and the fascination of the model-obstacle draws our thinking into a fixation on a reified, or what might be called "thingly," conception of reality (Girard uses the term *chosiste* [*Des choses*, p. 585]), but this is only a mythifying projection that serves to mask the reality of process.

In his *Philosophical Investigations,* Ludwig Wittgenstein said, "A *picture* held us captive. And we could not get outside it, for it lay in our language and our language seemed to repeat it to us inexorably."[11] Girard would probably find such a statement highly appropriate as a description of the way our reifying language reflects and reinforces the power of our reifying thinking, but he would also suggest that the only power such language has derives from the underlying mimetic process of which it is a sort of congealed shadow.

The tendency Ricoeur noted of metaphysical thinking to gravitate toward static abstractions in contrast to the thrust of metaphor toward the dynamic would also consequently be something that Girard would trace to the mimetic mechanism. Girard himself has spoken of this process of abstraction as an expression of the same tendencies that, building on the sacred "difference" discovered in the victim, give rise to the fixing of the mimesis of violence in religious rites: "From Aristotle to structuralism, all systems of static classification are the belated offspring of the ritual mentality. The recent emphasis on differential linguistics is but one more recipe for perpetuating that vast tradition, and behind this, one always finds essentialism, the fundamental Platonism of a philosophy which, from one end of its history to the other, remains faithful to tendencies deriving from the inspiration of ritual" (*La Route antique,* pp. 145–46).

The affinity of Lonergan's metaphysics for the mythic vision is evident from the fact that the supposedly entitative objects he particularly insisted on in the latter half of *Insight* and his later attack on Voegelin were exactly those that would matter most to what Girard calls "metaphysical desire": God and the human subject.[12] If what we seek above all else is the kind of "being" we can claim as our secure possession,

---

11. No. 115, p. 48e.

12. Lonergan's attack on Jaspers and Voegelin in the 1981 interview (discussed above in the Voegelin chapter) would seem suitable for analysis in Girardian terms as a rite of expulsion: the setting was a dialogue in a religious educational institution between a priest and a group of his coreligionists regarding the errors of two religious outsiders, and the shared conclusion of the group had much of the tone of a condemnation for heresy.

then we will be powerfully motivated to interpret this as objective and to attribute it both to ourselves (and therefore to man as such) and to the God we look to as its source. A less perspicacious thinker than Lonergan might also have sought support for his metaphysical desire in what he called the "naive realist" vision of a world of "already, out, there, now, real" things, but, as was discussed earlier, he rejected that in favor of a "critical realism" in keeping with the implications of generalized scientific method. Lonergan's approach to the objective world through an analysis of human "interiority" in terms of cognitional theory could be said therefore to have constituted a partial demythologizing of traditional metaphysics and epistemology. But he did not carry this demythologizing as far as Voegelin did. Voegelin's critique of the hypostatizing of the poles of our experienced "tension of existence" as "God" and "man" was a further step in exposing the mythic character of these images.

Ironically, Voegelin, despite his rather romantic conception of the authority of myth, would probably seem less mythic a thinker from Girard's point of view than Lonergan, who was so dismissive of myth—and probably for that very reason. Voegelin may not have reflected fully on the more sinister implications of myth, but at least he recognized its role in our thought, whereas Lonergan's rationalistic assumption that myth contracts as metaphysics advances seduced him into thinking that the two are neatly separable and that philosophy leaves myth behind.

The hypostatizing of the human subject as an objective reality is probably even harder to give up than the idea of an entitative God. Freud, for example, readily dismissed God as a "projection," but he was much less inclined to question the objective status of the human subject, even if he did disapprove of the fascination it tends to have for us. Freud's theory of "narcissism" was founded on the idea that the self exercises the same objective power to elicit desire as does a member of the opposite sex. He said, as was mentioned earlier, that man has two original sexual objects: one is the woman who nurtures him, the other himself. Freud looked upon the Oedipus complex, founded on object-desire for the mother, as a problem, but not a pernicious one; the libido needed only to be redirected to a different woman to become socially valuable. Narcissism, on the other hand, he stigmatized as inherently "regressive" and antisocial. He seemed to feel that the subject's power of self-attraction was virtually demonic and needed to be strenuously opposed. Girard has characterized this aspect of Freud's thought as a reflection of mythic thinking: "In the light of the mimetic theory one can easily see that the great division Freud makes between Oedipal object-desire on the one hand and narcissistic regression on the other cannot stand; it is rooted in Freud's strong tendency to discriminate between meritorious desires and unmeritorious ones and to turn loose on the latter the victimizing mechanisms which psychoanalysis is incapable of criticizing because it espouses them, because they remain foundational for it just as they remain foundational for all mythology" (*Des choses*, pp. 527–28).

Freudian psychology, too, like some of the other systems of thought we have been discussing, could be described as a partial demythologizing that stops short of actually extricating itself from the power of the mimetic mechanism. In his own treatment of the phenomena Freud classified under the heading of narcissism, Girard offers an alternative analysis that he believes not only can explain them fully but can account for the fear and fascination Freud himself felt in the presence of a narcissistic personality: "The intact narcissism of the other is the ineffable paradise where there seem to live beings who . . . give us the impression that no obstacle thwarts them and that they lack nothing. This impression . . . becomes blended with the impression that they have no need of us. . . . Their plenitude is assured; having nothing to desire beyond themselves, they attract all desires like magnets and force all men of duty such as Freud to desire them, at least a little" (p. 520). Freud consequently feared the magnetism of the narcissistic personality and felt a need to resist it.

In this, according to Girard, Freud fell victim to a myth of his own imagining. In reality there is no such personality; every human being feels the same inner emptiness and seeks to fill it in the same way: through the mediation of others. "The self-sufficiency" Freud believed in, says Girard, "is not to be found on this earth; it is the last glimmer of the sacred" (p. 521). Freud's coquette who seems so self-contained, even as she excites the desire of others, is herself dependent on their eyes to mediate for her the sense of her own desirability, on which her air of self-sufficiency is founded. She can desire herself only by inwardly imitating their desire for her, just as they imitate the desire they believe she feels for herself (pp. 513–14). In the case of Freud's theory of infantile "primary narcissism," which he thought of as the source of all of our self-interested behavior, Girard says Freud "confused, in sum, the most deceptive shimmerings of metaphysical desire with the elementary vital force" (p. 521).

Narcissistic self-absorption and self-sufficiency is a mythic vision of subjectivity, and one that seems to hold fascination for all of us, not just Freud. We all find it attractive, because at base we would all like it to be true; we would all like, at some level of our desiring lives, to be such a subject. "Object-oriented desire," says Girard, "dreams of intact narcissism because it dreams of that absolute and indestructible being who has the power of violence over all around him" (p. 521). It is this dream, Girard would probably say, that lies behind any philosophical theory that attempts to ground belief in an entitative subject. Any such theory is an attempt to close the circle of desire, uniting subject and object in a mythical self-sufficiency.

Girard's criticism of the idea of a metaphysical subject is more radical than that of any thinker we have considered so far. He has no use for the theory of a subject-entity in any of its traditional forms, either in philosophy or psychology. It was mentioned earlier that he rejected Freud's assumption regarding the power of objects to cause desire. He is no more inclined to speak of desire as originating from a subject. "I avoid speaking of a 'desiring subject,'" he says, "lest I give the impression of falling back into a psychology of the subject" (p. 428). The entire pattern of thought that gives rise to such thinking "rests on the heritage of romantic individualism, which is more alive now than ever despite the superficial criticisms it has been subjected to" (p. 428). They are all the more provocative in being closely linked in his thought to the idea of God and in being worked out primarily in connection with his discussion of the Judeo-Christian scriptures. The material for this is to be found primarily in *Des choses cachées* and *La Route antique*. In our earlier discussion of Girard's treatment of the themes of divinity and subjectivity it must have seemed that he would interpret both notions as simply mythic. In fact he considers almost all traditional thinking on either topic to be strongly imbued with mythologizing tendencies, but at the same time he does not consider that to be the whole of the matter. Rather he takes both topics quite seriously and thinks there is something genuinely important they point to, even if it is not easy to find a language for it that does not draw us back into the sacrificial mentality and the temptations of metaphysical desire.

His concern with both topics is a function of his belief that in our time we can no longer afford to indulge in violence and in the traditional remedies for it, which are themselves only controlled applications of its power. What interests Girard in the Judeo-Christian scriptures is the way they began from a mythological notion of the divine but also subjected it over time to a criticism that points beyond that—from a notion of God as the personification of supreme violence and coercive power to that of a radically nonviolent God, a "God of victims" who "could not impose his will on men without ceasing to be himself" (*La Route antique,* p. 226). Much of the biblical tradition consists of expressions of our all-too-human longing for a God who can exercise violence on our behalf, but gradually out of that very tradition, suggests Girard, emerged a radical critique of the idea of divine violence. It developed out of the gradually dawning realization that a truly world-transcendent God could not ask for sacrifices and could not be motivated by antagonisms and desires like our own; and it culminated, according to Girard's analysis, in the radically nonviolent God of Jesus and his Gospel, a God who does not intervene in the world by force and who would not impose what we could agree in calling justice, since our agreement and our justice are always founded on "mimetism" and mixed with vengeance (p. 226).

It is by the same process as that which led to the emergence of the idea of a truly transcendent, nonviolent God, Girard thinks, that genuine subjectivity also entered history. The two, in fact, are directly linked for Girard. In *Des choses cachées,* at a certain point in the dialogue he is carrying on with his two interlocutors, one of them, Jean-Michel Oughourlian, comments, "If I follow your reasoning, the genuine human *subject* can emerge only from the rule of the Kingdom; apart from that, there is never anything but mimetism and the '*interdividuel.*' Until then, the only subject is the mimetic structure itself," and Girard responds, "Precisely" (p. 292).

The term *interdividuel,* as was mentioned at the beginning of this chapter, is a Girardian coinage for the type of psychology he opposes to Freud's. It refers to the idea that we are not the "individuals" our romanticism would lead us to suppose. Rather our psychic life takes place as an interaction in a field of forces that is inherently multiple, articulated inwardly as a set of relations among imitator, mediators, and objects.[13] To say that the *interdividuel* is the real subject of our acts is to say that the process of mimetic desire itself is their hidden source, even if we would like to attribute them to a conscious and truly autonomous center of individual subjectivity within our personalities. At other points Girard also says that "violence . . . is always in the final analysis the true *subject* of every ritual, institutional, or other structure" (p. 306) or that mimetic desire is the subject (p. 428).

In reply to the question whether he is not implicitly hypostatizing desire, Girard denies that this is his meaning. What he thinks himself is that although the very notion of a "subject" reflects a naive conception of subjectivity, if one wishes to use that term more carefully, it can only refer in reality to the false, imaginary subjectivity of the mechanism of mimetic desire. In our ordinary usage, we use the term "subject" to refer to a supposed objectively real, autonomous, conscious source of intentions. This is what, for the purposes of the present discussion, we might term an "objective-subject." Girard, however, thinks even our conscious (or better, semiconscious) actions normally spring from a hidden source that itself is merely unconscious mimetic mechanism and blind violence. It would make his point clearer perhaps if Girard spoke of this mechanistic source not as a "subject" but a "quasi-subject," and

13. It is perhaps worth mentioning at this point, even if it anticipates a later discussion, that in his *Un Mime nommé désir* Jean-Michel Oughourlian has taken off from Girard's suggestive starting point to develop an extensive critique of the idea of a subject from the point of view of psychotherapy. He suggests that the idea of a psychological "ego" or "self" (*moi*) as a "subsistent structure of a monadic subject" is a mythic construction (p. 27) and that the "ego" or "self" is in reality a product of the movements of desire (p. 26). Traditional psychologies of intersubjective relation, he says, have begun with the assumption that prior to such relations there are preexisting subjects. Oughourlian replaces the notion of such a subject with that of what, following Arthur Koestler's *Janus*, he terms a "holon," by which he means a structured psychological unit in process (p. 32) that develops as a *moi* by way of and in absolute dependence upon the *interdividuel* relationship in which it is involved with another holon that becomes to it a model, obstacle, or rival. It is the relationship, in other words, that is fundamental, not the entities related. In contrast to traditional relational psychologies, he says, *la psychologie interdividuelle* "studies the *rapport interdividuel* which engenders by its movement even that in each holon that may be designated its *moi*. It is not the encounter of two selves that creates the relation; it is the relation that gives birth to each of the selves" (p. 305). The implications of Oughourlian's development of this line of analysis will be discussed further in the final chapter of this study.

in fact he does come quite close to making this very distinction when, elaborating on his idea of violence as *"le véritable sujet,"* the real subject of our action, he says that this is "the *Adversary par excellence* of the establishment of the Kingdom of God. It is the devil of tradition, he of whom theology affirms both that he is a subject and that nevertheless he is not one" (p. 306).

If the mimetic mechanism, then, is the false subjectivity underlying our illusion of autonomous individuality, where does Girard think genuine subjectivity is to be found? Oughourlian suggested, and Girard agreed, that it could be found only where the Kingdom of God is. In a further unfolding of the implications of this idea, Girard says, "If violence is the subject of every mythical and cultural structure, then Christ himself is the one subject who escapes from that structure in order to liberate us from its grip" (pp. 318–19). This, he says, is the real significance of the idea that Christ is God. Only when the nonviolent God breaks into our lives from within to overthrow the victimizing mechanism so that transcendent love becomes the source of our actions does our humanity become genuinely subjective for the first time. It becomes subjective in the sense that, with mimetic desire seen through and renounced, we can experience a new freedom consciously to choose a course of action that is free from its power. And the initiative for this can only come from beyond our ordinary humanity, which otherwise would be held firmly by the mechanism that has always controlled us:

> The arising of such a being from within a world entirely governed by violence and the myths of violence is impossible. To understand that one can only see and make known the truth if one takes the position of the victim, one must occupy that position oneself, and to do so in the required way, one must already possess the truth. One can only apprehend that truth, on the other hand, if one acts in a way that is contrary to the laws of violence, and yet one can do so only if one already apprehends it. All of humanity is locked in that vicious circle. This is why the gospels, the New Testament in general, and the theology of the first councils declare that Christ is God—not because he was crucified, but because he is God born of God from eternity. (Pp. 317–18)

The only truly conscious freedom, that is, and therefore the only genuine subjectivity we can experience, is that which the New Testament calls "Christ in us," the inward presence of the God of nonviolent love as the subjective principle of our actions. We like to think of ourselves as autonomous, individual subjects, but in the picture Girard sketches out on the basis of his reading of the New Testament, this is only a self-flattering illusion that our very emptiness leads us to cling to. Before the one source of genuine freedom enters our lives and becomes the fountainhead of true subjectivity—which is Christ's life in us—we are only the puppets of mimetic desire.

To cast this way of thinking in the language that would speak of "a subject," we would have to say that the incarnate Son of God is the true self of all mankind—the potential self of those still held captive in unconsciousness, and the actual self of anyone who rises to new life in him. Continuing in that language, and Girard himself has actually spoken in something very like this way, one could also say that just as in the life of the Kingdom Christ is the true self of redeemed mankind, so also in the kingdom of the Adversary, Sin is the true self of those in bondage: "At a certain depth there is no difference between our own secret and the secret of Others. Everything is revealed to the novelist when he penetrates this Self, a truer Self than that which each of us displays. This Self imitates constantly, on its knees before the mediator. This profound Self is also a universal Self" (Deceit, p. 298).

Such a way of thinking can only appear confused from the point of view of the ordinary mentality of mankind, which can be expected to try to improve upon it by straightening it out so that it will make sense. We would like such phrases to make sense in terms of our habitual patterns of thought, according to which we believe in autonomous subjectivity and radically individual selfhood, in a God of coercive power, in sacrificial substitution, and in the absolute difference between the sacred victim and ourselves. It is a natural human impulse to want to improve the story of the God who entered the world as a powerless victim and invited us to give up our claims to autonomous selfhood and share his very subjectivity, which he declared to be the only true life of man as well as God. It is out of this quite understandable and historically inevitable impulse that Girard believes the Christian religion began interpreting Jesus's death as an expiatory sacrifice, with all that this implies regarding divine violence and a sacred victim.

Girard calls this the "sacrificial reading" of the story of Jesus, and the religion springing from it he calls "historical Christianity" (Des choses, p. 324). He sees this remythifying sacrificial interpretation as beginning already in the New Testament itself, especially in the Epistle to the Hebrews, and he believes such textual refiguring was subsequently carried over into new victimizing action: " ... the persecuting character of historical Christianity is tied," he says, "to the sacrificial definition of the passion and redemption" (p. 325).

This, of course, makes it clear that Girard could hardly be an apologist for the traditional Christian religion. But at the same time it also shows why he is as much opposed to the antireligion that would make a new sacrifice of historical Christianity as he is to the sacrificial religion itself. If at the heart of the tradition is a new sacralizing of violence, there is also something else there that works in direct opposition to that: the New Testament's preservation of liberating insights into the source of violence. "Traditional Christian thinkers," he says, "recognize only the break between Christianity and all the rest of religion, but they have no way of explaining it. Anti-Christian thinkers recognize only the continuity, but without understanding what it really is" (p. 608). He goes on to say that he has found scarcely anyone except Paul Ricoeur who insists on taking both aspects of the tradition seriously, "especially in his fine work on *The Symbolism of Evil.*"

A valuable comparison can be made between the tenor of Girard's thought and that of Ricoeur in that work. As was discussed in the preceding chapter, Ricoeur engages there in a gradual exfoliation of the roots of human evil by tracing backwards from the speculative doctrine of Original Sin through multiple layers of metaphorical symbols toward an elusive, radically subjective source of evil, which he considers real in some sense but objectively unknowable. This, as we saw, makes for the ambiguity in Ricoeur's thought reflected in his use of paradoxical imagery, such as the "servile will" that is simultaneously enslaved and self-determining.

From a Girardian point of view this way of thinking would seem both true and incomplete. Its truth lies in the fact that the paradox negates the objectivistic implications of the imagery and thereby functions as a sign of the mystery of subjectivity. Its incompleteness lies in the fact that it does not distinguish sufficiently between what is actually a mystery and what is a problem that we need to penetrate. The true mystery of subjectivity for Girard is that of the genuine, transcendent subjectivity manifested in Christ. Sin, on the other hand, is a problem with a solution, and he believes the New Testament preserves, despite any residual mythologizing, the insights that solve it.

An example Girard gives special attention to is the New Testament's analysis of the *skandalon* or "stumbling block." This is an image he says few exegetes have ever discussed in more than a cursory manner, but in it he sees a particularly penetrating analysis of the power that binds us. This is the power of the *interdividuel,* and in particular of the fascination with the model-obstacle: "If one considers all the uses of the term . . . one cannot help but conclude that the *skandalon* is the obstacle in mimetic rivalry, the model inasmuch as he blocks the undertakings of the disciple and becomes for him an inexhaustible source of mimetic fascination" (p. 574). If the Biblical translators did not try so hard to find more "intelligible" alternatives for the term *skandalon,* it would be easier for us to see that it always refers to "the obsessive obstacle that excites under our feet mimetic desire, with all its vain ambitions and absurd resentments. . . . It is the temptation *par excellence* of the model who attracts us inasmuch as he is an obstacle and poses an obstacle inasmuch as he attracts us" (p. 574).

Children are especially vulnerable to the effect of such morbid fascination, says Girard, because they thirst avidly for models and submit to their authority with so little capacity for critical reflection; this is why Jesus emphasizes so strongly the evil of "scandalizing" them in Matthew 18:5–7. The power of the *skandalon* is shown as a temptation for Jesus as well in various passages, such as the scene in which he rebukes Peter, "Get behind me, Satan! You are a *skandalon* to me, because your thoughts are not those of God but those of men" (Matt. 16:23). Peter and the other disciples, moreover, make Jesus himself into a *skandalon* by interpreting him as a traditional messianic figure with power to triumph over his enemies by force.

They and those like them are even scandalized or "tripped up" by God, says Girard: "The God of the Bible is at one and the same time the unchanging rock, the refuge that never fails, and, for those intent upon idolatry, the obstacle *par excellence,* by the very fact that he deprives them of the altars that served them for support and assured the precarious equilibrium of their communities" (p. 580). This is a theme, he says, that was anticipated by Isaiah when he said of God: "He is the sanctuary and the stumbling-block and the rock upon which the two houses of Israel fall; a trap, a snare for the people of Jerusalem" (Is. 8:14). God and all the sacred imagery of the Biblical tradition constitute such a snare and a scandal: a temptation to idolatry and, through the Biblical critique itself, a wily undercutting of that very idolatry that leaves the idolizers in what amounts to a reverse image of the doublebind. This is the ironic effect of a demythologizing that emerges from the midst of the mythic tradition itself by what Girard believes is an inexorable logic in the mimetic process driving it toward its own exposure—Girard's equivalent of the providential philosophy of history Voegelin found in Augustine's image of exodus from the city of sin to the city of God. The New Testament completes the demythologizing of the stumblingblock and exposes the roots of our obsessiveness in a way that, if we can grasp its actual message rather than succumb to the temptations of a new mythology, still offers genuine liberation from it.

This exposure of the mechanism of the model-obstacle as the radical source of human evil offers a solution to the problem Ricoeur sensed in his paradoxes as well as a revelation of the mystery he sensed there also. It solves the problem of the enslaved will by showing how it is enslaved and also by making clear that it lacks the genuine subjectivity that would give it the power of conscious self-determination. The mechanism of self-enslavement is in reality no mystery, according to Girard, but is objectively knowable in the manner of a scientific hypothesis regarding the socio-psychological phenomenon of the *interdividuel*. What the exposure of this mechanism discloses is that, although it is "subjective" in the sense that it is within us, the root of human evil is not subjective at all in the sense of being a conscious source of free action. Rather it is the inner unconscious source of enslaved action.

The true mystery of subjectivity, on the other hand, is the consciousness that enters human life as transcendent love in the same moment that it breaks the power of the unconscious mechanism that held sway there. It is in the genuine subjectivity of conscious freedom that we can discover the mystery to which the "who" question referred to earlier points. The mechanism of mimetic desire, no matter what the power and complexity it can take on as it weaves itself into our lives, is only a "what." But the "who" is a mystery that Girard, too, finds himself forced to speak of, like Voegelin and Ricoeur, in the language of myth and metaphor, the symbolism of God as love and liberating light and of Christ as the incarnation of God.

Girard's writings so far touch only briefly on this mystery that catches us by surprise at the end of the journey through the labyrinth of the self. He has no special language of his own for it, but what his reflections point toward seems in fact very like what Voegelin used his images of existential tension and the pull of the golden cord to suggest: the idea that we are drawn ultimately not by any object but by the appeal of true subjectivity. We may mistakenly believe the source of the pull lies in some form of object, perhaps even an objectified God, but when we do, it is only the effect of our projecting outward a presence that is actually inward and unobjectifiable: the divine Beyond that Voegelin said is at the same time a divine Within. The same way of thinking seems suggested by Lonergan's idea of the transcendental notion, if what this really means, as was suggested earlier, is that we are drawn ultimately in intentional operations by an anticipation of what it would be like actually to perform them. It is also the meaning of Ricoeur's Heideggerian "preunderstanding" that is the dim image in our own incomplete subjectivity of the eternal *Verbum* we seek to express in our *verba*.

An implication of this line of thinking is that properly to appreciate the mystery of subjectivity one must find one's way past two pitfalls that seem to lie always in the path of our thought: objectivism and subjectivism. Perhaps one reason they are so difficult to avoid is that they are so closely linked. Objectivism we might describe as the belief that the ultimate factor in consciousness and in reality as a whole is objects. This can take the form Girard describes in his account of Freud's libido-psychology, or the form Lonergan called "naive realism," or it can also take the form of obsessions with objects of mimesis and desire. Subjectivism might seem its opposite, but in reality it is only more of the same: it believes there is a special type of object called a "subject," to which it attributes preeminent active and attractive power. Subjectivism is just the reverse face, one might say, of the objectivist coin.

One of the great values of Girard's analysis of human psychology is that it offers something that may be much more effective than a philosophical critique of these tendencies of thought. He makes it clear to us why both objectivism and subjectivism appeal to us so strongly: without the combination of ego-transcending insight and love which alone can grant us genuine subjectivity, we are incurable idolaters. A world without a point of focus, inward or outward, for our fascinations would be a world we could scarcely endure.

According to Girard's reading of the New Testament, Jesus is presented as breaking decisively with that fascination when he rejected Satan's appeal in the desert.[14] This was a temptation for Jesus to turn aside from the true God in order to possess all the objects of the world and rejoice in his own glory as an individual objective-subject. The implication is that unless we can do as Christ did and endure the emptiness left behind by the departure of the Adversary we will not be able to share the life he won for us by his victory. Nor will we even be able to think coherently about that life and the possibility of sharing it.

Perhaps it is the twin lure of objectivism and subjectivism that has made it so difficult for Christians to think in any but a metaphorical way about the saying that Christ's own subjectivity can be truly ours as well, that the incarnate Son of God can live in us and we in him. A passage in one of the interviews with Lonergan in *Caring About Meaning* seems an example of the slight awkwardness and embarrassment that so often seems to come into Christian thought when it is suggested that such Biblical expressions are to be taken seriously. As was discussed earlier, when Lonergan was teaching at the Gregorian University, he wrote a Latin treatise on "Christ as Subject" as a text for his course on Christology. That work was quite original for a Catholic theologian of his generation in broaching the question of the human subjectivity of Jesus, but it was also traditional in the sense that it interpreted Jesus as a divine-human "subject" in the conventional sense of the term (i.e., an objective-subject). In the interview Lonergan was asked about his interest in "Christ as person" and if his focus on the theme of "the subject" in his various writings was connected with that and with the idea of the Mystical Body. His answers seemed to reflect both an elusiveness of thought and an ambiguity of feeling that drew comment from one of the interviewers:

> C[harlotte] T[ansey]: You had a legitimation to go ahead with the notion of 'subject' because Christians were other Christs—would you say that?
>
> B. Lonergan: I wouldn't quote Mersch that far, you know. For me, phrases like that are repetitious: they *are* other Christs; *cor Christi, cor Pauli,* the heart of Paul is the heart of Christ; or, *ego*

14. Cf. Oughourlian's interpretation of the devil as mimetic desire in *Un Mime nommé désir,* pp. 97–98.

vivo, jam non ego sed Christus ["I live, yet not I but Christ..."
(Galatians 2:20)].
C.T.: I think we are now trying to find with you a pattern, or to sharpen
    one—but you outwit us at every turn.
B.Lonergan: Not intentionally.
C.T.: You are warning us not to oversimplify?
B.Lonergan: That would be one way of putting it.[15]

Of course to oversimplify the idea of the union of Christians with
Christ in a subjectivistic manner—an easy temptation in the tradition of
thought and language that prevails in our world—would be to invite an
ego-inflation that could be the worst possible way of yielding to the
power of the *skandalon*. Lonergan may well have felt this danger and
been wise in dodging it. In what Girard calls "historical Christianity"
the usual answer to this problem has been an objectivizing interpretation that makes idols of both Jesus and God.

But this too is a submission to the *skandalon*, even if it is a safer one
than the other for the Christian community. Unless a way can be found
to make sense of the idea of the new life in Christ in a way that is neither
objectivistic nor subjectivistic there will be no possibility of hearing the
liberating truth Girard thinks the Gospel expresses. One of the rare figures in the Christian tradition who has not only addressed this issue but
has made its paradox the center of his own philosophical reflections on
human subjectivity, is the one with whom the present study will conclude: Søren Kierkegaard.

15. *Caring About Meaning*, pp. 151–52.

CHAPTER 6

Søren Kierkegaard

Consciousness

as Incarnate Subjectivity

OF THE THINKERS this book studies, Kierkegaard is both the best
known—in the sense that he is widely read—and the most difficult to
know. It is not just that the problems he took up are inherently difficult
and that he strove to make us aware of that (one of his narrators,
Johannes Climacus, once said that his special mission in an age of systematic solutions was to make thinking difficult again).[1] It is also that
Kierkegaard pursued this end by driving his reader to reach beyond
ideas and arguments toward an existential self-discovery. He drives us,
that is, to realize our active involvement in a struggle for subjective existence. This is a struggle, moreover, that we are led to realize we share
with the author—or, to be more precise, with one or more of the author's *personae,* the masks or pseudonymous authors through whose
voices Kierkegaard addresses us and in whom he images for us not only
his own subjective presence but ours as well.

In one respect the difficulty of Kierkegaard's thought should be
reduced somewhat by the chapters that have preceded, since, as has
been discussed, several of the figures we have been studying—especially
Voegelin and Ricoeur—were influenced by Kierkegaard's
questions and his approach to philosophy. This should have the effect
of rendering his issues already familiar to some degree. A more direct
consideration of Kierkegaard's own treatment of the same issues should
make still clearer the nature of the problems his successors have been

---

1. *Concluding Unscientific Postscript to the Philosophical Fragments,* trans. David F.
Swenson and Walter Lowrie, pp. 165–67.

wrestling with. Kierkegaard himself was not concerned with offering definite answers to the problems he addressed. Rather he insistently called attention to them precisely as problems, and much of the line of inquiry we have been concerned with—especially that which has to do with the relation between the subjective and objective aspects or poles of consciousness—has been a prolonged response to the questions he raised regarding the earlier treatment of this theme in the tradition of Kant, Fichte, Schelling, and Hegel.

This focus in Kierkegaard on problems rather than on answers explains his characteristic tendency to speak to us through *personae* rather than in his own voice. He tried to make us aware of the complexity of the problems that interested him by getting us to look at them from a variety of angles. His writings considered collectively, therefore, tend to take on the character of an extended philosophical dialogue between different points of view rather than the more familiar one of a systematic exposition of one particular point of view.

This is not to deny, of course, that there are many specific philosophical claims that Kierkegaard advanced in his writings and that his various *personae* agree upon sufficiently that they may be said to represent a Kierkegaardian framework of thought. These, however, do not resolve the ultimate problems Kierkegaard sought to open up to us; rather they constitute essential points in the approach to those problems. An example that will be discussed shortly is Kierkegaard's conception of the nature of subjectivity and its relation to objectivity. Another is the distinction he makes between subjective and objective existence. These are matters he did not consider seriously controversial, even if he disagreed on them with the more fashionable thinkers of his time. With regard to the ultimate issues, on the other hand, such as the relation between man and God or between the believer and the savior—questions that reach toward the ultimate "who" at the core of subjective existence—his concern was not to persuade us of the truth of some solution but to elicit genuine philosophical wonder and active thinking. This means that the difficulty of Kierkegaard's thought is the difficulty of following him in his wonder, not the difficulty of figuring out how he might have brought that wonder to an end with an answer.

Even if this is acknowledged, however, it may be difficult for many readers to shake free from a desire to know "Kierkegaard's view," and some may find the present chapter rather frustrating because it does not

seek to develop and prove a particular interpretation of "what Kierkegaard meant" regarding the most searching questions he raised. Since
we have just finished considering the thought of a thinker, René Girard,
who had something to say about the kinds of desire that can grip us, it
may be worth taking a moment to consider how Girard's analysis of human psychology might be applied to the problem we tend to have in
reading Kierkegaard.

Girard emphasized the power of the instinctual drive that moves us to
imitate others, and he spoke of the resulting need we feel for what he
calls a "mediator." The mediator is a model we try to imitate in the
hope that through mimesis not only of his gestures but also of his intentions we may put on the power we feel him to have and may thereby acquire "real being." Without such a figure to imitate we feel vulnerable,
and we hope that a successful imitation will deliver us into a state of in-
vulnerability. This insight can be applied to our relation to an author
like Kierkegaard: whenever we approach a figure who has been ac-
corded prestige and authority by widespread recognition, we tend to
feel his power as a mediator. Sometimes we approach him admiringly
and seek to share in his glory through understanding and adopting his
ideas, in which case he becomes for us what Girard calls an "external
mediator." Or we may approach him with distrust or hostility, seeking
to master his thought only to dismiss it. In this case he becomes for us a
rival or obstacle, an example of what we saw Girard call an "internal
mediator." There are better ways to approach an author than either of
these, but it would be a rare reader who is fully immune to the attractive
power of a figure who, like Kierkegaard, has come to be so widely
quoted and admired in our world. It should hardly be surprising, therefore, if one finds oneself recurrently drawn to wonder "what Kierkegaard really intended" and even to feel existential anxiety over how one
can be certain one really knows that intention.

The latter problem, of how one can know with certainty the mind of
a past historical personage, is analogous to the one Kierkegaard addressed (or rather Johannes Climacus addressed) in the *Concluding Unscientific Postscript* when he took up the question whether historical
knowledge of the life of Jesus could attain certainty—and whether this
mattered. The simple answer to the first question is that all knowledge
of historical fact is only probable, so that certainty in history is an ever-

receding goal that one can approach only by an infinite process of approximation. What interested Kierkegaard more was why we feel that this matters, why such certainty fascinates us. In this, as we shall see, he seems to have anticipated Girard's critique of mediations as well as his critique of the conventional notion of a "subject." That discussion will have to wait, however, until we have considered a theme that Kierkegaard himself presents as an essential preliminary: that of human fallibility and fault, or, in his own more theological language, sin.

This is a theme as central to Kierkegaard's thought as to that of Ricoeur or Girard. In *The Sickness Unto Death*, which Kierkegaard published in 1849, his *persona*, Anti-Climacus, said, "I steadfastly hold to the Christian teaching that sin is a position [i.e., a positive reality, not a mere deficiency, or aspect of our finitude]—yet not as if it could be comprehended, but as a paradox that must be believed."[2] As an advocate of dogmatic belief, Anti-Climacus is the explicitly Christian counterpart to Johannes Climacus, the pseudonymous author of the *Philosophical Fragments* and *Concluding Unscientific Postscript*, who had approached Kierkegaard's topics, including the paradox of sin, from the point of view of the type of philosophy current in German universities in that period.

The two voices are not to be interpreted as antithetical, however, but complementary. As the Hongs wrote in their introduction to *The Sickness Unto Death*, "The prefix 'Anti' may be misleading. . . . It does not mean 'against.' It is an old form of 'ante' (before), as in 'anticipate,' and 'before' also denotes a relation of rank, as in 'before me' in the First Commandment" (p. xxii). Kierkegaard himself, in his *Journals*, described the relation in terms of degrees of ascent on a scale of understanding and spiritual development: "Johannes Climacus and Anti-Climacus have several things in common; but the difference is that whereas Johannes Climacus places himself so low that he even says himself that he is not a Christian, one seems to be able to detect in Anti-Climacus that he regards himself to be a Christian on an extraordinarily high level. . . . I would place myself higher than Johannes Climacus, lower than Anti-Climacus" (quoted in *Sickness*, p. xxii).

2. *The Sickness Unto Death: A Christian Psychological Exposition for Upbuilding and Awakening*, ed. and trans. Howard V. Hong and Edna H. Hong, p. 98.

Another way to state the relation between these *personae* can be taken from the meaning of the name Climacus, which comes from the Greek *klimakis,* meaning a staircase or ladder.[3] If Anti-Climacus stands above Johannes in the sense of having mounted higher, then for Kierkegaard it is because faith in the proper sense is not blind assent or dogmatism, but something that properly develops only on the basis of the fullest possible clarification of issues. Anti-Climacus represents in religion a position one can arrive at only after ascending the ladder of intelligent inquiry. There is a religiosity that favors incomprehensibility as an easy way of avoiding the demands of inquiry, but Kierkegaard considered this a sham; any earnest seeker of what Kierkegaard called "existential truth," which cannot itself be an object of intellection, must also be in earnest about understanding what *can* be understood. "Faith," as Johannes Climacus puts it, *"must* not *rest content* with unintelligibility; for precisely the relation to or the repulsion from the unintelligible, the absurd, is the expression for the passion of faith."[4]

The claim of Anti-Climacus that sin is a paradox that must be believed even if it cannot be comprehended is therefore not at all an expression of irrationalism. Rather he gives voice to a position arrived at by a thorough investigation of the possibilities of understanding, and he speaks in opposition to other, more common voices in the religious tradition that have assumed too easily that sin can be intellectually comprehended as though it were an idea. When Anti-Climacus says, "If all attempts to comprehend can just be shown to be self-contradictory, then the matter will fall into proper perspective" (*Sickness*, p. 98), behind this statement lies the work of an earlier *persona*, Vigilius Haufnensis of *The Concept of Anxiety,* who demonstrated at length that very self-contradictoriness.

Ironically, the latter work, which is subtitled "A Simple Psychologically Orienting Deliberation on the Dogmatic Issue of Hereditary Sin," as though it were to be an exposition of the familiar Augustinian doc-

---

3. The name alludes to St. John Climacus, a seventh-century anchorite of Mount Sinai who was famous for his learning and especially for his book, *The Ladder of Paradise,* a guide to the spiritual life in thirty steps.

4. *Concluding Unscientific Postscript to the Philosophical Fragments,* trans. David F. Swenson and Walter Lowrie, p. 540. This volume will subsequently be referred to as *Postscript.*

trine, presents a more thoroughgoing demolition of that speculative doctrine than even Ricoeur does in his essay "Original Sin: A Study in Meaning," referred to above in the chapter on Ricoeur.[5] In fact, the first part of *The Concept of Anxiety* takes up every explanation of sin that has been offered in the Christian traditions of both West and East and shows that all of them (and by implication any others that might be advanced) are necessarily self-contradictory—in that any explanation of sin must presuppose some cause for it, and the presupposition of a cause must negate the one thing that is absolutely essential if it is to be considered sin: that it has no objective cause.[6] The mistake in asking questions about sin, says Vigilius, lies in asking them as questions "directed to science"—that is, as questions about something objectively explainable.[7] Rather the question about sin is a question about oneself: "Every science lies either in a logical immanence or in an immanence within a transcendence that it is unable to explain. Now sin is precisely that transcendence, that *discrimen rerum* [crisis] in which sin enters into the single individual as the single individual. Sin never enters into the world differently and has never entered differently. So when the single individual is stupid enough to inquire about sin as if it were something foreign to him, he only asks as a fool, for either he does not know at all what the question is about, and thus cannot come to know it, or he knows it and understands it, and also knows that no science can explain it to him" (p. 50).

If one does "understand" sin, one does so not by way of a comprehension of ideas but by way of an earnest inward struggle. As Vigilius stated it in his introduction, "according to its true concept, sin is to be overcome" (p. 15). To understand sin one must not approach it in an attitude of objective curiosity; "the proper mood is earnestness expressed in courageous resistance" (p. 15).

5. In *The Conflict of Interpretations,* pp. 269–86.
6. Cf. Lonergan, *Caring About Meaning,* pp. 149–50: "If you have the distinction between the intelligible and the unintelligible, the chief instance of the unintelligible, of the surd, is sin. ('Why did Adam sin? why did the angels sin?' If there were a reason it would not be a sin.) It is a pure case of the irrational." Cf. also *Insight,* pp. 666–67, where Lonergan describes the basic sin as "contraction of consciousness" (with the effect that intelligent deliberation is precluded) and goes on to say that "all that intelligence can grasp with respect to basic sins is that there is no intelligibility to be grasped."
7. *The Concept of Anxiety,* ed. and trans. Reidar Thomte with the collaboration of Albert B. Anderson, p. 50.

In Kierkegaard's writings, sin is not an intentional object of any sort. Rather, to speak of sin is to speak indirectly and in a quasi-objectifying way about repentance. And repentance is subjective: it is an act one performs. The importance of repentance is that it is essential to the process in which, to use Kierkegaard's language, one comes to exist as a subject. As he put the matter in the religious language of Vigilius, "In turning toward himself, he *eo ipso* turns toward God, and there is a ceremonial rule that says that when the finite spirit would see God, it must begin as guilty" (p. 107). Or as he put it in the complementary philosophical language of Johannes Climacus, "the essential consciousness of guilt is the first deep plunge into existence, and at the same time it is the expression for the fact that an exister is related to an eternal happiness" (*Postscript,* p. 473).

That consciousness of guilt is an essential feature of the process of coming to exist, and that this involves a relation to an eternal happiness, is the heart of the matter. To understand what this means, however, we will first have to work out an understanding of a number of key notions in Kierkegaard's thought—among them existence, eternity, subjectivity, objectivity, and belief or faith.

It will be helpful to begin with a consideration of Kierkegaard's conception of objectivity—both because it is the simplest to grasp and because addressing it should help to correct the common misunderstanding of Kierkegaard as an irrationalist. That he should be thought so is probably due to the great emphasis he placed on the importance of subjectivity, as in his famous dictum, from the *Postscript,* that "truth is subjectivity."[8] Many who have heard this phrase but have not carefully read Kierkegaard himself assume that it implies a glorification of irrational arbitrariness. That this is not the case, however, Kierkegaard himself made quite clear.

The conception of subjectivity advanced in both the *Philosophical Fragments* and the *Postscript* is that of a process of conscious operations carefully carried out by a person genuinely concerned with truth. True subjectivity, therefore, is exactly the opposite of arbitrariness, which consists in deciding questions of truth and value without careful thought and serious intent. "It is commonly assumed," says Johannes

8. The phrase appears in the title of Part 2, Chapter 2, p. 169.

Climacus, "that no art or skill is required in order to be subjective" (*Postscript,* p. 116). The truth, he goes on to explain, is just the opposite, and the misunderstanding derives from the common failure to distinguish between being a subject in the proper sense and being "a bit of a subject" or a subject "so called" or "in the immediate sense," which is to say being just conscious enough to receive impressions, mouth conventional phrases, and leap on impulse to conclusions or outward actions without serious reflection: "When one overlooks this little distinction, humoristic from the Socratic standpoint and infinitely anxious from the Christian, between being something like a subject so called, and being a subject, or becoming one . . . then it becomes wisdom, the admired wisdom of our own age, that it is the task of the subject increasingly to divest himself of his subjectivity in order to become more and more objective. It is easy to see what this guidance understands by being a subject of a sort. It understands by it quite rightly the accidental, the angular, the selfish, the eccentric, and so forth, all of which every human being can have enough of. Nor does Christianity deny that such things should be gotten rid of; it has never been a friend of loutishness. But the difference is, that philosophy teaches that the way is to become objective, while Christianity teaches that the way is to become subjective, i.e. to become a subject in truth" (p. 117).

Far from wanting to suggest that true subjectivity is whimsicalness and heedlessness of objective truth, Kierkegaard maintained consistently that it is only a subject in the proper sense who can know truth at all, either objective or subjective. When Climacus speaks of "philosophy" as teaching that the way is to become objective, he is referring to the Enlightenment and idealist belief that knowing is a fundamentally passive process in which the empirically observable impresses itself on the observer or in which the logically necessary unfolds according to its laws before the gaze of disinterested reason. Kierkegaard's own claim is that only a concerned, interested inquirer can reason, deliberate, and decide and that when he does so, *that* is subjective existence. Far from being opposed to the objectivity that can be attained through actual subjective operations, Kierkegaard looks upon respect for objective truth in that sense as one of the marks of genuine subjectivity. The objectivity he especially objects to is the phantom objectivity of the rationalistic idealist, the mistaken belief that the supreme goal of thought is not the existential, but a panorama of logically necessary ideas.

Kierkegaard would agree in essence with Lonergan that true objectivity is, as we earlier saw Lonergan put it, "the consequence of authentic subjectivity, of genuine attention, genuine intelligence, genuine reasonableness, genuine responsibility" (*Method in Theology*, p. 265). He was not especially interested in natural science and its methodology, but there is no reason to think that he would have had any objection to the idea of its objective validity. His objection was to a different conception of "science" favored by the German Idealists of his time, whose ambition it was to render philosophy a science of that sort. This conception of "science" was "systematic" in the deductivist sense. It included, as Walter Kaufmann has explained, in *Discovering the Mind*, three central cognitive ideals: certainty, completeness, and necessity.[9] Its fountainhead for Kierkegaard's historical epoch was Kant's *Critique of Pure Reason*, where in his preface to the first edition Kant said, "Regarding certainty I have pronounced this sentence on myself: in this kind of consideration it is in no way permissible to *opine* and everything that as much as resembles a hypothesis is forbidden goods," and went on to say, "The perfect unity of knowledge of this kind that consists of nothing but pure concepts so that no element of experience . . . can have any influence on it and expand or augment it makes this unconditional completenesss not only feasible but also necessary" (quoted by Kaufmann). "To be sure, the dream of absolute certainty is older than Kant," says Kaufmann, "and can be traced back to Descartes, to Plato, and even to Parmenides, but it was Kant who impressed this trinity of certainty, completeness, and necessity on his successors, especially in Germany" (p. 186).

Whenever Kierkegaard spoke slightingly of objectivity or science, it was systematic objectivity according to this ideal of knowledge that he had in mind—for this is what the words meant in the language of his milieu. Far from objecting to the conception of experientially based objectivity Lonergan speaks for, Kierkegaard advocated it himself in opposition to deductivism. He may have used somewhat different language to speak of it, but it is clear that he believed, like Lonergan, that

9. Kaufmann, *Discovering the Mind*, 1:185–86.

the contingent reality of the objective world is known not through logical deduction but through a combination of experience, interpretation, and judgment.

Kierkegaard's most concise treatment of the theme of objective knowledge is to be found in the *Philosophical Fragments,* a work which, despite its title, is perhaps the most systematic of his writings. The book's speaker, as in its sequel, the *Postscript,* is Johannes Climacus.[10] The question of the nature and importance of objective knowledge not in the idealist but in a critical realist sense is implicit in the questions that appear on the title page of the book: "Is an historical point of departure possible for an eternal consciousness; how can such a point of departure have any other than a merely historical interest; is it possible to base an eternal happiness upon historical knowledge?" To phrase the issues involved in another way, one might ask the question, "Is there some essential link between contingent existence in time and the goal of our deepest longing (i.e., to enjoy eternal happiness) or is our involvement with the temporal dimension of life simply a distraction from our true life, which would be the contemplation of eternal ideas and their necessary connections?"

Still another way to put it is the question with which Climacus begins the first chapter: "How far does the Truth admit of being learned?" The meaning of the question must depend on whether truth is to be interpreted in strictly objective terms or also in terms of subjective life. If the only truth is objective truth, then all truth can be formulated, taught, and learned because all truth is commensurate with its objectifications. If there is also another, subjective sense of the word truth (here indicated by the capitalization of "Truth" in the above quotation from the

10. Regarding the question of the relation between Kierkegaard and Climacus, Niels Thulstrup suggests in his introduction to the Swenson-Hong translation that it definitely expresses Kierkegaard's own views and "cannot be considered a truly pseudonymous work." *Philosophical Fragments or A Fragment of Philosophy,* trans. David Swenson and Howard V. Hong, p. lxxxv. This volume will subsequently be referred to as *Fragments.* Thulstrup's suggestion does not necessarily conflict with what was said earlier about the difference between those points on which Kierkegaard did make consistent philosophical claims and those which he treated as ultimately problematic or, to use Marcel's term, mysterious. Climacus may speak a meaning close to Kierkegaard's own views much of the time, but he remains an explorer tentatively probing areas that lie beyond secure knowledge.

Swenson-Hong translation), there is a limit to the extent to which truth can be objectified.[11]

Implicit here is a debate between the idealist position mentioned above and Kierkegaard's Christian belief that man's eternal happiness is to be found not in the contemplation of a system of ideas but in active sharing of the contingent life God takes on in his incarnation. In this volume, however, Climacus shifts the scene of the confrontation from the nineteenth century to a sort of temporally unspecific classical present. In place of the Hegelians of Kierkegaard's own century, Climacus casts as his opponent the Socrates of Plato's *Meno*, and although what he opposes to it is belief in divine incarnation, the allusion to Christianity is veiled by references to "the God," and to an unnamed "Teacher" (implicitly Jesus).[12]

In the *Meno*, as was mentioned in the Lonergan chapter above, Socrates argued that all genuine knowledge is recollection and that the movement from ignorance to knowledge through inquiry is rather from apparent ignorance to a remembering of truths known in a former, supratemporal life. "Thus the Truth" according to the Socratic view, summarizes Climacus, "is not introduced into the individual from without, but was within him," and this implies, he goes on to say, a doctrine of the soul's "preexistence" (*Fragments*, pp. 11–12). The latter point is important, because the central issue, as far as Kierkegaard is concerned, is less how we can come to know cognitive objects than whether in coming to know ourselves as human beings we are rediscovering an existence we already have but have only lost sight of.

This is the deeper significance for Kierkegaard of the Platonic theme

11. Professor Howard Hong, the general director of the new Princeton edition of *Kierkegaard's Writings* kindly allowed me to see the new translation of *Philosophical Fragments* while it was in proof, and in what follows where the differences in translation seem interesting I will indicate them. The new translation does not follow the earlier one's practice of capitalizing key terms, such as Faith, New Birth, Reason, Repentance, the Teacher, the God, and so on. Since in some cases the device of capitalization may help to keep clear some of the distinctions Kierkegaard seems to have been concerned with, I will follow the old translation's usage in that regard. The distinction between subjective or existential "Truth" as compared with merely objective or informational "truth" is a major example. Another that will be discussed later is that between "faith" and "Faith." Still another is that between "the Moment" and "moments."

12. For extensive treatments of Kierkegaard's relation to Hegel and Hegelians, see Niels Thulstrup, *Kierkegaard's Relation to Hegel*, and Mark C. Taylor, *Journeys to Selfhood: Hegel and Kierkegaard*.

of "recollection" or *anamnesis*: do we have already an existence fundamentally our own which we need only trace our way back to along a trail of mythic symbols, or is our discovery of subjective existence something genuinely new—an awareness that is new of an existence that is new? The conception Climacus is sketching out—and here we are approaching one of Kierkegaard's ultimate issues—is the quite radical one that human beings have no existence of their own but only come to exist in the proper sense to the degree that they are "begotten" of God, living in God's incarnation.

The full exploration of that theme, however, has to wait until the ground for it is prepared. The approach Climacus takes is by way of asking how one can truly "know" the Teacher. This in turn leads to a distinction between objective and subjective knowledge. The ultimate problem is that of subjective knowledge of the Teacher. The initial focus, however, is the problem of the powers and limits of objective cognition.

In the *Fragments* this theme comes up as a question of the manner in which we can know the historical past. Whatever is factual, or contingent, is historical; because it is not necessary but something that simply has happened, the contingent is situated within the scheme of time, and it is known through a temporal process involving experience, interpretation, and judgment. Regarding abstract ideas, Climacus readily admits the claims of the idealists; it is possible to understand ideas and their necessary connections by logical reasoning alone. But in this case reasoning is an inquiry not into the factual but into the merely possible. It is what was referred to in the chapter on Lonergan as a "level two" operation, a purely formal analysis or explication of the contents of ideas.

Kierkegaard is as insistent as Lonergan or any other critical realist that the factual is known not through "pure reasoning" of this sort but by way of the act of judgment following upon critical reflection. Abstract reasoning knows the necessary, but the historical is what "has come into existence" and is therefore not necessary but contingent and uncertain. The inquirer's awareness of this uncertainty gives rise to what Climacus calls "the passionate sense for coming into existence: wonder" (p. 99). Wonder is the tension in subjectivity that moves one to reach from uncertainty toward factual knowledge. This is a movement beyond the immediacy of sensation and perception toward the historically contingent as known by a judgment of factual truth. When one knows the historical in this way, one does not have certainty in the formal sense, the certainty with which one knows the logically necessary, but rather one has "certitude," as Newman termed it, regarding what happens to be the case. It is such certitude Climacus refers to when he says, "Immediate sensation and immediate cognition have no suspicion of the uncertainty with which belief approaches its object, but neither do they suspect the certainty which emerges from this uncertainty" (p. 101).

The word "belief" in this passage, which is also translated in other passages as "faith," requires some explanation. Climacus uses the term in two ways: in the "direct and ordinary sense" and in the "eminent sense."[13] In this passage it is used in the "ordinary" sense (i.e., to refer to a judgment of contingent fact). Climacus says that "the organ for the historical must have a structure analogous with the historical itself; it must comprise a corresponding somewhat by which it may repeatedly negate in its certainty the uncertainty that corresponds to the uncertainty of coming into existence" (pp. 100–101). Despite the differences of language, this is exactly what Lonergan spoke of as "the isomorphism that obtains between the structure of knowing and the structure of the known" (*Insight*, p. 399). What both mean is that the objective reality of contingent fact is precisely that which can be reasonably affirmed through attentive inquiry and critical judgment.

Climacus goes on to give the "organ" of critical judgment the name "faith" (in "the ordinary sense"): "Now faith has precisely the required character; for in the certainty of belief [Danish: *Tro*, *faith* or *belief*] there is always present a negated uncertainty, in every way corresponding to the uncertainty of coming into existence. Faith believes what it does not see; it does not believe that the star is there, for that it sees, but it believes that the star has come into existence. The same holds true of an event. The 'what' of a happening may be known immediately, but by no means can it be known immediately that it has happened. Nor can it be known immediately that it happens, not even if it happens as we say in front of our very noses" (*Fragments*, p. 101).

"Faith" in this usage does not have a theological meaning (which would be what Climacus calls the "eminent" sense of the word), but

13. See the translator's footnote, p. 101.

refers simply to rational judgment on the basis of interpretation and evidence. What Climacus means is that the contingent world is not known through sensation or perception or through consideration of ideas alone, but through the particular act by which contingent factuality is always known, namely the act of critical judgment. That he says "belief is not a form of knowledge, but a free act, an expression of will" (p. 103) does not mean that belief is arbitrary, it only means that judgment is a consciously intended (hence "voluntary") operation distinct from the contemplation of ideas as such and their logical relations (which is what "knowledge" refers to in the passage just quoted). As was mentioned earlier, much of the common misinterpretation of Kierkegaard as an irrationalist is the result of not reading him carefully. To read him carefully on this point, one must be attentive both to how he uses his particular language and to how he relates it to the language in use in his philosophical milieu. To Kierkegaard's idealist opponents as he delineated them "knowledge," even of historical fact, meant logical certainty through a grasp of systematic necessity. To this way of thinking he opposed his insistence on the contingency of the factual and its apprehension through the conscious operations by which contingent events can be reasonably affirmed to have happened.

Thus far Kierkegaard is perfectly in accord with Lonergan regarding our knowledge of the objective world, except that he uses rather different terminology. If this were the whole of the matter, however, he would have little to contribute to the dialogue among the philosophers we have been examining. His real contribution emerges precisely at the point at which his accord with the critical realist position regarding objectivity reaches its limit. This is the point at which Kierkegaard insists on the absolute difference between subject and object. Lonergan, as we saw, claimed that the subject can be adequately objectified and known in the same way as any other real object. Kierkegaard, on the other hand, like his philosophical descendants, Voegelin and Ricoeur, maintains that no matter what sorts of analogy may be drawn between an actual subject and a hypothetical object of knowledge, subjectivity itself is unique and incommensurable with any objectification.

Not only does Kierkegaard deny that the subject as such is objectively knowable, but he emphasizes the contradiction and clash between the actuality of the subject as subject and our desire to know it in some objective manner. It is on this contradiction, moreover, that he believes human subjectivity is founded. This is why he places so much emphasis on the category of paradox. "[O]ne should not think slightingly of the paradoxical," says Climacus in the *Fragments*, "for the paradox is the source of the thinker's passion, and the thinker without a paradox is like a lover without feeling: a paltry mediocrity" (p. 46).

This, too, could be interpreted as evidence of irrationalism on Kierkegaard's part, but only if one does not attend carefully to his meaning. There are two reasons for the prominence of the theme of paradox in Kierkegaard. One is that in trying to find a way to speak of subjectivity in a milieu in which philosophical language was oriented almost exclusively toward the description of objects of perception or of intellection, he was driven to use the currently available language of philosophical discourse in ways it was not suited to. In this respect, Kierkegaardian paradox is a function of the breakdown of a language pushed beyond its capacity. This might be termed "accidental" paradox.

There is also another type of paradox in Kierkegaard's thought, however, and it is this that Climacus refers to as "the source of the thinker's passion." This we might term "essential" paradox—essential in that it stems from the structure of human consciousness itself, so that there is no way it could be resolved by reformulation in another language. The paradox that is the source of the thinker's passion, as Climacus goes on to explain, is the desire to attain what is truly other than thought: "The supreme paradox of all thought is the attempt to discover something that thought cannot think. This passion is at bottom present in all thinking . . ." (p. 46).

One way to explain this is to say that all thinking, moved as it is by the desire to know, seeks after the unknown. Now there is that which is unknown in an accidental sense: it is not yet known but can be known. It is not inherently a mystery, only a problem. But there is also that which is essentially unknown because it is unknowable: it cannot be rendered an object of understanding and *a fortiori* cannot be affirmed as an objective reality—and yet it is actual in the most proper sense of the word. This is subjective actuality itself, the presence and life of what Climacus calls "the God": "But what is this unknown something with which the Reason [new translation: "the understanding"] collides when inspired by its paradoxical passion, with the result of unsettling even man's knowledge of himself? It is the Unknown. It is not a human being, insofar as we know what man is; nor is it any other known thing. So let us call this unknown something: *the God*" (p. 49).[14]

What this means becomes clearer when we consider what Climacus says about God in the *Postscript:* "The existing individual who chooses to pursue the objective way enters upon the entire approximation-process by which it is proposed to bring God to light objectively. But this is in all eternity impossible, because God is a subject, and therefore exists only for subjectivity in inwardness" (p. 178). It is here that we discover mystery in the proper sense of the term.

The contrast with Lonergan on this point is sharp, and a consideration of the difference between them may help to correct any misleading implications that might seem to be contained in the reference to God as "a subject," as though he were an individual entity conceived according to what Girard would characterize as the false subjectivity of romantic individualism. What Climacus actually seems to mean is something much closer to Girard's own conception of transcendent subjectivity as the source of the life we are called to share with Christ: not that God is a superhuman individual, but rather that God is absolutely subjective and that his subjective presence is the objectively inscrutable, radically inward source of all true human subjectivity. God, that is, is not to be discovered in the objective pole of consciousness, but in the subjective pole; the existing individual's immediate experience of subjective actuality is his experience of the presence of God.

Lonergan, in connection with his own effort to prove the existence of God, says that "it is one and the same thing to say that God is real, that he is an object of reasonable affirmation, and that he exists" (*Insight,* p. 669). The line of thinking Kierkegaard explores through his *personae* leads in exactly the opposite direction: that God is not an object of any kind whatsoever, neither an object of sense, nor of intellection, nor of reasonable affirmation. This is why Climacus argues that the existence of God *cannot* be proven: "Whoever therefore attempts to demonstrate the existence of God . . . ," he says, "proves in lieu thereof something

14. The substitution of "the understanding" for "the Reason" in the new translation helps to make clear the link between Climacus's terms and the standard Kantian terminology, in which "understanding" (*der Verstand*) refers to the grasp and analysis of concepts, which in terms of intentionality analysis are strictly objective, while "reason" (*die Vernunft*) is associated more with subjectivity and a sense of the transcendent—rather as in Voegelin's discussion of the classical *nous* in his "Reason: The Classic Experience."

else..." (*Fragments,* p. 54); any proof would, by the very nature of proof, have to be proof of something objective, which is exactly what God is not.

In his own linguistic usage Kierkegaard does not ordinarily even say that God "exists," since he more commonly confines this term to human being, as when he has Climacus say in the *Postscript,* "God does not think, he creates; God does not exist, He is eternal. Man thinks and exists, and existence separates thought and being, holding them apart from one another in succession" (p. 296). What this would seem to mean is simply that the properly divine mode of being is that of subjectivity as such—God in his eternity is entirely active, the performer of the eternal operation that is his being, not passive or static. God does not respond, as a human being does, to experiential data that come to him as to a passive recipient; what God experiences, immediately and in its fullness, is the subjective act that is his eternal life.

As in Voegelin's image of man in the Metaxy, human existence, for Kierkegaard, is constituted as a tension between being and thought, the subjective pole and the objective. This is the basis of Kierkegaard's deepest objection to what he calls "the System," the Idealism he associated with Hegel and Hegelians. "The systematic Idea," says Climacus, "is the identity of subject and object, the unity of thought and being. Existence, on the other hand, is their separation" (*Postscript,* p. 112).

To exist humanly, in this conception, is to be concernfully and hence in an actively conscious way (i.e., "subjectively") engaged in an incessant striving toward the act of existence. Human existence is a passion to exist. This is incessant because existence as such in the full sense of the word, the eternal being of God, is inherently subjective, whereas to be human is to be structured as a relation between the subjective pole of consciousness (our experience of dynamic actuality) and the objective pole that is the necessary second factor in incarnation. If we were not oriented by the structure of incarnate subjectivity toward an objective pole of consciousness, we would not exist subjectively as human beings at all. The goal of our "existential pathos," as Climacus calls it, our deep longing for conscious existence, is one that we can pursue only through commitment to the demands of incarnation; our conscious existence *is* our active engagement in intentional operations, and these can take place only as relations between subjective and objective poles of consciousness. For us, the experience of existential presence is to be found only in, and as our intentional engagement with, time and the world—the life of incarnate subjectivity.

At the foundation of Kierkegaard's thought, therefore, is a distinction between two radically different meanings of the word "exist." At the end of the chapter on Lonergan, I suggested that a reader of *Insight* could easily get from that work the impression that existence is a property specifically of objects and of them only inasmuch as they can be judged actual by a critical knower, and this impression is only reinforced by Lonergan's later statement in *Method in Theology* that "*esse* ["to be" or existence] is reality affirmed in the world mediated by meaning" (p. 264). Kierkegaard makes a clear and absolute distinction between this sense of the term "existence," which I will call "objective existence," and another that I will call "subjective existence." The distinction was touched upon in earlier chapters with reference to Voegelin's emphasis on "existence as known from within" (i.e., subjectively) in comparison with Lonergan's emphasis on "existence as known from without" (i.e., objectively). Voegelin was concerned with knowledge "from within" of what he called "existential tension" and Kierkegaard called "passion."

The distinction between subjective and objective existence is treated in numerous places in Kierkegaard. An example is Climacus's discussion in the *Postscript* of the difference between what he considers existence in the proper and full sense, and existence in a loose sense of the word:

> It is impossible to exist without passion, unless we understand the word "exist" in the loose sense of a so-called existence. Every Greek thinker was therefore essentially a passionate thinker. I have often reflected how one might bring a man into a state of passion. I have thought in this connection that if I could get him seated on a horse and the horse made to take fright and gallop wildly, or better still, for the sake of bringing the passion out, if I could take a man who wanted to arrive at a certain place as quickly as possible, and hence already had some passion, and could set him astride a horse that can scarcely walk—and yet this is what existence is like if one is to become consciously aware of it. Or if a driver were otherwise not especially inclined toward passion, if someone hitched a team of horses to a wagon for him, one of them a Pegasus and the other a worn-out jade, and told him to drive—I think one might succeed. And it

is just this that it means to exist, if one is to become conscious of it. Eternity is the winged horse, infinitely fast, and time is a worn-out jade; the existing individual is the driver. That is to say, he is such a driver when his mode of existence is not an existence loosely so called; for then he is no driver, but a drunken peasant who lies asleep in the wagon and lets the horses take care of themselves. To be sure, he also drives and is a driver; and so there are perhaps many who—also exist. (P. 276)

Here, of course, Kierkegaard is alluding to what, as mentioned in his chapter, was also one of Voegelin's favorite texts, the episode in Plato's *Phaedrus* (246a–248c) where Socrates, after discoursing on the role of *eros* in the life of the soul, says that although it is impossible for a man to know *psyche* by direct vision, one may perhaps speak truly of it in a philosophical myth. Then he makes up the myth of the soul as a chariot driven by a horseman who has to try to guide the energies of two steeds, one of noble stock and the other of base, so that the noble steed's upward motion, countering the tendency of the other to seek solid ground, will carry the chariot toward the region where "true being dwells, without color or shape, that cannot be touched."[15] The appositeness of the myth to Kierkegaard's meaning is quite clear. "True being," which is without color, shape, or tangibility (i.e., without objectivity), and which can be reached only through the upward moving energy of *eros* (passion or existential tension), corresponds to what Kierkegaard considers existence in the proper sense of the word—that is, subjectivity. The tangible ground to which the base steed retreats is the objectivity upon which the thinker deficient in existential pathos tends to fall back.

If we consider Kierkegaard's adaptation of this imagery, his carter has two possible modes of existence. When he consciously drives the horses toward a goal, he is existing subjectively. When he does not, but is only drawn along as he lies unconscious, he exists objectively; he can be perceived and judged objectively real by an observer, but in his drunken stupor he lacks any subjective presence. He is present as an object to others, but as subject he does not exist. To state Kierkegaard's concept of objective existence in language like that of Lonergan's cognitional theory, objective existence is that which may be affirmed by a judgment of adequacy regarding a construing of a set of empirical data.

---

15. 247c, quoted from the translation by R. Hackforth in *The Collected Dialogues of Plato Including the Letters*, ed. Edith Hamilton and Huntington Cairns, p. 494.

Subjective existence, on the other hand, as Kierkegaard conceives it, cannot be an object of sense or of intellection or of rational judgment. It is experienced, but not as a datum of sense, nor is it to be found in any respect on the side of the objective pole of consciousness; it is experienced immediately at the subjective pole.

With this distinction clear, it is possible to decipher many paradoxical and initially perplexing statements in Kierkegaard's writings. When Climacus speaks in the *Fragments* of "the God" as "this Unknown, which does indeed exist, but is unknown, and insofar does not exist" (p. 55), this means that the God, who is present as the wellspring of subjectivity, does indeed exist subjectively, but not objectively. When he says in the same place, "The paradoxical passion of the Reason . . . comes repeatedly into collision with this Unknown" and "The Reason cannot advance beyond this point, and yet it cannot refrain in its paradoxicalness from arriving at this limit and occupying itself therewith," he is describing the intrinsic structure of human intentional consciousness, which is energized by a passion for existence in the subjective sense but which, because it is structured as a relation between subjective and objective poles, must always reach also in the direction of the objective. Wisdom develops as one realizes this, accepts it, and commits oneself faithfully to its demands, which are nothing other than the conditions of incarnate subjectivity. Wisdom, that is, is the realization both that the true goal of human life is subjective existence and that human (i.e., incarnate) subjectivity has the bipolar structure of intentional consciousness.

This is the same meaning Climacus expressed in the *Postscript* as the idea that "truth is subjectivity": "When subjectivity is the truth, the conceptual determination of the truth must include an expression for the antithesis to objectivity, a memento of the fork in the road where the way swings off; this expression will at the same time serve as an indication of the tension of subjective inwardness. Here is such a definition of truth: *An objective uncertainty held fast in an appropriation-process of the most passionate inwardness is the truth*, the highest truth attainable for an *existing* individual" (p. 182). If this were taken for a definition of objective truth, the truth of a statement about objective reality, it would be nonsense. The strictly subjective truth of which he is speaking, on the other hand, the "highest truth attainable for an *existing* individual," is subjective self-presence, conscious existence, the experienced "tension of subjective inwardness." It is "an objective uncertainty" because it can never be grasped as an object. The appropriation-process is intentionality itself, the inherent structure of human consciousness—an "appropriation-process" because human subjective existence takes the form of the intending that reaches from a subjective toward an objective pole; "passionate" because it is tensional through and through; "held fast" since the passionate intention to exist is of the essence of human being—if it ceased, the existing individual would be no more. The "fork in the road" is the realization of the distinction between subjective and objective existence as it pertains to this process—the realization that although the goal is subjective, its analogical images in the objective pole have an essential role to play in human consciousness. To exist in human subjectivity is to live the paradox that in order to become what one is as subjective, one must reach toward what one is not (the objective), but with the realization that while the objective is not itself our goal, to be human is to intend it.[16]

Paradox, as Climacus explains, is itself a product of intentional consciousness. It develops when one attempts to speak of subjective existence in language designed to describe objects. But that we use such language is not a mere accident, the result of our failure to design a more adequate language. We use it as a necessary instrument—necessary because it is a function of the intentional structure of human consciousness as a relation between subjective and objective poles. Subjective existence cannot itself be a paradox, because it is not an idea or proposition—it is immediately experienced dynamic actuality. It is only cast in the form of paradox when one attempts to speak of the experience of subjective existence as though it were an object of intentional consciousness. As Climacus puts it, "When subjectivity, inwardness, is the truth, the truth becomes objectively a paradox. . . . But the eternal essential truth is by no means in itself a paradox; but it becomes paradoxical by virtue of its relationship to an existing individual" (p. 183). Paradox in its true form is not, therefore, the result of a failure to express thought clearly; for one who realizes inwardly the existential truth that is subjectivity, paradox can be the truly adequate expression, in the

16. Cf. *Concept of Anxiety*, p. 150: "Having become truly earnest about that which is the object of earnestness, a person may very well, if he so wishes, treat various things earnestly, but the question is whether he first became earnest about the object of earnestness. This object every human being has, because it is *himself*. . . . "

language of intentional consciousness—and there can be no other human language—of the absolute difference between subject and object. This is the true wisdom of Socrates for Kierkegaard: he knew the difference between what he did understand and what he did not understand —between what was and what was not for him an object of intellection.[17] Subjective existence cannot be contemplated as an intellectual object; it can only be lived: "The Socratic ignorance gives expression to the objective uncertainty attaching to the truth, while his inwardness in existing is the truth" (p. 183).[18]

Another thing Climacus says in this passage from the *Postscript* is that his definition of truth as subjectivity, "an objective uncertainty held fast in an appropriation-process of the most passionate inwardness," "is an equivalent expression for faith" (p. 182). To understand what this means we will have to return to a consideration of the argument he unfolded in the *Philosophical,* where he distinguished between faith "in the ordinary sense" and "in the eminent sense." This will also offer an opportunity to explore further the implications of Kierkegaard's treatment of recollection or *anamnesis,* another of the major themes he shares with Ricoeur and Voegelin.

As was mentioned earlier, Kierkegaard's "faith in the ordinary sense" is simply the judgment of factual truth, the transition from idea to reality, or from understanding to knowing. To say that faith in this sense is a leap is simply to say that it is a transition from one kind of intentional operation to another quite different one. Far from claiming that Christian faith is a form of ungrounded factual belief (the popular parody of Kierkegaard's "leap"), Kierkegaard's line of thinking points in exactly the opposite direction. Not only does he not value arbitrary

---

17. See the epigraph of *Concept of Anxiety* and also *Postscript,* p. 495.

18. Cf. *Concept of Anxiety,* p. 143: "The most concrete content that consciousness can have is consciousness of itself, of the individual himself—not the pure self-consciousness [i.e., the self-contemplation aspired to by the Idealists], but the self-consciousness that is so concrete that no author . . . has ever been able to describe a single such self-consciousness, although every single human being is such a one. This self-consciousness is not contemplation . . . because he sees that meanwhile he himself is in the process of becoming, and consequently cannot be something complete for contemplation. The self-consciousness, therefore, is action, and this action is in turn inwardness. . . ." (This passage may well be the direct source of Voegelin's image of man as an actor in a drama he cannot stand outside of in the manner of a spectator, though another source in Kierkegaard for that image may also be *Postscript,* p. 141, where "world-history" is likened to a stage, with God as both royal spectator and royal actor.)

judgment, as was mentioned earlier in connection with his dismissal of "subjectivity" in the eccentric sense, he does not even suggest that well-founded rational belief can play more than an accidental role in the life of Christian faith. The leap of faith that is essential to Christianity as Kierkegaard conceives it is of an entirely different kind, and pertains to an entirely different meaning of the word "faith."

This is the point of Climacus's insistence in the latter part of the *Fragments* that there can be no disciple at second hand, which is exactly what a person who conceived of Christian faith as belief in the factual sense would be trying to be. It is also the point of his claim that the historical in the factual, objectively knowable sense can only be an occasion for the development of Christian faith, not its condition. Even if one believed the objective propositions of the incarnate God himself, this would not make one a disciple. Climacus comments on such a situation: "Wherever the Teacher appears the crowd gathers, curious to see, curious to hear, and eager to tell others that they have seen and heard him. Is this curious multitude the learner? By no means. Or if some one of the authorized teachers of that city sought him out secretly, in order to try his strength with him in arguments—is he the learner? By no means. If this teacher or that multitude *learn* anything, the God serves merely as an occasion in the strict Socratic sense" (*Fragments*, p. 71).

It is not just that the multitude or the member of the religious establishment does not properly believe the Teacher and therefore does not learn his objective teaching; rather, as Climacus says, even if those who approach him out of objective curiosity did believe in the factual truth of his teaching, such belief would never be more than incidental to discipleship. The Teacher is the God in the paradox of his incarnation, the eternal existing in time, which is to say, performing the contingent operations of intentional consciousness. An ordinary teacher or "forerunner" who teaches objective information about the Teacher, may "serve to arouse the learner's attention, but nothing more" (*Fragments*, p. 69). And this is true even of the Teacher himself to the extent that he imparts objective information or presents himself objectively. The Teacher's "merely historical" objective presence is only an occasion, objective and external, whereas what is essentially important about him is the manner in which he transcends the objective to become subjectively present as the animating principle of the concrete life of the believer. It is as the actuality of incarnate subjectivity to the degree that this takes place—wherever, whenever, and in whomever it actually occurs—that the Teacher is not just a "merely historical" occasion that may, as an external sign, arouse one's interest in eternal happiness, but is himself the condition that fulfills that interest. He fulfills it because his inwardly animating presence is precisely the existence for which we long.

Socrates claimed that he did not "beget" knowledge in his listener but only acted as a midwife, assisting externally by his words a process that took place within by a power other than his own. So also, even the Teacher himself, considered as an objective historical figure, is only an occasion whose external presence may assist at but cannot cause the inward begetting by which, as subjective presence, he comes to dwell within the disciple. The reason the Teacher is more than a sign or a midwife is that he is more than objective; he was and is the eternal in time, the incarnate presence of the deep source of all genuine subjectivity. "If this is not so," says Climacus, "then . . . the Teacher is not the God but only a Socrates, and if he does not conduct himself like a Socrates, he is not even a Socrates" (p. 72).

The theme sketched here, therefore, ties in with the question Socrates asks in Plato's dialogues: "Can truth be taught?" or as we saw Climacus phrase it in the opening sentence of the *Fragments,* "How far does the Truth admit of being learned?" (p. 11). Kierkegaard's answer is that objective truth can be taught but not subjective, that discipleship of the sort Kierkegaard has in mind is not an objective relation to the Teacher but a subjective one, and that faith in the sense of belief regarding factual truth therefore has nothing essential to do with it.

It is in connection with his treatment of the theme of true discipleship that Climacus presents the idea of "Faith" in the eminent sense, which was capitalized in the Swenson-Hong translation of the *Fragments* in order to distinguish it from ordinary or factual belief. The distinctive characteristic of Faith in this sense is that it is entirely subjective—not a subject's intention of an object, but the experience of subjective presence itself. The Teacher, in whom the disciple has Faith, is present for Faith not as an object of knowledge or speculation, but as subject.

Faith in this eminent sense can develop only after objective intentionality has been pushed to its limit in the thinker's passion for what we earlier saw Climacus refer to as the Unknown, which he also called "the

God" and "the Paradox" (pp. 63–67). When this limit has been reached, then and only then may there occur the "leap" that is not a judgment or an act of will, but a cessation of the effort to capture subjective presence as some sort of object. In discussing the true significance of the futile attempt to prove the existence of God, Climacus asks, "And how does the God's existence emerge from the proof? Does it follow straightway, without any breach of continuity? . . . As long as I keep my hold on the proof, i.e., continue to demonstrate, the existence does not come out, if for no other reason than that I am engaged in proving it; but when I let the proof go, the existence is there" (p. 53). As long as one is attempting to prove existence, that is, the existence one intends must be conceived of as objective. When one ceases to aim at subjective existence as though it were an object, on the other hand, then one can discover its subjective presence.

This "act of letting go" Climacus refers to explicitly as "a *leap*" (p. 53). It is a transition, that is, between qualitatively different conceptions of existence and stances in relation to it. It is not the sort of leap that marks the transition from understanding to judgment (faith in the ordinary sense), but a leap of an entirely different kind, a radical transition from the intention of an object to the experienced presence of transcendent subjectivity. As Climacus analyzes it, the attempt to prove the existence of God is founded on a confusion between objective and subjective existence, and the "letting go" is the acceptance of the gift of subjective existence as such, the discovery of the presence of God within the subjective pole of consciousness.

It is this letting go that constitutes the genuinely Christian leap of faith in Kierkegaard's thought. This is the equivalent in Kierkegaard of what we saw Voegelin refer to as "openness of existence." Far from being an irrational act of belief (which for Voegelin would be a symptom of "closed existence"), Kierkegaard's leap of "Faith" in the eminent sense is the discovery in inwardness of the presence of the living "Paradox" that is the "Moment" of the coming into subjective existence of the eternal in time: "But how does the learner come to realize an understanding with this Paradox? We do not ask that he understand the Paradox but only understand that this is the Paradox. . . . It comes to pass when the Reason and the Paradox encounter one another happily in the Moment, when the Reason sets itself aside and the Paradox bestows itself. The third entity in which this union is realized . . . is that happy passion to which we will now assign a name, though it is not the name that so much matters. We shall call this passion: *Faith*. This then must be the condition of which we have spoken, which the Paradox contributes" (pp. 72–73).

The last point, the bestowing of the condition for true discipleship and eternal happiness by the Teacher who is the living Paradox of incarnate subjectivity, connects Climacus's treatment of the theme of Faith with the Platonic theme of recollection. As was mentioned earlier, in the *Meno* Socrates proposes that to learn is actually to remember a truth known from a previous existence before one's life in this world. Climacus pointed out in the *Fragments* that the Socratic doctrine implies that "the Truth is not introduced into the individual from without, but was within him" so that "one who is ignorant needs only a reminder to help him come to himself in the consciousness of what he knows" (p. 11). Climacus alludes to this idea in the sentences immediately following his later designation of Faith as the condition that the Paradox contributes: "Let us not forget that if the Paradox does not grant this condition the learner must be in possession of it. But if the learner is in possession of the condition he is *eo ipso* himself the Truth, and the moment is merely the moment of occasion . . ." (p. 73).

The implication extends to the most fundamental issues and can help to bring them to light. It was mentioned earlier that the theme of recollection is connected with that of the immortality of the soul and its preexistence. What is most importantly at issue is whether each individual's subjective existence is actually eternal (and only forgotten or unrealized) or whether human existence is genuinely contingent. For if the Socratic position is correct, our life in time is only an illusion, because what we are in truth is eternal: "That the God has once for all given man the requisite condition [i.e., a subjective existence properly one's own] is the eternal Socratic presupposition, which comes into no hostile collision with time, but is incommensurable with the temporal and its determinations" (p. 77). Climacus's own position, he goes on to say, is that human subjective existence is not an illusion masking our eternal identity but is genuinely historical. It involves the eternal on the side of subjectivity, but it is itself intrinsically a life in relation to time, a life that has not just had a beginning at some point in the past but continues throughout its duration as a radically contingent coming into existence in the paradoxical Moment of incarnation: "The contradiction of our hypothesis is that man receives the condition in the Moment. . . . If the case is otherwise we stand at the Socratic principle of Recollection" (p. 77).

The Socratic principle would set aside the need for the Teacher, and Climacus agrees that insofar as a teacher does not confer the condition for the experience of subjective existence, the Socratic principle defines the proper relation between speaker and hearer. But if man does not possess a subjective existence all his own but receives it from the Teacher, the Teacher is no mere midwife but the actual present source and condition of the existence the disciple discovers as given to him in the Moment: "In order that he may have the power to give the condition the Teacher must be the God; in order that he may be able to put the learner in possession of it he must be Man. This contradiction is again the object of Faith, and is the Paradox, the Moment" (p. 77).

Again it would be easy to fall into an objectifying mode of thought and misinterpret the idea explored here as referring to a relationship of objective causality—as though the divine-human Teacher gives life to the disciple in the way a potter makes a pot, a Dr. Frankenstein his monster, or a Pygmalion his Galatea. This is not at all the idea Climacus is sketching out. What he is trying to account for is the radical subjective contingency of human consciousness, which he suggests stems from and itself manifests the subjective presence of the God. He is not saying that a superhuman individual who 1,800 years earlier was incarnate as the historical Teacher also at some point in our personal pasts objectively created us as human beings. Rather he is suggesting that the actual existence of each human being, in the proper or "subjective" sense, *actually is* the present human existence of the Teacher himself in the continuous union of time and eternity that is the process of his incarnation. The Teacher, in other words, does not cause our existence objectively but subjectively, constituting us inwardly as human individuals in such a way that he shares with us his own subjective presence and life.

This is why Climacus insists that the truly "contemporary" disciple— as compared with either an "immediate contemporary" or a supposed "disciple at second hand"—receives the condition (i.e., subjective existence) in "the Moment": "How does the learner then become a believer or disciple? When the Reason is set aside and he receives the condition. When does he receive the condition? In the Moment. What does this condition condition? The understanding of the Eternal. But such a condition must be an eternal condition.—He receives accordingly the eternal condition in the Moment, and is aware that he has so received it; for otherwise he merely comes to himself in the consciousness that he had it from eternity" (p. 79).

To understand what this means, one must realize that when Kierkegaard speaks of eternity, he is speaking both of the divine and of the subjective as such.[19] As he put it in *The Concept of Anxiety* (p. 151), "Inwardness is . . . eternity or the constituent of the eternal in man." Time, on the other hand, is objective in the sense of the word explored in earlier chapters of the present study: it is known objectively through intentional operations working upon the data of memory. Subjectivity is eternal precisely because it is not objective and therefore cannot be known as temporal or as an item in the objective scheme of time.

All of this follows from the fundamental principle of Kierkegaard's thought: the absolute difference between subject and object. God, as stated in the *Postscript,* is purely subject, not an object of any kind, and is known only in "inwardness" (i.e., in subjectivity). God, that is, *is* the eternal, and the word "eternity" refers to his presence. When God ("the Eternal" in the *Fragments*) enters into human existence in the Moment, this constitutes a "synthesis," as Climacus phrases it, of the eternal and the temporal, in that human existence is characterized by the intentionality that relates the subjective pole of consciousness (with its source in the eternal) to the objective pole, of which time is a function.

To say that the disciple "receives . . . the eternal condition in the Moment," therefore, and that he "is aware that he has so received it" is to say that his existence is genuinely contingent and that he realizes that in his reality as an historical individual he is not identical with the eternal God but is constituted as a set of contingent intentional operations energized by the "passion" that in human existence is both the image and the incarnation of the love of God. He realizes, that is, that human intentionality is not a possession of one's own but a gift rooted in the subjective presence of God.

---

19. In popular usage, of course, "eternity" is taken to refer to an enormous length of time. It did not mean that for traditional theology but was identified with God's own mode of being and was thought to be beyond time altogether, a qualitatively different conception from time of any length. Cf. Aquinas, *Summa Theologica,* I, q. 10, a. 1.

The "immediate contemporary" was one who, through his historical situation, was in a position to perceive the Teacher as an object of his senses, but this could not make him a contemporary in the sense Climacus is interested in. To be a contemporary in the truly significant sense is to share the Teacher's present, which is his subjective presence in the Moment.

The Moment to which Climacus refers is not a "moment" in the ordinary sense. It is not a particular segment, one among many, of objective time, a sort of temporal container of the incarnation of the God.[20] Rather it is the process of incarnation itself, the coming into historical existence of the Eternal as involved in and with time. As Climacus puts it, "If we posit the Moment the Paradox is there; for the Moment is the Paradox in its most abbreviated form" (*Fragments*, p. 64).

It is the inward experience of the life of the Moment that is bestowed when Reason (i.e., object-oriented inquiry) yields itself and the Paradox of the God's incarnate subjectivity bestows itself. The "understanding of the Eternal" that this bestowal conditions is the concrete realization of the subjective presence of the Eternal. It is not a form of objective knowledge, but Faith in the eminent sense: " . . . the Reason yielded itself while the Paradox bestowed itself (*halb zog sie ihn, halb sank er hin*), and the understanding is consummated in that happy passion . . ." to which Climacus says he gives the name of "Faith" (p. 67).

Exploring the relation of the Paradox to Faith as a sort of "understanding of the Eternal," Climacus suggests that in addition to its paradoxicalness as a synthesis of eternity and time, the Paradox is further paradoxical in that in Faith the disciple's knowledge of the God and of himself as begotten of the God is one with the God's knowledge of himself and of the disciple: "Only the believer, i.e., the non-immediate contemporary, knows the Teacher, since he receives the condition from him and therefore knows him even as he is known. . . . the Teacher must know everyone who knows him, and no one can know the Teacher except through being known by him" (pp. 84–85).[21] This paradoxically

20. Cf. *Concept of Anxiety*, p. 152: " . . . just as the road to hell is paved with good intentions, so eternity is best annihilated with mere moments."

21. Voegelin has an echo of this Kierkegaardian, and New Testament, theme in his essay "The Gospel and Culture," in his comment on Paul's warning in 1 Cor. 8:1–3 against the way in which human claims to know God can "puff up" rather than "build up": "The words are addressed to members of the Corinthian community who 'possess knowledge'

divine-human knowledge is strictly subjective, a knowledge entirely from within—not objective knowledge of a fact, but the experience of incarnate subjectivity. This is what it means, in Climacus's phrasing, to be "contemporary as a believer, in the autopsy of Faith" (p. 87): "autopsy" in Greek means "self-seeing" and here refers to the fact that in Faith one experiences inwardly the actual presence of the God and in doing so experiences one's own contingent subjective actuality.

Such knowledge is inaccessible to a mere perceiver—the "immediate contemporary"—who only happens, as an accident of his temporal situation, to know the Teacher from without, seeing him with his eyes or hearing him with his ears. It is similarly inaccessible to one who knows about the Teacher only "at second hand," acquiring objective information about him from others. But it is shared by every "real contemporary" in Faith: "When the believer is the believer and knows the God through having received the condition from the God himself, every successor must receive the condition from the God himself in precisely the same sense, and cannot receive it at second hand.... But a successor who receives the condition from the God himself is a contemporary, a real contemporary; a privilege enjoyed only by the believer, but also enjoyed by every believer" (p. 85).

How can this happen, however? How can the believer share not only objective information about the Teacher but the inward life and experience of the Teacher himself? It would seem that to do so would require the believer's annihilation and the replacement of his own subjective life with that of the Teacher. Climacus's answer is that in a sense this is indeed what happens. It was to this sense of the issue that we saw him alluding in the lines from the ending of Goethe's "Der Fischer," a poem about an angler enticed to drowning by a nymph: "Halb zog sie ihn, halb sank er hin,/ Und ward nicht mehr gesehen" ("Half drew she him, half sank he down, and never again was seen"). This was also, of course, a New Testament theme as expressed in the imagery of dying to self in order to rise to new life in Christ. There is a sense in which one must die in order to undergo what Climacus refers to as "the *New*

as doctrine and unwisely apply it as a rule of conduct; such possessors of truth are reminded that the knowledge which forms existence without deforming it is God's knowledge of man." In Donald G. Miller and Dikran Y. Hadidian, eds., *Jesus and Man's Hope*, 2:79.

Birth" that makes one a "new creature" (p. 23). But this rebirth, which Climacus also calls "Conversion" and "Repentance," could be a literal annihilation only if the one who underwent it had a prior existence of his own to lose in the process. In that case, however, we would be back once again with the Socratic conception: there could be no new birth, and repentance would be a remembering and rediscovery of one's own eternal being. The Teacher would be no more than the midwife of a rebirth that in none but a metaphorical sense could have any begetter.

The conception advanced in the *Fragments* is just the opposite. The change that takes place is what Climacus later speaks of, in his commentary on Aristotle's idea of *kinesis,* as "the coming-into-existence kind of change":

> In what sense is there change in that which comes into existence? Or, what is the nature of the coming-into-existence kind of change (*kinesis*)? All other change (*alloiosis*) presupposes the existence of that which changes, even when the change consists in ceasing to exist. But this is not the case with coming into existence. For if the subject of coming into existence does not itself remain unchanged during the change of coming into existence, that which comes into existence is not *this* subject which comes into existence, but something else. (P. 90)

The change that makes one a new creature, therefore, is truly a new birth and a begetting because it is a genuine beginning of existence, a transition not from one kind of being to another, but from nonbeing to being: "In the *Moment* man becomes conscious that he is born; for his antecedent state, to which he may not cling, was one of non-being. In the *Moment* man also becomes conscious of the new birth, for his antecedent state was one of non-being. Had his preceding state in either instance been one of being, the moment would not have received decisive significance for him . . ." (pp. 25–26). To understand *this* kind of change as a version of Platonic recollection, Climacus goes on to say, would be impossible because it would be quite simply inconceivable: "It would certainly be absurd to expect of a man that he should of his own accord discover that he did not exist [new trans.: "that he does not exist"]. But this is precisely the transition of the new birth, from nonbeing to being" (p. 27). Only one who undergoes this transition is in a position to make—through subjective experience, not objective inquiry—the discovery in question.

This discovery is what Climacus calls repentance. Because it is possible only from the point of view of the transition, repentance is by its
very nature retrospective. Insofar as the one who comes into subjective
existence looks back, he can look back only on what came before existence. What, however, could it be, if not a former existence, that he
looks back upon? Climacus uses two terms to speak of it: the religious
term, "Sin," and the more philosophical term, "Error." The two terms
are equivalent as he uses them and are linked in meaning by the way
they both involve a deviation from "Truth." In the *Fragments* Climacus
had not yet defined "Truth" as "subjectivity," but the meaning was implicit, and it was of course to render this central notion explicit that
Kierkegaard had his *persona* offer a *Concluding Unscientific Postscript*
to the *Philosophical Fragments*. If we keep that meaning of "Truth" in
mind, it is possible to follow the thread of Climacus's discussion of the
repentance from sin, the theme with which the present chapter began
but which had to wait until this point for a framework for its understanding.

What one discovers when one looks back in repentance is the Error
that for Kierkegaard is sin in the theologically significant sense of the
word (as compared with a mere violation of objective norms).[22] It is an
Error that stands directly opposed to the Truth. The Truth, of course, is
subjectivity, as is later spelled out in the *Postscript,* and subjectivity is
existence in the proper as compared with the loose sense. When Climacus speaks of the new birth as a coming into existence, he is speaking
not of objective but subjective existence—the conscious actuality that is
incarnate subjectivity. It is this that was missing from the one who undergoes the change in the Moment. The Truth into which the repentant
sinner becomes newly born is subjective existence, and the Error that
was his sin was its absence. The "new creature" who makes "the transition from non-being to being" obviously existed already in the objective
sense, and it is not impossible that he may have experienced some initial, minimal subjective presence and tension, depending on whether he
was in a drunken sleep or perhaps dimly awake.[23] But when he under-

22. I will continue to follow Climacus's usage in the Swenson-Hong translation and cap-
italize the terms "Truth" and "Error" as a reminder that he uses them with rather special
meanings.
23. This would seem to be what Climacus refers to when he speaks of "the fact that the
non-being which precedes the new birth contains more being than the non-being which

goes the "Conversion" that is his coming into existence in the proper sense, he experiences a new degree of subjective presence and actuality that makes him realize the difference between Truth and Error. And, in the existential pathos of his experience of the Truth that is the inward presence of "the God," he realizes this difference in such a way that he looks back on his Error with a grief that is the obverse of the love he now experiences:

> Insofar as the learner was in Error by reason of his own guilt, this conversion cannot take place without being taken up in his consciousness, or without his becoming aware that his former state was a consequence of his guilt. With this consciousness he will then take leave of his former state. But what leave-taking is without a sense of sadness? The sadness in this case, however, is on account of his having so long remained in his former state. Let us call such grief *Repentance;* for what is repentance but a kind of leave-taking, looking backward indeed, but yet in such a way as precisely to quicken the steps toward that which lies before? (P. 23)

Conversion and repentance become possible, that is, only when one knows the living Truth of divine love in the one way that, as that which can never be an object of intellection or *a fortiori* of judgment, it can be truly known: from within.

If the difference between Truth and Error is that between actual subjective existence and its absence, however, what contribution to our understanding does it make to call the latter Error? Why not just call it absence? And why speak of it as guilty? The idea of error, in the ordinary sense of the word implies a cognitive failure, and one that is not simply the absence of an act of correct understanding, but a positive misunderstanding. Also it will be remembered from the beginning of the present chapter that Anti-Climacus spoke of sin in *Sickness* as something positive, not a mere absence or function of our finitude, and presumably Climacus and Anti-Climacus would not, at least without explanation, hold entirely different conceptions of what can be meant by the term "sin." To understand why Error is not only an absence of understand-

----

preceded the first birth" (p. 25). He does not, however, give us enough clues really to know with certainty whether he intends the phrase as a reference to the distinction between objective and subjective existence, or perhaps, as will be discussed shortly, as a reference to the distinction between potential and actual existence.

ing but a positive misunderstanding for which the one who repents can take responsibility it will be necessary to consider some aspects of the issue that Kierkegaard does not himself make explicit.

To begin with, it will be helpful to consider what kind of cognitive error might underlie the existential Error that is sin for Climacus. Related to this is the question of what kind of intentional act a misunderstanding can be understood to be or involve—for if no subjective act at all were involved, how could the supposedly guilty one be considered in any sense responsible for it?

First let us consider the mistake itself. If Error is related to Truth as nonexistence to existence, then the error in Error, as one might call it, would have to be the mistaken belief that one did exist. The existence in question, however, is subjective not objective. The nonexistence, therefore, must also be subjective, so that the error would be not the belief in one's objective existence but in one's subjective existence.

A major source of the mistake at the heart of sin, furthermore, must be the confusion of subjective and objective existence that leads us to suppose that if we can reasonably believe ourselves to exist in the objective sense (the way the drunken peasant in the cart did), that implies we also exist in the subjective sense. Climacus would say that one does not come into existence as subjective by coming to know what one is as an object, but by coming to realize what one is not. One comes into existence subjectively, from his point of view, in a movement out of Error into Truth, where Truth is subjective existence and the Error that stands opposed to it is centered in the belief that one possesses a subjective existence of one's own other than that which is the presence in inwardness of the God who redeems us from sin and Error by giving us the new birth that is the Paradox of his life in us.

The latter belief is what we might term "egoism": the belief that one has an independent existence as an entitative subject, or what was referred to in the preceding chapter as an "objective-subject." What Climacus means when he speaks of the "existing individual" as "a subject" is not that he is such an entity, but that he is an individual instance of incarnate subjectivity. At the end of the last chapter I referred to Kierkegaard as exploring the question of what an "existing individual" is and is not. And what an existing individual is not, at least for Johannes Climacus, is a quasi-objective entity. Any human individual is, to be sure, objective in his physical reality; but as "existing" in

Kierkegaard's proper sense, he is characterized by the "inwardness" that is irreducibly subjective. The appropriation-process in which one holds fast to subjectivity in inwardness is not a process of becoming an objective entity; it is a process of coming into subjective existence through the life conferred inwardly by the subjective presence of the Teacher. It would be an easy step from thinking in the objectifying egoistic way to thinking that one need not look to the Teacher for anything but objective information about what relates to one's objective reality. One would forget that what one needs and longs for and must seek from the Teacher is not knowledge about objects but subjective actuality.

It is precisely this type of forgetfulness and failure that makes Error not only a cognitive mistake but sin. To be sure, there is a mistake involved: the mistake just referred to as egoism, the illusion that one is an entitative, quasi-objective subject with an existence properly one's own. This is the error of Error. The sin that holds one in Error is something more. The sin to which the egoistic illusion gives rise and to which it clings is not the failure to understand correctly but the failure to seek to understand. The two form a vicious circle: the blurring together of the subjective and the objective is the foundation of belief in egoistic self-hood, and that belief in turn founds the clinging to self that leads one to defend one's selfhood by claiming that existence is a possession of one's own—even if, in perhaps the subtlest of egoistic twists, one acknowledges in supposed humility that one received it at some point in the past as a gift from God. Whatever the twist, "[i]n the Socratic view," as Climacus says, "each individual is his own center, and the entire world centers in him . . ." (p. 14).

In the traditional language of the Christian religion, the claim to autonomous existence is at the core of what was called the sin of Pride. It was such an illusory, egoistic selfhood that Dante depicted in his *Purgatorio* as a great stone carried on their backs by the Prideful, a burden that they only had to set down to become free from. For Climacus, however, this is not one "sin" among others; in his vocabulary it is sin as such: "But this state, the being in Error by reason of one's own guilt, what shall we call it? Let us call it *Sin*" (*Fragments*, p. 19). Kierkegaard's emphasis with regard to sin is characteristically on the subjective factor. Sin in the proper sense is not for him an objective misdeed: it is the root of subjective failure.

Like Ricoeur (and Dante), Kierkegaard images sin as a kind of self-imposed captivity. The passage immediately following the one just quoted reads almost as if it anticipated Ricoeur's discussion of the "servile will." Climacus says of the one in Error by reason of his own guilt, "he might seem to be free; for to be what one is by one's own act is freedom. And yet he is in reality unfree and bound and exiled; for to be free from the Truth is to be exiled from the Truth, and to be exiled by one's own self is to be bound" (p. 19). He also goes on to say soon after this that "no captivity is so terrible and so impossible to break, as that in which the individual keeps himself" (p. 21). It is because the Teacher frees one from this "self-imposed bondage" and its consequent "burden of guilt" that Climacus says he can be called "Saviour," "Redeemer," and "Atonement" (p. 21; new trans.: "savior," "deliverer," "reconciler"). He also says that it is precisely because one is unable to free oneself from this captivity that one needs the Teacher as something more than a teacher of objective knowledge.

Why, however, should this be the case? If the bondage is self-imposed, why can one not simply let it go of one's own accord? Climacus himself asks this very question: "But since he is bound by himself, may he not loose his bonds and set himself free?" (p. 19). All Climacus has to say in this particular passage at the beginning of the *Fragments* is that "first at any rate he must will it" and that if he were capable of willing it, it would mean he already had the power to do so and need only be reminded of it by the Teacher, which would be a return to the Socratic position that we already possess eternal being and need only remember it.

This hardly seems an answer, however, and taken by itself it would only be begging the question. Climacus's real answer comes later in his discussion of the "offended consciousness" and the "acoustic illusion." This opens with the statement, "If the Paradox and the Reason come together in a mutual understanding of their unlikeness their encounter will be happy, like love's understanding, happy in the passion to which we have not yet assigned a name"—as we saw, he subsequently gives it the name of Faith (p. 61). Translated into the terms of intentionality analysis, this would mean: if the subjective presence of the incarnate God (the Paradox) and the intention of objective knowledge (the Reason) agree in an appreciation of the absolute difference (the unlikeness) between the subjective and objective poles of consciousness, their encounter will be satisfying as a fulfillment of their mutual intention, which is incarnate subjectivity.

Behind this idea lies Climacus's shortly preceding discussion of the mutual love between human intentionality and its eternal source: "... the Reason, in its paradoxical passion, precisely desires its own downfall. But this is what the Paradox also desires, and thus they are at bottom linked in understanding..." (p. 59). Reason, that is, seeks, as was mentioned earlier, to reach toward that Unknown which is not just relatively unknown (as would be an object not yet apprehended or verified) but which can never be objectively known because it is no object but subjective actuality itself. Reason reaches toward this inherently mysterious Unknown *as though* it were objective, because it is the nature of intentionality to do so. Doing so, however, it is always in peril of forgetting the metaphorical "as though" and beginning to think of what it reaches toward as literally objective. This is how it can happen that, as Climacus says, "the Reason, in attempting to determine the Unknown as the unlike, at last goes astray, and confounds the unlike with the like" (p. 57)—confusing, that is, the subjective with the objective. "[I]f man is to receive any true knowledge about the Unknown (the God)," he goes on to say, "he must be made to know that it is unlike him, absolutely unlike him," and even this surpasses the capacity of the Reason as such, which as positive knowledge can only know the objective. The entirely negative understanding of absolute unlikeness is possible only as the understanding that the Paradox itself has in the Moment of incarnation. But when one does, by the subjective presence of the Paradox, recognize the absolute unlikeness between subject and object, this intentional reaching that is the life of the Reason is not only harmless but good, since without intentionality there would be no human consciousness, hence no incarnation, which is the goal for which the Paradox bestows itself.

Considered in this light, Reason in the Kierkegaardian sense as the subjective intention of both objective truth and subjective "Truth" can only take place when the "unlikeness" between the two is understood. Otherwise one would be speaking of Reason in a loose or analogous way, as Climacus indicates when he introduces the idea of their possibly unhappy encounter as "Offense": "If the encounter is not in understanding the relationship becomes unhappy, and this unhappy love of the Reason if I may so call it (which it should be noted is analogous only to that particular form of unhappy love which has its root in misunderstood self-love . . .) may be characterized more specifically as *Offense*" (p. 61).

"Offense" here is an equivalent term for sin, and Climacus's analysis of it answers at least in part the questions raised earlier as to what kind of intentional act might be involved in sin and why the one who binds himself in sin lacks the power to loose himself from it. Climacus immediately goes on to say: "All offense is in its deepest root passive. In this respect, it is like that form of unhappy love to which we have just alluded. Even when such a self-love (and does it not already seem contradictory that love of self should be passive?) announces itself in deeds of audacious daring, in astounding achievements, it is passive and wounded. It is the pain of its wound which gives it this illusory strength, expressing itself in what looks like self-activity and may easily deceive, since self-love is especially bent on concealing its passivity" (p. 61).

The passivity referred to is lack of genuine subjective actuality. Subjective existence is conscious, intentional activity. The person whose behavior makes him seem active but who lacks subjectivity is in reality active only in an objective, outward sense. The difference is that between an intentional action—"self-activity" as Climacus calls it—and what we might call a "twitch" or "spasm." A spasm is not an intentional action, however vigorous its motion might be objectively. As Climacus describes the spasm in question, it is a reaction to pain, and its energy is the energy of the pain.

What, then, is the pain? The answer is obvious: it is the pain of longing for subjective existence. The longing, however, is actually experienced. It is not an illusion but the beginning, at least, of subjective existence. One might even describe it as the pain of birth; but in the case of Climacus's "Offense," which rejects the idea that one could even need a new birth into Truth, the pain is experienced as though it were the endless labor of a perpetual stillbirth. From the point of view of the unrepentant sinner's pride in his autonomous existence, the ultimate affront is to tell him precisely what he most needs to know: that he does not exist. This liberating truth, however, can only be realized in the past tense—that is, from the point of view of repentance and rebirth, which looks back on what came before with the realization that in actuality he did not yet properly exist in the subjective sense.

There is a clear link here between the thought of Kierkegaard and that of Girard, even if it may involve no direct influence. The point of linkage lies in the idea of "offense," which, as Climacus points out in a footnote, is a translation of the Greek *skandalon:* "This word comes from *skandalon* (offense or stumbling-block), and hence means to take offense, or to collide with something" (*Fragments,* pp. 62–63). Climacus does not mention, since he avoids all direct reference to Christianity, that the meaning he is interested in comes from the term's use in the New Testament in such familiar passages as: " . . . if thy right eye offend thee, pluck it out. . . . if thy right hand offend thee, cut it off, and cast it from thee" (Matt. 5:29–30); the words to Peter, "Get thee behind me, Satan: thou art an offense to me" (Matt. 16:23); or "But whoso shall offend one of these little ones which believe in me, it were better for him that a millstone be hanged about his neck, and that he were drowned in the depth of the sea" (Matt. 18:6).

In Girard's analysis, the *skandalon* that causes one to stumble or become blocked or fixated is what we saw him refer to as the model-obstacle, the figure of fascination who captivates us by his aura of power and prestige. The resulting blockage may take numerous forms. It may be that one submits to enchantment by the model and becomes his more or less willing slave. Or in a less obviously servile case, one may become his loyal supporter, share his dreams, and bask in his glory. Or it may be that one attacks the model and tries to wrest for oneself the power that gives him prestige in one's eyes. In any of these or similar cases the dynamics of the process tend to be quite unconscious, so that one emulates the model without even admitting to oneself that one has taken him as a model.

Climacus, as was noted above, describes Offense as rooted in "misunderstood self-love" and in the failure to appreciate the "absolute unlikeness" between the human and the divine and between the objective and subjective poles of consciousness. The same could be said of Girard's *skandalon*. Its essential quality is fixation upon a symbol of personal power and prestige, and its dynamism is essentially the energy of a longing to become invulnerable like the model, a figure who is always imagined as ontologically secure. This naive belief in the entitative status of the model as an autonomous human-divine objective-subject is founded on a tendency, increased by the power of the enchantment, to blur the subjective and objective together into the notion of an entity who has a subjectivity rooted in his own will alone and who also possesses a rocklike objective solidity. The resulting attitude toward the model, even when it takes on the form of abject submission, is always a form of "misunderstood self-love," in that the enchantment is with an image of oneself as one would like to be: invulnerable, powerful, and immune to fear or reprisal.

Climacus also describes the "offended consciousness" as "always passive" (p. 62) despite its claim to active power. What it wants above all else is to avoid acknowledging its own passivity and its radical dependency on the Paradox for any energy it has, and even for the minimal degree of existence it can be said to enjoy—since, as Climacus puts it, "offense comes into existence with the Paradox; *it comes into existence. Here again we have the Moment, on which everything depends*" (p. 64). The offended consciousness's claim is that it exists and acts out of its own autonomous energy as an independent objective-subject, and it clings to this status fiercely, even if its fierceness (as Anti-Climacus analyzes it in *Sickness*) is the mask worn by despair.

From the Girardian point of view, this claim might be spoken of as a sort of spasmic grasping after an image. It is essentially passive in that it takes place not as an expression of genuine intention but as a mechanism of the mimetic drive. Presented with such an image of personal power, whether by an encounter with a rival or through the influence of a misguided culture, the unwary individual is led by the sheer force of the mimetic drive into an unconscious attempt to appropriate that power for himself. Tripped up in this way, the individual comes to orbit about the stumbling-block—like the ass circling endlessly about the millstone in the parable in Matt. 18:6 as analyzed by Girard.[24] All of this is obscure to the individual, who in his very bondage believes himself free and powerful. The emulation is an unconscious mechanism of the mimetic drive, despite the fact that the claims it gives rise to are consciously voiced—even howled defiantly—to the world.

This provides the answer to the question asked earlier of what there could be of subjective intention in sin. The sin (Offense) is itself subjectively passive, merely a twitching away from the life that is longed for, but it takes place in a context in which at least a minimum of sub-

---

24. In the French version of the Jerusalem Bible that Girard quotes from, the passage reads: " . . . it would be better for him to have hung about his neck one of those millstones that the asses turn. . . . " Girard relates this image to that of the *skandalon* in *Des choses cachées*, p. 575.

jectivity is present—consciousness of the idol that fascinates it, or of its own defiance, or of a pain that may only seem pointless and frustrating. The one who experiences this pain may not understand it, but the longing itself is at least the beginning of subjective existence. As actual subjectivity this existential tension is the presence of the God in the Moment (i.e., in the process of incarnation). From Climacus's point of view, this bare minimum of subjective presence is shared by every person who is conscious at all. This is why he says in the *Postscript,* as was mentioned earlier, that everyone is at least "a bit of a subject": every person who is not lying like the drunken carter in complete unconsciousness experiences the tension or "passion" that is the necessary condition both for the pain of frustration, in the case of Offense, and for the happiness of satisfaction, in the case of Faith.

Climacus emphasizes that the illusory, egoistically conceived self that Offense clings to has no subjective existence of its own and that the energy of its spasms actually derives from the incarnation process of the God, in whom alone there is genuine subjective life and upon whom the illusory ego can only live parasitically. This is why Climacus refers to our impression of the ego's life as "an acoustic illusion," like that which can give us the feeling that a ventriloquist's dummy has a life of its own: "While therefore the expressions in which offense proclaims itself, of whatever kind they may be, sound as if they came from elsewhere, even from the opposite direction, they are nevertheless echoings of the Paradox. This is what is called an acoustic illusion" (p. 63). Even the offended consciousness's mistaken belief in its own objective selfhood derives its subjective energy from the Paradox: "But precisely because offense is thus passive, the discovery . . . does not derive from the Reason, but from the Paradox; for as the Truth is *index sui et falsi* [the criterion of itself and of the false], the Paradox is this also, and the offended consciousness [new trans.: "offense"] does not understand itself but is understood by the Paradox" (*Fragments,* p. 63).[25] "Offense," Climacus goes on to say, "is the mistaken reckoning, the invalid consequence, with which the Paradox repels and thrusts aside. The of-

25. Put in Girardian terms, "offense" (the stumbling block and our stumbling over it) would be mere unconscious mechanism, the opposite of the intentional operations motivated by the appetite for truth, which manifests the only real divine presence, that of the "god of victims." See *Des choses cachées,* bk. 2, ch. 4, "Amour et connaissance" ("Love and Knowledge"), pp. 393–97.

fended individual does not speak from his own resources, but borrows those of the Paradox; just as one who mimics or parodies another does not invent, but merely copies perversely" (p. 63).

This would also be Climacus's answer to Ricoeur's search for a way to discover the evil will. Ricoeur, to phrase his issue in the language being used here, was seeking to trace along a trail of paradoxical symbols toward a vanishing point of objectivity at which, through penetrating the paradox, one might hope to be able to catch a glimpse of the subjective intention of evil as the thing-in-itself at the core of fallen man. Climacus's comment on this quest would be that it is fruitless—and not for the Kantian reason that the thing-in-itself cannot be apprehended, but because the subjective intention of evil, precisely for lack of subjectivity, cannot exist.

Since, as we saw earlier, Kierkegaard also presented, through Anti-Climacus in *The Sickness Unto Death,* the idea that sin for Christianity is something "positive," not a mere absence, he would probably say also that one could reasonably attribute to the evil will as much objective existence as to the objective "subject" Lonergan argued for. But that, of course, is just the point: it is objective only, not subjective. Except in the loose sense of an "existence so-called," it does not exist. The reality of the evil will is merely that of what was referred to above as a spasm or twitch.

Perhaps the most helpful image in this case would be a cramp. A cramp is objectively real, and one experiences real pain in it, but it is not itself an intentional action, however energetic it may be. In the case of the evil will, the cramp is a grasping after the illusion of egoistic existence. The grasping is real or "positive," but it springs not from apprehension of an actual good but from a failure to understand what is truly desired. This is why Climacus says, in a note on his statement that "the offended consciousness does not understand itself": "In this sense the Socratic principle that sin is ignorance finds justification. Sin does not understand itself in the Truth, but it does not follow that it may not will itself in Error" (*Fragments,* p. 63). Sin's "willing itself" is the cramp. But its energy is borrowed parasitically from the God. Its only subjective actuality is that of the longing to exist subjectively, a longing that is itself actual but in error is misdirected toward what does not and cannot actually exist: one's supposed self conceived of as an objective-subject. The only subjective existence is that of the God in the Moment, and the only subjective actuality that the existing individual can ever have is that which the God brings into the Moment that is his incarnation.

The point Climacus is making here was later approached from an explicitly Christian angle in the well-known Deer Park episode of the *Postscript*. It is the absolute existential dependence of each person on the one source of all subjective actuality: every instance of immanent subjectivity is dependent on the transcendent, that which in immanent presence and contingent operations becomes Climacus's "the Paradox." To one who considers things from the point of view of the egoistic illusion, even if he might be trying to believe in his dependence on a transcendent source, it is only too easy to slip into interpreting the dependency in relative terms—as a belief that for some acts, such as "sins," minor good deeds, or morally indifferent actions, one has a "natural" power of one's own, while for special, heroic deeds or saintly virtues one depends on God.

In the Deer Park episode the issue is cast in the form of a question about what it could mean to speak of dependency on God in the case of something as simple as a holiday outing: "We ought always to bear in mind that a human being can do nothing of himself, says the clergyman; hence also when one proposes to take an outing in the Deer Park, he ought to remind himself of this, as for example, that he cannot enjoy himself; and the illusion that he surely is able to enjoy himself at the Deer Park, since he feels such a strong desire for it, is the temptation of his immediacy; and the illusion that he surely can take this outing since he can easily afford it, is the temptation of his immediacy" (*Postscript*, p. 422). (By "immediacy" here is meant a lack of reflectiveness; Kierkegaard's "immediate man" thinks that what he knows is what he perceives and that what he understands is whatever pattern of thought feels natural to him.)

Climacus then goes on to consider the many ways an individual might turn over in his mind the proposition that of oneself one can do nothing. The task of the individual, as he puts it, is "to understand that he is nothing before God" (p. 412), which is equivalent to his earlier description of the "new birth, from non-being to being" in the *Fragments* (p. 27) as requiring that the one undergoing it discover "that he did not exist." After considering the forms that a comparatively worldly relativizing of the idea might take, he considers the subtlest version of the error—a religious relativizing: "A man can do nothing of himself, this he should always bear in mind. The religious individual is in this situation—he is thus among other things also unable to take an outing in the Deer Park, and why? . . . It is because he understands hour by hour that he can do nothing. In his sickly condition, the religious individual is unable to bring the God-idea together with such an accidental finitude as the taking a pleasure outing in the Deer Park" (Postscript, p. 434). This, however, is only another version of the claim to independent selfhood, even if one in which the egoistic "offense" that was analyzed in the Fragments wears the disguise of religious humility.

Such humility, from the point of view presented in the Postscript, is one of the most refined and rarefied but also most stubborn forms that resistance to the Truth of the Paradox can take. For a person captivated by his own religious humility, the transition from this illusion into Truth would have to involve a realization that there is no impotent, ontologically separate created life, but only that which is the humanity of the incarnate God.

According to Climacus's analysis of this captivity and the potential liberation from it, the religious person has to be delivered from the illusion that he possesses, and is bound in, a defective egoistic life of his own: "He feels the pain of this [his inability to take an outing in the Deer Park], and it is surely a deeper expression for his impotence that he understands it in relation to something so insignificant. . . . The difficulty is not that he cannot do it, humanly speaking, but the difficulty is first and foremost, to attain to a comprehension of his inability, and so to annul the illusion, since he should always bear in mind that he can do nothing of himself—this difficulty he has conquered, and now there remains the second difficulty: with God to be able to do it" (pp. 434–35).

As Climacus put it in the Fragments, sin and error are parasitically dependent on the subjectivity of the God in the Moment. This is why the Moment is both a "moment" in the temporal sense and also something more: it is "filled with the Eternal" (p. 22), uniting eternity and time. In its eternal aspect the Moment is the subjective presence of what Climacus calls the God. In its temporal aspect the Moment is the process in which, energized by presence of the God, the contingent operations that constitute incarnate subjectivity take place. That sin and error exist at all depends on the incipient divine presence that is experienced, whether one realizes it or not, as a longing for the fulfillment of the movement of incarnation. When this process reaches fulfillment, when the full range of intentional operations on all existential levels is actualized, then the Moment can be called "the *Fullness of Time*" (p. 22). Sin and error are merely a deflection of the energy that would fulfill this movement. Nothing they can do, however, since they lack any life of their own, can ever reduce the Moment to a mere moment of objective time, even though that is the direction in which they twist.

The Moment, therefore, is always a movement toward the fullness of time in incarnation. Every instance of incarnate subjectivity, however incomplete or distorted, remains at least a beginning. To bring this conception of human existence to full clarity it will help to consider how Climacus represents the movement from lesser to greater actualization of subjectivity as taking place.

It was mentioned above that one of the themes of the *Fragments* is Aristotle's conception of *kinesis* as a "coming-into-existence kind of change" (p. 90). In that volume the importance of this theme is emphasized, but it is still treated rather abstractly. One of the values of the *Postscript* as a supplement to the *Fragments* is that it fleshes out this theme as a concrete process of transition from one stage of existence to another.

This movement is a process of actualization, of coming into existence in the proper sense. Toward the end of the chapter on Voegelin, I suggested that the Aristotelian idea of a movement from potentiality to actuality might serve to counterbalance the tendency of Voegelin's favored Metaxy metaphor to image human existence as an inevitable deficiency longing for an unattainable sufficiency. The Metaxy image tends to locate "being" at the further pole of a tension or Eros that must always long for it because it must always fall short of it. Inherent in this rather spatialized image—whether it is Plato, Voegelin, or Ricoeur who uses it—is a tendency to cast the matter in static terms: being is imaged as a stasis "beyond" the realm of movement between the poles; man's state of deficiency is essentially static in its inescapability; and time, as the moving image of eternal stasis, is essentially an illusion, a cognitive distortion of the really real. To speak of a movement from potentiality to actuality or from lesser to greater fullness is also to use a metaphoric image, but it may be a less misleading one, and on the whole Kierkegaard tended to favor it. It has the advantage of emphasizing the dynamism of the actual rather than the stasis of the ideal.

Kierkegaard also made frequent use of the similarly metaphoric image of synthesis, as when he had Climacus say in the *Postscript:* "Existence is a synthesis of the infinite and the finite, and the existing individual is both infinite and finite" (p. 350). It is important not to misinterpret his idea of "synthesis" (Greek: "putting with") as that of a fusion; he deliberately used the term with its Greek connotation of a combination of elements that continue to remain distinct and different. Hegel is frequently described as thinking about a fusion of "thesis" and "antithesis" into a "synthesis," but, as was mentioned in the chapter on Lonergan, this was not actually Hegel's language. What Hegel talked about was "mediation," which he conceived of as an overcoming and negation of the sort of genuine difference that Kierkegaard continued to insist upon. Kierkegaard chose to use the term "synthesis" specifically to differentiate from Hegel's his own way of thinking, with its insistence on the absolute difference between the subjective and objective, infinite and finite, eternity and time.[26]

The implication of the image of synthesis as Kierkegaard used it is that any instance of incarnate subjectivity unites (without annihilation of difference) the subjective (the infinite) and the objective (the finite) in the intentionality that has the subjective as one pole or aspect and the objective as the other. Kierkegaard's term for this synthesis, which I refer to as "intentionality," was "spirit": "Man is a synthesis of the psychical and the physical; however, a synthesis is unthinkable if the two are not united in a third. This third is spirit" (*Concept of Anxiety,* p. 43). The same meaning, of course, was expressed in the *Fragments* as the idea that the Moment is a synthesis of the eternal (the subjective pole) and time (the objective).

The image of synthesis and the image of actualization share the important characteristic that they imply the involvement of both poles in that in which they are united. To speak of a synthesis is to speak of something that may involve distinctions of opposite aspects but that in itself is nevertheless one. And the image of a movement of actualization, though it is in one respect "a transition from not existing to existing" (*Fragments,* p. 91), encompasses nonetheless the notion of an increase in what is *already* existential presence. The actualization of a potential adds what might be called new existential content, but it does not have

26. Cf. *Concept of Anxiety,* pp. 10–12, and Taylor, *Journeys to Selfhood,* pp. 170–72.

to imply that before the new actuality there was no existential content whatsoever. The development of subjectivity can be described as a process in which the range of subjective operation, hence of actual subjective presence, increases by degrees. This would be the process Lonergan was referring to in his lecture on "The Subject" when he said, "For we are subjects, as it were, by degrees" (*Second Collection*, p. 80). For Kierkegaard, the process of becoming an existing individual, which is one of coming into subjective existence, is a process of becoming increasingly what to some degree one already is. It is not a change from being one kind of thing to another but an increase in subjectivity—from "a bit of a subject" (*Postscript*, p. 116) to more of one.

This, then, would be Kierkegaard's answer regarding both the value and the limitations of the Metaxy image, as he himself, speaking through Climacus, made clear in the *Postscript:* "It is with this view of life as it is with the Platonic interpretation of love as a want; and the principle that not only he is in want who desires something he does not have, but also he who desires the continued possession of what he has" (p. 110). Climacus went on there to say: "One might . . . by way of misunderstanding set up an antithesis between finality and the persistent striving for truth [i.e., subjectivity]. But this is merely a misunderstanding in this sphere" (p. 110). The persistent tension and striving that is essential to human existence is not, as Climacus images it, a matter of deficiency longing for an unattainable sufficiency; it is, in the life of Faith, a continuous subjective striving for an increase of the subjective presence that is already enjoyed.

For one who has not already found his way into Faith, on the other hand, or as Climacus might prefer to say, for one who has not yet been discovered by the Paradox, that incipient, relative plenitude of presence may not be experienced as enjoyment. It may, as in the case of one who flees toward the illusion of egoistic selfhood, be experienced as a torment. Or it may, by one who stumbles along in confusion, be experienced as something like a nagging, elusive question that hints at some other possibility of life. As Climacus describes it concretely, the process of entry into Faith begins as a movement through a sequence of stages of existence, and at various points on the journey the one making it is likely to experience both discomfort and perplexity. The stages themselves, as specified in the *Postscript,* move from the aesthetic to the ethical, then to "ethico-religious" existence ("religiousness A"), and finally to "paradoxically" or "dialectically" religious existence ("religious-ness B").

This schema of the stages of existence—in the simplified form that reduces it to the aesthetic, the ethical, and the religious—is probably Kierkegaard's most widely known single theme, even among many who may not have read his actual works. It is the one specifically Kierke-gaardian theme to which Lonergan has referred in print, for example.[27] I will try to summarize the theory of the stages as simply as possible. The aesthetic and ethical stages are fairly straightforward. The term "aesthetic" in this case refers to feeling and immediacy. For the person thinking in the aesthetic mode, the good, for example, is simply what is immediately pleasing, what feels or seems good to one who asks no fur-ther questions. Regarding questions about the real, the aesthetic person tends to assume that reality is the object of perception. Characteristi-cally he tends toward passivity in relation to whatever interests him: the good is what gives him good feelings; the real is what impresses itself on his perceptual faculties; and so on. Ethical existence, in contrast, is more reflective and also makes more demands on itself for active exer-tion. Regarding his central concern, the question of the good, the ethical person wants to *be* or *do* good and approaches this task by way of ques-tions that would carry no force for the aesthetic type, such as whether what is immediately pleasing might or might not be truly satisfying over the longer run or whether it is in accordance with one's obligations.

The emphasis in Kierkegaard's discussion of the ethical is rather on the latter than on the former point. From the Kantian point of view prevalent in Kierkegaard's philosophical milieu, the question of deep and lasting satisfaction would probably have seemed only a refinement of aestheticism, not a truly ethical question. What seemed more urgent and preoccupied Kierkegaard's archetypally ethical figures, such as

27. *Insight*, p. 624. Frederick Crowe, the former director of the Lonergan Center at the University of Toronto, said in his book, *The Lonergan Enterprise,* p. 90, that an interest in Kierkegaard would be good background for a reading of Lonergan's *Method.* Lonergan does not himself seem to have read much if anything of him, however. At a con-ference at the University of Santa Clara in 1984 in honor of Lonergan's eightieth year, Fa-ther Crowe talked about sources of evidence for Lonergan's own reading. During the question period following his lecture, I had the opportunity to ask Father Crowe if there is any evidence that Lonergan read Kierkegaard. He answered that he knew of none and that since Kierkegaard was in the air in the 1950s, Lonergan's reference to the Kierkegaar-dian stages of existence might well be based on what he had heard rather than read.

Judge William in *Either/Or* or the Knight of Infinite Resignation in *Fear and Trembling*, was how a fact or action could be located in an intelligible scheme of obligations. The Kantian goal was the transcendence of moral egoism, and Kant interpreted religion as a practical aid to this goal. Kierkegaard, however, had a very different conception of both Christianity and the transcendence of egoism. His Knight of Faith, as sketched in *Fear and Trembling*, was a person who not only made the infinite resignation of the ethical man but also reverently accepted all possibilities of enjoyment back again as gifts. In this respect religious existence as depicted there combined features of the aesthetic and the ethical in a way that would have scandalized the Kantians, to whom the Knight of Faith would probably have seemed a mere hedonist or, in the words W. H. Auden used in his Kierkegaardian sonnet sequence "The Quest," "too like a grocer for respect."[28]

The treatment of religious existence in the *Postscript* is considerably more complex than that in the earlier works, involving as it does Kierkegaard's further distinction between the two levels or types of religiousness referred to above as "religiousness A" and "religiousness B." The religiousness of the earlier Knight of Faith would in the later terminology be a version of religiousness B, which Climacus considers the only type corresponding to genuine Christian faith.[29] Religiousness A, on the other hand, is a version of ethical existence, and stands at the point of transition from the ethical to the life of Faith. It is religious in that it is concerned with what it takes to be the relation between man and God. It is ethical in that it is concerned with right action in obedience to God. It falls short of what for Climacus is religiousness in the proper sense, however (that of religiousness B) in that it misconceives both God and man as well as the relation between them. It aims at a self-transcendence in which the self, considered both as transcending and as transcended, is conceived of in the egoistic mode as an independently existing objective-subject, which carries the ironic implication that its concern with self-improvement through moral effort is really only a refinement of egoism. Its misconception of God is similarly egoistic in that the God it thinks of as demanding the ethical is merely

---

28. *Collected Poetry*, p. 260.

29. Cf. *Postscript*, p. 505, note: "... faith belongs essentially in the sphere of the paradoxic-religious.... all other faith is only an analogy."

another entity not essentially different from itself, even if better and more powerful. The ethico-religious idea of self-transcendence, in other words, amounts to no more than the subordination of one egoistically conceived entity to another.[30]

A further complication is that these two forms of religiousness as described thus far do not exhaust the picture. Although Climacus does not distinguish any other by name, there is at least an implicit distinction between religiousness A in the genuinely ethical mode and a more naive, basically aesthetic religiousness that he refers to as "immediate": "An immediate religiosity rests in the pious superstition that it can see God directly in everything; the 'awakened' individual has impudently made arrangements for God's presence wherever he himself happens to be, so that as soon as you catch sight of him you may be sure that God is there, because the 'awakened' individual has Him in his pocket" (*Postscript*, pp. 451–52). What he means is that such a person believes he has a capacity to sense the presence of God everywhere in the world as though the divine were simply a special aspect of things; he has God "in his pocket" in that he has reduced him to something perceptible or imaginable. "The aesthetic," says Climacus, "always consists in the fact that the individual imagines that he is busy grasping after God and getting hold of Him, and in the conceit that the individual is pretty smart if only he can get hold of God as something external" (p. 498).

Such aestheticism is not limited entirely to those who emphasize feeling. The intellectualizing dogmatist is no more than another version of the aesthetic type in that he too reduces the divine to a form of object—in his case an object of intellection. God, being pure subjectivity, cannot, for Kierkegaard, be in any sense or measure an object of intentional operations. God is not merely difficult to understand, he is absolutely impossible to understand, because he is not an intellectual object at all, and any effort to get an intellectual grasp of him would ex-

---

30. In terms of the Girardian framework discussed in the preceding chapter, such subordination would amount to a self-sacrificial abasement before an "external mediator." This might have some social advantages over the war between internal mediators, but from Girard's point of view a religion that interpreted the relation between man and God in such a way would miss the point of the Christian faith and of its conception of God as the "God of victims" rather than one who demands sacrifices. In this respect, despite the lack of direct influence, there is a definite affinity between Girard's critique of what he called "historical Christianity" and Kierkegaard's own "attack upon Christendom."

press only misunderstanding of the divine and a fundamental missing of the point of Christianity. This would be what Climacus calls an attempt "to push Christianity back into the aesthetic sphere (in which unwittingly the hyper-orthodox especially are successful) where the incomprehensible is the relatively incomprehensible . . ." (p. 499).

Humor, which for Climacus marks the boundary between religiousness A and B, protects against such naiveté by reminding one that God is absolutely different from and incommensurable with anything in the objective realm—the sensible, the perceivable, the conceivable, or the verifiable. "Religiosity with humor as its incognito," he says, "is . . . a synthesis of absolute religious passion . . . with a maturity of spirit, which withdraws the religiosity away from all externality back into inwardness, where again it is absolute religious passion" (p. 452). Humor, or its lesser cousin, irony, reminds the aesthetic person that God is not an object of feeling or contemplation, as it also reminds the ethical person both that God is not a behavioral ideal and that even if he were, the ethicist could do nothing to attain him.

Humor would also be the most effective antidote to the quasi-tragic notion that human existence is trapped in an inescapable state of unfulfillable longing. What Kierkegaard would probably say of Plato's Metaxy metaphor is that it is not the ultimate symbol of the human condition but rather one that expresses what human existence must seem like when considered from the point of view of the ethico-religious stage of existence and not yet from the point of view of the Paradox.

That both the aesthetic and the ethical are ultimately laughable from Climacus's point of view might make it seem that he would think the movement from the former to the latter involves no truly significant development. It is true that the transition to religiousness B must leave both behind in essentially the same category, that of finitude or object-oriented consciousness. But there is one respect in which the development from the first to the second prepares for the final transition in a way that is absolutely essential. This is that ethico-religiousness is the necessary foundation for repentance, which Climacus says "belongs in the ethico-religious sphere, and is hence so placed as to have only one higher sphere above it, namely, the religious in the strictest sense" (p. 463). Repentance, that is, is the portal into religiousness B, which is the life of the Paradox itself.

What repentance is essentially for Climacus, as was explained earlier in this chapter, is sorrow regarding failure. It looks back with regret on the life one has lived and does so because it also experiences the present love of the true life that in one's egoism one has failed to understand or appreciate. It is an essential step in the preparation for the new birth because it is a function of the letting go of what impedes it.

Nor can repentance ever be left entirely behind. Incarnate subjectivity as we experience it involves, among other things, memory. Even in the perspective of religiousness B, one's life in time is made up of layers corresponding to the existential stages. The individual always discovers himself within a framework of memory and therefore of time. And in proportion as he considers his memories of deeds done or left undone from the point of view of concerned consciousness—or "passion"—he will always find them to fall short. Always the repenter finds a past life as the background of his present, and this past always includes a false beginning: " . . . the task is presented to the individual in existence, and just as he is ready to cut at once a fine figure (which only can be done *in abstracto* and on paper, because the loose trousers of the abstractor are very different from the strait-jacket of the exister) and wants to begin, it is discovered that a new beginning is necessary, the beginning upon the immense detour of dying from immediacy, and just when the beginning is about to be made at this point, it is discovered that there, since time has meanwhile been passing, an ill beginning is made, and that the beginning must be made by becoming guilty and from that moment increasing the total capital guilt by a new guilt at a usurious rate of interest" (p. 469).

For one who discovers himself as living in time, therefore, repentance is not an accident to be sloughed off, but an essential element in the process by which one comes into subjective actuality. "Repentance," says Climacus, " . . . does not, from the religious point of view, wish to be allotted its duration, and then be past and over, the uncertainty of faith does not have its period, then to be relegated to the past, the consciousness of sin does not have its time, then to be past: for in that case we go back to the aesthetic" (p. 467, note).

Religiousness B, in which one discovers the "forgiveness of sins," takes place on the basis of the development of self-understanding that in its initial expression is consciousness of guilt and subsequently develops into consciousness of sin. Repentance, too, therefore, has its stages. The reason that for Kierkegaard the consciousness of guilt is "the first deep plunge into existence" (p. 473), as was mentioned earlier, is that it develops in the ethical stage as a function of the realization that what one longs for is not some worldly thing or sensation but a life—not an object but subjective actuality. The reason it is only the first plunge is that it remains captive to the illusion that the act required would be that of an autonomously striving ego. With the transition from the idea of guilt to that of sin the emphasis shifts from self-disapprobation to the love of what the self falls short of, from a retrospective focus on one's own failure to an anticipation of the presence of the God. As Climacus puts it, " . . . the consciousness of guilt still lies essentially in immanence, in distinction from the consciousness of sin. In the consciousness of guilt it is the selfsame subject which becomes essentially guilty by keeping guilt in relationship to an eternal happiness, but yet the identity of the subject is such that guilt does not make the subject a new man, which is the characteristic of the breach" (p. 474). This breach, when it comes, is the new birth that is the paradox of religiousness B.

As a point of transition from religiousness A to B, repentance is closely related to humor, which, as was mentioned above, marks the boundary between them. The ability to consider oneself in the light of humor is at the heart of repentance as Kierkegaard conceives it. That is, the process of repentance, as a turning from the seduction of the ego toward the Truth that is the living presence of the Paradox, is not complete until humor regarding the pretensions of the ego penetrates and shatters its defenses. As Climacus puts it, "The different existential stages take rank in accordance with their relationship to the comical, depending on whether they have the comical within themselves or outside themselves . . ." (p. 463). The "immediate" consciousness has the comical outside itself, he goes on to say; irony is the light of humor uncomprehended by its victim. When the victim becomes capable of laughing inwardly at himself, his fascinations, and even his ideals, the egoistic vision that captivates us in both the aesthetic and the ethical stages begins to lose its hold. The new birth into paradoxical religiousness cannot take place until that hold has been broken, and both humor and repentance are thrusts of the force that breaks it.

The force itself is insight. What the insight is an understanding of, however, is not an idea or intelligible form. In its initial stages, in the transition from the aesthetic to the ethical, the liberating insight takes shape as the negative realization that the objects one thought one longed for were not really what one wanted. In the transition from the ethical to the religious, it is the negative understanding referred to in the *Fragments* as the realization that one "did not exist," that the autonomous ego-entity one believed one was is in actuality a phantasm. It is an understanding, that is, not of what one is, but of what one is not.

If there is anything like a positive intellectual content to this insight it would have to be phrased as the understanding that the only actual incarnate subjectivity is that of what in the *Fragments* was called "the God in time," that in God alone we live, move, and have our being. Even this, however, must not be misinterpreted as a positive understanding of an idea. God is not an object, but purely subjective and therefore cannot be an element in an objective pattern of relations. The substantive foundation of the realization of existential truth is not an act of intellection, but the experience, unencumbered by egoistic illusion, of subjective actuality. The insight contributes to the realization in the strictly negative way that it frees one from that encumbrance. It does so by bringing to clarity the fact that the subjectivity one experiences as one's only actual conscious life is not one's own creation but a discovery and a gift. One experiences that presence and life in the strictest "inwardness" or subjectivity. One does not sense, feel, understand, or know it objectively, because it is in no way objective. The understanding that emerges from humor and repentance is, therefore, the purely negative understanding of what subjective existence is not. Once one realizes what it is not, one can cease to try to grasp it as though it were some form of experiential, intellectual, or entitative object or, in the *Postscript*'s phrase, a form of "externality." This combination of negative insight with experienced subjective presence that I just referred to as a realization of existential truth is exactly what Climacus meant by Faith, in the eminent sense, in the *Fragments*.[31]

Who, then, if not an entitative subject, has the insight? There are two ways this could be answered. Climacus's way of putting it, drawing on the language of the Christian tradition, is that God has (or one might better say, "does") the insight, but in such a way that it is also fully the act of the human individual. This is what for the *Fragments* is the Paradox that bestows itself in the Moment: the very life of the God who is present in Faith. The only genuine human subjectivity, that is, is that of

31. It is also what Voegelin meant by "openness" or "open existence."

the Paradox, the God who enters into existence in the Moment that is his incarnation. "The paradoxical edification," as it is phrased in the *Postscript,* "corresponds . . . to the determination of God in time as the individual man . . ." (p. 498).

The other way Kierkegaard might have spoken would have been in strictly negative terms: that no entity has the insight; rather insight is a process, not an entity. This way of speaking has been used extensively in the Buddhist tradition, especially in the Madhyamika and Yogacara schools of thought.[32] Kierkegaard, of course, could hardly have taken that linguistic option in his milieu. Christians have always spoken of the divine in positive, quasi-entitative terms, even if they have sometimes insisted that such language must be analogical.[33]

Medieval theologians had a maxim, *analogiae claudicant* ("analogies limp"), meaning that all analogies, however helpful they might be, carry misleading implications. In this case what is misleading, from the point of view of the Kierkegaardian analysis, would be the implication that God is objective—since as our earlier discussion of cognitional theory made clear, to speak of a real entity is to speak of what must at least in principle be a conceivable and verifiable object of some sort. This is not at all, it should be equally clear, what Kierkegaard's line of analysis moves toward. When his *personae* use the term "God," they are not referring, as they insistently remind us, to any kind of object at all but to the irreducibly subjective source of all subjective presence.

To speak in such a way, however, borders for most of us on unintelligibility. The language we ordinarily use is so thoroughly involved with an interpretative framework that does not make Kierkegaard's strict distinction between subject and object that we cannot begin to talk about "a subject" without slipping into conceiving of that subject as some sort of entity. To speak of the God's coming into existence in the Moment as identical with that of the individual in his new birth in the Moment precipitates in the imagination a picture of the collision or fusion of two entities.

32. See, for example, Frederick J. Streng, *Emptiness: A Study in Religious Meaning,* and Diana Y. Paul, "The Structures of Consciousness in Paramartha's Purported Trilogy," *Philosophy East and West* 31, no. 3 (July 1981): 231–55. Some other recent works that take up this theme are Robert Magliola, *Derrida on the Mend,* and Mark C. Taylor, *Erring: A Postmodern A/theology.*

33. See, for example, St. Thomas Aquinas, *Summa Theologica,* I, q. 13.

The major problem of Kierkegaard's work as a writer was to find a way to speak of what has always been the central mystery of the Christian faith: that God is able to become man and in doing so to redeem man from egoistic captivity. Kierkegaard's challenge was to find a language that would enable him to point his reader into this mystery without causing him to fall into one or the other of two traps that seem always to attend any effort to speak of it: the idea that God and man are two different things, or the even more dangerous error that they are the same thing. Kierkegaard's answer to this problem was to insist on the paradoxical character of any language for mystery, as when he had Climacus say regarding the idea of "the determination of God in time as the individual man" that "[t]he fact that it is not possible to think this, is precisely the paradox" and emphasized "Christianity's affirmation that the paradox it talks about cannot be thought, and thus is different from a relative paradox which at the utmost presents difficulty for thought" (*Postscript,* p. 498). "The characteristic mark of Christianity," he says, "is the paradox, the absolute paradox" (p. 480). To say that the eternal God has come into existence in time and become truly a man is to say what for ordinary language is necessarily a contradiction, a uniting of incompatible categories; and yet to say anything less would be, for Kierkegaard, to reduce Christianity to simply another version of paganism.

This may sound very much like saying that to be a Christian is to believe nonsense. Of course, as we saw, Kierkegaard's *personae* maintain that the existential Paradox is not a linguistic paradox but rather that linguistic paradox is what happens to language that attempts to treat the existential as though it were objective. But if the only way one can follow Kierkegaard's path is by speaking in language that breaks down into self-contradiction or else by leaving language behind, the attempt to do so might seem at best questionably advisable or even intellectually irresponsible. I have tried to show that Kierkegaard is not in reality the antirationalist he is often taken to be, but it must be admitted that at a certain point he drops the effort to communicate in intelligible language and that there is at least a possibility he does so too early.

There are important questions even a person sympathetic to Kierkegaard's way of thinking might wish to continue to wrestle with before deciding that language can never develop resources with which to address them, and some of these may even have a direct bearing on the existential quest he urges upon us. To speak of realizing that one "did not exist," for example, necessarily gives rise to certain questions that are directly relevant to understanding both what that proposition means and what alternatives of more adequate understanding Kierkegaard might wish us to pursue.

One of these questions, which Kierkegaard never specifically addressed, is that of what we can properly mean by the idea of "a person" and how this relates to that of "a subject." If the central theme of Christianity, as Kierkegaard emphasizes, is that God is the eternal subject who enters history by becoming a human individual or person, then it would seem important to understand what exactly the differences and similarities are between a person and a subject. This could help, for example, to indicate the difference between the God in time and the sinner he redeems while at the same time making clear why and how their real union or mutual involvement in the Moment could be possible. It would also help to clarify the relation between the drunken peasant drawn along in his cart and the other who consciously drives his horses. Would one not wish to say that the unconscious peasant remains in some sense a real human person, even if as subject he does not actually exist? Is not the sinner, who is called to realize that in his unrepentance he "did not exist," nevertheless a sinner and therefore in some psychological sense real in his error?

Another closely related question, therefore, is one that has been raised several times before: that of the relation of existence to reality. In our normal use of language we assume that these terms are directly related or even perhaps identical: that reality exists and that existence is real. Lonergan's way of thinking, as we saw, would be compatible with such a statement. Kierkegaard's, on the other hand, is quite different, but his explanation of just how it differs stops short of full explicitness. The key would seem to be that Kierkegaard's insistence on the absolute difference between subject and object implies a parallel difference between existence and reality: existence as subjective and reality as objective. With that difference in mind, one might meaningfully say what for ordinary usage would seem nonsensical: that reality does not exist and that existence is not real. To make clear that this is indeed the best way to speak of Kierkegaard's issues and to render explicit what such language can mean would be to free his meanings—as well, perhaps, as those of Voegelin, Ricoeur, and other thinkers in the existential tradition—from the trap of linguistic paradox that sometimes makes them seem nonsensical, irrational, or arbitrary. To deal with such questions will be one purpose of the next chapter.

CHAPTER 7

The Differentiation and Integration

of Consciousness

in the Individual and in History

DURING THE COURSE of this study, certain themes have emerged as central to understanding the phenomenon of consciousness. In the broadest perspective, all of the discussion can be seen to point in the direction of a challenge to play well, as Voegelin has put it, our role in the drama of being. The various thinkers we have considered, despite their differences of approach or emphasis, have shared a basic conception of where the challenge in this principally lies: in a differentiation of consciousness leading toward a new, more reflective integration of the human agent as a rational and responsible performer of the intentional operations that constitute specifically human existence.

Any human being comes into the world with both a capacity and a need to engage in some sort of action, even if it is only to cry out for nurture or affection. As the individual develops this capacity, he also gradually becomes increasingly reflective in its exercise. In the earliest stages of human development there is a kind of initial integration of consciousness around impulse that makes conscious action of a rudimentary sort possible and enables it to take place with a minimum of internal hesitation or disturbance. As reflectiveness develops, this initial smoothness of response and operation may falter as the individual becomes more capable of considering questions regarding the field of possible action and the variety of paths that could be pursued through it.

One possible response to this is to retreat from the challenges of reflectiveness and to seek recovery of the lost paradise of spontaneous impulse. Another possible response, even if it is difficult to carry out consistently, is deliberately to cultivate a maximum of reflectiveness and the differentiated awareness of experience and operation that this makes possible. The figures we have been considering would all agree that the latter path is preferable, and all share a hope that the integration of consciousness it seeks will offer the best fulfillment of the aspiration to active human existence they believe stirs within each of us.

The challenges of differentiation and integration of consciousness are lived through on the level of society and culture as a whole, as well as on that of the individuals within it. Each person's capacity for the development of reflective consciousness is inevitably affected by the level of reflectiveness attained by others in his or her historical milieu and by their attitudes toward it. A culture can encourage or discourage critical reflection and the development of a capacity for rational judgment and decision. As individuals meet or evade these challenges, their examples can serve to guide or misguide others, as can also the adequate or inadequate philosophies they develop to elucidate or obscure the possibilities that consciousness opens up to us.

The challenges involved in humanly conscious existence have faced every person who has ever been capable of reflection, perhaps as far back as the emergence of our species. The increasing differentiation of consciousness on the part of at least some human beings in different historical ages has raised the level of challenge over time. Voegelin, as we saw, discussed in his *Order and History* the challenges presented in the ancient world by the experience among leading figures of what he termed the "pneumatic" or spiritual and the "noetic" or intellectual differentiations of consciousness, Israel and Greece respectively. Our own age, it would also seem fair to say, experiences these challenges with a special acuteness. The development of modern methods of inquiry and the rapid communication now possible not only of discoveries but also of questions forces far more of us than might in an earlier age have done so to become aware, as Kierkegaard phrased it in reference to the special wisdom of Socrates, of the difference between what we do know and what we do not know, and this in turn drives us to reflect on consciousness and the question of how we come to know at all.

It seems to have been easier for people in earlier ages spontaneously to generate mythic maps of reality and to put trust in them. In the process of becoming more reflectively aware of our cognitive procedures, we have been trying for centuries to develop maps that would be as objectively accurate and as free from the symbolism of mythic imagination as possible. In the natural sciences this has not been inherently difficult—at least for those who have been willing to commit themselves to the task. In the human sciences, on the other hand, it has been more difficult, and the extent of its possibility is one of the main points of contention we have seen among the figures treated in this book. Polanyi, Lonergan, and Girard in particular have all declared an explicit concern with the problem of developing a genuinely scientific science of man that would at the same time do justice to all that distinguishes man from other phenomena of nature. The others have shared that concern to a degree, but with greater cautiousness about the dangers of possible reductionism.

Much of the controversy between Lonergan and Voegelin, for example, and implicitly between Lonergan and other existential thinkers such as Jaspers, Kierkegaard, and Ricoeur, could be said to revolve about the possibility of a radical demythologizing of such an image of human existence as that which Plato called the Metaxy or the Between. As was discussed earlier, Voegelin claimed against Lonergan that there is something about man that only philosophical myth of Plato's sort can do justice to. The central symbol in a truly adequate philosophical myth for Voegelin was the Between, imaged as a region between the merely biologically human and the divine. The central phenomenon of consciousness for him was the "existential tension," as he termed it, that we become aware of as an experienced dynamism in the area between these poles. As we saw in the chapter on his thought, Ricoeur, too, drew on Plato's image of the Between to sketch out the problem of understanding the specifically human, and Kierkegaard was thinking along similar lines when he imaged man as "a synthesis of infinite and finite" (*Postscript*, p. 350).

In an attempt to demythologize such imagery, Lonergan aimed at reconceiving its terms as metaphysical concepts grounded in a cognitional theory. This involved a conception of man as an entitative subject, with Voegelin's Platonic Beyond interpreted as a (or rather "the") divine subject conceived of in what, at least in Lonergan's *Insight*, seems to have been a similarly entitative mold. Much of the last few chapters was devoted to considering the limitations of such an approach to the problem in the light of the objections raised by such existential thinkers as Jaspers, Voegelin, Ricoeur, and Kierkegaard.

The groundwork for another possible approach was also sketched in the discussion of Girard's ideas about the social psychology of desire. The way Girard and similar thinkers, such as his collaborator, Jean-Michel Oughourlian, would probably address the problem of demythologizing the image of the Metaxy would be to interpret it as imaging various facets of the relationship between an imitator and his model. Considered from this point of view, there is no entitative "subject" or "self" that could serve as the proximate term of the relation between man and "the Beyond." Rather man as we know him, or what "self" there is, takes shape in the "interdividual" relationship between imitator and model. In this respect, at least, they agree with Voegelin, for whom *psyche* was not a thing or a part of one, but an activity—a process of dynamic interaction between the poles of the Metaxy. As Girard and Oughourlian would put it, the "self" is not an entity at all, but a function, an aspect of a process of relationship in which the dynamic principle is the mimetic drive that motivates each of us on the level of prereflective acts. Similarly, "the Beyond" or the remote term of the relation that constitutes "the Between" is a cipher for all the qualities associated with the mediator: true "being," prestige, or, in the final analysis, power.

From a Lonerganian point of view, to say that the Metaxy is mythic is simply to say that it is not the expression of a fully developed and verified system of concepts. From the Girardian point of view, it is to say that it is a symbolic construct that functions both to image and conceal a network of relationships that are essentially social and concerned with the acquisition or the holding of power, which means ultimately the capacity to exercise violence without danger of retaliation. It is characteristic that Lonergan would define myth as the opposite of metaphysics (*Insight,* p. 543) and mythic consciousness as that which is "incapable of guiding itself by the rule that the impalpable act of rational assent is the necessary and sufficient condition for knowledge of reality" (p. 538). It is equally characteristic that Girard would interpret myth as the naive encoding of the structure of the "sacrificial crisis" and its resolution.

For Lonergan, myth is a simple cognitive error about the objective world; for Girard it is a fateful and pregnant one about the social world. In the system defined by the mythic vision, Girard's sacrificial crisis finds its resolution in the collective murder of an ambiguous scapegoat-god, and the naiveté of the mythic encoding is essential to the ambiguity upon which this process relies for its traditional resolution. By masking the fact that the victim is in actuality only that—a victim—and not the superhuman source of both collective violence and reconciliation, the mythic vision makes traditional society possible. Whether that is any longer a viable procedure in a world in which the forces of violence have become powerful enough to destroy all of us is another question, on the other hand, and one Girard thinks it is time to raise.

In the argument between Lonergan and Voegelin, Girard would agree with Voegelin that myth expresses a meaning that is not to be dismissed as a failed effort at a conceptual system. On the other hand, he would also want to argue, as was discussed earlier in the chapter on his thought, that the symbolism of the Metaxy is also in need of critical analysis lest the meaning it encodes remain in darkness, where it can vitiate our efforts to understand our lives and to break free from the cycle of violence that has held us in its grip throughout history. For Girard it would probably seem characteristic not only of certain aspects of Voegelin's thought but also of mythic thinking as such that Voegelin should place such emphasis on the Platonic notion of *philosophia* as the philosopher's realization that wisdom (*sophia*) is attainable only by the gods. He would share Voegelin's belief that one must be on guard against the temptation to self-deification, but he would be wary of letting that wariness itself become simply another trap by which the mythic vision binds us to its sacrificial scenario.

Voegelin had reason to warn of the dangers of what he called "gnosticism," by which he meant an attempt to overleap the human condition and claim an unjustifiable moral and cognitive perfection or preeminence.[1] Voegelin's historical studies made use of the concept of gnosticism in this sense to analyze the various mass movements and revolutionary faiths that have enchanted whole societies in the modern world and precipitated them into the "holocausts" and "cultural revolutions" that have littered our recent history with corpses.

That analysis expressed an important truth, but from a Girardian point of view it might seem rather rough, or even crude. It explains such movements as the result of a kind of arrogant overreaching, which in

---

1. For a discussion of Voegelin's concept of gnosticism, see Webb, *Eric Voegelin*, pp. 198–207.

certain respects it is, but it does not explain the psychological dynamics of "interdividual" desire and rivalry that are also involved there, and it supposes perhaps too easily that social victimization is the result of an accidental "derailment" rather than what is possibly a structural feature of society—at least as long as societies are made up predominantly of people who are unaware of the unconscious mechanisms that drive them in their grasping after power.

Rather than interpreting true wisdom as a "divine" quality beyond our reach, Girard believes that there is a genuinely liberating (and in that quite different sense "divine") wisdom that is not only attainable but urgent. Voegelin's identification of wisdom with the Beyond and of man's life in the Between with perpetual longing might well seem to Girard less an expression of properly human humility than an evasion of what for him would be the properly and imperatively human quest for wisdom, which is to unmask and bring to light the mimetic mechanism that must otherwise control us inexorably, driving us to act out again and again in the realm of social reality its endless, sanguinary variations on the theme of sacrificial victimization.

To make use of myth, from this point of view, is to play with fire. Myth can give symbolic expression to a range of human reality that would escape the net of metaphysics, but it does so in a way that is seductive. It shows us our violence, but it does not unmask it fully, and even what it shows it continues to entice us with. Voegelin's discussion of gnosticism, moreover, sometimes has a mythic flavor of its own, in Girard's sense of the word—casting the "gnostics" as the villains of history and thereby tempting us to slip more or less unconsciously into the role of its heroes, in a melodramatic script pitting "us" against "them." In one respect, the concept Voegelin developed was a tool of demystifying analysis; in another it continued to function as an unwitting expression of the ancient mythic scenario of sacrifice. The ironic result in Voegelin's personal history was that having been chased from his Austrian homeland by what he analyzed insightfully as a movement of "gnostic activists" (the Nazis), he sometimes found himself in later life wondering what to make of some of the enthusiasts he attracted who seemed at times to want to make a new witch-hunt of the search for modern gnostics.

Girard would probably agree in the end, therefore, with Lonergan that whatever else it may involve, "mythic consciousness is the absence

of self-knowledge" (*Insight,* p. 542)—even if they offer different interpretations of exactly what it means to say this.

Considered as a corrective to the different forms of naive trust in
myth that are possible for those insufficiently critical either of objective
theories of the world or of their own subjective operations and motives,
both Lonergan and Girard make points that need to be appreciated and
remembered. Voegelin, Ricoeur, and Kierkegaard, on the other hand,
would also claim with good reason that just as myth or metaphor may
be naively misused, it would be equally naive to conclude that they can
ever be completely dispensed with. There are areas of questioning about
the subjective dimension of consciousness in particular that the language of myth has functioned historically to open up for exploration.

Voegelin's interpretation of the image of the Metaxy, for example, involved much more than just an idea of the Beyond as an unattainable
objective. It was also an image that could be used to elucidate the structure of consciousness as involving inescapably both objective and subjective dimensions. Even the image of the unattainable Beyond contributes to that meaning of the philosophical myth. Plato's Beyond as interpreted by Voegelin is not, after all, to be best understood as representing an exalted sort of object, even if such connotations tend to accompany its imagery. The myth, rather, uses its images to objectify what
would not otherwise be imaginable but which is also not in actuality an
object at all. Voegelin's idea at least, whatever Plato's may have been, is
that the Beyond is unattainable as an object precisely because it is not
an object—"not to be found among the things of the external world,
nor among the purposes of hedonistic and political action"—but irreducibly subjective.[2] Understood in such a way, a myth like that of the
Metaxy would be only accidentally and for the uncareful reader or
hearer a source of misdirection. Interpreted carefully it can serve to
guide us at least to some degree in the exploration of existential possibilities.

This exploratory role of myth and metaphor in thought—as compared with the socio-psychological role Girard criticizes—has been crucial to the development of our capacity to ask the very sorts of question
that the thinkers studied in this volume have been inquiring into. There
is no reason to suppose they will not continue to play such a role in the

2. "Reason: The Classic Experience," in *Anamnesis,* p. 96.

future history of human thought, and indeed for the exploration of the irreducibly subjective and hence inherently mysterious they would seem indispensable. At the very least, thinkers such as Voegelin and Ricoeur have shown in their historical studies that a sensitivity to mythic meaning can play an important role in the quest for self-knowledge.

The various figures studied here have diverged in some important ways on what fully developed human consciousness and self-knowledge must involve. All of those discussed, on the other hand, agree that it is this that we must seek above all else. In their ways of seeking it, moreover, they may be said to share, despite their differences of emphasis, the broad outlines of a theory of human consciousness. All of them agree that consciousness is not a mere fact but a calling and a task, and all of them would urge us, along generally similar lines, to pursue this task actively as the best hope we have for playing well our roles in the drama of human existence.

Let us consider then in conclusion what are the issues and points of convergence that have emerged from the preceding discussion as a whole and what may be consolidated from them. The issues turn upon several key questions: the manner in which consciousness may be construed as involving subjective and objective aspects or poles; the relation and possible distinction between existence and reality; and the possible ways of understanding what can be meant by the term "person."

One of the most fundamental assumptions shared by all these thinkers is that we experience consciousness as involving a distinction between subjective and objective poles and that in some manner this is essential to its structure. It was primarily the realization of this distinction, for example, that Voegelin used the phrase "differentiation of consciousness" to refer to. We saw Michael Polanyi discuss this issue in terms of a distinction between focal and subsidiary awareness or between explicit and tacit dimensions of consciousness. Polanyi's point, to which I think the other thinkers studied here would subscribe, is that human consciousness is always structured as a relation between the tacit dimension of consciousness and the specified or focal objects its activity bears upon.

Lonergan shared with Polanyi a conception of consciousness as a dynamic relation between subjective and objective dimensions. His own emphasis was on the possibility of organized pattern in that dynamism. The "differentiation of consciousness" he analyzed consisted of the realization of the distinctions and relations that can be discovered among the intentional operations that constitute the dynamism of inquiry in all of its modes—experiential, intellectual, rational, and ethical. The other thinkers studied in subsequent chapters also, as I tried to show in discussing them, appreciated the types of distinction Lonergan developed with his own special explicitness, and they also understood the normative pattern of relations Lonergan believed constituted rational and responsible human existence.

At the very least, therefore, and setting aside for the moment the more specifically spiritual problem of the manner in which consciousness may be required to relate itself to itself, the present book's inquiry into the elements of an adequate philosophy of consciousness leads to the conclusion that consciousness can be understood as the experience of performing structured combinations of intentional operations that relate the elements of experience to one another in intelligible patterns and that also relate the subjective or "tacit" dimension of consciousness to an objective dimension or pole.

What it means to speak of a distinction between subjective and objective dimensions or poles of consciousness, on the other hand, has been a major point of dispute among the thinkers here studied, just as it has among many others in the philosophical tradition. Does it mean, in particular, that there is a "real" entity, a unitary metaphysical "substance," the "subject," who confronts a world of "objects"? Or does it mean something quite different? Until one begins to probe it in depth, the idea of a "subject," equivalent in meaning to the term "person," probably seems almost self-evident. If consciousness involves intentional acts after all, common sense would say, then the acts must be intended by *somebody,* and even a thinker who carries his inquiries far beyond the scope of commonsense thinking will probably have some difficulty letting go of the idea that he himself, the inquirer, is some sort of ontologically stable, unitary entity.

It would be repetitious at this point to sum up all the ways the thinkers studied here have attacked this issue (and sometimes attacked each other over it). To establish the advantages of dispensing with the notion of an entitative subject, perhaps it will be sufficient to point out a few simple problems any attempt at a metaphysical solution must run into.

To begin with, the existence of an entitative subject as a "real" object can only be known by the procedures of rational inquiry, and it should hardly seem controversial at this point, after all the discussion of intentionality analysis and cognitional theory that has preceded, to say that this must involve experiential data, the development of a clear and adequately encompassing hypothesis by which to explain the data, and a method of testing the hypothesis that can establish it as valid. It is perhaps less obvious, but equally crucial to the question, that to be satisfactorily proven the hypothesis must not merely be found to construe a set of data but must also be found to be needed as a hypothesis and to offer a better explanation than can competing hypotheses. It must also show itself able to take into account not only the data used to support it but also any relevant data and alternative interpretations that might challenge it.

The data Lonergan offered as evidence for the objective existence of a subject of consciousness as a metaphysical hypothesis are the intentional operations that subject must be supposed to perform. One obvious problem, however, with the attempt to validate the hypothesis of a continuously self-identical ontological subject by the supposition that one is needed as the performer of such operations is that the necessity of the supposition itself can be questioned. To suppose that operations must be performed by an operator may be merely to beg the question at issue. This supposition may even itself be explainable as the result of the seductive power of the language we are accustomed to using—a language that habitually casts processes as transactions (indicated by verbs) between subjects and objects (indicated by nouns and therefore cast in the mold of entities). There is nothing inherently self-contradictory (even if it may sound odd to common sense) about a process that simply takes place as a process, without any need for entities to "do" it.

As was mentioned in the introduction to the present book, this problem with such an approach to the question of the entitative reality of a "self" or subject was pointed out by William James in 1891 in his *Principles of Psychology*. The pertinence of James's remarks to the present discussion and to what will follow is sufficiently great to make it worth quoting the concluding summary of his chapter "The Consciousness of Self":

The consciousness of Self involves a stream of thought, each part of which as "I" can 1) remember those which went before, and know the things they knew; and 2) emphasize and care paramountly for certain ones among them as "me," and *appropriate to these* the rest. The nucleus of the *"me"* is always the bodily existence felt to be present at the time. Whatever remembered-past-feelings *resemble* this present feeling are deemed to belong to the same *me* with it. Whatever other things are perceived to be *associated* with this feeling are deemed to form part of that me's *experience*; and of them certain ones (which fluctuate more or less) are reckoned to be themselves *constituents* of the me in a larger sense,—such are the clothes, the material possessions, the friends, the honors and esteem which the person receives or may receive. This me is an empirical aggregate of things objectively known. The *I* which knows them cannot itself be an aggregate; neither for psychological purposes need it be considered to be an unchanging metaphysical entity like the Soul, or a principle like the pure Ego, viewed as "out of time." It is a *Thought*, at each moment different from that of the last moment, but *appropriative* of the latter, together with all that the latter called its own. All the experiential facts find their place in this description, unencumbered with any hypothesis save that of the existence of passing thoughts or states of mind. The same brain may subserve many conscious selves, either alternate or coexisting; but by what modifications in its action, or whether ultra-cerebral conditions may intervene, are questions which cannot now be answered.[3]

(To such questions, as we shall see shortly, Jean-Michel Oughourlian has attempted to offer some answers.)

The mere fact that there are intentional operations, therefore, does not necessarily establish that they are intended or performed by an entitative subject. One way to construe the structure of consciousness, and one that has the advantage of simplicity, is simply to say that it is a bipolar process of which the subjective aspect is constituted of intentional operations (James's "Thought") while the objective is constituted of whatever those operations bear upon: experiences, ideas, and so on. If only for the sake of simplicity alone, rational inquiry following the principle of parsimony would have reason to favor such a model.

3. *Great Books of the Western World*, 53:258–59; emphasis in original.

From this point of view, what goes on as subjective process can be said to constitute human "existence" (i.e., the flow of intentional operations that is experienced as the human process of "existing"). The "real," on the other hand, as determined by such operations, can only be found within the framework of the objective pole of consciousness. The flow of operations is experienced from within, in what Polanyi called the subsidiary or tacit dimension, and cannot, therefore, be rendered a focal object or a set of such objects. Since this subjective pole or aspect of consciousness is not reducible to any combination of construable objects, it cannot properly be used as data for a hypothesis. It would be both unnecessary and misleading, therefore, to construe it as "real" or as an entitative "subject."

Another problem with the supposition of a metaphysical subject, which may give even greater cogency to the simpler hypothesis, is that one can find further empirical data, beyond the mere fact of intentional operations, that would be difficult to square with the idea of such an entity. In his *Un Mime nommé désir,* which applies Girard's theory of mimetic desire to the analysis of a variety of psychological phenomena, Jean-Michel Oughourlian offers, in the process of analyzing some empirical cases, a thoroughgoing criticism of the idea of a "subject." He suggests in its place the hypothesis that consciousness actually occurs as a function of desire (p. 138) and that the best use of the term "subject" (*"le véritable sujet,"* p. 156) would be as a reference to desire and the system of feelings and memories that become organized around it. From his consideration of a case exemplifying the phenomenon sometimes called "possession," for example, he draws the following conclusions:

> —It is desire that is the subject of the discourse [i.e., the words spoken by the individual in the state of possession].
> —Desire is, by its movement, constitutive of the self.
> Only a new anthropology that depicts the self as forming and producing itself ceaselessly as a *desire-self* [*moi-du-désir*], will enable us to understand that the subject of the discourse is desire itself and that the subject of action is the self of that same desire. (Pp. 166–67)

Since Oughourlian construes desire in turn as a mimetic process that takes place between two human individuals (which, as was mentioned above in the Girard chapter, he calls "holons" to avoid the connotations of such terms as "person," "self," or "subject"), this also means that the "self" is not to be identified with the individual but is strictly a function of the "interdividual" relationships he or she becomes involved in. New relationships can result in a radically new organization of desire and memory and therefore in a new "self" that may, in the extreme case, be experienced as completely other than the one that preceded. In some cases the new self simply replaces the old, in which case one sometimes speaks of "rebirth" or radical renewal. In other cases the old self may alternate with the new one and object to its competing presence. This is precisely what happens, according to Oughourlian, in cases of possession. As Oughourlian interprets it, exorcism is the attempt to drive out the "self" experienced as alien by the dominant personality system.

To invoke the phenomenon of possession as evidence in such a discussion might seem to wander rather far from the realm of scientific inquiry, especially since in its traditional interpretation possession is a highly mythologized notion and also because instances of the phenomenon have always been unpredictable in their manifestations. Except by way of the repeated patterns Oughourlian thinks they display when they happen to occur, they would hardly seem to meet the usual requirement that experimental evidence be replicable by further investigators.

Oughourlian himself places more weight on the evidence offered by the phenomenon of hypnosis, which *is* fully replicable in the case of any hypnotizable individual and which itself serves to further clarify, he believes, the underlying mechanism of the phenomenon of possession. According to Oughourlian, hypnosis "constitutes the concrete revelation of the interdividual relationship [*le rapport interdividuel*] and of mimetic desire" and "is the verification of all the hypotheses formulated" in his volume (p. 274). He also says that hypnosis provides the acid test by which to prove that "the self is a mythic notion": " . . . any other anthropology [than that of interdividual psychology] would render completely unintelligible, and hence mysterious, hypnotic phenomena" (p. 252).

For the experimental particulars of such phenomena, Oughourlian draws principally on cases recorded in the works of Pierre Janet and other classic investigators of hypnosis. The most striking examples have to do with the role of memory in the hypnotic state. In the ordinary view, the "subject" or "self" is regarded as a perduring, unitary entity that may be temporarily eclipsed or displaced (for example, in sleep or in a coma) but which nevertheless returns always as the same self on waking and which might be said to "have possession," through memory, of all the experience it accumulates over time.

Like James, Oughourlian thinks this is a fundamentally false conception. The evidence hypnosis offers against it is that, in cases of deep trance, the hypnotic state demonstrates patterns of memory the ordinary conception of selfhood cannot explain, but which Oughourlian says can be explained quite well by the theory of interdividual mimesis.[4] Janet found that the memory of a deeply hypnotized individual obeyed what he formulated as three "laws," all of which would be difficult to reconcile with the hypothesis of a unitary subject: (l) complete forgetfulness during the normal waking state of everything that took place during somnambulism, (2) complete remembrance during a new state of somnambulism of everything that took place during preceding somnambulisms, and (3) complete remembrance during somnambulism of everything that took place during the waking state.[5]

Oughourlian's explanation is as follows:

Hypnosis is a process in which the attention of the hypnotized is given over without reserve to a prestigious other, the hypnotist. Whereas in our ordinary interdividual relations, there is always mutual influence between the respective "holons" in the relationship, in the case of hypnosis the mimesis is unidirectional: the hypnotized imitates the gestures and more importantly the intimated desires of the hyp-

---

4. The scientific literature on hypnosis includes descriptions of many levels of hypnotic trance, from very light to very deep. On the lighter levels of trance the phenomena of state-dependent memory that are important to Oughourlian's discussion do not occur. They are well documented, on the other hand, in cases of deep trance. For an early discussion of the variety of levels of trance that are possible, see Hippolyte Bernheim, *De la suggestion et de ses applications à la thérapeutique,* 2nd ed. revised and augmented, Octave Doin, ed. (Paris, 1888), 1:1–29, translated in Maurice M. Tinterow, *Foundations of Hypnosis: From Mesmer to Freud* (Springfield, Ill.: Charles C. Thomas, 1970), pp. 438–59. The levels Bernheim lists are, in progressive degrees of depth: somnolence, light sleep, deep sleep, very deep sleep, light somnambulism, and deep somnambulism. The phenomena Oughourlian focuses on are characteristic of the level Bernheim calls "deep somnambulism."

5. Pierre Janet, *L'Automatisme psychologique,* p. 88, quoted in Oughourlian, *Un Mime nommé désir,* p. 296. As was explained above, these findings apply to cases of deep trance. In the case of a light trance, as well as that of self-hypnosis, the continuity between hypnotic and nonhypnotic consciousness is not radically broken.

notist, while the hypnotist experiences no comparable pull toward imitation of the hypnotized. Also, in ordinary interdividual relations the sense of actual or potential rivalry always makes for a certain mutual wariness on the part of each holon, whereas in hypnosis the hypnotized yields completely to the model.

According to Oughourlian's hypothesis, consciousness is an attribute of the self, and the self in turn is a function of desire (p. 291). Memory plays an essential role in consciousness and the formation of the self, since it serves to focus or register the desire around which the self forms while excluding through forgetfulness competing patterns of desire. The same systematic process of memory and forgetfulness also serves to exclude any awareness that the desire does not originate within the supposed self but in the relationship with the other. In hypnosis the hypnotized is aware only of the desires of the hypnotist, but apprehends them entirely as his or her own. The result is the formation of a new "self": "...each dialectic of desire engenders a psychogenesis, a memory, and hence a self" (p. 291).

This process of psychogenesis is not, according to Oughourlian, unique to the hypnotic state, but is essentially the same as that which takes place in the ordinary case as well. A young child relates to its parents or other models in pretty much the same way that the hypnotized does to the hypnotist. In the case of hypnosis, one might say, the intense dependency and malleability of the child returns even to an adult.

The reason Oughourlian gives for the discontinuity of memory noticed in cases of deep trance by Janet is that the old or habitual self, lacking the pattern of experience, desire, and hence of memory around which the new self has taken shape, has no consciousness in common with the new self. The new self, on the other hand, registers the experience that comes to it once it takes shape, including that which comes through the perceptual capacities of the holon during the normal waking state when the old self has returned to control of the organism. The old self receives the same experience, but assimilates it in its own manner (i.e., into its own system of desire and memory): "But once the holon is 'reawakened,' the desire-self returns as it was, with its consciousness and memory. This memory is the memory of the old self of the old desire; it was formed *before* the new memory, that of the new self of the new desire. It cannot therefore remember the experience of the new self; it can at best only foresee it" (p. 297).

This has the important implication that, as Oughourlian puts it, "the somnambulistic state is always future in relation to the habitual state of the holon" (p. 297). The reason is that psychological time, like the self that experiences it, is a function of desire: "Psychological time, which is . . . desire-time [le temps-du-désir] as the self [le moi] is a desire-self [moi-du-désir] . . . is not subject to the laws of physical time. It is movement that constitutes time. The movement of universal gravitation constitutes physical time. The movement of universal mimesis constitutes psychological time or memory, just as it also constitutes sociological time or history" (pp. 298–99).

The same principle applies to the phenomenon of rehypnosis of the hypnotized. According to the evidence of Janet's experiments, it is possible to hypnotize an individual and then go through the hypnotic process again with the new self that has developed under hypnosis.[6] This results in the formation of a further hypnotic "self" who is able to remember his own experiences and those postdating his psychogenesis, but whose experiences are inaccessible to either of the preceding selves—the habitual waking self or the first hypnotized self. What might seem the counterevidence of instances of posthypnotic recall during the waking state, in fact, turn out on examination not to be that at all. Rather, during the moments of recall, the relevant hypnotic self returns to consciousness and then subsides again, with the result that the preceding self has no memory of what took place during the interval.

The implications for the present study are profound and give rise to questions that must seem disturbing from the point of view of the commonsense picture of personality. For one thing, if Oughourlian's Girardian anthropology is sound, it makes the conventional idea of the "self" or "subject" seem indeed mythological and lends support to the existential camp among the figures we have been considering. But in doing so it renders every question regarding personhood highly problematic. If we cannot answer the "what" question with a theory of an entitative subject, we also cannot answer the "who" question in any simple manner

6. Oughourlian, *Un Mime nommé désir*, p. 298, referring to Janet, pp. 98–103. Again, this applies in cases of very deep trance.

either. If the desires we experience and identify ourselves with are to be understood as functions of the interdividual relation, if they do not originate in ourselves but in the other we unwittingly model ourselves on and who is himself equally dependent on the interdividual, then "whose" desires are they? Or again following Oughourlian and Girard, if we distinguish between natural and artificial appetites, classifying the latter but not the former as "desires," then one may wonder what types of appetite would remain if liberation from desire were possible, and "whose" they might then be said to be.

These are not questions either has addressed in a systematic way, but the passages on the Johannine Logos and the divine love in *Des choses cachées* pertain to it. There Girard spoke of an "epistemology of love" in certain passages of the New Testament, such as: "He who loves his brother abides in the light and has in him no occasion of scandal, but he who hates his brother dwells and walks in darkness; he knows not where he goes, for the darkness blinds his eyes."[7] Commenting on this passage, Girard says that "the love of which John speaks escapes from the hate-filled illusions about doubles" (i.e., from the combat of rival desire-selves). It does so by seeing through the illusory assumptions about selfhood, one's own and that of others, on which its framework of thought is founded.

From Girard's point of view, therefore, the knowledge and truth that matter ultimately are not those that pertain to theoretical understanding of the world of objects, but those that grow out of an inward realization and have the power to free us from the compulsions of a false subjectivity. This alone, he believes, can make possible peace and love between concrete human individuals, and it is only with reference to this experience of living truth that one may speak in a genuinely nonmythological way of the presence of God:

> No purely 'intellectual' process can lead to true understanding, since the supposed detachment of one who contemplates the enemy-brothers from the height of his wisdom is in the final account illusory. All human wisdom is illusory in proportion as it has not confronted the ordeal of the enemy-brothers. . . . Love alone is truly revelatory, because it escapes from the spirit of retaliation and vengeance that still clings to and limits

7. 1 John, 1:9–11, quoted by Girard, *Des choses*, p. 394.

that disclosure in our world in order to use it as a weapon against the double. Only the perfect love of Christ can accomplish without violence the perfect revelation toward which we all are advancing, in spite of everything, but on a path that runs through the dissensions and divisions correctly foreseen by the evangelical text. (P. 394)

To speak in this way of the wisdom of Christ as an inner principle of liberation and new life is to return to the paradoxes we were left with at the end of the chapter on Kierkegaard, but perhaps with a better basis for winning an intelligible meaning from them. Johannes Climacus spoke in *Philosophical Fragments* of a crucial realization that one "did not exist," and this must have seemed a perplexing notion when it was mentioned earlier. In the light of Oughourlian's critique of the idea of selfhood, however, perhaps it may seem less so. To realize that the selves whose presence we experience are not substantial entities but "desire-selves" and that they can change or multiply, even within the life of a single "holon," can help free us from the compulsion to defend our selfhood that grips us in the combat with our "enemy-brothers." It is the egoistic belief that the very existence I enjoy is identical with my imagined "self" that leads me to fight to protect that self against any threat from a rival. The "self" conceived in this way is in reality a compactly apprehended amalgam of our experiences of organic life, memories, desires, anticipations, and mythic images of the heroic roles we play in the melodramas of our daydreams. From the point of view of the insight that sees through this conception, on the other hand, what is threatened is no substantial reality but an illusory self-perception, an interpretation unconsciously generated in the interdividual process. When we come to understand this we are in a position to let go of it and recognize that the fundamental dynamism of consciousness, the true life that moves in each of us, belongs to no substantial "self" at all, since no such self exists.

To look at human personality in this way may also help us to grasp what Climacus was pointing to when he spoke of the subjective presence of the Teacher in the learner as that which makes a disciple "contemporary" with him in the reflective as compared with the "immediate" sense—when it becomes, that is, the eternal condition he shares with the Teacher in the Moment. Kierkegaard seems to have been pointing toward much the same conception of the presence of

Christ as Girard suggests when he had Climacus say "Whoever received the condition received it from the Teacher himself, and hence the Teacher must know everyone who knows him, and no one can know the Teacher except through being known by him" (*Fragments*, p. 85). In the Moment, one might say, there is one life, which is that of "the God in time" as he becomes concretely incarnate in diverse historical situations. Or to phrase it in more Girardian terms, the only true subjectivity, which emerges in our lives only in proportion as we become free from the myth of substantial selfhood, is that which Girard called, in the earlier quotation, *"l'amour parfait du Christ."* "Love, like violence," he says, "abolishes differences" (*Des choses*, p. 384), but it does so not by the mob's irrational merging of identities but by the power of truth, and brings the peace of genuine brotherhood in place of rivalry.

Kierkegaard's idea of true contemporaneity with the Teacher as the subjective discovery of his presence in the Moment finds an echo in Girard's interpretation of what it means to find true subjectivity in Christ: "To recognize Christ as God is to recognize in him the one being capable of transcending that violence which until his coming had transcended man absolutely. If violence is the subject of every mythic and cultural structure, Christ himself is the one subject who escapes from that structure to free us from its grip" (pp. 318–19).

Both Kierkegaard and Girard use the language of the Christian faith to talk about what (or "who") can be said to emerge as the subjective principle of consciousness in proportion as egoism is transcended. It might seem to many readers, however, that to use that type of language is to flirt dangerously with a myth that still retains a considerable power of seduction in our culture. Both of these figures would probably be sympathetic to such a caution. Girard's criticism of "historical Christianity" and Kierkegaard's of "Christendom" show their awareness of the temptations that religiousness is subject to. Still, it has only been in religious thought—even if only on its most critically reflective as well as spiritually sensitive level—that any language at all has been developed for the discussion of the radical contingency of human selfhood and the possibility that selfhood might be transcended. If one wishes to explore such matters, there seems no alternative but to begin with the language of those who have explored it before—which means, again, that to explore the philosophy of consciousness one can hardly help becoming engaged on a certain level with the traditional languages of myth and religion. In doing so, however, one has good reason to keep in mind the dangers that can accompany any enterprise of thinking that seeks to tap the power of such language. W. H. Auden, who as both poet and religious thinker was sensitive to these perils, once said that "a Christian ought to write in Prose/For poetry is Magic."[8] He also added, however, that such magic could be used to exorcise as well as to enchant. The only way to ensure that religion and mythology will function as beneficent forces in human life, one might say, is to maintain a clear awareness of their power to seduce as well as to liberate.

The pervasive ambiguity of religious thinking as well as its possible continuing value can be well illustrated by further consideration of the phenomenological approach of Mircea Eliade, whose influential study, *The Sacred and the Profane,* was discussed briefly above in the chapter on Girard. Eliade speaks of all religiousness as rooted in a certain experiential pattern, the sense of the sacred. This he describes as a sense of awe and fascination (simultaneous fear and attraction) before what is felt to be mysterious, powerful, and "wholly other." According to Eliade's way of analyzing it, the sense of the sacred is rooted in "an unquenchable ontological thirst."[9] "Religious man," he says, "thirsts for *being.*"[10]

This image of an unquenchable "thirst" seems to refer to the same experience as Voegelin's term "existential tension," and in both cases the point of the analysis is similar: the "tension" or "thirst" is a fundamental human experience, and the attempt to escape it would be both misguided and fruitless; rather the proper way to relate to it is to accept it as essential to the human condition and be guided by the imagery that declares "the gods" alone to enjoy an experience of existence beyond tension.[11]

---

8. Epigraph to *Collected Shorter Poems, 1927–1957.* For a discussion of Auden's poetry and religious thought in this connection, see Webb, *The Dark Dove,* pp. 239, 257–58.

9. *The Sacred and the Profane: The Nature of Religion,* p. 64.

10. Ibid. In this and subsequent quotations from Eliade, the emphasis is Eliade's.

11. Voegelin and Eliade in fact read and appreciated each other's work, as I learned in conversations with each in 1976. What they shared was a conviction that the experience in question is universal and central to the understanding of human existence. As will be explained below, however, they diverged in important respects regarding how the experience should be interpreted.

What, however, is this thirst precisely a thirst for? Or to put it another way, what is "being" for religious man? Eliade's own answer to this question, in the passage that was cited above in the Girard chapter, is ambiguous: " . . . religious man deeply desires *to be,* to participate in *reality,* to be saturated with power" (p. 13). Eliade's formulation invites two quite different interpretations: one in Lonerganian terms, the other in Girardian, depending on whether the key word is taken to be "reality" or "power."

To take the Lonerganian approach first, let us consider the implications of another formulation by Eliade: "Religious man's desire to live *in the sacred* is in fact equivalent to his desire to take up his abode in objective reality, not to let himself be paralyzed by the never-ceasing relativity of purely subjective experiences" (p. 28). If one accepts Lonergan's analysis of the idea of "objective reality," this is properly understood as that which is attained through satisfactory completion of the distinct but interrelated operations of attention, interpretation, and critical judgment regarding the accuracy of the interpretation of a set of experiential data. Naive realism, as Lonergan termed it, assumes reality to be known by immediate experience or perception ("taking a look"); but from the point of view of the more differentiated critical consciousness, the level one operation of the "look" does not give one the real, but only a perceptual impression. Much of our life, however, is made up of perception, which consists of uncritical packaging of experience, and most of the time we are content with this. Critical reflection only comes into play when we feel a need for it, which happens when we notice some discrepancy between one perception and another—as when the stick that looks bent in the water feels straight to the hand.

From this point of view, the "profound nostalgia" (p. 65) Eliade says motivates religious man to seek the sacred as a guarantee of the real would seem to be at least in part a nostalgia for experience undisturbed by the need for critical reflection. It would seem a nostalgia, that is, for a life comfortably embedded in the uncritical, undifferentiated consciousness that we experience when sensation and habits of mind come together to form our perceptions.

Considered from this angle, Eliade's tripartite schema of "the 'system of the world' prevalent in traditional societies" (p. 37) looks like a way of dealing indirectly and uncritically with the problem of the three-leveled structure of knowing. As Eliade summarizes this "system," it involves a "break" in ordinary space or time "symbolized by an opening by which passage from one cosmic region to another is made possible (from heaven to earth and vice versa; from earth to the underworld)." The "heaven" of this schema is the realm of the gods, the abode of the "really real," and the source of true order or form, while the "underworld" serves as an image of chaos and the danger of dissolution. The "earth" stands between them and shares in the characteristics of each: a partial participation in true order as human beings and the cosmos imitate a divine pattern, but also a partial lack of order, since the divine patterns are never perfectly reproduced in this world. These mythic levels of being would seem to parallel the objective poles of the three basic levels of intentional operation: the formless confusion of mere experience, the clearer but still bewildering realm of multiple possible interpretations, and the secure reality of a verified interpretation.

If this suggestion is correct, religious man's "longing to take up his abode in objective reality" and thereby escape from the "nausea" (to borrow Sartre's suggestive image) he feels in the midst of "never-ceasing relativity" would seem a nostalgia for the naive security he felt before the first stirrings of reflective consciousness began to make him uncomfortably aware that the world as merely perceived is not the only one there is. Similarly, religious man's abhorrence of "purely subjective experiences" would seem the initial discomfort one can feel at the dawning realization that consciousness involves subjectivity in the sense in which that term has been used in this study: the conscious, critically reflective performance of intentional operations. To have to know reality through critical operations and in the limited and always relative way such operations make possible may seem disorienting to one who tends basically toward the perceptionism of the naive realist. It is not surprising, therefore, that Eliade's *homo religiosus* could find appealing the idea of an opening into a higher realm through which the "really real" can reach into the world to impress itself as "objective reality" on an essentially passive recipient (i.e., on one who is not subjectively active in the sense of consciously and purposefully performing the operations of inquiry).

Turning, however, to a Girardian approach to the same phenomenon, the key phrase in Eliade's explication of religious man's desire "to be" becomes "to be saturated with power." So also, the "sense of the sacred" becomes the complex of fear and attraction one feels before a powerful "mediator" or the cultural image of one. The religious life, in turn, becomes from this point of view a sacrificial self-abasement that is ambiguously both an act of surrender and an attempt to merge with the mediator and thereby participate in his power. Hence Girard identifies the sacred itself, as we saw in his chapter, with violence.

Both approaches, the Lonerganian and the Girardian, can throw light on the phenomena Eliade describes, but at the same time there would also seem to be something more to the experience of "unquenchable ontological thirst" than merely nostalgia for naive cognitive complacency, on the one hand, or an expression of our fascination with violence on the other. It may be, as was discussed earlier, that Voegelin's own image of the experience as a "tension of existence" reaching for a divine "Beyond" carried some of the connotations of "mediation" in Girard's sense, but this was clearly not all that this imagery meant for Voegelin. His primary emphasis in his discussion of the experience in question was on the dynamism of consciousness itself, in the fullness of its dimensions—a fullness that encompassed rational reflection and responsible decision. It was not associated in any way in Voegelin's thought with a nostalgia for naive realism, which would be an aspect of what he described as gnostic escapism. Rather, Voegelin's "tension of existence," especially as he explained it in "Reason: The Classic Experience," was clearly associated in his thinking with noetic as well as with pneumatic differentiation of consciousness. He conceived of it as the experience, that is, of an inner imperative to the development of full rationality in relation to the world as well as spiritual openness in relation to what he called the "divine ground" of existence.

Religious man's "unquenchable ontological thirst" or his deep desire "to be" may, therefore, point in either of two directions: backward toward a flight from reflective consciousness or forward toward its greater development. To the extent that it points forward, the experience would correspond in most respects to that which Lonergan referred to as "the force of the question" or the "transcendental notion"—the force that, in Lonergan's thought, moves us to perform intentional operations.

This association of the "thirst" for being with the energy of intentional operations may serve as a clue to the solution of some problems that the sources considered above have left us with. One is the question of what role there might be for the idea of self-discovery in a framework of thought that submits the idea of a self to a deconstructive critique. The other is how to develop a more differentiated understanding of the role of desire in human existence than the Girardians or other critical analyses of desire, such as that in Buddhist thought, have to offer. Buddhist psychology usually speaks quite negatively of desire, interpreting it as the root of all existential misconstruction (*avidya*) and all of the human suffering that this entails. Girard, as we saw on the other hand, makes an explicit distinction between desire and appetite, so that he does not condemn the appetitive aspects of human existence altogether.[12] Still, Girard and the Girardians have said very little about what kinds of appetite are genuine and legitimate as compared with the artificial appetites (i.e., "desires") that interdividual mimesis and competitiveness give rise to.

A further development of this crucial distinction could help greatly to clarify what is needed for an adequate differentiation and integration of consciousness. If the category of "appetite" is expanded to include Voegelin's "existential tension" or the Lonerganian "transcendental notions," then self-discovery at least in the sense of the experiential discovery of genuine appetite will be seen as essential to the process of breaking free from misconstructions and gaining the existential actuality for which we genuinely thirst. Whatever else it may connote, the language of much religion and myth can also be interpreted as conveying intimations of the possibility of precisely this sort of liberating insight.

The language of religion and myth has been needed historically and probably always will be because in addition to the tasks of differentiating the bipolar structure of consciousness and the diverse intentional

12. For the sake of full clarity, however, it should be said that Buddhist pronouncements on desire tend to give a more negative impression of the Buddhist view of human appetite than is really warranted. In practice the Buddhist tradition also makes an implicit distinction of its own between desire and appetite that is very similar to Girard's. A Buddhist saint (bodhisattva) remains capable of experiencing appetite and enjoying its satisfaction, and in fact may enjoy such satisfaction all the more for being liberated from "desire." Unfortunately the failure to make this distinction explicit leads many Western readers to assume that Buddhism recommends a virtually suicidal rejection of the world. Girard himself seems to have made this assumption: in *Des choses cachées* (p. 552) he says that "in the great religions of the East" the critique of mimetic desire and the violence it gives rise to leads to a wish to escape from them completely through an absolute renunciation of all worldly undertakings, an escape into what Girard characterizes as "a sort of living death."

operations by which the subjective pole can relate to the objective, there is also the question, which was temporarily put to one side earlier, of how consciousness is called upon to relate itself to itself. In addition to the requirements of objectivity, that is, there is also a strictly inward aspect to the differentiation and integration of consciousness that must involve the individual on all levels.

This includes the process of actively realizing, through experiential insight and what in religious language is called "repentance," the difference between genuine existential appetites and the artificial desires entangled with the illusory selfhood that ordinarily holds us captive. This is a process of discovering what one truly loves and the sort of life one most deeply longs for, and its articulation in consciousness requires a language adequate to such love, longing, and repentance. Such a process of meditative elucidation of the depths of one's life is what is needed in practice to clear the way for the emergence of an active and effective appetite for actual existence.

This is not an appetite for the illusory existence of a mythically imagined self as an entity for whom the quest to "exist" is in reality a struggle for power over rival selves. Rather, when it is adequately understood, it will be discovered as an appetite for the genuine actuality of intentional operations motivated ultimately by self-transcending love. For a life lived in the light of such an understanding of one's genuine (as compared with artificial and unconsciously mimetic) longings, the true goal of our "ontological thirst" will be discovered not to be an object of any kind, but the subjective existence constituted of such operations. These in turn, moreover, will not, from this point of view, be seen as proceeding from a reified "self," but rather from an irreducibly mysterious source in the subjective dimension of consciousness.

Taking all these considerations into account, perhaps the best way to use the rather problematic term "person" in the context of an adequate philosophy of consciousness would be to use it to refer to the total system consisting of the human organism (Oughourlian's "holon") and its mental as well as physical functions—and including also its depths of spiritual mystery. A person, considered in this manner, could be said to have both outward or objective and inward or subjective aspects, depending on whether he (or she) is considered as the object of empirical, intellectual, and rational operations or as constituted by the subjective process of performing such operations.

In this sense, our "reality" consists of everything that can be objectively known about us. It is in the experience of performing our operations, on the other hand, that we may be said to "exist" in the humanly important sense of the word. The existence for which we experience genuine appetite (rather than artificial "desire") is not the objective existence of an objective entity but the subjective existence that is our actual life. The discovery of such genuine existential appetite would seem to be the true goal of the "hermeneutic of recovery" described by Ricoeur.

Even if subjective existence is the goal of our true longings as human beings, on the other hand, the objective existence of the human organism and its instrumental role in the subjective operations we can concretely perform must not be dismissed. Without eyes there could be no seeing. Without ears there could be no hearing. Without legs there could be no walking. So also without a central nervous system there could be no experiencing, interpreting, or judging, and without these in turn there could be no deciding or acting. Considered in this manner, a human "person" cannot be reduced either to his "real" or to his "existential" aspects.

Even something as seemingly objective as what we call one's "body" can be seen to share in the irreducible ambiguity that characterizes human existence. It is here, where we touch on the theme of incarnation, that Polanyi's idea of "indwelling" and the functional character of subsidiary awareness can reveal its full significance. Polanyi spoke, as we saw in the first chapter, of the manner in which we indwell physical objects and make them "form a part of our own body" as they become instruments of our conscious presence.[13] The person using a probe, as he put it, focuses his attention at the tip of the probe, so that he has a subsidiary awareness of the probe itself and of the sensations in his fingertips. In this way he incorporates it into his life in such a way that he may be said to incarnate himself in it, just as he does in his organism, his thoughts, his words, and his gestures. All of these function as elements in the life of the "person," who cannot be identified with or reduced to any one element or set of elements, but lives in and through all of them.

13. *Personal Knowledge*, p. 59. See also Mary Gerhart, "Paul Ricoeur's Notion of 'Diagnostics': Its Function in Literary Interpretation," *Journal of Religion* 56 (1976): 139–40.

Similarly, to shift to the point Oughourlian emphasizes, a person is not psychically complete as an isolated holon, but becomes the person he is in his relations with others. One could even say that the "person" as such comes into being in the process of incarnating himself—in his organism, in his "body" in Polanyi's extended sense, in his manifold operations, and also in his "interdividual" relationships.

In the latter aspect of a person's life the mimetic drive plays a major role, plunging him into dramas of adulation or conflict and producing the desire-selves that we commonly take to be the core of personality, but which both Oughourlian and the Buddhists consider so problematic.

The interdividual may be found to have its own ambiguity as well, however. There can be circumstances—when the models available are of the right sort, as in the case of the saint's *imitatio Christi*—in which the interdividual dimension of human life can lead to possibilities beyond the adulatory or conflictual alone. If Polanyi's concept of indwelling is extended to *le rapport interdividuel,* it can point toward a conception of genuinely fraternal human life in which the mimetic can function not as a source of conflict or domination but as the essential basis of mutual involvement in sympathy and affection—even, perhaps, as an instrument of the love of God.

Such a broadening of the Girardian concept of the "interdividual" would seem needed, in fact, if Girard himself is to be able to make sense of the possibility of our mutual involvement in the love of God as he has interpreted it in his comments on the first epistle of John (*Des choses,* p. 394). The mimetic drive may form personality in the mode of egoistic selfhood, but in the case of a differentiation of consciousness that culminates in self-transcending love, it may also issue into the selflessness of the saint or bodhisattva and the emergence in their persons of a life from beyond the world—which would also be, in Kierkegaard's language, the life of the God in time as experienced in the Moment. To the extent that it can be realized, this would be a life in which consciousness could be defined as the presence of God, and God in turn could be defined as the one source of life of whom our individual lives are the finite gestures. Considered in this way, Voegelin's image of the drama into which we are called as players would blend well into Kierkegaard's image of the theaters of God:

The ethical development of the individual constitutes the little private theater where God is indeed a spectator, but where the individual is also a spectator from time to time, although essentially he is an actor, whose task is not to deceive but to reveal, just as all ethical development consists in becoming apparent before God. But world-history is the royal stage where God is spectator, where He is not accidentally but essentially the only spectator, because He is the only one who *can* be. To this theater no existing spirit has access. If he imagines himself a spectator here, he merely forgets that he is himself an actor on the stage of the little theater, who must leave it to the royal spectator and actor how He will use him in the royal drama, *drama dramatum.*[14]

It would also be easy, of course, to slip once again from such a view of transcendence and human personhood into a mythic vision of the replacement or manipulation of an old, egoistic self by a new "transcendent" one. Whenever the insight that liberates from egoism is given voice it seems almost inevitably to fall victim to a renewed mythologizing. Considered in such a remythifying manner, the process Saint Paul referred to as "putting off the old man" in order to "put on Christ" would be interpreted as though it had to do with successive states of "possession" in the sense Oughourlian has been concerned with.[15] Oughourlian coined the term "adorcism" as the opposite of exorcism to refer to the manner in which religions, and cultural traditions generally, try to induce the acceptance of authorized models as a way of controlling the personality. Read in this way, Paul might seem to be speaking in such passages of a combination of exorcism and adorcism—the driving out of an old sinful "self" and the conjuring in of a new sinless one. It is of course possible that Paul may have meant something as "mythic" (in the Girardian sense) as this, but if so, this would not amount to genuine redemption of the actual human person, but merely his replacement or possession by another, more approved "self."

Traditions of religious culture have seemed on the whole to prefer exorcism and adorcism to the challenge of an insight that would expose the reifying implications of their mythological imagery and neutralize them so that the elements of genuine insight in the mythology may do

14. *Concluding Unscientific Postscript,* p. 141.
15. Cf. Rom. 13:14; Gal. 3:27; Eph. 1:24; Col. 3:9.

their proper work. Just as what Girard has called "historical Christianity" calls for a self-sacrifice that can have the ironic effect of reinforcing the sense of egoistic selfhood even as it condemns it—as sacrality in Girard's view always tends to do with its victims—so too historical Buddhism seems ironically to have tended to canonize the selfhood whose reality the more reflective level of the tradition has always denied. On the level of the popular tradition Buddhism has seen the old Indic mythology of reincarnation, interpreted as the transmigration of perduring selves into new bodies, eclipse the much more central and distinctively Buddhistic doctrine of *anatman* ("no self").

To be fair to it, however, Buddhism seems to have fared somewhat better on the whole in its historical tradition than Christianity has. Those voices that have been authoritative over time in the Buddhist tradition have always been those that reminded the faithful of the critique of egoism with which it began. The Christian tradition has tended historically to give a relatively greater prominence to the voices of figures who were more intent on using its heritage of mythic imagery as a weapon against perceived enemies of its exclusivistic claims to authority than they were on testing the limits of its metaphors. The institutional authorities of "Christendom" have usually felt suspicious of such probing thinkers as Kierkegaard, and to the extent that Kierkegaard himself has finally become widely acceptable among Christians, it seems to be through a reading that avoids the real challenge in his thought.

That challenge is, in Kierkegaard's own phrasing, to become "an existing individual." It is also, as he further described it, "to become a Christian." What he meant by the latter phrase, however, was precisely the opposite of submission to authorities and abasement before an object of adorcism.

If he is not read carefully, it would be easy to misunderstand Kierkegaard's advocacy of the imitation of Christ as an exhortation to adorcism. His own writings make clear, on the other hand, that such "admiration," as he himself termed it, would at best be the attitude of what Climacus called religiousness A, which is not yet Christianity. And it might not even be that, but simply an evasion of the serious demands of ethical existence—which means it would actually be a form of aestheticism pretending to be something higher. "O Lord Jesus Christ," Kierkegaard wrote in 1851 in his comparatively late, nonpseudonymous work, *Training in Christianity,* "Thou didst not come to the world to be served, but also surely not to be admired or in that sense to be worshipped. Thou wast the way and the truth—and it was followers only Thou didst demand. Arouse us therefore if we have dozed away into this delusion, save us from the error of wishing to admire Thee instead of being willing to follow Thee and to resemble Thee" (p. 227). "Only the 'followers' are the true Christians." he went on to say (p. 247); "The 'admirers' have in fact a pagan relationship to Christianity."

The problem with admiration and worshipful self-abasement, from Kierkegaard's point of view, is that although they are a form of relation to what is higher, they treat the higher as an object and make the objective relation an end in itself. "[A]dmiration is a deceitful relationship, or may readily become such," as Johannes Climacus put it in the *Postscript*: "One need not be a psychologist to know that there is a certain disingenuousness of spirit, which seeks to protect itself against the ethical impression precisely by means of admiration" (p. 321). The real challenge, both ethical and religious, is to exist. For one who has not yet become an existing individual to attempt to lay down his existence as a sacrifice on the altar of an object of admiration would only be to offer a phantom existence to a phantom God.

Such a way of thinking—whether in its Christianized form or in that of the adorcism of any authorized cultural model—may have the advantage for society that it replaces the dangers of what we have seen Girard call "internal mediation" (the imitation of potential rivals) with the safety of "external mediation," which places the model beyond rivalry. It also has the disadvantage, on the other hand, that it is simply another variation on the ancient, sacrificial, sanguinary myth in which reified "subjects" are cast as objects either of hatred or of worship.

That myth has had its uses in history, and in the past it may, at least some of the time, have done more good than harm. Quite apart, however, from the question Girard raises about the dangerousness of the sacrificial mentality in our present historical situation, the power of its myth effectively to win adherents is rapidly being undermined by a variety of developments within the cultural traditions it has cradled.

Considering the cultural situation of modernity in the most positive light—perhaps an exaggeratedly positive light—in its aspect, that is, as an age of science and critical reflection, one might say that the old path of external mediation can hardly seem a viable alternative to anyone who has reflected carefully on the issues considered by the thinkers who have been the focus of the present study. Once one has realized that all genuine understanding, judgment, and decision—which is to say, genuine human existence in Kierkegaard's sense—depend on one's own active performance of subjective operations, there is no way one can seriously expect the answer to the existential challenge of human life to come from one's relation to an object of admiration. When one realizes the difference between differentiated and compact consciousness and between critical and uncritical subjectivity, there is no way one can consciously choose mythic thinking in the sacrificial, reifying, and deifying mode for oneself, even if it may be all too easy to slip back into unwittingly when reflective consciousness flags.

Of course it is also possible—if one disregards Girard's warnings about the inherent dangers of such thinking—that one might choose for the sake of social control, like Dostoyevsky's Grand Inquisitor, to recommend "external mediation" and self-sacrifice for the masses. This avenue too, however, is in the process of being closed off by a feature of modern culture that Kierkegaard had already discussed as early as 1846 in his *Two Ages*.

This work analyzes the cultural situation of "the present age" and predicts the direction in which it will develop. The situation Kierkegaard describes is one in which a "leveling process" motivated by pandemic enviousness has been tearing down every figure of eminence and admiration, every possible form of recognized leadership and authority. This leveling itself is evil because it grows out of an impulse to destroy or deny every possible superior quality lest one feel oneself inferior. Yet it is a process in which God is directing history toward the emergence of potentially universal existential actuality.

As Kierkegaard puts it, this ambiguous structure in history, formed as it is by the dynamic of envy, "is dialectically opposite to the systematizing that makes the generation, preformed in the men of excellence, the supporting factor for individuals" because "it now turns polemically against individuals"; but it does so, he says, "in order to save every single individual religiously."[16] In the old order of culture, heroes or figures of admiration were able to give the individual the feeling that

16. *Two Ages: The Age of Revolution and The Present Age, A Literary Review*, trans. Howard V. Hong and Edna H. Hong, p. 107.

through participation in their eminence—sharing their attitudes, opinions, passions, and so on—he too could possess their qualities. Or else they simply followed their leaders like sheep. In "the present age," on the other hand, as the possibility of admiration becomes closed off, people have to band together as "a public" in order to find the courage to think: "Formerly the ruler, the man of excellence, the men of prominence each had his own view; the others were so settled and unquestioning that they did not dare or could not have an opinion. Now everyone can have an opinion, but there must be a lumping together numerically in order to have it. Twenty-five signatures to the silliest notion is an opinion" (p. 106).

Under the new cultural conditions, leadership and authority in the former mode are, of course, impossible, but in the irony of what Kierkegaard sees as a providential process this opens the way for a new mode of leadership that can have the maieutic effect of assisting each person to rise to the challenge of subjective existence. Whereas before, he says, "the non-commissioned officers, company commanders, generals, the hero (that is, the men of excellence, the men prominent in their various ranks, the leaders) were *recognizable.* . . . now the men of excellence, the leaders . . . will be without authority precisely because they will have divinely understood the diabolical principle of the leveling process. Like plainclothes policemen, they will be *unrecognizable,* concealing their respective distinctions and giving support only negatively . . ." (p. 107). The true leaders in the divinely intended course of history, that is, must hide their eminence in order not to tempt people to admiration and to escape into vicarious existence. "Like secret agents . . . they are unrecognizable (without authority) because of their apprehension of the universal in equality before God, because of their acceptance of the responsibility for this at all times . . ." (p. 107).

This will enable the process to complete its providential course, precipitating the mass of humanity into a spiritual wasteland in which no one will any longer be able to find any alternative to the divine challenge to come into existence:

> When the generation, which in fact has itself wanted to level, has wanted to be emancipated and revolt, has wanted to demolish authority . . . when the generation momentarily has entertained itself with the broad vista of abstract infinity, which no elevation, none whatsoever, disturbs, and in-

stead there is "nothing but air and sea"—that is the time when the work begins—then the individuals have to help themselves, each one individually. It will no longer be as it once was, that individuals could look to the nearest eminence for orientation when things got somewhat hazy before their eyes. That time is now past. They either must be lost in the dizziness of abstract infinity or be saved infinitely in the essentiality of the religious life. (Pp. 107–8)

The leveling process itself, therefore, must continue, and the servants of God must not seek to impede it, even if "every good man will have times when he could weep over its hopelessness" (p. 109). Rather those who understand it must keep silence and let the leveling proceed, because "God permits it and wants to cooperate with individuals, that is, with each one individually, and draw the highest out of it" (p. 109).

The irony of the historical process Kierkegaard describes recalls that alluded to by Girard in *Des choses cachées,* when he talks about how the modern opposition to the West's religious tradition is itself forcing a disclosure of its true, antisacrificial import: "Modern thought in this respect is reminiscent of those innumerable diggers of the desert in Deutero-Isaiah, all those slaves whose power is increased in our own day by magnificent bulldozers, who do not even know why they are leveling the mountains and filling the valleys with such strange frenzy. They have scarcely heard anything of the great king who is to pass in triumph on the road they are preparing" (pp. 397–98). He then proceeds to quote in English from the King James version of the Bible: "The voice of him that crieth in the wilderness, Prepare ye the way of the Lord, make straight in the desert a highway for our God. . . ."[17]

That even Girard turns to the language of myth at such a point, of course, is a further indication that mythic language is not in itself a problem, but only the way we habitually draw it into the framework of an objectifying, reifying, and "sacrificial" (in Girard's sense) mentality. At the end of the journey in which the objective, or what Voegelin called the noetic, dimension of consciousness is elucidated, what comes inevitably into view is its complementary subjective or spiritual dimension, and there has never been any language yet with which to communicate a sense of that realm, its challenges, and its imperative calling

17. He quotes Isaiah 40:3–8.

than that of analogical symbols and especially religious and mythological symbols such as those of Christianity or those that Voegelin drew from Plato.

The spiritual challenge has to do essentially with the manner in which consciousness is called to commit itself to itself—that is, to its own inherent structure and dynamism. As Voegelin discussed it, this is a matter of yielding and giving oneself to the tension of existence rather than fleeing from it. Such flight would be an attempt to evade objective reality as well as subjective existence. To respond in love to the divine calling, on the other hand, is to decide for existence in the full, human sense of the word—to be willing to live spiritually as well as to live and act in the world of reality.

As Voegelin interpreted them, Plato's philosophical myths orient us toward the development of consciousness, imaged as an ascent in being. This was the thrust of his interpretation of Plato's fable of the golden cord of Nous: there is a subjective dimension, imaged in the fable as a vertical dimension of movement, in which man experiences a sacred and imperative calling (imaged as a divine pull from above). This image and that of the Metaxy had the value of serving to represent consciousness as involving both horizontal and vertical dimensions, both of which are essential to specifically human existence. The horizontal dimension is the intention of objective reality as knowable through the exercise of our powers of noetic inquiry. The vertical is the "pneumatic" or spiritual dimension, that in which the call to consciousness itself is heard and heeded or else eclipsed and evaded. Neither of these dimensions, distinct as they are, can exist apart from the other—hence Voegelin's dictum quoted above in his chapter: "To move within the *metaxy*, exploring it in all directions and orienting himself in the perspective granted to man by his position in reality, is the proper task of the philosopher" (*Anamnesis,* p. 107).

All of the other thinkers here studied would agree with this, I believe, since, whatever their differences of emphasis, they have all shared the fundamental belief that consciousness can be adequately understood only in terms of both of its dimensions together—whether one speaks of these as objective and subjective, intellectual and spiritual, horizontal and vertical, or any other pair of images that can suggest what it is that must be differentiated within consciousness in order that it may eventually be adequately integrated.

The humanity that gave rise to the sacrificial mentality and mythology analyzed by Girard—a humanity that is of course far from being yet extinct—manifested a compact consciousness rather than one integrated in the present sense, and it was this very compactness that expressed itself in readiness to project evil outward onto alien objects. But for a person who has tasted and thirsts for more of the subjective actuality that constitutes genuine human existence, the old mentality cannot be a conscious option. For such a person the sacrificial script is not the truth of the drama that calls us to rise to our best possibilities. To one who has tasted even briefly the freedom of a life in which there can be neither masters nor slaves nor "enemy-brothers" but only companions in suffering and joy, to one who has consciously lived the drama of human existence to the point that its real challenges and possibilities have begun to come clear, there is no deliberate choice possible but to proceed as best one can in the pursuit of truth, both objective and subjective—the truth of reality and the truth of existence.

Bibliography

Abrams, Meyer H. *Natural Supernaturalism: Tradition and Revolution in Romantic Literature.* New York: Norton, 1973.

Adorno, Theodore W. *The Jargon of Authenticity.* Translated by Knut Tarnowski and Frederic Will. Evanston: Northwestern University Press, 1973.

Altizer, Thomas J. J. "A New History and a New But Ancient God? A Review-Essay." *Journal of the American Academy of Religion* 43 (1975): 757–64.

Aquinas, St. Thomas. *The Summa Theologica of St. Thomas Aquinas.* Translated by Fathers of the English Dominican Province. Revised by Daniel J. Sullivan. *Great Books of the Western World,* vols. 19 and 20. Chicago: William Benton, 1952.

Aristotle. *The Basic Works of Aristotle.* Edited by Richard McKeon. New York: Random House, 1941.

Auden, Wystan Hugh. *Collected Poetry.* New York: Random House, 1945.

———. *Collected Shorter Poems, 1927–1957.* New York: Random House, 1966.

Benz, Ernst. "Theogony and the Transformation of Man in Friedrich Wilhelm Joseph Schelling." In Joseph Campbell, ed., *Man and Transformation: Papers from the Eranos Yearbooks,* 5. Princeton: Princeton University Press, 1964.

Bleicher, Joseph. *Contemporary Hermeneutics.* London: Routledge and Kegan Paul, 1980.

Brown, Peter. *Augustine of Hippo: A Biography.* Berkeley and Los Angeles: University of California Press, 1967.

Butler, B. C. "Lonergan and Ecclesiology." In Philip McShane, ed., *Foundations of Theology: Papers from the International Lonergan Congress 1970*, pp. 1–21.

Byrne, Patrick H. "The Thomist Sources of Lonergan's Dynamic World-View." *The Thomist* 46 (1982): 108–45.

Cobb, John B., Jr. *Beyond Dialogue: Toward a Mutual Transformation of Christianity and Buddhism.* Philadelphia: Fortress Press, 1982.

Collins, James. *The Mind of Kierkegaard.* Princeton: Princeton University Press, 1983.

Conn, Walter E. "Bernard Lonergan on Value." *The Thomist* 40 (1976): 243–57.

Copleston, Frederick. *A History of Philosophy*, vol. 7 (1). New York: Image Books, 1965.

Crowe, Frederick. *The Lonergan Enterprise.* Cambridge, Mass.: Cowley, 1980.

Davis, Charles. "Lonergan and the Teaching Church." In Philip McShane, ed., *Foundations of Theology: Papers from the International Lonergan Congress 1970*, pp. 60–75.

Derrida, Jacques. *Speech and Phenomena and Other Essays on Husserl's Theory of Signs.* Translated with an introduction by David B. Allison. Preface by Newton Garver. Evanston: Northwestern University Press, 1973.

Doran, Robert M. "Aesthetic Subjectivity and Generalized Empirical Method." *The Thomist* 43 (1979): 257–78.

———. *Jungian Psychology and Lonergan's Foundations: A Methodological Proposal.* Washington, D. C.: University Press of America, 1979.

———. *Subject and Psyche: Ricoeur, Jung, and the Search for Foundations.* Lanham, Maryland: University Press of America, 1980.

———. "Subject, Psyche, and Theology's Foundations." *Journal of Religion* 57 (1977): 267–87.

Douglass, Bruce. "A Diminished Gospel: A Critique of Voegelin's Interpretation of Christianity." In *Eric Voegelin's Search for Order in History*, edited by Stephen A. McKnight. Baton Rouge and London: Louisiana State University Press, 1978.

Drucker, Peter Ferdinand. *Adventures of a Bystander.* New York: Harper and Row, 1979.

Dulles, Avery, S. J. Review of Lonergan's *Method in Theology. Theological Studies* 33 (1972): 553–54.

Dumouchel, Paul, ed. *Violence et vérité: Autour de René Girard.* Paris: Grasset, 1985.

Dumouchel, Paul, and Michel Deguy. *René Girard et le Problème du mal.* Paris: Grasset, 1982.

Dumouchel, Paul, and Jean-Pierre Dupuy. *L'Enfer des choses: René Girard et la logique de l'économie.* Paris: Éditions du Seuil, 1979.

Dupuy, Jean-Pierre. *Ordres et désordres: Enquêtes sur un nouveau paradigme.* Paris: Editions du Seuil, 1982.

Eliade, Mircea. *The Sacred and the Profane: The Nature of Religion.* Translated by Willard R. Trask. New York: Harcourt Brace, 1959.

Ermarth, Michael. "The Transformation of Hermeneutics." *Monist* 64 (1981): 175–94.

Freud, Sigmund. *Group Psychology and the Analysis of the Ego.* In *The Standard Edition of the Complete Psychological Works of Sigmund Freud.* Edited and translated by James Strachey. 24 vols. (London: Hogarth Press, 1953–66), 18:105.

Gadamer, Hans-Georg. "Heidegger and the History of Philosophy." Translated by Karen Campbell. *Monist* 64 (1981): 434–44.

———. *Philosophical Hermeneutics.* Translated and edited by David E. Linge. Berkeley and Los Angeles: University of California Press, 1976.

———. *Truth and Method.* New York: Seabury Press, 1975.

Garrett, Jan Edward. "Hans-Georg Gadamer on 'Fusion of Horizons.'" *Man and World* 11 (1978): 392–400.

Gelwick, Richard. *The Way of Discovery: An Introduction to the Thought of Michael Polanyi.* New York: Oxford University Press, 1977.

Gerhart, Mary. "Imagination and History in Ricoeur's Interpretation Theory." *Philosophy Today* 23 (1979): 51–68.

———. "Paul Ricoeur's Notion of 'Diagnostics': Its Function in Literary Interpretation." *Journal of Religion* 56 (1976): 137–56.

Gill, Jerry H. *On Knowing God.* Philadelphia: Westminster Press, 1981.

———. "Of Split Brains and Tacit Knowing." *International Philosophical Quarterly* 20 , no. 1 (March 1980): 49–58.

———. "Reasons of the Heart: A Polanyian Reflection." *Religious Studies* 14, no. 2 (June 1978): 143–57.

Girard, René. *Critiques dans un souterrain.* Paris: Grasset, 1976.

———. *Deceit, Desire, and the Novel: Self and Other in Literary Structure.* Translated by Yvonne Freccero. Baltimore: Johns Hopkins University Press, 1965.

————, with Jean-Michel Oughourlian and Guy Lefort. *Des choses cachées depuis la fondation du monde.* Paris: Grasset et Fasquelle, 1978.

————. *La Route antique des hommes pervers.* Paris: Grasset, 1985.

————. *The Scapegoat.* Translated by Yvonne Freccero. Baltimore and London: Johns Hopkins University Press, 1986.

————. *Violence and the Sacred.* Translated by Patrick Gregory. Baltimore and London: Johns Hopkins University Press, 1977.

Gombrich, Ernst Hans. *Art and Illusion: A Study in the Psychology of Pictorial Representation.* 5th ed. London: Phaidon, 1977.

Gram, Moltke S. "Gadamer on Hegel's Dialectic: A Review Article." *The Thomist* 43 (1979): 322–30.

Gueguen, John A. "Voegelin's *From Enlightenment to Revolution*: A Review Article." *The Thomist* 42 (1978): 123–34.

Hall, Ronald L. "Wittgenstein and Polanyi: The Problem of Privileged Self-Knowledge." *Philosophy Today* 23 (1979): 267–78.

Hallowell, John H. "Existence in Tension: Man in Search of His Humanity," *Political Science Reviewer* 2 (1972): 181–84. Reprinted in *Eric Voegelin's Search for Order in History,* edited by Stephen A. McKnight. Baton Rouge and London: Louisiana State University Press, 1978.

Hans, James S. "Hans-Georg Gadamer and Hermeneutic Phenomenology." *Philosophy Today* 22 (1978): 3–19.

————. "Hermeneutics, Play, Deconstruction." *Philosophy Today* 24 (1980): 299–317.

Ihde, Don. *Hermeneutic Phenomenology: The Philosophy of Paul Ricoeur.* Evanston: Northwestern University Press, 1971.

Innis, Robert E. "Art, Symbol, and Consciousness: A Polanyi Gloss on Susan Langer and Nelson Goodman." *International Philosophical Quarterly* 17 (1977): 455–76.

————. "Hans-Georg Gadamer's *Truth and Method*: A Review Article." *The Thomist* 40 (1976): 311–21.

————. "The Logic of Consciousness and the Mind-Body Problem in Polanyi." *International Philosophical Quarterly* 13 (1973): 81–98.

James, William. *Essays in Radical Empiricism and A Pluralistic Universe.* In one volume. Edited by Ralph Barton Perry. Gloucester, Mass.: Peter Smith, 1967.

————. *The Principles of Psychology.* In *Great Books of the Western World,* vol. 53. Chicago: William Benton, 1952.

Jaspers, Karl. *Philosophy.* Translated by E. B. Ashton. 3 vols. Chicago and London: University of Chicago Press, 1969–71.

―――. *Reason and Existenz: Five Lectures.* Translated with an introduction by William Earle. New York: Noonday Press, 1955.

Johnson, John F. "The Relationship Between Direct and Reflective Understanding As an Issue in Lonergan's *Insight.*" *Kinesis* 10 (1980): 87–91.

Joy, Morny. Review of Paul Ricoeur, *Time and Narrative,* vol. 1. *Religious Studies Review* 12 (1986): 247–51.

Kaufmann, Walter. *Discovering the Mind.* Vol. 1: *Goethe, Kant, and Hegel.* New York: McGraw-Hill, 1980.

―――. *Discovering the Mind.* Vol. 2: *Nietzsche, Heidegger, and Buber.* New York: McGraw-Hill, 1980.

―――. *Discovering the Mind.* vol 3: *Freud versus Adler and Jung.* New York: McGraw-Hill, 1980.

―――. *Hegel: A Reinterpretation.* Notre Dame: University of Notre Dame Press, 1978.

Kepnes, Steven D. Review of Paul Ricoeur, *Time and Narrative,* vol. 1. *Religious Studies Review* 12 (1986): 247–51.

Kierkegaard, Søren. *The Concept of Anxiety: A Simple Psychologically Orienting Deliberation on the Dogmatic Issue of Hereditary Sin.* Edited and translated by Reidar Thomte with the collaboration of Albert B. Anderson. Princeton: Princeton University Press, 1980.

―――. *Concluding Unscientific Postscript to the Philosophical Fragments: A Mimic-Pathetic-Dialectic Composition: An Existential Contribution.* Translated by David F. Swenson and Walter Lowrie. Princeton: Princeton University Press, 1941.

―――. *Journals and Papers.* Vol. 2: *F–K.* Edited and translated by Howard V. Hong and Edna H. Hong, assisted by Gregor Malantschuk. Bloomington and London: Indiana University Press, 1970.

―――. *Philosophical Fragments or A Fragment of Philosophy.* Translated by David F. Swenson and Howard V. Hong, Introduction and commentary by Niels Thulstrup. Princeton: Princeton University Press, 1962.

―――. *Philosophical Fragments; Johannes Climacus.* Edited and translated with introduction and notes by Howard V. Hong and Edna H. Hong. Princeton: Princeton University Press, 1985.

―――. *The Sickness Unto Death: A Christian Psychological Exposition for Upbuilding and Awakening.* Edited and translated by Howard V.

Hong and Edna H. Hong. Princeton: Princeton University Press, 1980.

———. *Training in Christianity*. Translated with an introduction and notes by Walter Lowrie. Princeton: Princeton University Press, 1967.

———. *Two Ages: The Age of Revolution and The Present Age, A Literary Review*. Edited and translated with an introduction and notes by Howard V. Hong and Edna H. Hong. Princeton: Princeton University Press, 1978.

Kirby, John, and William M. Thompson, eds. *Voegelin and the Theologian: Ten Studies in Interpretation*. Toronto Studies in Theology, vol. 10. New York and Toronto: Edwin Mellen Press, 1982.

Kirkland, Frank M. "Gadamer and Ricoeur: The Paradigm of the Text." *Graduate Faculty Philosophy Journal* 6 (1977): 131–44.

Kitchener, Richard F. "Piaget's Genetic Epistemology." *International Philosophical Quarterly* 20 (1980): 377–405.

Kroger, Joseph. "Polanyi and Lonergan on Scientific Method." *Zbornik Slovenskeho Narodnaho Muzea. Serie: Historie* (Bratislava) 21, no. 1 (1977): 2–20.

———. "Theology and Notions of Reason and Science: A Note on a Point of Comparison in Lonergan and Polanyi." *Journal of Religion* 56 (1976): 157–61.

Lawrence, Frederick. "Gadamer and Lonergan: A Dialectical Comparison." *International Philosophical Quarterly* 20 (1980): 25–47.

Lefort, Guy, with René Girard and Jean-Michel Oughourlian. *Des choses cachées depuis la fondation du monde*. Paris: Grasset et Fasquelle, 1978.

Lindenfeld, David F. *The Transformation of Positivism: Alexius Meinong and European Thought, 1880–1920*. Berkeley and Los Angeles: University of California Press, 1980.

Locke, John. *An Essay Concerning Human Understanding*. Edited by Alexander Campbell Fraser. In *Great Books of the Western World*, 35:85–395. Chicago: William Benton, 1952.

Lonergan, Bernard J. F. *Caring About Meaning: Patterns in the Life of Bernard Lonergan*. In *Thomas More Institute Papers*, vol. 82. Edited by Pierrot Lambert, Charlotte Tansey, and Cathleen Going. Montreal: Thomas More Institute, 1982.

———. *Collection: Papers by Bernard Lonergan, S. J.* Edited by Frederick E. Crowe, S. J. New York: Herder and Herder, 1967.

————. *De Constitutione Christi Ontologica et Psychologica.* Rome: Gregorian University Press, 1956.

————. *De Deo Trino: Pars analytica.* Rome: Gregorian University Press, 1961.

————. *Grace and Freedom: Operative Grace in the Thought of St. Thomas Aquinas.* New York: Herder and Herder, 1971.

————. *Insight: A Study of Human Understanding.* 3rd ed. New York: Philosophical Library, 1970.

————. *Method in Theology.* New York: Herder and Herder, 1972.

————. *Philosophy of God, and Theology.* Philadelphia: Westminster Press, 1973.

———— "Reality, Myth, and Symbol." In *Myth, Symbol, and Reality*, edited by Alan M. Olson, pp. 31–37.

————. *Second Collection.* Edited by William F. Ryan, S. J., and Bernard J. Tyrell, S. J. Philadelphia: Westminster Press, 1974.

————. "Theology and Praxis." In Catholic Theological Society of America, *Proceedings of the Thirty-Second Annual Convention* Toronto, 1977, pp. 1–16.

————. *The Way to Nicea: The Dialectical Development of Trinitarian Theology.* Translated by Conn O'Donovan. Philadelphia: Westminster Press, 1976. [Translation of Part 1 of *De Deo Trino.*]

Lovejoy, Arthur O. *The Great Chain of Being: A Study of the History of an Idea.* Cambridge, Mass., and London: Harvard University Press, 1936.

MacIntyre, Alasdair. *After Virtue.* Notre Dame: University of Notre Dame Press, 1981.

McKnight, Stephen A., ed. *Eric Voegelin's Search for Order in History.* Baton Rouge and London: Louisiana State University Press, 1978.

McPartland, Thomas J. "Horizon Analysis and Historiography: The Contribution of Bernard Lonergan Toward a Critical Historiography." Ph. D. dissertation, University of Washington, 1976.

McShane, Philip, ed. *Foundations of Theology: Papers from the International Lonergan Congress 1970.* Notre Dame: University of Notre Dame Press, 1972.

————, ed. *Language, Truth, and Meaning: Papers from the International Lonergan Congress 1970.* Notre Dame: University of Notre Dame Press, 1972.

Magliola, Robert. *Derrida on the Mend*. West Lafayette: Purdue University Press, 1984.

Malantschuk, Gregor. *Kierkegaard's Thought*. Edited and translated by Howard V. Hong and Edna H. Hong. Princeton: Princeton University Press, 1971.

Mann, Thomas. *Joseph and His Brothers*. Translated by H. T. Lowe-Porter with an introduction by the author. New York: Knopf, 1948.

Marcel, Gabriel. *The Mystery of Being*, vol. 1. Chicago: Henry Regnery, 1960.

————. *Tragic Wisdom and Beyond, including Conversations between Paul Ricoeur and Gabriel Marcel*. Translated by Stephen Jolin and Peter McCormick. Evanston: Northwestern University Press, 1973.

Margolis, Joseph. "Puzzles Regarding the Cultural Link Between Artworks and Criticism." *Journal of Aesthetic Education* 15 (1981): 17–32.

Martin, Graham Dunstan. "The Tacit Dimension of Poetic Imagery." *British Journal of Aesthetics* 19 (1979): 99–111.

Mathews, William. "Lonergan's Economics." *Method: Journal of Lonergan Studies* 3, no. 1 (March 1985): 9–30.

Misgeld, Dieter. "On Gadamer's Hermeneutics." *Philosophy of the Social Sciences* 9 (1979): 221–39.

Moore, George Edward. *Philosophical Studies*. New York: Harcourt Brace, 1922.

Newman, John Henry. *An Essay in Aid of A Grammar of Assent*. Edited by Charles Frederick Harrold. New York: Longmans, Green and Co., 1947.

Niemeyer, Gerhart. "Eric Voegelin's Philosophy and the Drama of Mankind." *Modern Age* 20 (1976): 28–39.

Oakley, Francis. *Omnipotence, Covenant, and Order: An Excursion in the History of Ideas from Abelard to Leibniz*. Ithaca and London: Cornell University Press, 1984.

Olding, A. "Polanyi's Notion of Hierarchy." *Religious Studies* 16 (1980): 97–102.

Olson, Alan M. "Myth, Symbol, and Metaphorical Truth." In Alan M. Olson, ed., *Myth, Symbol, and Reality*, pp. 99–125. Notre Dame: University of Notre Dame Press, 1980.

Opitz, Peter J., and Gregor Sebba. *The Philosophy of Order: Essays on History, Consciousness, and Politics* [For Eric Voegelin on His Eightieth Birthday, January 3, 1981]. Stuttgart: Klett-Cotta, 1981.

Oughourlian, Jean-Michel, with René Girard and Guy Lefort. *Des choses cachées depuis la fondation du monde.* Paris: Grasset et Fasquelle, 1978.

Oughourlian, Jean-Michel. *Un Mime nommé désir: Hystérie, transe, possession, adorcisme.* Paris: Grasset et Fasquelle, 1982.

Pagels, Heinz. *The Cosmic Code: Quantum Physics as the Language of Nature.* New York: Simon and Schuster, 1982.

Paul, Diana Yamaguchi. *Philosophy of Mind in Sixth-Century China: Paramartha's Evolution of Consciousness.* Palo Alto: Stanford University Press, 1984.

———. "The Structures of Consciousness in Paramartha's Purported Trilogy." *Philosophy East and West* 31, no. 3 (July 1981): 231–55.

Piscitelli, Emil J. "Paul Ricoeur's Philosophy of Religious Symbol: A Critique and Dialectical Transposition." *Ultimate Reality and Meaning* 3 (1980): 275–313.

Plato. *The Collected Dialogues of Plato Including the Letters.* Edited by Edith Hamilton and Huntington Cairns. Princeton: Princeton University Press, 1961.

Polanyi, Michael. *Knowing and Being: Essays by Michael Polanyi.* Edited by Marjorie Grene. Chicago: University of Chicago Press, 1969.

———. *Personal Knowledge: Towards a Post-Critical Philosophy.* Corrected edition. Chicago: University of Chicago Press, 1962.

———. *Science, Faith, and Society.* Chicago and London: University of Chicago Press, 1964.

———. *The Study of Man.* Chicago and London: University of Chicago Press, 1959.

———. *The Tacit Dimension.* Garden City, N. Y.: Doubleday, 1966. New York: Anchor Books, 1967.

Rasmussen, David M. "From Problematics to Hermeneutics: Lonergan and Ricoeur." In Philip McShane, ed., *Foundations of Theology: Papers from the International Lonergan Congress 1970,* pp. 236–71.

Ricoeur, Paul. *The Conflict of Interpretations: Essays in Hermeneutics.* Edited by Don Ihde. Evanston: Northwestern University Press, 1974. (Originally published in French, 1965.)

———. "Conversations between Paul Ricoeur and Gabriel Marcel." In Gabriel Marcel, *Tragic Wisdom and Beyond, including Conversations between Paul Ricoeur and Gabriel Marcel.* Translated by Stephen Jolin and Peter McCormick. Evanston: Northwestern University Press, 1973.

————. *Essays on Biblical Interpretation.* Edited by Lewis S. Mudge. Philadelphia: Fortress Press, 1980.

————. *Fallible Man: Philosophy of the Will.* Translated by Charles Kelbley. Chicago: Henry Regnery Co., 1965. (Originally published in French, 1960.)

————. *Freedom and Nature: The Voluntary and the Involuntary.* Translated with an introduction by Erazim V. Kohák. Evanston: Northwestern University Press, 1966. (Originally published in French, 1950.)

————. *Freud and Philosophy: An Essay on Interpretation.* Translated by Denis Savage. New Haven and London: Yale University Press, 1970. (Originally published in French, 1965.)

————. *Gabriel Marcel et Karl Jaspers: Philosophie du mystère et philosophie du paradoxe.* Paris: Temps Présent, 1948.

————. *History and Truth.* Translated with an introduction by Charles A Kelbley. Evanston: Northwestern University Press, 1965. (Originally published in French, 1955.)

————. *Husserl: An Analysis of His Phenomenology.* Evanston: Northwestern University Press, 1967.

————. *Karl Jaspers et la philosophie de l'existence.* With Mikel Dufrenne. Paris: Editions du Seuil, 1947.

————. *Political and Social Essays.* Edited by David Stewart and Joseph Bien. Athens: Ohio University Press, 1975.

————. *The Reality of the Historical Past.* The Aquinas Lecture, 1984. Milwaukee: Marquette University Press, 1984.

————. *The Rule of Metaphor: Multidisciplinary Studies of the Creation of Meaning in Language.* Translated by Robert Czerny with Kathleen McLaughlin and John Costello. Toronto, Buffalo, and London: University of Toronto Press, 1977.

————. *The Symbolism of Evil.* Translated by Emerson Buchanan. Boston: Beacon Press, 1967. New York: Harper and Row.

————. *Temps et récit.* Vol. 3: *Le temps raconté.* Paris: Editions du Seuil, 1985. [The untranslated third volume of his *Time and Narrative.*]

————. *Time and Narrative,* vols. 1 and 2. Translated by Kathleen McLaughlin and David Pellauer. Chicago and London: University of Chicago Press, 1984, 1986.

Ryan, William F. J. "Intentionality in Edmund Husserl and Bernard Lonergan." *International Philosophical Quarterly* 13 (1973): 173–190.

Sagan, Eli. *At the Dawn of Tyranny: The Origins of Individualism, Political Oppression, and the State*. New York: Alfred A. Knopf, 1985.

Sala, Giovanni. "The *A Priori* in Human Knowledge: Kant's *Critique of Pure Reason* and Lonergan's *Insight*." *The Thomist* 40 (1976): 179–221.

Sandoz, Ellis. *The Voegelinian Revolution: A Biographical Introduction*. Baton Rouge and London: Louisiana State University Press, 1981.

————, ed. *Eric Voegelin's Thought: A Critical Appraisal*. Durham: Duke University Press, 1982.

Sartre, Jean-Paul. *Nausea*. Translated by Lloyd Alexander. New York: New Directions, 1949.

Schelling, Friedrich Wilhelm Joseph von. *Schellings Werke*. 6 vols. Edited by Manfred Schröter. Munich: C. H. Beck and R. Oldenbourg, 1927–28.

Schuchman, Paul. "Aristotle's Phronesis and Gadamer's Hermeneutics." *Philosophy Today* 23 (1979): 41–50.

Schürmann, Reiner. "The Loss of Origin in Soto Zen and Meister Eckhart." *The Thomist* 42 (1978): 281–312.

Searle, John. *Intentionality: An Essay in the Philosophy of Mind*. Cambridge: Cambridge University Press, 1983.

Shmueli, Adi. *Kierkegaard and Consciousness*. Princeton: Princeton University Press, 1971.

Skousgaard, Stephen. *Language and the Existence of Freedom: A Study in Paul Ricoeur's Philosophy of Will*. Washington, D. C.: University Press of America, 1979.

————. "Revisiting Fundamental Ontology: Ricoeur versus Gadamer." *Tulane Studies in Philosophy* 29 (1980): 119–32.

Smith, Marc. "Religious Experience and Bernard Lonergan." *Philosophy Today* 23 (1979): 359–66.

Smith, P. Christopher. "Gadamer's Hermeneutics and Ordinary Language Philosophy." *The Thomist* 43 (1979): 296–321.

Streng, Frederick J. *Emptiness: A Study in Religious Meaning*. Nashville: Abingdon Press, 1967.

Taylor, Charles. *Hegel*. Cambridge: Cambridge University Press, 1975.

Taylor, Mark C. *Erring: A Postmodern A/theology*. Chicago and London: University of Chicago Press, 1984.

————. *Journeys to Selfhood: Hegel and Kierkegaard*. Berkeley and Los Angeles: University of California Press, 1980.

Thulstrup, Niels. *Kierkegaard's Relation to Hegel.* Translated by George L. Stengren. Princeton: Princeton University Press, 1980.

Tracy, David. *The Achievement of Bernard Lonergan.* New York: Herder and Herder, 1970.

Tyrell, George N. M. *Man the Maker: A Study of Man's Mental Evolution.* New York: E. P. Dutton, 1952.

Voegelin, Eric. *Anamnesis.* Translated and edited by Gerhart Niemeyer. Notre Dame and London: University of Notre Dame Press, 1978.

————. "Configurations of History." In Paul G. Kuntz, ed., *The Concept of Order,* pp. 23–42. Seattle and London: University of Washington Press, 1968.

————. "Equivalences of Experience and Symbolization in History." In *Eternità e Storia: I valori permanenti nel divenire storico* pp. 215–34. Florence: Valecchi, 1970.

————. *From Enlightenment to Revolution.* Edited by John H. Hallowell. Durham: Duke University Press, 1975.

————. "The Gospel and Culture." In Donald G. Miller and Dikran Y. Hadidian, eds., *Jesus and Man's Hope,* 2:59–101. Pittsburgh: Pittsburgh Theological Seminary, 1971.

————. *The New Science of Politics: An Introduction.* Chicago: University of Chicago Press, 1952.

————. "On Hegel: A Study in Sorcery." *Studium Generale* 24 (1971): 335–68.

————. *Order and History.* Vol. 1: *Israel and Revelation.* Baton Rouge: Louisiana State University Press, 1956.

————. *Order and History.* Vol. 2: *The World of the Polis.* Baton Rouge: Louisiana State University Press, 1957.

————. *Order and History.* Vol. 3: *Plato and Aristotle.* Baton Rouge: Louisiana State University Press, 1957.

————. *Order and History.* Vol. 4: *The Ecumenic Age.* Baton Rouge: Louisiana State University Press, 1974.

————. *Order and History.* Vol. 5: *In Search of Order.* Baton Rouge: Louisiana State University Press, 1987.

————. "The Origins of Scientism," *Social Research* 15 (1948): 462–94.

————. *Die politischen Religionen.* Vienna: Bermann-Fischer, 1938.

————. *Die Rassenidee in der Geistesgeschichte von Ray bis Carus.* Berlin: Junker and Duennhaupt, 1933.

————. "Response to Professor Altizer's 'A New History and a New But Ancient God?'" *Journal of the American Academy of Religion* 43 (1975): 765–72.

Webb, Eugene. *The Dark Dove: The Sacred and Secular in Modern Literature.* Seattle and London: University of Washington Press, 1975.

———. *Eric Voegelin: Philosopher of History.* Seattle and London: University of Washington Press, 1981.

———. "Eric Voegelin's Theory of Revelation." *The Thomist* 42 (1978): 95–122. Reprinted in Ellis Sandoz, ed., *Eric Voegelin's Thought: A Critical Appraisal,* pp. 157–78.

———. "The Pneumatology of Bernard Lonergan: A Byzantine Comparison." *Religious Studies and Theology* 5, no. 2 (1985): 13–23.

———. "Politics and the Problem of a Philosophical Rhetoric in the Thought of Eric Voegelin." *Journal of Politics* 48 (1986): 260–73.

Wilhelmsen, Frederick D. "The New Voegelin." *Triumph* January 1975, pp. 32–35.

Wittgenstein, Ludwig. *Philosophical Investigations.* 3rd ed. Translated by G. E. M. Anscombe. New York: Macmillan, 1958.

Worgul, George S. "The Ghost of Newman in the Lonergan Corpus." *Modern Schoolman* 54, no. 4 (May 1977): 317–32.

Index

Actuality: and potentiality (Aristotle),
127; subjective, 263, 278, 318. See also
Actualization; Existence, potential vs.
actual
Actualization, 270, 271–72; in history
(Kierkegaard), 314–16
Adam, in Ricoeur, 146
Admiration (Kierkegaard), 312–13,
314–15
Adorcism (Oughourlian), 311–12, 313
Aeschylus, 168, 169–70
Aestheticism, 312; in Ricoeur, 165–68
Altizer, Thomas J. J., 154n
Analogy, 280, 317; Lonergan and
Ricoeur on, 158–59
Anamnesis. See Recollection
Anatman, Buddhist doctrine of, 312
Anaximander, 122, 209
Aporia, 176–77
Appetite, existential, 307–8; in
Kierkegaard, 242
Appetites and needs: distinguished from
desire (Girard), 184–85, 307
Aquinas, 23, 156; on grace, 128;
compared with Lonergan, 129
Aristophanes, 168–69
Aristotle, 44, 56, 61, 156, 164, 166–67,
169, 170, 202, 208, 212, 270;
compared with Plato, 127–28;
compared with Lonergan, 129.
See also Metaphysics, Aristotelian
Auden, W. H., 182n, 274, 303

Augustine, 29, 172, 174; argued for
persecution of heretics, 182

Bacon, Francis, 33
Bad faith: Ricoeur on, 147
Bateson, Gregory, 192
Being: proportionate (Lonergan), 78–79,
82; interpreted as power (Girard), 193,
228, 287, 304
Belief: Lonergan and Kierkegaard on,
110; in the sense of rational judgment
(Kierkegaard), 238–39
Bentham, 28
Benz, Ernst, 133–34
Bergson, Henri, 17; mentioned, 12
Between, 286, 289. See also Metaxy
Beyond, the (Voegelin), 126, 208, 287,
289; defined, 96; also a "divine
Within," 106; not an object, 290
Bible: Girard on, 221–22, 316. See also
Adam; Christ; Devil; Jesus; Satan
Body, 309; in Polanyi, 43–44, 45,
51–52; as conceived by Lonergan, 78
Boehme, Jacob, 132
Brentano, Franz, 32
Broz, Josip. See Tito, Marshal
Buddhism, 280, 307, 312

Care (Heidegger and Ricoeur), 172, 173,
174
Catharsis, 208; Ricoeur on, 167–68
Certitude (J. H. Newman), 59, 238

Christ: Girard on, 218–19, 224;
    Lonergan on, 66, 224–25; as true
    subject, 302; saint's imitation of, 310,
    312. *See also* Christology; Jesus
Christianity, 18–24; "historical"
    (Girard), 219–20, 225, 302, 312
Christology, 18–19, 66
Cognition: passivist theory of, 55; tacit
    (Polanyi), 64–66. *See also* Cognitional
    theory; Perceptualism
Cognitional theory (Lonergan), 60
Common sense: as a "realm of meaning"
    in Lonergan, 74, 75, 78, 79, 83; in
    Voegelin, 131
Comte, Auguste, 31
Consciousness: as a term, 4–10; as
    constituted of subjective and objective
    poles, 6, 44, 73, 79, 161, 177, 227,
    242, 245, 271, 291–92; defined by
    Lonergan, 66–69; undifferentiated
    (Lonergan), 80; as conceived by
    Girard, 183; radical contingency of
    (Kierkegaard), 252–53; and society,
    285; as a function of desire
    (Oughourlian), 295, 298; compact,
    318. *See also* Differentiation of
    consciousness; Noetic differentiation;
    Pneumatic differentiation
Conversion (Kierkegaard), 255–56, 258
Cords, golden and iron: image in Plato,
    96–97; interpreted by Voegelin, 99,
    101, 102, 105, 173–74, 223, 317
Critical realism, 213, 304; in Ricoeur,
    156–57; in Kierkegaard, 234–35,
    237–38
Crowe, Frederick, S. J., 273n

Dante, 260–61
Dasein: Jaspers, 111–13; Heidegger, 172
Davis, Charles, 101
Deconstruction, 163, 206, 211, 307
Deformation of symbols. *See* Symbols,
    deformation of
Demystification, 18, 206, 289
Demythologizing, 207, 287; Girard on,
    211, 215, 222; in Lonergan, Voegelin,
    and Girard, 213; in Freud, 214
Derrida, Jacques, 207, 210
Descartes, 32, 33, 39, 58, 138, 139;

Polanyi's criticism of, 40; mentioned,
    36, 234
Desire: mimetic or triangular (Girard),
    183; metaphysical (Girard), 184, 185,
    193–94, 212, 228; and the self
    (Oughourlian), 295, 298–99. *See also*
    Appetites and needs
Desymbolism (Girard), 204
Determinism, 80
Devil: in Ricoeur, 146; as mimetic desire
    (Oughourlian), 224n. *See also* Satan
Difference: as origin of culture (Girard),
    196; as a cognitive principle (Girard),
    212
Differentiation of consciousness, 5–6,
    285, 291, 317–18; in Lonergan,
    72–73, 76, 80. *See also* Noetic
    differentiation; Pneumatic
    differentiation
Divinity: as symbol of power (Girard),
    193
Doctrinization (Voegelin), 124. *See also*
    Symbols, deformation of
Doran, Robert M., 104–5
Dostoyevsky, 314
Double-bind (Girard), 192
Doubles (Girard), 195
Drama: as image for human existence
    (Voegelin), 92–93, 98, 99–100,114,
    203–4, 284; in Voegelin and
    Kierkegaard, 247n, 310–11. *See also*
    Aeschylus; Aristophanes; Euripides;
    Narrative form; Sophocles; Tragedy
Drucker, Peter, 26–29
Dualism: Cartesian, 7; in the imagery of
    Voegelin, 120–22, 125, 129, 136,
    174; in myth of the exiled soul
    (Ricoeur), 145–46; Ricoeur's freedom
    from, 173–74
Dulles, Avery, S. J., 109n
Duty (Lonergan), 88

Egoism, 259–60, 269, 272, 274, 279,
    281, 301–2, 311–12; as rooted in
    "acoustic illusion" (Kierkegaard),
    266–67
Einstein, Albert, 34, 57, 58, 84
Eliade, Mircea, 185–86, 303–6
Embodiment (Ricoeur), 172–73. *See*

also Incarnation

Emergence: Polanyi, 48; Lonergan, 82

Emplotment (Ricoeur), 167, 178

Entity, theoretical (Lonergan), 80

Envy, 314

Epistemology (Lonergan), 60.
  See also Love, epistemology of

Eros, 244. *See also* Passion; Tension,
  existential

Essentialism: Girard on, 212

Eternity, 178

Eternity (Kierkegaard), 253

Eudaimonia (Aristotle), 129

Euripides, 168

Evil: myths of the origin and end of
  (Ricoeur), 145–47

Evil, human, 16, 17, 144, 146–47;
  mimetic mechanism as the source of
  (Girard), 222; Kierkegaard on, 267

Existence: as term, 88–89; as conceived
  by Voegelin, 107; as conceived by
  Ricoeur, 158, 161–62; subjective vs.
  objective (Kierkegaard), 227, 243–46,
  250, 257, 259–60; open vs. closed
  (Voegelin), 250; radical contingency of
  (Kierkegaard), 252–53, 268–70;
  potential vs. actual (Kierkegaard),
  257n23, 260; as a synthesis
  (Kierkegaard), 271, 286; stages of
  (Kierkegaard), 272–78; as a process of
  intentional operations, 295

Existence, human: drama as image for,
  92–93

Existence, subjective, 93, 95, 162, 163,
  226, 317, 318; in Kierkegaard,
  232–33, 251, 263, 266; as the
  presence of God (Kierkegaard), 240;
  "coming into" (Kierkegaard), 257,
  268; as challenge, 315–16. *See also*
  Actualization; Existence, potential vs.
  actual; Existence and reality; *Existenz;
  Existenzerhellung*

Existence and reality: Kierkegaard, 282;
  distinction between, 295, 309, 318

Existence [*Dasein*] analysis (Jaspers),
  111–13

Existential: definition of term, 86; in
  Lonergan's use, 89

Existentialism, 95; Ricoeur on, 143–44.

See also Existenz; Existenzerhellung

Existential tension. *See* Tension,
  existential

Existenz: term in Jaspers, 100, 102; as
  subjective existence, 102

Existenzerhellung (Jaspers): as a term,
  100; likened to prayer 110;
  distinguished from "existence
  analysis" and metaphysics, 111–12,
  113; Girard and, 211

Exorcism: as interpreted by Oughourlian,
  296; adorcism distinguished from, 311

Experience: as conceived by Lonergan,
  54–55, 66–69

Externality: as term in Kierkegaard, 279

Faculty psychology: rejected by Lonergan
  and Ricoeur, 158

Faith: as defined by Lonergan, 87; "in the
  eminent sense" and "in the ordinary
  sense" (Kierkegaard), 110, 238–39,
  247–48, 249, 251, 254; postcritical
  (Ricoeur), 141–42; hermeneutic
  (Ricoeur), 181; as conceived by
  Kierkegaard, 230, 272, 274; leap of
  (Kierkegaard), 248, 250; as passion
  (Kierkegaard), 251, 261; the
  "autopsy" of (Kierkegaard), 255

Fermi, Enrico, 83–84

Fichte, Johann Gottlieb, 153; mentioned,
  12, 227

Focal and subsidiary awareness (Polanyi),
  11, 38–39, 42–45, 98–99, 172, 291;
  correlated with "inner" and "outer,"
  57; correlation with part-whole
  relation, 76

Forgiveness of sins (Kierkegaard), 277

Fraser Spiral: illustration, 63;
  implications for cognitional theory,
  63–66, 72

Freedom: in the tragic and Adamic myths
  (Ricoeur), 146–48; as constituent of
  personhood (Ricoeur), 148

Freud, 17, 32, 137, 150, 184, 197,
  213–15; Voegelin's and Ricoeur's
  attitudes toward, 141; theory of
  religion,188–89; theory of the
  unconscious, 189–90; mentioned, 14.
  See also Oedipus complex

Gadamer, Hans-Georg, 12
Gill, Jerry H., 47n22
Girard, René, 5, 13–14, 17, 136, 166, 168, 169, 182, 224, 286–89; influence in France, 30; conception of consciousness, 183; on appetites and needs, 184–85, 307; on external and internal mediation, 187–88, 210, 228, 313, 314; compared with Freud, 188–92; on the unconscious, 189–90; conception of divinity, 193; and doubles, 195; on hominization, 196–98; on "founding murder," 199; conception of myth, 201, 205; compared with Voegelin, 202, 204; compared with Ricoeur, 203, 220–21; and desymbolism, 204; compared with Lonergan, 210–11; and essentialism, 212; critique of Freudian psychology, 213–15, 223; on God, 215–16, 218; conception of genuine subjectivity, 218–19, 222, 223; on sin and human evil, 219, 220–22; on historical Christianity, 219–20, 225, 302, 312; on the Bible, 221–22, 316; critique of objectivism and subjectivism, 223–25; compared with Kierkegaard, 263–65, 266n; his epistemology of love, 300–301; contrasted with Eliade, 305–6; on Buddhism, 307n; philosophy of history, 316; mentioned, 125, 229, 295. *See also* Being; Demythologizing; Desire; Metaphysics; Mimesis; Model-obstacle; Religion; Victimizing mechanism
Gnosticism: Voegelin's critique of, 121, 125, 126, 129, 288
God: as conceived by Lonergan, 108–9, 241; as conceived by Schelling, 134; Girard's conception of, 210, 215–16, 218, 300–301; as object of metaphysical desire, 212; as a "projection" (Freud), 213; objectified, 223; as conceived by Kierkegaard, 240–42, 275–76; as "egoistically" conceived, 274–75; incarnation of, 310. *See also* Divinity
Goethe, Johann Wolfgang von, 32

Good: of order (Lonergan), 87
Guilt: in the thought of Kierkegaard, 232, 278

Hayek, Frederick, 28
Hegel, Georg Wilhelm Friedrich, 22–23, 32, 55–56, 58, 59–60, 135, 177, 236n; in Ricoeur, 150, 154n; cognition as active process, 153; in Voegelin, 154n; mentioned, 12, 13, 227
Heidegger, Martin, 172, 173, 174, 208; mentioned, 12
Heisenberg, Werner, 58
Helvetius, 29
Hermeneutic circle, 152
Hermeneutics: of suspicion, 14, 16–17, 18, 141–42, 181, 210; of recovery, 18, 309; of faith (Ricoeur), 141, 181, 210; of self-discovery (Ricoeur), 145; Ricoeur on, as exploration of subjectivity, 171–72
Hierarchy: of being (Polanyi, Lonergan), 45–46, 82; of time (Ricoeur), 174, 179
History: as conceived by Voegelin, 106–7, 132–33; philosophy of (in Augustine, Ricoeur, and Voegelin), 179–80, (in Kierkegaard) 314–16, (in Girard) 316
Hobbes, Thomas, 4–5
Hominization: Girard on, 196–98
Hume, David, 31
Humor: Kierkegaard on, 276, 278
Husserl, Edmund, 6, 8
Hypnosis: Oughourlian's theory of, 296–99
Hypostatizing: Voegelin's criticism of, 107, 117, 129

Idealism, 7, 233, 236; in Hegel, 135
Idolatry: Ricoeur's critique of, 141, 150; Girard's critique of, 223–25
Immediacy: Lonergan, 75; Kierkegaard, 268
In-Between. *See* Between; Metaxy
Incarnation, 20, 242–43, 248–49, 259, 281, 309, 310; of the Son of God, 224. *See also* Body; Paradox, incarnation as; Subjectivity, incarnate
Indwelling (Polanyi), 172–73, 309; as a

cognitive principle, 41–42, 44–45
Integration of consciousness, 285,
317–18
Intentionality, 271; term, as used by
Voegelin, 101
Intentionality analysis: likened to
existence analysis (Jaspers), 111–12
Intentional operations, 10–11; Lonergan,
60–62, 69; Ricoeur, 156–57; do not
imply an "operator," 293–94; as
energy, 306
Interdividual [Interdividuel]. See
Psychology, interdividual
Interdividual relation (Oughourlian),
296–99
Interiority, 213; as a "realm of meaning"
in Lonergan, 73, 79, 83; compared
with Polanyi's "tacit dimension," 76
Inwardness (Kierkegaard), 110, 260, 279.
See also Subjectivity
Irony: Kierkegaard on, 276, 278
Isomorphism between knowing and
known (Lonergan), 238
It, the (Voegelin), 133

James, William, 7–10, 293–94
Janet, Pierre, 297–99
Jaspers, Karl, 95, 100, 102–3, 110–13,
114, 118, 181, 286; compared to
Marcel, 109; mentioned, 13, 211
Jesus: problem of historical knowledge
about (Kierkegaard), 228–29, 237.
See also Christ
Judgment, rational: Lonergan, 61;
Ricoeur, 157
Jung, Carl, 104

Kant, Immanuel, 39, 58, 104, 164, 209,
234; Polanyi's criticism of, 40;
influence on Voegelin, 130–31, 180;
influence on Ricoeur, 149–52,
154–57; mentioned, 8, 12, 13, 36, 227
Kantianism, 274; Lonergan's critique of,
151–55; "post-Hegelian," in Ricoeur,
154
Kaufmann, Walter, 56, 234
Kierkegaard, Søren, 13, 118, 253, 279,
285, 286, 290, 310–11; not an
irrationalist, 15, 230, 232, 239–40,

250; influence of, 102; on belief, 110,
238–39; on inwardness, 110, 260,
279; pseudonymous authorship, 226,
227–30; the problem of historical
knowledge, 228–29, 237; on faith,
230, 248, 250–51, 255, 272, 274;
objectivity and subjectivity, 232–35,
237–38; compared with Lonergan,
234, 238–41; mystery and problem in,
235n; Socrates in, 236, 285;
recollection in, 236–37, 256;
existential appetite, 242; subjective
and objective existence, 243–46, 250,
259–60, 263, 278; incarnate
subjectivity, 248–54, 257, 262,
266–67, 270–72, 277, 279–80; on
conversion, 255–56, 258; sin and
error, 257–61, 263, 269–70;
compared with Ricoeur, 261, 267; on
acoustic illusion, 266–67; immediacy,
268; spirit in, 271; stages of existence,
272–78; types of religiousness,
274–78, 312–13; irony and humor,
276–78; sin and guilt, 277, 278;
differences between subject and
person, existence and reality, 282;
Christendom, 302; on admiration,
312–15; philosophy of history,
314–16; mentioned, 182, 211, 225.
See also Moment; Paradox; Passion;
Reason; Repentance; Socratic
principle; Truth
Knight of faith (Kierkegaard), 274
Knowing: "from without" and "from
within," 87, 89, 243, 258. See also
Knowledge, of God
Knowledge: distinguished from
experience (Lonergan), 54–55; of God
(Kierkegaard), 254–55, 302
Known unknown (Lonergan), 107
Koehler, Wolfgang, 32

Language: theological, 18; myth as, 91,
97, 101; philosophical and mythic,
114, 119, 124; and linguisticality
(Ricoeur), 142, 157, 161; metaphoric
vs. speculative discourse (Ricoeur),
159–63; referential function of
(Ricoeur), 163–64; seductive power

of, 212, 293; of paradox (Kierkegaard), 246–47; tends toward objectification, 280; value of mythic and religious, 302–3, 308, 316–17

Leap: in being (Voegelin), 114; of faith (Kierkegaard), 248, 250

Leibniz, Gottfried Wilhelm von, 35

Lindenfeld, David F., 31–32

Linguisticality (Ricoeur), 142, 157, 161. See also Language; Word of God and word of man

Locke, John, 5, 6, 31, 33, 58

Lonergan, Bernard J. F., S. J., 5, 6, 12, 23, 107, 272, 286, 287–88, 304; on philosophy, 3–4, 96; on positivism, 4; compared with William James, 7; on subject and object, 8, 121; compared with Polanyi, 14–15; as Christian theologian, 21; compared with Hegel, 22; interest in economics, 30; on relativity theory, 35; and Polanyi, 52, 53–58; conception of experience, 54–55, 66–69; and J. H. Newman, 59; on difference between cognitional theory, epistemology, and metaphysics, 60; on Christ, 66, 224–25; definition of consciousness, 66–69, 72–73, 76, 80; on theory, 73, 79, 83; immediacy in, 75; sublation, 76–77; distinction between immediate and mediated knowing, 77–78; distinction between "body" and "thing," 78; on proportionate being, 78–79, 82; definition of faith, 87; on duty, 88; compared with Voegelin, 93–121, 129, 132, 212n; on Jaspers, 97, 100, 212n; criticized by Charles Davis, 101; Doran on, 104–5; on mystery, 107–110; argument for the existence of God, 108–9, 241; criticized by Avery Dulles, S. J., 109n; distinction between mystery and problem, 110; on "adoration," 110; compared with Jaspers, 113; on myth, 114–16, 212, 287–88, 289–90; criticism of Platonism, 120–21; Aristotelian-Thomistic background, 121; compared with Aquinas, 129; conception of person, 138–39, 148; critique of

Kantianism, 151–53; compared with Ricoeur, 155–62; on analogy, 158–59; rejection of faculty psychology, 158; compared with Girard, 210–11; on metaphysics, 212–13, 287; demythologizing in, 213; on sin, 231n; conception of subjectivity and objectivity, 234; and Kierkegaard, 234, 238–41 267, 273n. See also Intentional operations; Interiority; Knowledge; Object; Scotosis; Subject; Transcendental notion

Love: Ricoeur on, 143; transcendent, 222; epistemology of (Girard), 300–301; as liberation from egoism (Girard), 302; as existential appetite, 308; of God (Girard), 310; as response to existential calling, 317

Lovejoy, Arthur O., 23

Luminosity (Voegelin), 101, 107, 122

Mach, Ernst, 31, 32, 34–35

Marcel, Gabriel, 16, 110, 181; distinction between mystery and problem, 16, 107–8, 109; mentioned, 211

Mécanisme victimaire. See Victimizing mechanism

Mechanism: as a philosophical theory, 80

Mediation (Girard), 187–88, 210, 228

Merleau-Ponty, 12

Metaphor, 16, 290; Ricoeur on, 145, 158–63

Metaphysics, 287, 289, 292–93; Lonergan's, 60, 212–13; Aristotelian, 79; scholastic, 85, 101; as conceived by Jaspers, 111–12; criticized by Voegelin, 124, 128; Girard on, 207, 210, 211, 287. *See also* Desire, metaphysical

Metaxy (Plato): in Voegelin, 9–10, 116–17, 126, 174, 242, 270–71, 276, 287, 290, 317; in Ricoeur, 138, 139–40; and tragic vision of life, 143–44

Michelson-Morley experiment, 34

Mill, John Stuart, 32

Mimesis: Ricoeur, 164, 168; in Freud, 190; Girard, 190, 211, 207;

Oughourlian, 297. *See also* Desire, mimetic
Mises, Ludwig von, 28
Model-obstacle (Girard), 192–93, 221–22, 264–65
Moment, the (Kierkegaard), 250–54, 262, 266, 268, 269–70, 280, 302
Murder, as origin of society: in Freud 189; in Girard, 199
Mussolini, 27
Mystery, 308; in Voegelin, 107; Ricoeur on, 158–59; problem of finding language for, 281–82
Mystery and problem, 18, 25, 178, 222, 240, 241; distinction between (Marcel), 16, 108; Lonergan on, 110; in Kierkegaard, 235n
Myth, 16, 18, 85, 91, 97, 119, 285–91, 303, 316; philosophical, 22–23, 114–16, 126, 208; Lonergan's view of, 114–15; in Schelling, 133–35; as an expression of precomprehension (Ricoeur), 138; as symbolic language (Ricoeur), 147; Girard's conception of, 201, 205; and Lonergan's metaphysics, 212; as language for subjectivity, 222
Mythic thinking: in Lonergan, 212; in Freud, 214

Naive realism, 223, 304; Ricoeur's critique of, 157; Girard critical of, 210–11. *See also* Critical realism
Narcissism: Freud's theory of, 213–14, 215
Narrative form: Ricoeur, 163–65; as a metaphor for human existence, 179–80
Newman, John Henry, 59, 238
Newton, Isaac, 35, 58, 61
Nietzsche, Friedrich, 102, 208
Noetic differentiation of consciousness (Voegelin), 5, 114, 306, 316–18
Now: human (subjective) vs. abstract (objective) (Ricoeur), 173, 176

Object (Lonergan): as "already, out, there, now, real," 75, 78, 213; theoretical, 78
Objective-subject, 217, 224, 259, 267,

274. *See also* Egoism
Objectivism and subjectivism, 223, 224
Objectivity: Kierkegaard's conception of, 232, 234–35; and Lonergan's, 234
Ockham, William of, 23–24, 58
Oedipus complex (Freud): Girard's critique of, 188–92
Offense: Kierkegaard, 261–66, 269; Girard, 264
Olding, A., 47–51, 75–76, 77, 80
Open and closed existence (Voegelin), 17, 123, 141
Order (Voegelin), 123; Schelling as source of Voegelin's conception of, 134–35
Original Sin: Ricoeur on,143, 144, 182; Girard on, 220–21; Kierkegaard on, 230–31
Otto, Rudolf, 185, 186
Oughourlian, Jean-Michel, 5, 17, 197n, 287, 295–99, 308, 310; on adorcism, 311–12, 313; on desire, 224n, 295, 298–99. *See also* Psychology, interdividual

Pagels, Heinz, 57, 83–84
Paradox (Augustine and Ricoeur), 176, 178
Paradox (Kierkegaard), 230, 266, 272, 301; distinction between essential and accidental, 240; as a function of language for subjectivity, 246–47, 280–81, 283; incarnation as, 248, 250–51, 254, 259, 261, 262, 276, 280; as "religiousness B," 276, 278; as "the characteristic mark of Christianity," 281
Parmenides, 234
Parsimony. *See* Principle of Parsimony
Participation in being (Voegelin), 92, 97–98, 115–17
Pascal, Blaise, 138
Passion: Polanyi, 29; Kierkegaard, 242, 243, 245–46, 251, 253, 263, 277
Perceptionism. *See* Perceptualism
Perceptualism, 57–59, 152–53, 156–57
Periagoge. See Plato
Pericles, 168
Person, 51–52, 292, 308–9, 310; Ricoeur on, 148; and subject, 282

Philosophy: as a term, 3–4; Lonergan's conception of, 3–4, 96; linguistic, 4; Christian, 19–24; Voegelin's conception of, 96; Ricoeur's conception of, 138–39; as rooted in religion (Girard), 207
Piscitelli, Emil J., 103, 151–52
Plato, 61, 95, 118–19, 120–21, 138, 140, 167, 190, 207–8, 249, 272, 286; *periagoge*, 115–16; compared with Aristotle, 127–28; mentioned, 234, 270
Plato, works by: *Phaedrus*, 22–23, 122, 126, 128, 244; *Meno*, 54, 236, 251; *Laws*, 96–97; *Philebus*, 116–17; *Symposium*, 116–17, 126
Pneumatic differentiation of consciousness (Voegelin), 114, 306, 316–18
Pol, Otto. *See* Polanyi, Otto
Polanyi, Adolph, 27
Polanyi, John, 21, 26n, 27n, 31n
Polanyi, Karl, 26, 27–28
Polanyi, Laura, 27
Polanyi, Michael, 11, 12, 29, 80, 98, 286, 291; on positivism, 14, 31–37; and Lonergan, 14–15, 52, 53–58, 64–67, 71–72, 76–77, 83; and Christianity, 20–21; Drucker's description of, 28; criticism of Kant, 40; and Descartes, 40; on "body," 43–44, 45, 51–52; compared to Aristotle, 44; on "otherness," 44; on hierarchy of being, 45–46; distinction between process and act, 46–47; on emergence, 48; on relativity theory, 58; on tacit cognition, 64–66; and the functional character of subsidiary awareness, 67, 309; criticized by A. Olding, 75–77. *See also* Focal and subsidiary awareness; Indwelling; Interiority; Teleology
Polanyi, Otto, 26–27
Polarity, tensional, 172
Polarized vision: Girard on, 201, 208
Popper, Karl, 39–40
Positivism, 4; Polanyi on, 14, 31–37; historical origins of, 31–32
Possession: as interpreted by Oughourlian, 296, 311

Power: interpreted as plenitude of being (Girard), 193, 228. *See also* Desire, metaphysical; Sacred
Precomprehension or preunderstanding (Ricoeur), 138, 140, 171–72, 223
Primary symbolism (Ricoeur), 145. *See also* Voegelin, on primary and secondary symbols
Principle of parsimony, 294
Problem. *See* Mystery and problem
Process and act: Polanyi's distinction between, 46–47
Proportionate being. *See* Being, proportionate
Psychology, interdividual, 5, 184, 216–17, 221–22, 296–99, 310
Public, the (Kierkegaard), 315

Quantum theory, 84
Question, The (Voegelin), 118

Rasmussen, David, 103–4
Reality: as conceived by Lonergan, 108–9; distinguished from existence, 109–10, 161, 176, 295, 309, 318; as what can be known by intentional operations, 128, 295; and existence (Kierkegaard), 282
Reason: Voegelin's conception of, 106; Kierkegaard's conception of, 254, 262
Recollection: in Ricoeur, 140; in Kierkegaard, 236–37, 256
Reference: as theme in Ricoeur, 164
Reification, 308, 313; Ricoeur's opposition to, 139; Girard on, 212. *See also* Hypostatizing
Religion: Girard on, 186–87, 189, 192–94, 205; and adorcism (Oughourlian), 311–12
Religiousness, types of (Kierkegaard), 274–78, 312–13
Repentance, 137, 308; Kierkegaard on, 232, 255–58, 263, 276–78
Revelation: distinguished from "information" (Voegelin), 95; distinguished from reason (Voegelin), 106; love as (Girard), 300–301
Ricardo, David, 28
Ricoeur, Paul, 12, 14, 104, 136, 202,

209–10, 286, 290; compared with
Voegelin, 17–18, 138–43, 179–80;
and Christianity, 21, 143; political
interests, 30; influenced by Jaspers and
Marcel, 103; on myth, 138, 147; on
person or subject, 139–40, 148, 150,
151, 158–59, 162–63; and Freud,
141; critique of idolatry, 141, 150; on
hermeneutics, 141, 145, 171–72, 181,
210; on symbolism, 141, 142,
159–60, 182; language and
linguisticality, 142, 157–64; on love,
143; on tragedy, 143–44, 146, 166;
existentialism in, 143–44; on
metaphor and metaphoric discourse,
145, 158–63; Adam in, 146;
inclination toward hermeneutics of
faith, 147, 181–82; on wager,
148–49, 151; Kantianism in, 149–57,
162, 164–66, 180; critical realism in,
155–57; compared with Lonergan,
155–62; on existence, 158, 161–62;
rejection of faculty psychology, 158;
on mystery, 158–59; on narrative
form, 163–65; on mimesis, 164, 168;
on teleology, 165; aestheticism in,
165–68; on catharsis, 167–68; on
incarnate subjectivity, 171–76; on
care, 172, 173, 174; on subject and
object, 172; on time, 173–76,
178–79; Word of God and word of
man, 179, 181–82; on transcendence,
181; compared with Girard, 203, 204,
208, 220–21; and the problem of
human evil, 222; compared with
Kierkegaard, 261, 267; mentioned,
125, 211, 226, 229, 230, 239, 270,
283. See also Dualism; Embodiment;
Emplotment; Metaxy;
Precomprehension; Tension
Rivalry (Girard), 194, 318
Romanticism: in Voegelin, 135, 208;
Girard on, 166, 186, 213, 215, 216; in
Ricoeur, 203, 208

Sacred, the: ambiguity of, 182, 196;
Girard on, 184, 192–94, 200, 214;
Eliade on, 185–86, 303–6
Sacrifice, 19, 314; Girard on, 196,

199–201, 219–20, 318
Sagan, Eli, 197–98
Sartre, Jean-Paul, 12, 305
Satan, 224, 264. See also Devil
Scapegoat: in Plato, 207–8. See also
Victimizing mechanism
Schelling, Friedrich Wilhelm Joseph von,
209; influence on Voegelin, 130,
132–35; mentioned, 12, 13, 227
Schlick, Moritz, 31
Schopenhauer, Arthur, 130, 131
Scotosis (Lonergan and Voegelin), 94,
138
Scotus, John Duns, 55, 58, 153
Seeking and being drawn (Voegelin), 116,
130. See also Tension, existential.
Self, 287, 311–12; as term, 88; Ricoeur's
conception of, 139; as conceived by
Oughourlian, 296–99; reified, 308,
313. See also Egoism
Sin: Kierkegaard, 230–32, 257–61, 267,
268, 269–70, 278; Lonergan, 231n.
See also Offense; Original Sin
Skandalon (Girard), 221–22, 225,
264–65. See also Offense
Society: and consciousness, 285
Socrates, 22, 249, 251; in Kierkegaard,
236, 285
Socratic principle, the (Kierkegaard),
251–52, 256, 261
Sophocles, 202–3
Spirit (Kierkegaard), 271
Story: in Schelling and Voegelin, 133.
See also Narrative form
Structuralism, 163, 212
Subject: existential (Lonergan), 15, 129;
entitative, 19, 100–101, 292–93;
defined by Lonergan, 68–69, 84–86,
158; truncated (Lonergan), 81; as
term, 88; Ricoeur on, 150, 151,
158–59, 162–63; as conceived by
Kierkegaard, 259–60, 266;
distinguished from person, 282;
reified, 292, 295, 313; as conceived by
Oughourlian, 295
Subject, human: as object of metaphysical
desire, 212; hypostatizing of, 213, 215,
217–18; Oughourlian and Girard on,
216

Subject and object: as terms, 10–11; Ricoeur on relation between, 172; absolute difference between (Kierkegaard), 239, 253, 261, 282. *See also* Existence and reality

Subjective and objective dimensions of consciousness: correlation with mystery and problem, 16

Subjectivism. *See* Objectivism and subjectivism; "Who" question

Subjectivity: of the historical Jesus (Lonergan), 66, 224; existential, 130, 218; and eternity, 178; mystery of, 222; Kierkegaard's conception of, 232–34; Lonergan's conception of, 234. *See also* Inwardness; Now

Subjectivity, incarnate, 52, 171–76, 218, 242–43, 248–54, 257, 262, 266–67, 270–72, 277, 279–80. *See also* Incarnation

Sublation (Lonergan), 76–77

Subsidiary awareness (Polanyi), 67, 309. *See also* Focal and subsidiary awareness.

Substitution (Girard), 200–201

Symbolism: inherent ambiguity of, 125, 135–36; "gives rise to thought" (Ricoeur), 159–60

Symbols: deformation of (Voegelin), 107; of existential order or disorder (Voegelin), 122; primary and secondary (Voegelin), 123–25, 134–36; in the thought of Ricoeur, 141, 142, 159, 182; Ricoeur on "transcendental deduction" of, 149–50; revelatory function of, in Ricoeur and Voegelin, 180. *See also* Desymbolism

Tacit dimension (Polanyi), 15, 38, 64–66, 85, 98, 291

Tacit knowing (Polanyi), 64–66

Teleology: Polanyi, 50–51; Lonergan, 87; Ricoeur, 165

Tension, existential (Voegelin), 6, 96, 97–98, 116, 117, 119, 126, 130, 172, 208, 223, 242, 243, 246, 272, 286, 306, 307, 317; compared with Lonergan's "transcendental notion,"

118; parallel in Ricoeur, 138–39, 180; in Kierkegaard, 237, 266; in the phenomenology of the sacred, 303, 306. *See also* Care (Heidegger)

Theophanic event (Voegelin), 122, 130

Theory: as a "realm of meaning" in Lonergan, 73, 79, 83

Thing: as conceived by Lonergan, 78

Time: Augustine and Ricoeur on, 174–76, 178–79; psychological (Oughourlian), 299

Tito, Marshal, 27

Tragedy: Ricoeur on, 166; Voegelin's theory of, 168–70; Girard on, 201–5

Tragic vision: Ricoeur on, 143–44, 146; Ricoeur's affinity for, 154n

Transcendence: as a "realm of meaning" in Lonergan, 86–87; Voegelin on, 99; Ricoeur, 181

Transcendental notion (Lonergan), 70–71, 118, 121, 223, 307

Truth: subjective, as a mode of existence, 118; historicity of (Voegelin), 119; "of existence" (Voegelin), 126; in metaphor and narrative (Ricoeur), 163; existential, 179–80; objective and subjective, 249; subjective (Kierkegaard), 257, 259, 261

Unconscious, the: Girard's theory of, 189–90

Unknown, the (Kierkegaard), 245; as the ultimate goal of reason, 262

van der Leeuw, Gerardus, 185

Victimizing mechanism (Girard), 18, 19, 195–97, 201, 206–7. *See also* Sacrifice, Girard on

Vienna Circle, 31

Vitalism, 81; Polanyi criticized for, by A. Olding, 49–51

Voegelin, Eric, 5–6, 12, 15, 16, 25, 85, 174, 209, 270, 285, 290, 306, 316, 317; on noetic and pneumatic differentiation of consciousness, 5, 114, 306, 316–18; on existential tension, 6, 96, 97–98, 116, 117, 119, 126, 130, 172, 208, 223, 242, 243, 246, 272, 286, 306, 307, 317; and

William James, 8–10; compared with Ricoeur, 17–18, 138–43, 179–80; on open and closed existence, 17, 123, 141; and Christianity, 19–20, 142–43; criticism of Hegel, 22–23, 154n; on philosophical myth, 22–23, 114–16, 126, 208; unwarranted reputation as a "conservative," 29; on relativity theory, 35; drama and story in, 92–93, 98, 99–100, 114, 133, 203–4, 247n, 284, 310–11; on participation in being, 92, 97–98, 115–17; compared with Lonergan, 93–121, 129, 132; conception of revelation, 95, 106; conception of philosophy as existential *zetema*, 95–96, 102; interpretation of Plato's golden and iron cords, 99, 101, 102, 105, 173–74, 223, 317; on intentionality, 101; luminosity, 101, 107, 122; conception of reason, 106; the divine Within, 106; on mystery, 107; conception of existence, 107; against hypostatizing, 107, 117, 129; compared with Marcel and Jaspers, 109; leap in being, 114; the Question, 118; the historicity of truth, 119; problems with his emphasis on mythic language, 119–35; on gnosticism, 121, 125, 126, 129, 288; tragic tonality in, 121–22, 128, 131; theophanic event, 122, 130; on primary and secondary symbols, 123–25, 134–36, 140–41; on doctrinization, 124; on metaphysics, 124, 128; on existential truth, 126, 179–80; theory of spontaneous symbolization, 128–29, 130–36; influence of Schelling, 130, 132–35; common sense in, 131; concept of "the It," 133; romanticism in, 135, 208; and Freud, 141; philosophy of history, 106–7, 132–33, 179–80; theory of tragedy, 168–70; compared with Girard, 202, 204, 288–89; demythologizing in, 213; compared with Kierkegaard, 287; conception of *psyche*, 287; mentioned, 211, 213, 226, 239, 283, 284. *See also* Beyond; Dualism; Metaxy; Scotosis; Symbols

Wager: as theme in Ricoeur, 148–49, 151
"Who" question, the, 85, 171, 182, 222, 227, 299. *See also* Subject; Subjectivity
William of Ockham. *See* Ockham, William of
Within, the (Voegelin), 106
Wittgenstein, Ludwig, 212
Word of God and word of man (Ricoeur), 179, 181–82

Zetema (Voegelin), 95, 102

DATE DUE

20 '97			